RELUCTANT EMPIRE

RELUCTANT EMPIRE

BRITISH POLICY
ON THE SOUTH AFRICAN
FRONTIER 1834–1854

BY JOHN S. GALBRAITH

UNIVERSITY OF CALIFORNIA PRESS
Berkeley and Los Angeles 1963

UNIVERSITY OF CALIFORNIA PRESS / BERKELEY AND LOS ANGELES, CALIFORNIA

CAMBRIDGE UNIVERSITY PRESS / LONDON, ENGLAND

TO W. ROSS LIVINGSTON

PREFACE

THIS NARRATIVE belongs to the genus of imperial rather than of South African history. Its preoccupation is with British frontier policy, not with the internal history of Cape Colony and adjacent territories. Subjects of such importance to South African history as the anticonvict agitation and the introduction of representative government are mentioned only to the extent that they are relevant to the theme.

Initially my intention was to study the influence of the missionary movement on policy at the Cape, but I soon abandoned this approach. Earlier investigations had led me to expect a far greater coherence in the "missionary factor" than I actually found. W. M. Macmillan's books, *The Cape Colour Question* and *Bantu, Boer, and Briton,* were important pioneering works. But in demolishing hoary legends, they presented other interpretations which are also open to question. The letters of Dr. John Philip and the correspondence of the London Missionary Society, on which Professor Macmillan relied to a considerable extent, are ex parte evidence. The role of Philip in South African history has, I think, been exaggerated by excessive dependence on his own assessment of his contribution. South African historians have collided on the issue of Philip's integrity while agreeing on his influence, for good or for ill. But conclusions based upon Philip's letters must be modified by evidence in the archives of the London and Methodist Missionary societies, the Public Record Office, and other depositories.

To assert that Philip's significance has been overstated is not to imply that he was inconsequential. He and the missionary society he represented were powerful forces. In this study, their power will be weighed in relation to other influences on colonial policy.

If this work has a thesis, it is that throughout the two decades under consideration zeal for retrenchment conditioned the basic decisions of imperial policy. But the conventional interpretation in terms of the clash of "economics" and "humanitarianism" is an oversimplification. The factors underlying the decisions of imperial administrators at the

Cape are not easily reducible to neat, clean categories. In this book I
hope to provide some sense of that complexity.

For inspiration and assistance I owe much to many persons. C. W.
de Kiewiet, an outstanding scholar and teacher, excited my interest in
the motivation of imperial policy in South Africa. My research was
made more pleasant and profitable by the kindness of Mr. Kenneth
Timings, Public Record Office; Miss Irene Fletcher, London Missionary
Society; Mr. J. E. Fagg, Prior's Kitchen, University of Durham; and
many others. The Ford Foundation, by sponsorship of an earlier research project in southern Africa, contributed substantially to my
knowledge of the area. For comments and criticisms on the manuscript
I wish to thank my colleague, Professor Leonard Thompson; Professor
Gerald S. Graham, King's College, University of London; and my wife,
Laura Galbraith. For her assistance in editing, my thanks to Mrs. Grace
H. Stimson.

The map on page 153, copied from Eric Walker, *A History of
Southern Africa,* is reproduced with the permission of the publishers,
Longmans, Green, and Company.

Finally, I express appreciation to the Social Science Research Council for the financial assistance that made this study possible.

J. S. G.

CONTENTS

MAPS

SIMPLICITY IS THE MOST DECEITFUL
MISTRESS THAT EVER BETRAYED MAN.

The Education of Henry Adams

Chapter I

INTRODUCTION

VIEWED FROM CAPE TOWN, Table Mountain seems almost flat, but its surface is rocky and uneven. Remoteness from an era also creates a false sense of symmetry. Much of the study of nineteenth-century imperial history has been characterized by distance not only from the period but from the facts. Grand generalizations have been accepted which upon close analysis have proved to be exaggerated, undocumented, or untrue.

The familiar phenomenon of pyramiding upon the works of previous authorities has produced an impressive mass of literature resting upon faulty foundations. Until the recent past, students of British Empire history described imperial policy in the middle years of the nineteenth century in terms of a conflict of "Little England," liberal imperialist, and "humanitarian" influences.[1] The documentation underlying this conception was derived largely from such sources as blue books, parliamentary debates, books by political theorists of the day, newspapers, and magazines. Such evidence, of course, was valuable, but without archival research it presented a distorted impression of the character of imperial policy.

It is true that some writers insisted that the Empire was an expensive anachronism, and that some statesmen in moments of petulance—likely to be incited by an expensive and unproductive war—complained that the colonies were a "mill-stone round our necks." But selections from a statesman's speeches or from his correspondence can exaggerate the contradictions inherent in the nature of the politician's profession. Acceptance of the language of partisan politics likewise can produce a gross enlargement of the range of the political spectrum. Sir William Molesworth and W. E. Gladstone denounced the colonial policy of Lord John Russell and the third Earl Grey, but the distance between their views was in fact small. The London *Evening Mail* perceptively

---

[1] For a more detailed discussion of this subject, see my article, "Myths of the 'Little England' Era," *American Historical Review*, LXVII (Oct., 1961), 34–48.

observed, after one spirited exchange between Molesworth and the Russell government, that if actions rather than words were to be trusted, Molesworth had no more ardent supporters than the very ministers who attacked him for his alleged "Little England" views,[2] for all agreed on the principle of colonial self-government and the reduction of British expenditures for colonial purposes.

In the middle years of the nineteenth century, British traders enjoyed a freedom of access to the markets of the world unparalleled before or since. During those halcyon days few could dispute the prevailing conviction of the inevitability of progress, with Britain in the van. Progress connoted the discarding of all that was wasteful, inefficient, and outworn. It also involved the restriction of government functions—which were essentially unproductive—to the barest minimum, and an insistence on rigorous economy. The perennial aversion to payment of taxes thus received philosophic sanction. The dedication to retrenchment, on the part of Parliament and "the people who mattered," circumscribed the range of action of a secretary of state. He knew that while debates on "colonial policy" might empty the House of Commons or reduce it to utter boredom, proposed levies upon the Treasury for colonial purposes were certain to undergo most critical scrutiny and could jeopardize the life of the government. When great commercial interests were concerned, as in the Opium War of 1839–1842, a government might use force to support trade, but such intervention was exceptional. The British trading empire in general remained outside the purview of governmental action.

Zeal for minimal expense affected the British Army far more than the Royal Navy, which enjoyed a special status as the protector of the British Isles and of the trade lanes of the world. Because the navy required bases there was no serious opposition to the maintenance of naval stations, and none contested the importance of retaining Table Bay and the adjacent anchorages in False Bay. But beyond these harbors was a hinterland, control of which led to endless expense without compensating returns. Imperial governments sought a means of escape from burdens that grew ever heavier, as European cattle farmers spread into the interior and became embroiled in conflicts with tribal peoples. The third Earl Grey's statement of the dilemma he faced as secretary of state for colonies echoed those of his Dutch and British predecessors:

Few persons would probably dissent from the opinion that it would be far better for this country if the British territory in South Africa were confined

---

[2] *London Evening Mail*, April 11, 1851.

to Cape Town and to Simon's Bay. But however burdensome the Nation may find the possession of its African dominions, it does not follow that it can now cast them off, consistently with its honour and duty. It has incurred responsibilities by the measures of former years, which cannot be so lightly thrown aside.

If from the moment of the conquest of the Cape from the Dutch, the British Government had resolutely adhered to the policy of preventing any advance of the then Colonial frontier, and of limiting, instead of increasing, the extent of territory that was occupied by British subjects, I believe it would not have been impossible (though certainly it would have been very difficult) by judicious measures to have accomplished this object.[3]

The directors of the Dutch East India Company had spoken similarly in 1661 when they had instructed Jan van Riebeeck that any idea of enlarging the colony beyond the limits of the Cape peninsula should be abandoned, and van Riebeeck had sought to accomplish this object by planting a great thorn hedge. The hedge had the advantage of being cheap; it had the liability of being ineffectual. Neither thorn hedges nor other "judicious measures" deterred the wanderings of the cattle Boer, and where he went governmental jurisdiction soon followed.

To the economy-minded it was intolerable that British resources should be poured out for worthless deserts, but expansion at the Cape seemed to have the inevitability of a natural law. The *Times* expressed its indignation in an editorial in 1853:

Once embarked on the fatal policy of establishing a frontier in South Africa and defending that frontier by force, there seems to be neither rest nor peace for us till we follow our flying enemies and plant the British standard on the walls of Timbuctoo. To subdue one tribe is only to come in contact with another equally fierce, impractical [sic] and barbarous. . . . So long as the Governor of the Cape shall have a large military force at his disposal, supported at the expense of this country, we doubt not that he will always find enemies against whom to direct it, and so long as we encourage our colonists, relying on our military protection to scatter themselves over a vast continent without the support of a concentrated population, we must expect every succeeding mail to bring us the same tale of losses and disasters.[4]

The moral was clear; the only means by which Britain could free itself from the incubus was to withdraw military protection, leaving

---

[3] Earl Grey, *The Colonial Policy of Lord John Russell's Administration* (2 vols.; London: Bentley, 1853), II, 248.

[4] *Times*, Feb. 28, 1853. It should be noted that "the Cape" is used to apply to the entire colony, not only to the Cape peninsula. In this book I shall also use the term to apply to both. The meaning should be clear from the context.

the colonists to defend themselves. In the 1850's governments were not yet prepared to go to that extreme, though by the Sand River and Bloemfontein conventions they abdicated responsibility beyond the Orange River. But, like their predecessors, both Dutch and British, neither were they willing, even had they been able, to expend the financial and human resources necessary to produce order on the turbulent frontiers of southern Africa. By emphasizing economy in administration of the Cape while asserting jurisdiction over a huge territory with a frontier stretching over hundreds of miles, Britain incurred huge expenditures, exacerbated racial friction, and contributed to periodic wars that were an ever-increasing drain on the British Treasury.

British policy in southern Africa was influenced not only by material but by humanitarian considerations. The tremendous force displayed by the Saints in the abolition of slavery within the Empire did not evaporate with emancipation; concern for the "backward races" was a continuing preoccupation of Exeter Hall, and the Cape and its environs were an important field of endeavor for the powerful London and Wesleyan missionary societies. But the power and the cohesion of the "humanitarians" should not be exaggerated. At times the Wesleyan and the London societies were openly hostile to each other, and the advice they offered governors for the resolution of the "native problem" was frequently contradictory. The Select Committee on the Aborigines, which was dominated by its chairman Thomas Fowell Buxton, quoted approvingly from the sermon of one evangelical minister that "it is our office to carry civilization and humanity, peace and good government, and above all, the knowledge of the true God, to the uttermost ends of the earth." [5] Those objectives were not necessarily harmonious, and the committee's report was of little use as a guide to policy; indeed, it was virtually ignored.

An individual might in different situations be labeled a "humanitarian" and an advocate of economy. James Stephen, described by his biographer as a "Christian humanitarian," [6] fits that description as well as any statesman of his day. But in his counsel on policy in Cape Colony, Stephen as permanent undersecretary of state for colonies advocated retrenchment with all the vigor of the most ardent disciple of Cobden and Bright. The third Earl Grey at times expressed views

[5] *Report from the Select Committee on Aborigines (British Settlements)*, 1837, p. 76.

[6] Paul Knaplund, *James Stephen and the British Colonial System* (Madison: University of Wisconsin Press, 1953), p. 17.

indistinguishable from those advocated by the missionary societies when he sought to promote the organization of tribes north and west of the Vaal River for defense against the Boers; on other occasions his philosophy seemed to be akin to that of the Chancellor of the Exchequer. These differences in emphasis do not necessarily imply a contradiction. "Humanitarians" and "Exchequer minds" were not at opposite ends of a spectrum of opinion. Few nineteenth-century humanitarians would have been prepared to demand large levies on the British Treasury for promoting the welfare of "backward peoples"; they shared with the generality of the British middle classes a deep aversion to tax burdens for any purpose, colonial or domestic. They might contribute—and many did contribute generously—in time and money to the work of a private society, but as merchants, manufacturers, professional men, or landowners they expected rigorous economy in their government's budget. To them, as to Gladstone, economy was a religion.

Had there been no intervention by the British government, the Boers would either have reduced the Bantu to subjection or would have been exterminated by them. The alien power of Britain prevented establishment of a social order that would have been the product of relative power within South Africa. Humanitarianism often had the strength to frustrate practices repugnant to British morality; it did not have the force—perhaps it did not have the inclination—to go further. The negative accomplishments of Great Britain in South Africa were impressive; the abolition of slavery and the freeing of the Hottentots from legal subservience were proud achievements of the humanitarian spirit. By the abolition of the commando system, Britain frustrated the slaughter of the Bantu by the Boers. But it did not impose an alternative system of order in accordance with humanitarian principles.

The attempt to reconcile the humanitarian impulse with "due regard for economy" contributed to aggravation rather than to solution of the frontier problem. British intervention on the frontiers was weak and ineffectual. Though justified in terms of protection of the native against the European and the maintenance of order, intervention accomplished neither, and Britain found itself impelled to make war on the people it had vowed to protect. Sir George Clerk stressed this contradiction when he wrote the Duke of Newcastle in 1854:

One of the reasons generally assigned for extending British dominion in South Africa has been to prevent the extinction of the rights of the Natives. The knowledge that British dominance has thus been enlarged, proves acceptable in England. The extension makes manifest our power, the motive our benevolence. After a while the measure becomes costly. Enquiry follows, and it then is evident that the conquest has been the occupation of wastes almost uninhabitable, attended with constant inconvenience and expense to the State, arising from nothing less than the extinction of the rights of those Natives to protect whom it was the motive or the pretext for the extension of authority. . . .[7]

James Stephen repeatedly hammered on the theme that southern Africa was worse than worthless with the exception of its seaports and their immediate hinterlands. In this position he was in agreement with practically every official since the days of Jan van Riebeeck, but he was forced to acknowledge that it was now impossible "to recede from the position we have taken there." [8] The basic dilemma that plagued him and his superiors was demonstrated in their response to Sir George Napier's plea as governor of Cape Colony that Port Natal be annexed to protect the tribes of that area against the emigrant Boers, and to prevent the harbor's falling into the hands of an alien power. Stephen believed Natal to be as worthless as the Cape and he was convinced that the assertion of British sovereignty would be of no benefit to the natives and would probably contribute to greater misery, as it would set the Boers again in motion and would lead to collisions with other tribes. The possession of the port alone was impracticable, for Great Britain would inevitably become embroiled in feuds between settlers and tribesmen and would be forced to intervene.[9] Yet Stephen himself agreed that it was in the British interest to retain possession of Cape Town, Simon's Bay, and Port Elizabeth, where his corollary also applied that possession of the ports implied control of the country beyond.

Lord John Russell was much more inclined to support imperial expansion than was Stephen. In 1839 he asserted that he was "not in principle adverse to the extension of our colonies, the Crown, & of the strength and wealth of the Empire—Their extension may sometimes

---

[7] Clerk to Newcastle, Jan. 14, 1854, C.O. 48/364, P.R.O.

[8] See, for example, his minute on Napier to Russell, Sept. 21, 1840, confidential, C.O. 48/208, P.R.O.

[9] Minute by Stephen, Feb. 15, 1841, on Colonial Land and Emigration Board to Stephen, Feb. 11, 1841, C.O. 48/215, P.R.O. Stephen wrote a few months later: "I have no doubt that by far the least evil of all if it were practicable would be to abandon as worthless the whole of the Colony except the Seaport Towns and their immediate neighbourhood. This of course is not practicable. . . . Nations never can recede willingly from any measure of apparent aggrandizement however absurd it may really be" (minute on Napier to Russell, June 1, 1841, C.O. 48/212, P.R.O.).

be inevitable, often advantageous." [10] But there were certain conditions under which Russell believed that expansion should be rejected. He asserted that

Two of the most prominent of these circumstances are

1. Where the occupation of territory hitherto held by aboriginal tribes must lead to flagrant injustice, cruel wars, & protracted misery—

2. Where the burthen of occupation is so great as to require a large expenditure for which there is no prospect of an adequate compensation. For an increase of troops cannot take place without an increase of establishments, nor an increase of expenditure without an increase of the burthens of this country.[11]

Both of these proscriptions applied with particular force in southern Africa, yet the extension of British jurisdiction continued until the withdrawals of 1852 and 1854. For an explanation of this seeming paradox, purely economic analysis is of little value. In some areas of "formal" and "informal" empire it is true that financial and commercial interests were able to summon British power to their assistance, even though the costs of intervention outweighed the benefits to British society as a whole. In the first half of the nineteenth century, however, the Cape attracted little interest among British bankers and merchants; the value of its exports and imports was insignificant, and its potentialities as a market were unimpressive. In 1834 the Cape imported goods worth £332,420 from Great Britain, and its exports to Britain were valued at only £238,258.[12] The "Cape lobby" in Britain was composed primarily of shipping interests, principally in the City of London, but their influence on British policy was negligible with the possible exception of Natal, where representations that the country was fertile and well adapted for colonization stimulated the interest of the Colonial Office. Even in that territory commercial influence was not decisive.[13]

Reviewing the history of British policy at the Cape, Earl Grey expressed the opinion that the fateful commitment had been made in 1819 when the Chancellor of the Exchequer had secured the consent of Parliament to a grant of £50,000 to assist in the settlement of British unemployed in the zuurveld adjacent to the Bantu tribes of south-

---

[10] Minute by Russell, Nov. 30, 1839, on Borradale to Secretary of State for Colonies, Nov. 18, 1839, C.O. 48/204, P.R.O.

[11] Ibid.

[12] Cape Colony, Imports and Exports for 1834, C.O. 53/71, P.R.O.

[13] See, for example, Borradale to Russell, Nov. 18, 1839, with enclosed memorial, signed by shipowners and others interested in southern Africa, C.O. 48/204, P.R.O.

eastern Africa. The settlement of 5,000 immigrants in this territory
was justified by the ministry of the day as an economy measure; it
would relieve British society of the burden of surplus laborers who
might become assets in their new roles as farmers and pastoralists, and
would interpose a barrier to the restless Kaffirs which would enable the
imperial government to reduce expenditures for frontier defense. On
these justifications the government had secured the general support of
the House of Commons, and even Joseph Hume, who prided himself
upon being a watchdog of the Treasury, had expressed regret that the
project had not been expanded. This "economy" measure, Grey contended, was among the most expensive in the history of the British
Empire. To place settlers with flocks and herds in the neighborhood
of warlike tribes to whom cattle were an irresistible attraction in the
expectation of producing order, he asserted, was lunacy. The conditions thus created were akin to those on the Anglo-Scottish border
centuries earlier. Rather than being collected in villages where they
could have defended themselves, the settlers had scattered over the
country on large farms; instead of being a bulwark of order their
presence was a stimulus to disorder. Short-run economy brought long-
run huge expenditures. As the settlers had been planted in this turbulent territory with governmental assistance, Britain could not without
dishonor refuse them military protection in peace and in war. Neither
could it, without doing violence to Christian morality, allow the
Europeans to fall upon the Kaffirs, but was required to use its power
to enforce on both sides respect for each other's rights:

> Nor do I think that a Christian Nation would be justified, in throwing off
> the responsibility which Providence has cast on the British Government,
> by the power placed in its hands in this part of Africa, and in deliberately,
> and with open eyes, incurring the fearful consequences which must arise,
> from leaving the Settlers and the Kaffirs to struggle for possession of the soil.[14]

This sense of obligation to honor and to "Christian morality" was
widely shared. William Porter, attorney general of the Cape, much
esteemed by his contemporaries as a keen legal mind but not usually
thought of as a "humanitarian," expressed deep regret at the withdrawal of British influence to the south of the Vaal by the Sand River
Convention of 1852, which he thought involved "reversal of what was
so long a cherished and in its principle a most noble policy and one
which had been maintained at no small cost of blood and treasure." [15]

---

[14] Grey, *op. cit.*, II, 249–254.
[15] Memorandum by Porter, Aug. 4, 1852, enclosure in Cathcart to Secretary
of State for Colonies, no. 34, Nov. 14, 1852, C.O. 48/328, P.R.O.

This was not cant; to refer to such expressions as "sounding brass and tinkling cymbals, signifying nothing" would be to misinterpret Victorian society.

British statesmen, like Sisyphus, seemed condemned to everlasting frustration in their efforts to achieve order in South Africa. Among the secretaries of state for colonies were some of the most gifted politicians of their era, among them Lord Stanley and Lord John Russell. Earl Grey made the study of colonial problems his preoccupation, yet he and all the rest failed to promote stability at the Cape. They failed not because they did not understand the problems they confronted; they and their staff had a clearer perception of the characteristics of the Cape society than did the settlers themselves. They failed because the characteristics of British society and the magnitude of the problem made success impossible. General George Cathcart, as governor of Cape Colony, described their dilemma when he wrote to Grey in 1854:

> The truth is that designs so vast and benevolent as the care of the Tribes in the interior of Africa, by means of the extension of British Magisterial powers to protect them is [sic] worthy of the humanity and the civilization of Great Britain; but the idea of our Laws being there rendered effectual without the introduction of permanent, remote, and costly establishments, though often arising from nothing else than a want of reflection, is sometimes conceived either in utter ignorance of the subject or in the vain ambition of establishing a mere semblance of supremacy.[16]

A succession of ever more expensive Kaffir wars seemed to demonstrate that humanitarianism, instead of transforming the savages of southern Africa into orderly inoffensive Christians, made them more formidable adversaries. Massive imperial expenditures in these wars brought only temporary respites. The conclusion seemed inescapable that intervention benefited neither the tribesmen, who demonstrated their hostility in a most emphatic manner, nor the settlers, who lost their self-reliance and became ungrateful mendicants. Under these circumstances Britain sought to transfer to the colonists responsibility for their own protection and to withdraw imperial jurisdiction into a narrower compass. As events demonstrated, this policy also was unavailing.

---

[16] Cathcart to Grey, Nov. 30, 1854, C.O. 48/364, P.R.O.

Chapter II

MEN AND MECHANISMS
IN IMPERIAL POLICY

To PRODUCE FIRE a burning glass must have focus; so also must the critics of a government's policies. When the American colonies erupted in revolution against the royal authority, the Whigs conveniently attributed the breach to the wrongheadedness of George III and his Tory ministers. When the formal administration of colonial policy was assigned to the Colonial Office, the opposition explained the disasters of imperial policy in terms of the deficiencies of the minister and his advisers. The convention was accepted that secretaries of state in the Colonial Office usually were mediocre politicians, deficient in intelligence and in energy and almost totally devoid of knowledge of the empire they were appointed to administer. A later, more sophisticated generation found the culprit to be the "system." Bureaucracy, the multiplication of personnel and offices, frustrated the objects it was avowedly established to advance. Charles Dickens, in this sense a pioneer of twentieth-century social science, invented the Circumlocution Office as the epitome of slavish dedication to routine and divorcement from constructive accomplishment:

The Circumlocution Office was (as everybody knows without being told) the most important Department under Government. No public business of any kind could possibly be done at any time, without the acquiescence of the Circumlocution Office. Its finger was in the largest public pie, and in the smallest public tart. It was equally impossible to do the plainest right and to undo the plainest wrong, without the express authority of the Circumlocution Office. If another Gunpowder Plot had been discovered half an hour before the lighting of the match, nobody would have been justified in saving the parliament until there had been half a score of boards, half a bushel of minutes, several sacks of official memoranda, and a family-vault full of ungrammatical correspondence, on the part of the Circumlocution Office.[1]

---

[1] Charles Dickens, *Little Dorrit* (London: Hazell, Watson, and Viney, n.d.), p. 95.

Civil servants and politicians undoubtedly joined in the approval of this witty, perceptive thrust at the characteristics of other civil servants and politicians. The personnel of the Colonial Office had been frustrated by the dilatoriness of the Treasury, the Bureau of Ordnance, and other departments; it was a source of wry amusement that others should recognize the baneful influence of these offices. To critics of colonial policy, the description perfectly fitted the Colonial Office. Had not Charles Buller also satirized the noxious atmosphere of Downing Street where men with colonial grievances were doomed to grow gray while they awaited answers to their problems?

Between 1834 and 1854, however, the capacities of bureaucracy for delay were as yet undeveloped, for the system was in its infancy. Certainly important decisions were unduly delayed by interoffice communications, but the fault was usually an inadequacy rather than a superfluity of personnel, or occasionally the languor of a minister or the inefficiency of his subordinates.

The Colonial Office of this period was deficient in neither intelligence nor industry, nor did it lack understanding of colonial problems. Its most vehement critics were men obsessed with a cause. After reading one governor's defense of his policies against the criticism of Downing Street, James Stephen noted:

> I observe that the Writer labours under the disadvantage common to almost all Colonists who speculate on the affairs of the Colony to which they belong—a disadvantage analagous to that of a short-sighted man the strength of whose vision within his own range of sight is compensated for by the narrowness of the horizon over which his eye ranges—or more analagous perhaps to the views which the Garrison of a besieged Town take of the conduct of a Campaign on which their own fate depends, and which in their estimate is well or ill-managed just as it contributes to their immediate relief or the reverse.[2]

The Colonial Office in the 1830's was, like other departments, in a process of transition. The day was passing when offices of government could be regarded as sinecures for the sons of favored families, and relaxed inefficiency as the characteristic of government service. In that dying era, clerkships had given an air of respectability to the lives of young aristocrats who were otherwise, in fact still, devoted to pleasure

---

[2] Minute by Stephen, March 17, 1841, on Napier to Russell, confidential, Sept. 8, 1840, C.O. 48/213, P.R.O. Though the minute is attached to Napier's dispatch, it apparently refers to another letter, Venning to Wood, Oct. 30, 1840, private, C.O. 48/208, P.R.O.

and "idle pursuits." Appointments had served political interests, the only qualification for a clerkship being the ability to write legibly. Advancement was by seniority, and the system tended to stifle what little imagination and industry an official might possess. But in the 1830's good family and political connections were no longer enough; ability had become as important a qualification as influence.[3]

This change had not occurred suddenly. After the Napoleonic Wars governments had been concerned with financial reform, one of the corollaries of which was greater efficiency in governmental departments. But, with the appointment of Lord Goderich as secretary of state for war and colonies in the government of Earl Grey, a new zeal for efficiency became evident in the Colonial Office. This emphasis probably originated with young Viscount Howick, the future third Earl Grey, who in his first administrative position as parliamentary undersecretary for colonies in his father's government had early established himself as one of a "ginger group" of young idealists dedicated to the rationalization of government and the infusion of energy into its operations. Such activity was disturbing to those who sought the quiet life, and Howick was unpopular with his more leisurely colleagues who felt that after the passage of the Reform Bill of 1832 they should be allowed to rest. In the Colonial Office Howick was a powerful influence until, in 1834, he resigned in disgust at the decision of the government to accept gradual rather than immediate emancipation of the slaves; thereafter he continued to exercise considerable influence on colonial questions from his position as secretary at war in the Melbourne ministry from 1835 until his resignation in 1839.

Howick found two kindred spirits among the permanent officials of the Colonial Office, Henry Taylor and James Stephen. Taylor, an irreverent young man like his contemporary Howick, was a clerk in the West Indian department. Stephen, slightly older than his associates, had been legal counsel in the Colonial Office since 1813. To Howick and Taylor the contrast between the old corrupt days of influence and inefficiency and the hoped-for new era of dedicated public service was symbolized by the conflict between the permanent undersecretary, R. W. Hay, and Stephen.

Hay, who had been appointed to his position in 1825, the first official to bear the title, was a well-meaning, friendly man with no visible claims to justify his appointment other than an engaging per-

---

[3] Taylor to Villiers, April 2, 1832, Grey Papers, Prior's Kitchen, University of Durham.

sonality and association with prominent families. Further, he was a Tory serving a Whig government. Stephen, on the other hand, seemed to Howick and Taylor a paragon of the ideal public servant—able and industrious, gifted with organizational ability and with an incisiveness that could cut through a mountain of paper and lay bare the essentials.

In the formulation of policy Howick sought advice from Stephen rather than from the Permanent Undersecretary. Although Hay continued to carry on quasi-official correspondence with governmental officials throughout the Empire, his influence was gone; he was in effect quarantined. Stephen in 1834 was appointed assistant undersecretary, but owed no allegiance to his official superior. The relations between the two men naturally became intolerable, but Hay, perhaps hoping that a Tory government would restore him to power, refused to resign. After the departure of Howick from the Colonial Office, Hay in his wounded pride occasionally sought to assert his authority, whereupon Stephen would refuse to participate in any functions beyond those of department counsel. This war of nerves continued for years. Lord Glenelg as secretary of state virtually ignored Hay and reposed entire confidence in Stephen, but he could not bring himself to demand Hay's resignation; and Hay refused to accommodate him.[4]

Stephen, Taylor, and the parliamentary undersecretary, Sir George Grey, regularly informed Howick of what was going on in the Colonial Office; and he importuned Melbourne and Glenelg to end an impossible situation by dismissing Hay. Finally, in 1836, Glenelg, confronted with an ultimatum from Stephen that he intended to resign, dismissed Hay, and Stephen became officially what he had already been in fact, permanent undersecretary of state, a position he was to occupy for the next eleven years.

The judgment of Stephen's contemporaries accords with more recent evaluations by historians in only one respect: Stephen's contributions to the organization of the Colonial Office and to the formulation of imperial policy were impressive. Charles Buller wrote a famous satire of him as "Mr. Mother-Country," who lived in a world of blue books and dispatches, divorced from the realities of life but exercising a baneful influence over colonial policy. Buller's opinion was widely shared by those who sought to promote a more flexible relationship

---

[4] Howick explained Glenelg's temporizing in terms of his fear that the Tories, when they returned to office, would retaliate by dismissing his brother-in-law, who held a position in the Home Office (Howick's Journal, Jan. 18, 1836, Grey Papers). More likely, his lack of decisiveness toward Hay reflected Glenelg's disinclination to face hard decisions.

between the colonies and Great Britain. The *Colonial Magazine* wrote
in 1841:

The permanent under-secretary, Mr. Stephen, is a man of plodding industry, a lawyer of much subtlety, fluctuating as a weathercock in politics, alter-
nately democrat and despot, and who possesses the confidence of no one
colony in the empire. Under Mr. Stephen are many clerks, not one of whom
is known to have ever been in any colony, whose names are entirely unknown,
and who with much tact move the puppets who are put forth as the responsible advisers of the crown. This is our colonial policy and government.[5]

Stephen's intimate friends agreed that he dominated the Colonial
Office, but to them he was a giant figure who with selfless dedication
to duty had created the constructive policies for which others had
received the credit. Charles Greville wrote to Taylor on the occasion
of Stephen's retirement:

. . . here is a man with stupendous powers of mind and great acquirements,
who has devoted himself to the public service; in a manner the most modest
and conscientious consenting to occupy a subordinate situation, casting aside
all personal ambition, indifferent to that public admiration and applause
which are dear to most men, and satisfying himself with the approbation of
his own conscience, and the regard and esteem of the few who are really
acquainted with his great qualities and powers.[6]

Recent investigations have demonstrated that Stephen was neither
a dull unimaginative clerk nor "Mr. Oversecretary." [7] He was a highly
competent public servant, a master of the art of précis writing, whose
long experience with colonial questions had given him a surer grasp
of imperial problems than any of his superiors, with the possible
exception of the third Earl Grey. By his powers of dissection he was
able to influence the decisions of secretaries of state, particularly if
the secretary disliked the tedious, exhausting, and time-consuming
tasks of reading voluminous state papers. Even a conscientious secretary

---

[5] *Colonial Magazine*, IV, no. 16 (1841), p. 405.

[6] Greville to Taylor [1847?], in Edward Dowden, ed., *Correspondence of Henry
Taylor* (London: Longmans, Green, 1888), p. 166.

[7] See Paul Knaplund, *James Stephen and the British Colonial System* (Madison:
University of Wisconsin Press, 1953); E. Trevor Williams, "James Stephen and
British Intervention in New Zealand, 1838–40," *Journal of Modern History*, XIII
(March, 1941), 19–35; W. L. Burn, *Emancipation and Apprenticeship in the
British West Indies* (London: Cape, 1937); Paul Knaplund, "Mr. Oversecretary
Stephen," *Journal of Modern History*, I (March, 1929), 39–66; and J. C. Beagle-
hole, "The Colonial Office, 1782–1854," *Historical Studies, Australia and New
Zealand*, I (April, 1941), 170–189.

of state could not read all of the mass of material that flowed into the Colonial Office in ever-increasing volume, and also attend to his other responsibilities.[8] Not only did Stephen read it, but he digested it and retained its essentials for future reference. Such a mind was a priceless asset. But to suggest that Stephen dictated colonial policy is grossly to overstate his influence and to understate the powers of the secretaries of state under whom he served. Stephen was always a subordinate, available for advice and information, but never presuming to attempt to usurp power that did not properly belong to his office. Had he been so inclined, he would have been promptly rebuked, for secretaries of state, however indolent or active they might be, were jealous of their authority.

Some ministers, notably Glenelg and Grey, held Stephen in high esteem and valued his opinions, whether or not they agreed with him. Stanley disliked him and made important decisions without consulting him. Russell considered him a pernicious influence, a man who had contributed to the problems of the Empire by his lack of respect for colonial self-government.[9] But all of them, willingly or grudgingly, conceded his high sense of public duty and his unusual mental powers.

It was the fate of Stephen to be permanent undersecretary in an era when the traditional structure of empire was being subjected to attack. The outcome of this conflict was a more flexible relationship between Britain and her colonies, but in the meantime much bitterness was engendered among the supporters of colonial self-government against those who opposed their cause. Stephen became the scapegoat for attacks on the old order. Ministers changed frequently, but Stephen remained in an exposed position, pilloried as a living symbol of reaction. Publicly he displayed indifference to his detractors, and his lack of response contributed to the legend that he was insensitive to abuse. In fact he suffered torture, and the wounds never healed. During all the years he had served in the Colonial Office, as counsel and as undersecretary, he wrote Howick in 1845, he had never been free from obloquy because of his alleged dictation of colonial policies. He had been silent because vindication would have involved a breach

---

[8] During his secretaryship Grey had an inventory made of dispatches and letters received in the Colonial Office. The totals were as follows: 1822–5,195; 1823–4,961; 1824–7,941; 1846–10,049; 1847–11,443; 1848–12,018 (Grey Papers).

[9] Russell wrote: "It was the fault of Stephen that instead of being Under Secy *for* the Colonies, he was *more* Under Secy *against* the Colonies. If we cry stinking fish, it is no wonder our customers are few" (Russell to Grey, March 16, 1848, Grey Papers).

of confidence, but now in his waning years his good name was important, if not to him, to his children.[10] No one could read this letter
without recognizing that here was a highly sensitive human being who
had suffered for his virtues rather than for his sins. He was a dedicated
public servant who deserved the emulation of his successors as permanent undersecretary.

Stephen's passion for precision made him impatient with the deficiencies of his staff, and he could scourge a subordinate who was guilty
of slipshod work.[11] His zeal for efficiency, however, did not extend to
the reorganization of the permanent establishment, which remained
essentially unaltered throughout his tenure in office. It was not until
1850, three years after Stephen's retirement, that significant organizational reforms were effected. Before 1855 the personnel of most government offices won their initial appointments by patronage rather than
by merit alone; the Colonial Office differed only in that the quality
of its appointees was usually higher than in most other departments.[12]

Since the reforms of 1821–1825 the Colonial Office had been divided
into one general and four geographical departments: North American,
West Indian, African, and Mediterranean. In 1843 another department was added, the Miscellaneous. Each of the geographical departments was under a senior clerk who reported to the permanent undersecretary. The permanent staff, which numbered only twenty-five in
1833, did not substantially increase during Stephen's tenure. The clerk
in charge of the African division was George Barrow, who had been
appointed in 1825 through the influence of his distinguished father,
Sir John, and who demonstrated during his long years of office that the
genius of the parent is not necessarily conferred upon the son. Young
Barrow showed no aspirations to rise beyond his station; he remained
an uninspired subordinate, capable of summarizing documents with a
fair degree of precision but devoid of any inclination to present an
idea of how problems might be resolved. So far as the formulation of
policy at the Cape was concerned, therefore, the significant officials
were Stephen, the parliamentary undersecretary, and the secretary of
state.

Among the parliamentary undersecretaries in the period between

---

[10] Stephen to Howick, Feb. ——, 1845, Grey Papers.

[11] Even Taylor, his most devoted admirer, was forced to admit that Stephen was a
most difficult master (Taylor's comments to Grey, Aug. 2, 1847, Grey's Journal, Grey
Papers).

[12] R. B. Pugh, "The Colonial Office, 1801–1925," in *The Cambridge History of
the British Empire*, III (Cambridge: University Press, 1959), 717.

1834 and 1854 only two might be considered important in their contributions to South African policy: Sir George Grey, who served under Lord Glenelg, and Benjamin Hawes, under Lord Grey. Both these men, because their superiors were in the House of Lords, had the responsibility of defending the government's colonial policy in the Commons. Sir George Grey was an able and energetic politician who took his position seriously; his advice was influential in the formulation of the celebrated Glenelg dispatch reversing Governor D'Urban's annexation of territory to the Kei River. Hawes, less talented than Sir George, and serving under a colonial secretary who was far less inclined to seek advice, nevertheless did not hesitate to express his opinions with vigor on issues of colonial policy, even when he knew they were at odds with the views of Earl Grey. Generally, however, between 1834 and 1854 the parliamentary undersecretary made little distinctive contribution to the formulation of policy. The important decisions were made by the secretary of state in consultation with the permanent undersecretary.[13]

The myth of "King Stephen" involved a corollary, that the secretaries of state for colonies were "either well-intentioned nonentities or men of first class ability who took this minor office as a step toward higher place." [14] This conclusion will not bear examination. Certainly the colonial department did not confer as much prestige on its possessor as did the Foreign Office or the Exchequer, but neither was it a minor office to be filled by political hacks or young men on the make. The price of incompetence in colonial policy was too high to risk appointment of a mediocrity or worse. The office might not add much glitter to the accomplishments of a government, but it could be the means of its embarrassment or even defeat. Between 1815 and the Crimean War, no other department gave so much grief to the budget makers as did the Colonial Office. Henry Wood, Chancellor of the Exchequer, wrote to Grey in 1847, "I do wish you had a petty Ch. of Ex. in the Colonial Office, for your money concerns are more troublesome than

---

[13] One innovation of Stephen's which makes possible such a generalization is the practice of minuting of dispatches. Although it is not true that he originated the practice, minuting as a general procedure began with his appointment as permanent undersecretary.

[14] E. L. Woodward, *The Age of Reform, 1815–1870* (Oxford: Clarendon Press, 1938), p. 351. Before 1854 the control of the offices of War and Colonies was assigned to a single secretary of state. But most of the secretary of state's attention was directed to colonial affairs, and he seems rarely to have exercised close supervision over military matters. Examination of the confused administrative relationships in the army makes the disasters of the Crimean War understandable.

all the other departments in Westminster. . . ." [15] Other keepers of the keys to the Treasury would have endorsed Wood's opinion.

Certainly the seals of the Colonial Office were held by some young politicians who later achieved even greater eminence. Russell held the office for two years in the second Melbourne government, Stanley for almost five in the Peel ministry, and Gladstone for a few months in the same administration. But Russell was forty-seven when he became colonial secretary, and was already a power in the government as its leader in the House of Commons; Stanley was forty-two and had already achieved a brilliant reputation; and Gladstone's short tenure at the age of thirty-six was terminated by the dissolution of the ministry. None of these treated his responsibilities lightly. Russell retained a lively interest in colonial matters long afterward; as prime minister he sometimes seemed to be acting as an overseer to the incumbent, Earl Grey. Gladstone also continued to give close attention to colonial problems after he left office.

Earl Grey, who served for six years, was a difficult colleague whose rigidity of opinions and bluntness of expression made him unpopular on both sides of the house, but not even his severest critics ever expressed doubts as to his ability or his public spirit. His enemies, who were many, called him haughty and arrogant; they mistook his temper. With Grey the welfare of Britain and the Empire overrode all other considerations; he thought little of the private concerns or sensitivities of other individuals or of himself when opposed to the public interest. Henry Taylor, who was intimately acquainted with him for decades, wrote that "when public interests have permitted it, I have not known any man more careful of the interests and feelings of those serving under him in the Colonies, or more truly liberal in his manner of dealing with them." [16]

Of the lesser-known ministers, Thomas Spring-Rice, the colonial secretary in the first Melbourne administration, certainly was no mediocrity in the eyes of his associates; he was selected as Chancellor of the Exchequer in the reconstituted Melbourne government in 1835. Taylor stated that he had known "few men . . . whose knowledge of all sorts of subjects, literary and political, was more extensive, and none who could acquire knowledge, and make it ready for use, more swiftly as well as effectively." James Stephen said of him, "If

[15] Wood to Grey, April 9, 1847, Grey Papers.
[16] Taylor to Editor, *North British Review*, May 1, 1852, in Dowden, *op. cit.*, p. 197.

you multiply his matter into his velocity you get a very considerable momentum." [17]

The Duke of Newcastle, who served in the office between 1852 and 1854, was a capable administrator and an influential politician. Though his association with the war department after its separation from the Colonial Office in the Crimean War was a disaster, the responsibility for tragic maladministration was not his alone, but was shared by the entire administration and its predecessors who had allowed the military establishment to fall into decay.

Lord Normanby and Sir John Pakington served too briefly to demonstrate their talents; but Normanby had been Lord Lieutenant of Ireland and moved from the colonial department to the Home Office, while Pakington, whose appointment in the Derby government of 1852 was generally regarded as a travesty, served as First Lord of the Admiralty in the Derby ministries of 1858 and 1866.

The legend that secretaries of state were incompetent or indifferent seems to be personified in one minister, Charles Grant, Lord Glenelg, who held the office between 1835 and 1839. One of the few subjects on which Radicals and Tories could agree was that Glenelg was totally unqualified to hold office. He was "sluggish and somnolent," [18] "a poor nervous incapable man," [19] "notoriously incompetent," [20] "vacillating and procrastinating." [21] Disasters in Canada and confusion at the Cape, his detractors alleged, were largely the responsibility of this heavy-lidded, apathetic nonentity. Crises that would have roused others to action scarcely caused him to lose a day's sleep.[22] The *Times*, which in the 1830's was a rowdy, brawling antagonist of the Whig government, found in Glenelg a perfect target for its satire. In a leading article in 1836 it wrote of him:

Observing, from the Court Circular, that poor Lord Glenelg is still unreleased from his languors at the Colonial Office, we are extremely loth, just at the commencement of the shooting season, to disturb that autumnal variety of the *otium cum*, wherewith we doubt not he is preparing to *brace* himself

[17] Henry Taylor, *Autobiography* (2 vols.; London: Longmans, Green, 1885), I, 211.

[18] *Ibid.*, p. 147.

[19] Howick's Journal, Jan. 6, 1838, Grey Papers.

[20] Molesworth in House of Commons, March 6, 1838, *Parliamentary Debates*, 3d series, XLI, 481.

[21] William IV's characterization (Spencer Walpole, *The Life of Lord John Russell* [2 vols.; London: Longmans, Green, 1889], I, 268).

[22] The sneer was originally Lord Brougham's; like many others of Brougham's poisonous witticisms, it was delightedly repeated by the malevolent gossips of the day.

for the relaxation of another session, if the Ministry shall survive to see one. Disturb, did we say? No, that may not be; for happily or unhappily, it is the curious peculiarity of this piece of official still-life, that while wielding habitually a mischievous influence unknown to that condition, his Lordship possesses withal a more than ordinary share of its unconsciousness and imperturbability.[23]

This characterization of Glenelg was a misrepresentation, but, like the libel of Stephen, it gained weight by repetition. The allegation that he was somnolent seems to have originated in a meeting of the cabinet at Holland House early in the first Melbourne administration. After dinner the ministers had returned to continue a detailed discussion of the phraseology of a bill, but the combination of food, wine, and tedium had a soporific effect, and when Lady Holland looked into the room after the meeting was over she found Melbourne and Glenelg asleep on sofas on opposite sides of the room.[24] Melbourne had other attributes upon which the wits could concentrate; but poor Glenelg, whose private life was above reproach, was ridiculed as the man who slept at cabinet meetings.

Glenelg was not a distinguished colonial secretary, but he was far from incompetent. Even his most violent enemies occasionally admitted grudgingly that his intellectual powers were far above the ordinary. Christopher Bird, former colonial secretary at the Cape and an intimate friend of Governor D'Urban, whom he believed to have been a victim of Glenelg's misguided policies, nevertheless described Glenelg, in a letter to D'Urban, as "a man of great talent" and "an excellent scholar." [25] Glenelg's outstanding faults, which infuriated activists like Howick and Russell, were a lack of decisiveness, a reluctance to commit himself to a line of policy until he had acquired all the relevant facts, and an excessive preoccupation with the details of composition of his dispatches. His temperament was that of a scholar, an excessively fastidious scholar, not that of an administrator.

Glenelg came to office when Canada was on the brink of revolt, the West Indies were in turmoil as the aftermath of emancipation, and the Cape was embroiled in a Kaffir war. Glenelg, like Stephen, became

---

[23] *Times*, Sept. 10, 1836.

[24] Memorandum by Russell, n.d., PRO 30/22/11, P.R.O. This was not the only instance of a sleeping cabinet; another and more famous instance occurred on the evening of June 28, 1854, during the Crimean War (see Alexander William Kinglake, *The Invasion of the Crimea* [8 vols.; Edinburgh: Blackwood, 1863–1887], II, 94, and App. I).

[25] Bird to D'Urban, private, March 4, 1839, D'Urban Papers, VII, Cape Archives.

a sacrificial victim. If the Empire was in turmoil the colonial minister and his permanent undersecretary must obviously be responsible, as the decisions on colonial policy were theirs to make. Perhaps it was as a fellow sufferer that Stephen called Glenelg "the most laborious, the most conscientious and the most enlightened of Colonial Secretaries," [26] but the praise was not entirely unmerited. Glenelg was no puppet under the control of his able subordinate; he made his own decisions after long and arduous study of the facts. That this consideration was too long and too arduous was perhaps his most serious fault.

In the period between 1834 and 1854, secretaries of state for colonies were not inferior either in capacity or in industry to other ministers of cabinet rank. Few departments of the government could boast of subordinates as capable as theirs. The disasters that aroused Parliament from its habitual apathy toward colonial matters were the product neither of ignorance nor of incompetence in the Colonial Office. Dispatches were written and policies were enunciated only after the most thorough study. The department was no mere devourer of blue books, devoid of understanding of the flesh-and-blood realities of colonial societies, registering its conclusions on the basis of paper research. Perhaps on occasion the Colonial Office did give insufficient weight to the opinions of the man on the spot. Perhaps in its understanding of the wider context which he did not see, it sometimes was unable to understand sufficiently the peculiar problems that he had to face. The Colonial Office, however, was subject to two limitations beyond its control: the dictates of British society, and its distance in time and space from the colonies.

Before the end of 1850, when steamships began to be regularly employed, communications with the Cape were almost entirely by sailing ship. Dispatches in both directions usually awaited the adventitious sailing of a warship or a merchantman. The time of the journey varied considerably, depending on such factors as weather and the character of the ship, but normally about three months were required, so that a minimum of half a year elapsed between a governor's request for guidance and his receipt of a reply. Under these circumstances Downing Street confided wide responsibilities to governors, restricting itself to broad statements of policy. The basic limitation imposed upon a governor's freedom of action—that he must have "due regard" for economy—was not departmental but was laid down by the mandate of the government, Parliament, and the electorate. The resources permitted him were small, and the responsibilities were great; the

[26] Burn, *op. cit.,* p. 139.

decisive voice in British colonial policy in the nineteenth century was the mandate of the budget.[27]

Because South Africa was valued by the government as a naval base, governors at the Cape until 1854 were, with one exception, professional soldiers who viewed the problems of the frontier from the standpoint of military security. A keenly perceptive politician has said: "Give a general any situation and he'll find strategic significance in it. I don't trust generals' appraisals of strategic significance." [28] This suspicion of generals is to an extent applicable to the policies of the military governors of the Cape, who sometimes were overly dominated by considerations of strategy and tactics, but the fundamental cause of failure did not lie with them. Nor did it rest with their superiors in Downing Street. It was inherent in the conjunction of exalted ends and meager means which British society imposed upon policy in southern Africa.

Another, but secondary, cause of difficulty was division of responsibility. In the nineteenth century the functions of government, though steadily increasing, were few, and the number of offices and office-holders was small. But the characteristics of bureaucracy were already observable in embryonic form. An agency created to be a means to an end tended to become an end in itself; an official assigned to expedite business became another echelon of obstruction. Imperial policy became the responsibility of a number of departments, each of which by its veto or, more commonly, by its inaction, could complicate the problems of the Colonial Office. In this negative sense, major participants in colonial policy were the Treasury, the Board of Ordnance, and the commander in chief of the Horse Guards. As students of colonial policy have usually concluded that the Colonial Office itself was efficiently administered during the regimes of Stephen and his successors as permanent undersecretary, they have tended to seek another villain as the cause of delay. The usual selection for this role has been the Treasury. In this conclusion they agree, probably not coincidentally, with Stephen himself. Stephen fumed that "it does not take less than two months to obtain an answer from the Treasury to Letters from this Office." [29]

Certainly such delays did occur; what should be surprising is that

---

[27] For a most effective expression of this viewpoint, see C. W. de Kiewiet, *The Imperial Factor in South Africa* (Cambridge: University Press, 1937), p. 9.

[28] N. Khrushchev, as quoted in the *Sunday Times* (London), Nov. 15, 1959.

[29] E. Trevor Williams, "The Colonial Office in the Thirties," *Historical Studies, Australia and New Zealand,* II (May, 1943), 150.

they were not more protracted, for the responsibilities of the Treasury were great and its staff was small. In 1831 the requirement was instituted that the Treasury must be consulted in the appropriation of public money for colonial purposes; previously such decisions could be made by the colonial secretary alone. Thereafter decisions were often delayed for months, sometimes even for years, but the conclusion that the Treasury was primarily responsible has never been documented and is probably unfair. Charles Trevelyan, the permanent head of the Treasury, was no myopic ledger slave; he was one of the ablest civil servants of his day, and in fact was called upon to assist in the re-organization of the public service shortly after Stephen's retirement. Some of his subordinates no doubt held up important decisions by an excessive preoccupation with details, but the main causes of delay seem to have been inadequate staff and ineffective liaison. For the latter Stephen must bear some share of the responsibility. In 1843, during a protracted stalemate encompassing several offices, Stephen complained that officials of the various departments were "all writing to each other on the subject," while "no one hand grasps and weaves together all the scattered threads of this intricate series of letters." For such a task Stephen himself would seem to have been the logical selection.[30]

When departments beyond the Colonial Office and the Treasury were concerned, opportunities for delay were naturally multiplied. One instance of an almost complete breakdown of communications occurred over the project for providing barracks accommodations for troops on the frontiers of Cape Colony. So long as the troops had been regarded as a field force, their officers could employ them in the erection and repair of living quarters; but when the buildings became the property of the public, jurisdiction passed to the ordnance department, and soldiers were no longer permitted to make repairs because any unauthorized changes in the structure subjected the personnel responsible to a claim for damages. Consequently, buildings decayed while the miserable inmates cursed the government. The medical officer at Fort Willshire reported in 1821 that the roofs of the barracks and the hospital needed repair; he made the same report with increasing emphasis in 1828, 1830, and 1833, with no results. In 1833 he wrote:

The Barracks remain in the same dilapidated state, nothing in the shape of repairs having been attempted. Works were commenced at the beginning of the year, but after taking off part of the roof &c, their further proceedings

---

[30] Pugh, *op. cit.*, p. 727.

were stopped. I feel myself called upon in this place to state, that the Hospital, owing to the badness of the roof, is scarcely fit to accommodate the patients, every storm or even slight fall of rain drenches them in their beds, without any means of avoiding or escaping from the descending drops which find their way through the sieve-like roof.[31]

With perhaps a trace of sarcasm, the medical officer pointed out that the commissariat department provided tarpaulins to protect grain from the weather and that, if repairs were impossible, perhaps such protection might be provided for the sick soldiers in the hospital. In some other frontier stations there were no barracks at all, the soldiers being housed in wattle and daub huts which were probably better protection against the elements than leaky, drafty tenements. Significantly, the only places where barracks accommodations were adequate were at headquarters stations in Cape Town and on the frontier.[32]

It would be an overstatement to say that the process of authorization moved at a snail-like pace. The first requests for new barracks at the Cape were transmitted to the Colonial Office in 1828. By 1841 no perceptible progress had been made, and two-thirds of the frontier force remained unprovided with barracks! In 1844 the senior engineering officer at the Cape, in an inspection of the frontier, found that of the proposed defenses and barracks accommodations authorized in 1837, only one-third had been completed; and if this rate of construction continued, another fourteen years would be required for completion, by which time the original construction would be in a state of decay.[33]

Such a breakdown in administration, incredible even in the present era, was not the fault of any office or of any individual. It was the product of zeal for economy and of division of the responsibility for frugality among a number of different departments. Until the beginning of the nineteenth century responsibility for a decision would have been assumed by the prime minister, whose orders would have ended all discussion among the departments concerned. But with the increase of public business during and after the Napoleonic Wars, the head of the government was no longer able to devote his personal attention to such matters. During the war the secretary of state for war and colonies exercised the power of decision, but with the peace, the system disintegrated into a competition among a number of

---

[31] Extract from Report on Sickness and Mortality among the Troops serving at the Cape of Good Hope, n.d., Grey Papers.

[32] Ibid.

[33] C.O. to Trevelyan, Sept. 10, 1841, C.O. 48/215, P.R.O.

departments, each jealous of its prerogatives. Rather than regarding themselves as coöperative agencies engaged in a common service, they viewed one another as competitors; in fact, all were "rivals for the praise of retrenchment and frugality," for which genuine economy was continually sacrificed.[34]

On such matters as military construction, five sets of correspondence were required: between Colonial Office and governor, Ordnance and their officers, Colonial Office and Treasury, Colonial Office and Ordnance, and Treasury and Ordnance. Thus five distinct series of letters were being written at the same time on the same subject matter. The result was chaos; as no one office or individual had the power of final decision, the various departments became enmeshed in a complicated correspondence which absorbed their energies and the public money while projects remained in abeyance. It seemed that the departments had become entangled in a circulating correspondence almost entirely divorced from the avowed objects, and that the purpose of a department had become the perpetuation of itself and the defense of its interest. Consequently men died and thousands of pounds were lost while departments deliberated. In Jamaica, for example, troops perished from exposure to the elements while clerks in Westminster debated over the exact expense to be authorized for barracks to house them. Purely in economic terms the process was wasteful, for the cost of replacing the casualties was higher than the cost of constructing even the most sumptuous quarters.[35]

One example of this dreary routine illustrates the nature of the problem. In 1832 Lieutenant Colonel R. Thomson submitted plans for the defense of the Cape's eastern frontier to the inspector general of fortifications. The master general and the Board of Ordnance which finally considered the case a year later declined to come to any decision until the new governor of the Cape, Sir Benjamin D'Urban, had visited the frontier and reported on the desirability of the project.[36] But before he could perform this task a Kaffir war broke out. After the end of hostilities Lieutenant Colonel Lewis of the Cape Engineers prepared another plan at the behest of D'Urban; but before any action was taken, D'Urban was replaced by Sir George Napier. The Colonial Office requested Napier to make another survey, and in 1838 he sub-

---

[34] Colonial Office memo based on Napier to Glenelg, July 12, 1838, C.O. 48/189, P.R.O.

[35] *Ibid.*

[36] Thomson to D'Urban, May 26, 1838, D'Urban Typescript, Provincial Library, Cape Town.

mitted a plan for fortifications which he estimated would cost the Treasury £19,435. The secretary of state, Lord Normanby, transmitted this proposal to the Treasury and to the Board of Ordnance with the recommendation that the governor be authorized to proceed with the construction of these works, which he considered absolutely necessary. The Board of Ordnance, however, in examining Lewis' and Napier's plans, reported that it found Lewis' proposals in some respects superior, and requested further information. Normanby thereupon ordered Napier not to undertake any additional expenditures until he received further instructions. During the prolonged silence that followed, Napier had further consultation with Lewis on defense of the frontier and in February, 1840, submitted a memoir by Lewis proposing the formation of military villages of pensioners and settlers as the best system for the protection of the border against the depredations of the Kaffirs. Lewis' proposals were referred to the general commanding in chief, Lord Hill, who found it completely unacceptable, contending that these pensioner villages would probably "be the present discomfort and future ruin" of the inhabitants.[37] This issue became intertwined with the earlier correspondence, thus contributing to general paralysis.[38] One cannot read the interoffice correspondence of this era without wonderment that a system so hostile to efficiency could have been tolerated for so long.

But after due weight has been given to the characteristics of ministers, the contributions of this or that public official, and the dead weight of bureaucratic inefficiency, it must be acknowledged that these were not the basic determinants of imperial policy. The course pursued by Britain at the Cape was not decided by the accidents of domestic party politics or by the peculiar attributes of the minister who happened to be the incumbent. It was dictated by forces of far greater moment.

Basically imperial policy sought to serve the interests of British industry and commerce; in this context the Cape was important only in relation to the riches of the East. As the interior was considered the "most sterile and worthless" in the whole Empire,[39] with no pos-

---

[37] Memo on Napier to Glenelg, July 12, 1838, C.O. 48/189, P.R.O. This system was later tried by Harry Smith, and Hill's prophecy was proved correct.

[38] See, for example, minutes on Napier to Normanby, Aug. 19, 1839, C.O. 48/201; Ordnance to Stephen, Feb. 3, 1840, C.O. 48/209; minutes on Trevelyan to Stephen, Feb. 27, 1840, C.O. 48/209; and Treasury to C.O., Dec. 14, 1841, C.O. 48/215, all in P.R.O.

[39] Minute by Stephen, Feb. 19, [1841?], on Napier to Glenelg, July 12, 1838, C.O. 48/189, P.R.O.

sibilities for commercial exploitation, parsimony was particularly enjoined on the government. But side by side with this cold appraisal of national interest was a sense of higher destiny, a recognition of obligation to the peoples under British jurisdiction, of which the missionary movement was one, but only one, expression. These material and spiritual forces at times seemed diametrically opposed, pointing to contrary lines of policy. Certainly British statesmen were keenly aware of this duality. Melbourne in 1838 sent Russell a copy of Buxton's *The Slave Trade and Its Remedy,* advising him to read it carefully because it would be the manual of the Saints during the next session of Parliament and the government must do its best not to antagonize them. "But," he added, "it is impossible not to feel that religion, morality, law, eloquence, cruisers will all be ineffectual, when opposed to a profit of cent. per cent. and more." [40] At the Cape the material interest was not profit, but its obverse, economy. In an analysis of British policy in southern Africa there is a temptation to emphasize this clash of material and spiritual forces. Such an approach has the great merit that it produces maximum dramatic effect; it has the decisive defect that it is a gross oversimplification. The problems of South Africa were, as they have continued to be, complex; and British policy was not determined simply by the interaction of opposites, with the lines of policy being the mere resultant of forces. Just as it is true that "the moods of a thinking man in politics are curiously evasive and difficult to describe," [41] so also are the motives of governments.

---

[40] Melbourne to Russell, Sept. 3, 1838, in Lloyd C. Sanders, *Lord Melbourne's Papers* (London: Longmans, Green, 1889), pp. 376–377.

[41] H. G. Wells, *The New Machiavelli* (London: Odhams, n.d.), p. 234.

Chapter III

SOUTHERN AFRICA IN 1834

SOME SAY THE DEVIL sits upon the peak which bears his name, smoking his pipe and surveying his South African domain.[1] Few have seen him, but the evidence of his presence is overwhelming. Only a malignant spirit intent on using humanity for grisly amusement could have conceived the tragedy of South African history. It was fated that Boers and Bantu could neither live together nor prosper separately. Environment was conducive to racialism in an economically interdependent society. Other societies had achieved order through the elimination of the weaker by the stronger civilization; in this land such a resolution of conflict was impossible. The virile Bantu could be dominated, at least for a time; they could not be exterminated or reduced to social insignificance as had the Australian aborigines or the North American Indians. Nor did the Europeans wish to exterminate them, for their labor was essential to the South African economy in all phases of its development—pastoral, mining, and industrial. The Europeans subjugated the Africans, who became in time a rightless proletariat, condemned to serve the white man's requirements with little return for themselves. Britain assumed control of the Cape at a time when humanitarian influences were exerting an increasing influence on imperial policy; humanitarianism and economy further complicated interracial relations and spread the virus of racial conflict into areas hitherto untouched.

The ecology of southern Africa could not be basically altered by the intervention of any alien authority, certainly not by that of the British government of the nineteenth century. Natural factors exerted far too strong an influence to be constructively controlled by the efforts of a few officials, however perceptive they might be.

South Africa was the graveyard of political reputations, not because

[1] How long the Devil has been there is a matter of speculation, but his partner Jan van Hunks arrived quite recently; the "folk tale" of their smoking match seems to have originated in the twentieth century (see Dante Gabriel Rossetti, *Jan Van Hunks*, ed. John R. Wahl [New York: New York Public Library, 1952]).

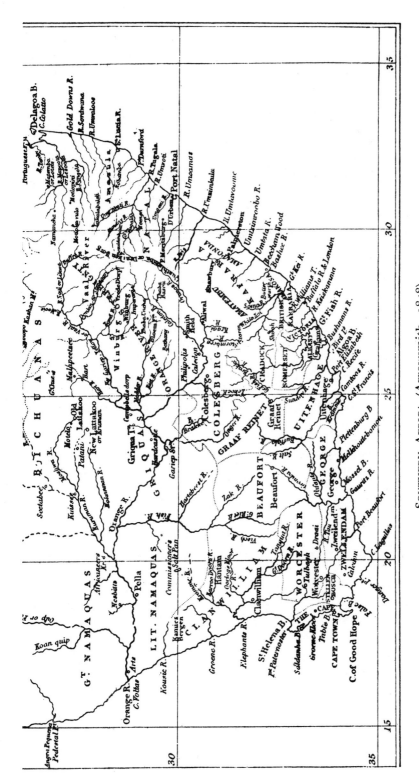

Southern Africa (Arrowsmith, 1848)

of lack of intelligence either in Downing Street or in Cape Town's government house, but because the problems with which officials had to wrestle were inherently insoluble. Every governor between 1834 and 1854 left the Cape frontiers in a more inflamed condition than he had found them; and three, Sir Benjamin D'Urban, Sir Peregrine Maitland, and Sir Harry Smith, were ruined. South African policy was not the cause of Lord Glenelg's downfall, but his name has been held in obloquy by white South Africans from his day to the present; and the Cape frontier contributed to the defeat of the Russell government in 1852 and wrecked the political career of Earl Grey, the most knowledgeable colonial secretary of the nineteenth century. Dias had been prophetic when he had called that ill-omened landfall Cabo Tormentoso.

South Africa, except for a narrow strip along its eastern coast, is a vast plateau varying from 3,000 to 6,000 feet above sea level, interspersed with flat-topped *tafelberg* and *spitzkop* hills which relieve the otherwise dead monotony of the landscape, but offer no obstacles to travel once the bordering mountain barrier has been breached. This rampart stretches from the Roggeveld Mountains on the southwest to the formidable Drakensberg on the east, rising to heights of more than 10,000 feet. The mountain ranges bordering the Cape peninsula provide scenery of spectacular beauty, and the Drakensberg chain, particularly in the land now called Basutoland, throws up majestic peaks veiled in blue which excite the admiration of the least imaginative of observers. But to the trek Boer searching for a path to the interior plateau for his stock and wagons, the mountains offered acute frustrations. When the ordeal was over and the promised land had been gained, the wandering pastoralist had isolated himself from coastal influences; traffic in goods and, more important, in ideas was meager until the mountains were tamed in the mid-nineteenth century by modern roads with relatively easy gradients.

The mountains constituted a boundary between two utterly different worlds. The well-watered southwestern Cape, the first area of European habitation, is atypical of most of southern Africa by almost any criterion; it is a smiling land of flowers and vineyards, where winter rains are more than adequate and drought is unknown. Along the coast eastward from the Cape peninsula rainfall is more evenly spread through the year, but, particularly in the eastern districts of the colony, there are periodic visitations of drought. In the border areas of white-Bantu contact, this blight made its destructive contribution to race conflict.

The great bulk of the territory embraced by the present Republic of South Africa suffers from uncertain rainfall and deficient soil. About four-fifths of it has an average annual rainfall of less than 25 inches and, except for the coastal belt of the Cape, the rainy season is in the summer when evaporation is greatest. In approximately two-fifths of the area, drought is to be expected in about one year of every three, and in most of the other years it is an ever-present specter. In the mountains, rainfall may be copious. Evelyn Valley in the Amatola Mountains of the eastern Cape has an average rainfall of 73 inches, and Belvedere in the Transvaal Drakensberg, 81 inches. The heaviest official annual precipitation in the mountains around the Cape is on Table Mountain, with an average of 75 inches, and unofficial readings in the Drakenstein Range have been as high as 200 inches. But in that part of the plateau named by the Hottentots the Karroo, the "dry country," the mean annual rainfall is only 10 inches, and even this scant precipitation is seldom attained in the western drought lands on the verge of the Kalahari. The Karroo is a region of violent contrasts. For much of the year the earth is parched and baked by the sun and ravaged by the west wind which not only sucks up the little remaining moisture but sweeps up the precious topsoil. The dust-laden air catches the sun's rays at sunset, transforming the drab scene into a riot of exotic colors. The price for this spectacle is exorbitant, for the desert marches perceptibly eastward each year.

Rain usually comes to this thirsty land in storms of great intensity; dry gullies become torrents, and the rush of water tears deep gashes in the land and washes away the soil that the drought has laid bare. The Orange River, which in the dry season sometimes is little more than a string of stagnant pools, becomes in the rainy season a torrential flood, sweeping the soil of Africa into the ocean. In this vast wilderness of the interior plateau a new species of humanity came into being, the cattle Boers, children of the Karroo just as are the thorn bushes that dot the landscape.

When Britain reconquered the Cape in 1806, the existence of such people was of no concern to the new overlords. What mattered was the possession of Cape Town and its adjacent harbors. But Great Britain had acquired not only an anchorage but a colony of between 120,000 and 130,000 square miles, which on its northeastern border faced problems of great magnitude and complexity. Along the Fish River the leading edge of white settlement had already encountered the southernmost extension of the Xosa tribes, and this turbulent border was soon to be further disturbed by a catastrophe to the north. In the country

beyond the Tugela River in modern Natal, Dingiswayo, King of the
Abatetwa, had fashioned his impis into a perfectly disciplined fighting
force, which under his successor Chaka, chief of the Zulus, would fall
upon the tribes of the coast, stabbing and burning, leaving death and
desolation, and, either directly or through others whom his wars had
driven into flight, producing eruptions as far away as Nyasaland to the
north and Bechuanaland to the west. This was the *Mfecane,* the crushing, a disaster of cataclysmic proportions, and the reverberations
rolled across the borders of the Cape. Remnants of tribes flying south-
westward before the Zulus pressed in upon the Xosa people, contributing to the roiling of the already troubled frontier. British governors knew little of the nature of the eruptions to the northeast, but
were caught up in their consequences. From the perspective of Cape
Town, the problem was one of producing a stable border at minimum
expense; but a stable border was not possible so long as the society on
one side was in a condition of instability. Governors were driven to
various expedients in their efforts to produce order on both sides of
the boundary; they were doomed to failure because failure was inherent in the magnitude of the problems with which they had to contend and the paucity of resources at their disposal.

In 1834, except for tiny clusters of population around Cape Town,
Grahamstown, and a few other villages, Cape Colony was largely
wasteland. On the interior plateau a few specks of humanity wandered
with their wagons and their herds, engulfed by the vast expanses of
the wilderness. Of so little consequence was this desert that the boundary of the colony from the Atlantic Ocean to the Orange River was no
more than a random line scratched jaggedly across the map. Because
colonies must be delineated, Lord Macartney had proclaimed a boundary in 1796, and this line had been reconfirmed in 1805, but it had
never been officially surveyed. From the Buffels River in the northwest
to the Orange River it skirted the southern edge of a country presumed
from travelers' descriptions to be a desert waste, for "the most part as
barren a desert as can be found upon the Earth's crust," [2] and inhabited
only by a few Bushmen.

The boundary to the east and southeast from its point of intersection
with the Orange was somewhat better delineated by a river and mountain line to the watershed of the Amatola Mountains. By contrast with
the uncertain inland boundary, that between the mountains and the
coast seemed well defined, but this precision was only apparent. The

---

[2] This description is that of the surveyor general, Charles C. Michell, enclosure in
Smith to Grey, Dec. 8, 1847, C.O. 48/279, P.R.O.

eastern line contributed to conflict rather than stability, for it possessed none of the characteristics that should be the requisites of a boundary; it was unilaterally imposed, it was vague, and it was inadequately defended.

The first attempt to draw a line between the colony and the Bantu tribes had been made by Governor Joachim van Plettenberg, who in 1778 decreed the upper Fish River as a boundary with the acquiescence of some petty Xosa chieftains who almost certainly did not understand the implications of the agreement and in any event had no power to make commitments for anyone beside themselves and their immediate followers. The Fish River, which was eventually decreed as the boundary for its entire length, was a most unsatisfactory line of demarcation. For most of the year it was a mere trickle which presented no difficulties for the crossing of men and animals. Its banks, clothed with dense vegetation, offered ideal cover for marauding parties; in its middle reaches it ran parallel rather than at right angles to the coast, and in a westerly direction, favorable to the Xosa rather than the colonists. Consequently, Plettenberg's successors chose to regard a northern tributary, the Kat River, as the true Fish River boundary, without, of course, consulting the tribes. The Fish River did not reflect a true boundary between the Bantu and the colonists, for numerous tribesmen lived in the territory west of the Fish which Plettenberg had assigned to the colony. Consequently, when efforts were made to dislodge the tribesmen, they resisted, and the frontier for the next thirty-five years was in almost constant disorder.

Lord Charles Somerset's attempt in 1819 to create a stable boundary was no more successful. By an oral agreement with Gaika, whom he chose to recognize as the paramount chief of the Xosa, the densely wooded area between the Fish and Keiskama rivers, with the exception of the vaguely defined Tyumie Valley which remained in Gaika's possession, was declared neutral, to remain depopulated of both colonists and tribesmen. This *cordon sanitaire* was to be preserved by a fort on the Keiskama and by military patrols. As the treaty was not reduced to writing, controversy inevitably arose over its terms. Somerset, who had initially referred to the territory as "neutral," soon described it as "ceded." In 1821 Acting Governor Rufane Donkin induced Gaika to permit a settlement of ex-officers in his area; at the same time Makomo and his tribe were allowed to return to the upper Kat River from which they had been expelled; and in 1825 Somerset permitted Pato, Kama, and Kobus of the Gonukwebe tribe to reëstablish themselves in the neutral territory. In 1834, consequently, the boundary of

the colony was assumed by the government in Cape Town to be the
Keiskama River. The basis for this claim was dubious indeed, and to
the west of this line lived thousands of tribesmen occupying land on
sufferance, in the view of the British authorities, but, in their own
conception, by right. On the colonial side of the Fish River the live-
stock of the farmers wandered over extensive pasturages, inadequately
watched, a sore temptation for the cattle-loving Bantu. The conditions
were there in abundance for another major eruption.

Cape Colony was by any material standard a great liability. Its
frontier, particularly between the mountains and the Indian Ocean,
was a cause of anxiety and expense, and there were few assets beyond
the harbors of the Cape peninsula. In 1834 the total white population
of the colony was only 117,858; slaves who were emancipated in the
course of the year and became apprentices totaled 36,169. So-called
"Hottentots"—for the original possessors of that name had been
mixed with other racial strains—were not listed in the official statistics,
but were approximately as numerous as the white inhabitants. Cape
Town was a village of 19,387 persons, of whom 13,804 were white.[3]
The significance of the colony as a field of British commercial activity
is reflected in the following statistics of trade for the year: [4]

Estimated Value in Pounds

IMPORTS

	From Great Britain	British colonies	United States	Foreign
Cape Town	275,049	27,200	4,349	86,229
Simon's Town	503	3,338	5,391	392
Port Elizabeth	56,868.4	3,430.10.3		19
	£332,420.4	£33,968.10.3	£9,740	£86,640
Total imports	£462,768.14.3			

EXPORTS

	To Great Britain	British Colonies	United States	Foreign
Cape Town	171,319			
Simon's Town	5,797		(Not itemized)	
Port Elizabeth	61,142.4			
	£238,258.4	£111,556	£4,664	£15,324
Total exports	£369,802			

[3] Annual Report of Cape for 1834, C.O. 53/71, P.R.O. The tax rolls of 1831–32
listed 48,672 male and 44,043 free colored inhabitants, but a large number of the
latter had no fixed residence (*Missionary Register* [Jan., 1835], p. 21).

[4] Cape Colony, Imports and Exports for 1834, C.O. 53/71, P.R.O.

Of the exports from the colony, only two commodities, wool and wine, were of much importance. But Cape wines had acquired the reputation of being inferior, and the market for them in Britain and in foreign countries was declining.[5] The export of wool, on the other hand, was rising sharply, partly as a result of the development of the industry in the eastern districts after 1820. The Cape exported only 9,000 pounds of fine wool in 1816, but by 1840 the quantity had soared to 750,000 pounds.[6] Impressive as this increase was, however, Cape production was small by comparison with the great wool-producing countries of the world.

Not only was the Cape of little commercial significance, but there seemed to be little prospect for improvement. After the British occupation all hopes for the development of the colony as a market had proved illusory. Sir George Yonge in 1800 had written to Henry Dundas that "the importance of the Cape grows in Its every Hour. It is and will become the Centre of Commerce with India, America and Europe." [7] Richard Plasket had been somewhat nearer the truth when he stated in 1827 that the colony "never can be looked upon as anything but a half-way house betwixt India and England." [8]

British control of the Cape benefited some firms, notably the shipping interests, for even after the repeal of the Navigation Acts almost all the colony's exports and imports were transported in British ships.[9] But the drain on imperial resources dwarfed all benefits to individual entrepreneurs. Military expenditures were a source of constant anguish to economy-minded chancellors of the Exchequer hounded by economy-minded Parliaments. When the Cape was captured in 1806, the imperial force left for the defense of the colony was approximately 4,000 men. Gradually, under pressure from Westminster, this establishment was reduced until at the beginning of 1834 only 1,789 men remained, of whom 1,034 were stationed in Cape Town. In addition, the imperial government maintained a corps of Hottentots which in 1834 numbered 234 rank and file, 35 noncommissioned and commissioned officers, and 200 horses. The expense of this unit, the Cape Mounted Rifles, had been borne technically by the revenues of the colony until 1828, when

---

[5] The decline in wine exports to Britain was accentuated by a reduction in British tariff preferences.

[6] Borradale to Russell, March 25, 1841, C.O. 48/215, P.R.O.

[7] Yonge to Dundas, March 29, 1800, private and confidential, in G. M. Theal, *Records of Cape Colony* (36 vols.; Cape Town: G.P.O., 1899–1907), III, 94.

[8] Plasket to Hay, Jan. 21, 1827, *ibid.*, XXX, 113. "Never" in this instance was forty years, before the diamond discoveries.

[9] In 1855 exports were valued at £1662,936, of which £622,325 were carried in British ships (C.O. 53/91, P.R.O.).

for constitutional and financial reasons the government decided to bring all colonial corps under the supervision of Parliament and to pay them from imperial funds, with the understanding that the charges would then be repaid by the respective colonial governments. No such payments had been made by Cape Colony because of its inability to support even its civil government.[10] In 1834 the total revenue of the colonial government was £119,583 and the expenditure was £120,925, of which £608 was listed as being in support of military defense. A balance sheet like this was well calculated to produce acute pain in the Treasury chambers of Westminster, particularly when it was recognized that the Cape was likely to remain a mendicant for the foreseeable future. The government secretary at the end of 1835 informed the governor that "our Treasury is ebbing fast," particularly black intelligence when the public debt amounted to £264,768.[11] British expenditure for the defense at the Cape, even after the reduction of troops to a mere skeleton establishment, was at no time less than £100,000 per year, and during the numerous Kaffir wars it rose sharply. In 1834 the total imperial expenditure at the Cape for military purposes was £114,875,[12] and the war that erupted at the end of that year cost the British Treasury an additional £154,000.[13]

Faced with these unpleasant statistics, British ministers and their advisers not unnaturally regarded the barren wastes of southern Africa with keen distaste. James Stephen could see no rational justification for straining the Treasury to benefit a population "as numerous as the inhabitants of one of the second rate towns in England," who persisted in wandering into the interior and, when they became involved in conflict, expected the home government to provide for them the same effective protection as their fellow subjects in the United Kingdom.[14] Governors of the colony heartily agreed, for beyond the relatively civilized environs of Cape Town there stretched hundreds of miles of nothingness, at the end of which lay a turbulent frontier. At best they could expect vexation; at worst they would become embroiled in a war that was certain to be costly, and equally certain to reflect no credit on the reputation of the governor as commander in chief, for it would be a war without glory. Their tribal foes were regarded in Britain and

---

[10] Memorandum (1834) on history of Cape defenses, unsigned, C.O. 537/145, P.R.O.

[11] C. F. J. Muller, *Die Britse Owerheid en die Groot Trek* (Cape Town: Juta, [1948]), pp. 29–30.

[12] Revenue and Expenditure of Cape Colony for 1834, C.O. 53/71, P.R.O.

[13] Muller, *op. cit.*, p. 29.

[14] Minute, Stephen to Smith, May 29, 1841, on Napier to Russell, March 16, 1841, C.O. 48/211, P.R.O.

in the colony as contemptible adversaries, whose primitive weapons were no match for cannon and muskets. But they were an elusive foe who would not stand to be slaughtered; and burning their huts and crops and killing their cattle, while eventually effective in reducing them to temporary impotence, could not be translated even by the most talented pen into brilliant military action. This service, said one soldier, is "most humiliating," and "the true soldier is almost ashamed when he has to report the killing of a flying enemy who will not fight, and his own imitation of the barbarian Cattle-Stealer and house burner." [15]

The inhabitants of the colony for the defense of which these wars were fought and these expenditures incurred seemed to British observers to be unworthy of imperial protection. Whatever their opinions on the policy Britain should pursue in southern Africa, Britons for the most part accepted certain stereotypes of the various racial elements. The specific characteristics assigned to these groups differed from those accepted outside South Africa in the twentieth century, but there were the same downright judgments devoid of understanding of the South African environment. The Boers were uncouth, vicious, benighted barbarians whose actions made a mockery of the Christian religion which they professed. The *Birmingham Reporter* wrote that "civilized Christians in South Africa have been nothing better than a horde of plundering and sanguinary banditti," and the *Spectator* in 1834 described the treatment of aborigines as "one of the darkest and bloodiest stains on the pages of history, and scarcely any is equal in atrocity to the conduct of the Dutch Boers, ably seconded, according to Pringle, by some of the most degraded of the English settlers." [16] When British officials arrived in Cape Town, their opinions usually underwent a modification. From their associations with burghers they were led to admit a wide variation in the characteristics of the Dutch-speaking settlers, but the trek Boers of the interior, with whom they had little or no contact, continued to exist only as types rather than as flesh-and-blood human beings. In this view they were supported by a substantial number of the residents of Cape Town, who, far from the scene of conflict, were able to preserve a high degree of detachment. It was not coincidental that the one newspaper expressing a "liberal" point of view on race relations and frontier policy, the *South African Commercial Advertiser,* was published in Cape Town.

---

[15] Enclosure in Maitland to Grey, Jan. 26, 1847, C.O. 48/271, P.R.O.

[16] George E. Cory, *The Rise of South Africa* (5 vols.; London: Longmans, Green, 1921–1930), III, 282.

The capital of the colony, several hundred miles from the frontier, lived in a world almost as insulated from racial violence as Great Britain itself. True, many of the burghers were slaveowners, for most of the slaves of the colony were kept in Cape Town and adjacent rural areas; and in the polyglot population of whites, Malays, Hottentots, and Negroes in varying degrees of admixtures color had become a badge of servitude. But the social hierarchy was well defined and widely accepted; and the subordinate castes were docile. Consequently, the racialism of Cape society, while deeply embedded, expressed itself in a soft and relaxed fashion. Further, the community as a port of call for vessels to and from the East was much more subject to cosmopolitan influences than the rest of the colony. Its mild climate made of the Cape peninsula a favorite place of retreat for retired servants of the East India Company, government officials, and army officers. Wynberg and Rondebosch, villages a few miles away, were favorite havens.[17] These retired officials exerted an additional leavening influence. Visitors to Cape Town frequently expressed surprise that a community the majority of whose white population was Dutch should be so "English" in appearance and characteristics.[18] They were superficially correct, but beneath the English veneer Cape Town was neither English nor African. Its back was to the continent and it faced an oceanic world. This environment strengthened the sense of remoteness which British officials felt toward the settlers in the interior and on the frontier. Likewise, to the frontiersmen government from Cape Town was government at a distance in both the geographical and the spiritual sense. Neither Cape Town nor Downing Street could possibly understand their problems. The *Volksraad* of the Boer republic of Natal expressed this attitude in extreme but not uncharacteristic language when it responded to Sir George Napier's ultimatum in 1842. They committed their cause to God, asserting:

We are aware of the power of Great Britain, and it is not our object in any way to defy that power; but we can at the same time as little allow that violence instead of right shall triumph over us, unless we shall have exerted

---

[17] Reference to this colony of retired officials is made in a memorandum by R. Smith, Oct. 16, 1841, C.O. 325/38, P.R.O. Before 1848 officers of the East India Company as well as those of the imperial army enjoyed the privilege of settling in certain colonies with remissions of purchase money of from £200 to £600, according to length of service (see *Cape Monitor*, Oct. 23, 1852).

[18] R. Montgomery Martin, who visited it in the 1830's, wrote that Cape Town had a more English appearance, with the exception of Sydney, than any other colonial city he had seen (*Statistics of the Colonies of the British Empire* [London: Allen, 1839], p. 474).

all our efforts to resist such violence. We do not accuse the British government of intending this, but experience has taught us that the wrong and groundless projects (as it is again manifest that the case is in our regard) having their origin in a far distant country have but too often brought to bear measures that are oppressive and unjust.[19]

These were the words of men with no doubts about the rectitude of their position or the morality of their way of life. But neither humanitarian condemnation nor Boer self-justification provided much insight into the anatomy of the trek Boers' character. In many respects they resembled their North American contemporaries who pioneered the West. Like the American frontiersmen, Boer families migrated for various reasons—some in the hope of finding a better life in the great beyond, some because of personal problems from which they sought release, some to escape the law. On both frontiers men were dominated by a restiveness under civilization and all that it implied, and by a longing for an anarchic freedom. For both Boers and frontiersmen, this freedom implied the right to do as they pleased. Both had a sense of divinely ordained superiority which justified slaughter of the natives and seizure of their lands. These similarities should not be overstated, for there were significant differences. The sparse Indian population of North America did not provide resistance comparable to that of the Bantu. The Sioux, the Apaches, and other tribes were a minor obstacle as compared to the power of the Xosa, the Matabele, or the Zulus. The pioneer of the American West was never so isolated from the world as was the cattle Boer of the high veld. The trek Boer's links with his past were his Calvinistic faith, his Bible, and his weapons, all the equipment he needed to face the problems of life on the veld.

As pastoralists the trek Boers were unprogressive; their way of life remained essentially unchanged over the generations. Travelers from Europe found them indolent and ignorant, slipping back from civilization to barbarism. The poorest of them lived in huts hardly distinguishable from those of the natives, and the homes of even the most energetic and well-to-do were primitive by comparison with the white-gabled houses of the Cape. One traveler of the 1840's, describing the "miserable hovels" of so many sheep farmers, explained this lack of the amenities partly in terms of the Boers' assumption that a house was an unnecessary luxury until a man was married and had a family.[20] The *lekker lewe*, the "lotus life," seemed a repudiation of civilization.

---

[19] *Volksraad* to Napier, Feb. 21, 1842, in John Bird, *The Annals of Natal* (2 vols.; Pietermaritzburg: Davis, 1888), I, 192.

[20] Alfred W. Cole, *The Cape and the Kafirs* (London: Bentley, 1852), p. 86.

Such observations, while correct so far as they went, were misrepresentations. Although the Boers of the far interior were unlettered and many were illiterate, they were not without regard for education. Sir George Clerk, who visited frontier families beyond the Orange River in the 1850's, was impressed by the number of Boers who maintained tutors for their children either from their own resources or jointly with other families. He found no instances of similar exertion by English settlers in remote districts. The Boers also subscribed freely to maintain clergymen when they could be had. As to their alleged indolence, Clerk pointed out that the veld was fit only for grazing and that the pastoral life was not characterized by intense activity. But the extension of the frontier into the lands of a formidable native population was not the work of indolent men; rather it had required the utmost vigilance and activity.[21]

Certainly the life of the trek Boer produced impressive physical specimens. The men were not uncommonly from 6 feet 2 inches to 6 feet 6 inches in height, and broad and muscular in proportion; and the women were worthy mates for these giants. Well might the natives look upon them as a race of supermen.[22]

From the beginning it was inevitable that there should be conflict between the trek Boers and the officials who sought to control them. To governments in Cape Town the extension of the line of settlement created more serious problems. Wherever the trek Boer went disorders erupted. It was incomprehensible that men should leave good homes and prosperous farms for the wilderness for any other than political reasons. Obviously, therefore, the primary motive must be disaffection; some officials used the stronger word "disloyalty." But the movement of the trek Boers from the eighteenth century until the Great Trek of the 1830's was political only in the sense that it was a flight from established authority, any established authority. It was a repudiation of the settled life and the ordered existence. This the comfortable inhabitant of the Cape peninsula could never understand.[23] When the government at Cape Town was seized by the British the alienation became even deeper, but the conventional emphasis of English humanitarianism versus Boer racialism is only a partial explanation. There would have been conflict between English governors and Boer frontiersmen even

---

[21] Memorandum, private, by Sir George Clerk, May 22, 1857, C.O. 537/150, P.R.O.

[22] For a discussion of the characteristics of treks and trekkers, see P. J. van der Merwe, *Die Trekboer in die Geskiedenis van die Kaapkolonie (1657–1842)* (Cape Town: Nationale Pers, 1938).

[23] Cole, *op. cit.*, p. 122.

if there had been no "humanitarian" movement. Sir George Clerk argued that the fundamental cause of British-Boer animosity was British arrogance:

This has been at the root of all the difficulties in the Cape Colony. Within it, Boers are the pith of the people. Governing that Boer community in an exclusively English fashion, English in its superciliousness, English in its abuse of patronage, we disdained to cherish their municipal institutions, or to care to be just to them in an essential matter. By such neglect or contempt we engendered hatred of us in a race, in whose character naturally there is more in common and in sympathy with ours than we find in any other people.[24]

This observation also was a partial truth. British governors and Boer frontiersmen were fated to collide because the governors were British, but also because they were governors. They might come to an understanding when their interests were in harmony, as in the 1850's when the Boer desire for freedom and the British desire for order at minimum expense led to an accommodation. In 1853 Governor Benjamin Pine of Natal expressed a viewpoint which was becoming general among British administrators when he wrote:

The existence of the Dutch Boers in South Africa is a great fact, which can never be lost sight of. They exist as a mighty engine, so far as the natives are concerned, for good or for evil. Do what we may, they must and will exercise an immense influence over the destinies of the Natives of South Africa, and upon the policy to be pursued towards them by this Government depends the question whether their influence shall be a benefit or a curse.[25]

The attitude of the British government could not be precisely the same toward the English settlers on the eastern frontier as toward the Boers, for the government was itself responsible for the settlement, which it had hoped would serve as a buffer against the Bantu tribes. The plan was ill-conceived. The zuurveld on which the colonists were settled was not suited to agriculture; many of the 5,000 settlers in the original migration left the land and moved to the towns, and most of those who remained turned to sheep or cattle raising. Consequently, the eastern border was thinly settled by widely separated pastoralists, with knots of population in Grahamstown and other villages. Rather than being a buffer, the settlement became an irresistible attraction to Bantu cattle thieves, a source of turmoil rather than security, requiring protection rather than providing it.

---

[24] Memorandum, private, by Sir George Clerk, May 22, 1857, C.O. 537/150, P.R.O.
[25] Pine to Newcastle, June 3, 1853, C.O. 179/29, P.R.O.

Because the colonists had been planted there by a British government, and financed by a parliamentary grant, Great Britain had no
alternative but to defend them. Every government recognized this
obligation, but it was not to be expected that the beneficiaries of this
protection should be regarded with affection. The settlers' strident
insistence on the need for greater protection evoked a counterstatement
that they themselves were contributing to the peril. Merchants of
Grahamstown, British officials alleged, were warmongers because they
reaped huge profits from the sale of supplies to the army, and an irresponsible press magnified every incident into a threat of a Kaffir invasion. Sir Benjamin D'Urban became the darling of the settlers because of his aggressive prosecution of the Kaffir war of 1834–1835, his
annexations of the territory to the Kei River, and his repudiation by
the Colonial Office which the colonists considered to be dominated by
pseudo humanitarianism. But in his private correspondence D'Urban
was vehement in his denunciation of the "firebrands" of Grahamstown.
He considered the *Grahamstown Journal* a purveyor of rumors that
poisoned the atmosphere and made peace difficult, if not impossible.[26]
To a confidant he wrote in the spring of 1835: "The atmosphere of
Graham's Town is charged with Panic, and it explodes on every sort
of improbable fancy from time to time, and these stories once set agoing
multiply and grow as they run." [27] Grahamstown connoted to Cape
governors political intrigue, dissidence, psychotic alarmism, and a
preoccupation with profit making which was peculiarly repulsive in
time of war. One of D'Urban's closest friends, Colonel Josias Cloete,
called the people of the Albany settlement a "money eating race." [28]

Conflict with the tribesmen bred in the English settlers a racial outlook not essentially different from that of the Boers, although it expressed itself in somewhat different language. Robert Godlonton, editor
of the *Grahamstown Journal* and one of the most influential spokesmen
of the eastern province, told an audience at Bathurst: "To them [the
eastern province settlers] was committed the task of colonizing Kaffirland, that was a work allotted to them evidently by Providence, and he
was persuaded that so long as they followed its leadings, acting in all

---

[26] On a clipping from the *Grahamstown Journal* in 1842, in which the paper
expressed the hope that "warfare [in Natal] has been brought to a close," D'Urban,
now in retirement, wrote: "It will have been brought to a close if those firebrands
do not rekindle it." When the paper stated that everything had been done to
exasperate the Boers, D'Urban commented, "This Paper and several others has done
its utmost" (D'Urban Papers, Private Letter Book I, Cape Archives).

[27] D'Urban to Thomas, March 24, 1835, *ibid.*

[28] Cloete to D'Urban, private, July 20, 1841, D'Urban Papers, VI, Cape Archives.

their dealings on principles of mercy and justice, so long would the blessing of God rest upon them and their posterity." [29] This identification of land-grabbing with the will of God was blasphemous to those who sought to defend the natives against the rapacity of the Europeans. Missionaries, particularly those of the London Missionary Society, were emphatic in their denunciation of this mentality and in turn became an object of aversion to the settlers. One missionary, a Wesleyan, wrote: "It is a lamentable fact that not only ignorant African Boers but even enlightened Englishmen when they come into the interior of Africa, are too apt to disregard native rights, and demean themselves as if they really believed that heaven had irrevocably decreed the everlasting degradation of the black races." [30]

There was misunderstanding between the British government and its agents and the white settler population of southern Africa, and between the western Cape and the frontiersmen, for each existed in a different environment, and each converted its own interests and objectives into universal moral standards. When British public opinion condemned the farmers for harsh treatment of the natives, a spokesman of the settlers could reply that in the "land of true Benevolence" notices were posted before gentlemen's parks and gardens, "MAN TRAPS AND SPRING GUNS." [31] Such a reply, of course, made no contribution to mutual understanding, and indeed no communication was possible. Each community lived within its own compartment.

To the British industrial-commercial community and the government that represented it, South Africa was important because of the harbors of Good Hope. The interests of Britain required no more than the protection of this peninsula, but the colonists perversely persisted in expanding into the interior and in the process collided with native races, creating obligations for the government which were totally unproductive and imposing a heavy drain on the British taxpayer. The evangelicals of Britain denounced this intrusion of Europeans into the territories of the tribes as contrary to morality and justice. The governors of the Cape were charged to maintain order, and they were predisposed to make judgments upon men and movements on the basis of

---

[29] Remarks by Godlonton, Aug. 16, 1847, in *Documents Relative to the Question of a Separate Government for the Eastern Districts of the Cape Colony* (Grahamstown: Godlonton and White, 1847), p. 96.

[30] Cameron to Secretaries, Wesleyan Missionary Society, July 21, 1850, in Methodist Missionary Society Archives (hereafter referred to as MMS). Cameron was stationed at Thaba Nchu and was referring to that area, but his comments applied to the settlers generally.

[31] *Friend of the Sovereignty*, Feb. 17, 1851.

the extent to which they contributed to or worked against this object.
Sir Harry Smith, who was more forthright in his expression of emotions
than most, called Andries Pretorius a "shrewd, sensible man" [32] when
he accepted the governor's authority, and a villain when he rebelled
against it. It was not Pretorius' characteristics that had changed, but
his relationship to Smith's objectives.

The trek Boer regarded those who resided in the land that Providence
had assigned to him in much the same light as the Israelites had regarded the men of Canaan, and an alien government that sought to
stay his hand was a tyrant in league with the powers of darkness. Those
who preached the false doctrine of the equality of races were evil men;
in the 1790's the Dutch East India Company had sent Landdrost
Honoratus Maynier to the frontier to impose control upon the Boers'
relations with the natives, and the Boers had driven him out; nineteenth-century Boers were no more inclined to accept restraints on
what they regarded as their inherent rights and freedoms by an alien
government dominated by the same false doctrines.

The English settler of the eastern border considered that he had a
right to the protection of his flocks and herds against marauding Kaffirs,
and that such thievery should be severely punished by government.
Like the Boers, he coveted the land of the Bantu, and, though he might
express himself less harshly, he shared the conviction that the superior
race to which he belonged had a prescriptive right to lands occupied
by more primitive peoples.

Beyond the frontier, but already in conflict with the settlers on the
eastern frontier, were the masses of the Bantu tribes, far stronger adversaries than the Hottentots with whom the first settlers had contended.
Like most other primitive peoples, the Hottentots had been demoralized by contact with Europeans. Their social structure had disintegrated. Those who survived the white man's bullets and his diseases
became servants of the whites, landless laborers whose condition frequently was virtually indistinguishable from that of the slaves, and indeed in many instances more degraded, for masters felt less sense of
obligation for the Hottentots' well-being than they did for their legal
possessions. Some masters treated them ill, others well; but they were
consigned to a position of permanent inferiority, constituting a docile
labor supply that existed to perform menial tasks for the white aristocracy. Eventually the Bantu would also be subjected, but in the process,
unlike the Hottentots, they not only retained their vitality but grew in
numbers. Their labor became indispensable to the whites' economy, but

---

[32] Smith to Grey, Feb. 10, 1848, C.O. 179/4, P.R.O.

their numbers made them a constant threat to the security of the white minority. In 1834, however, few Bantu were employed on the farms of the settlers. They remained as they had been since the initial clashes, an enemy to be feared in possession of land that was coveted.

Like the Boers, the Bantu were trekkers, a seminomadic people, primarily pastoral but also practicing a primitive agriculture which rapidly exhausted the soil. Their origins are a subject of controversy. Until recently there was general agreement that their homeland was in the Great Lakes region of east central Africa,[33] but evidence based on linguistic analysis suggests that they may have originated in west Africa on the borders of Nigeria and the Cameroons.[34] Those who entered South Africa migrated in a number of waves, extending over a long period and in a sequence that remains somewhat uncertain. Though Dutch outriders from the Cape encountered Bantu parties at the end of the seventeenth century, the first major collision between the tribes and the settlers occurred in the 1770's on the eastern coast in the vicinity of the Fish River. The coastal tribes with whom the colonists came into conflict had arrived in the vicinity no later than the last quarter of the seventeenth century, perhaps earlier.

These tribes the colonists called Kaffirs.[35] They included a group of related tribes, the Xosa, including the Gcaleka, Ngquika (Gaika), Ndlambe (Slambie), Gonukwebe, and other clans.[36] The tribes sprang from heterogeneous origins. They were originally offshoots of the Nguni who had migrated into the Natal area in the fifteenth or sixteenth century, but with admixtures of other people. Among the inhabitants of the territory into which the Xosa moved were the strongest of the Hottentots, the Gqonaquas, larger, stronger, and darker than their fellows. These people were absorbed into the Xosa tribes in varying de-

[33] See, for example, I. Schapera, "The Native Inhabitants," in *The Cambridge History of the British Empire*, VIII (Cambridge: University Press, 1936), 40.

[34] This hypothesis, which is widely accepted, particularly in the United States, was first presented by Joseph H. Greenberg. See his "Africa as a Linguistic Area," in William R. Bascom and Melville J. Herskovits, eds., *Continuity and Change in African Cultures* (Chicago: University of Chicago Press, 1959), pp. 15–27.

[35] The term comes from the Arabic *kāfir*, "unbeliever." The word "Bantu," meaning people, was coined by W. H. Bleek (see J. H. Soga, *The South-Eastern Bantu* [Johannesburg: Witwatersrand, 1930] pp. 11, 60). Andries Stockenstrom, who knew the Bantu perhaps as well as any white man in the early nineteenth century, stated that the term "Kaffir" was properly applied only to the Xosa (*Report of the Select Committee on the Kafir Tribes*, 1851, p. 443).

[36] Tribes usually took their name from a great chief or other hero. Membership in a tribe depended fundamentally on loyalty to a chief, and the size of a tribe rose or fell as a chief gained or lost in popularity.

grees. A large number of them amalgamated with a section of the Xosa to form the Gonukwebe tribe. The Gonukwebe were subsequently looked down upon by the Xosa as a bastard race, but the "pure" tribes also received infusions of Hottentot blood, the proportion being generally largest in the western areas where there was more contact. To the east and northeast of these tribes were the Tembu and the Mpondo.

Although the Xosa recognized a hierarchy of chiefs, the authority of a chief beyond his immediate tribe was small and was far from absolute within it. The dignity of the paramount chieftaincy did not confer with it the power to compel obedience from inferior chiefs. Further, tribes frequently split as a result of disputes over the succession to a deceased chief. In their early negotiations with the tribes, European officials assumed a degree of Bantu organization far beyond that which existed; and the failure of the chief to punish offenders they considered proof of bad faith. The standard by which they judged a chief was his fidelity to the interests of the Cape government; resistance to its will was treachery.

European colonization of southern Africa was fatal to the independent tribal system; European culture, European government, European interests made its destruction inevitable. Wars were merely the dramatic symptoms, the death throes of a society already mortally afflicted. However able and resolute the chiefs might be, they could not delay the process; rather, by their efforts to resist the inevitable, they accelerated it. The tragedy of the Bantu tribal society is epitomized by the fate of Makomo, a man who in his qualities of mind and his characteristics as a leader merits comparison with the great Basuto chief, Moshesh. In the mountain fastnesses of Basutoland he might have become renowned as a master soldier; instead, he became a victim of the brandy bottle.

In 1834 Makomo was the regent of the Gaika tribes (Sandile, the heir apparent, being yet a minor). Between thirty-five and forty years of age, he was in the fullness of his physical and intellectual powers. During the few years since the death of Gaika he had acquired an influence far beyond that inherent in his formal authority. By other chiefs and by Europeans alike he was recognized as a man of rare force and subtlety. To the chiefs his advice was compelling; to the government officials and to colonists he was a menace. Even twenty years later, when sodden with drink, he was impressive enough to win the admiration of Governor Grey as "the greatest politician and best warrior in Kaffraria." [37]

_____
[37] Grey to Grey, Feb. 22, 1855, C.O. 48/365, P.R.O.

For Makomo there could be no peace. His regency would end with the majority of a lame youth, deficient in courage and intelligence, who had no other claims to leadership than the accident of birth. More clearly perhaps than any other chief, Makomo saw the submergence of the tribes and the loss of their lands before the inexorable advance of the Europeans. They might passively accept their fate or they might fight. In 1834 he chose to fight and most of the chiefs of the Gaika and Slambie tribes acknowledged his leadership. The war convinced him of the futility of struggle against superior weapons and organization, and he tried to withdraw into the colony to seek a life of retirement at Fort Beaufort. But in the colony he found no rest; excluded from the white society, he rapidly became demoralized, consuming his property and his moral fiber in the canteens. To escape being an object of derision, he finally returned to his people. When war was imminent in 1846 he counseled his chiefs against it, and when his advice was rejected he sought asylum in the colony and was refused. In 1851 he joined what he must have known was a hopeless cause, conducted a brilliant guerrilla campaign which won him the reluctant admiration of his enemies, and then returned to oblivion. No man, however able, could save the Xosa people from their fate; nor could Makomo save himself.

Among the eastern Xosa lived the Fingoes (Mfengu), the remnants of tribes that had been uprooted and disorganized by the wars of Chaka in the 1820's. Contrary to widespread colonial opinion, they were not "slaves" to their protectors, but they were held in contempt by the Xosa. A missionary to one of the Xosa chiefs described them as a "very poor degraded nation," esteemed no more than dogs. They were harder workers than the Kaffirs, he said, "but very great eaters." [38] The last observation was relevant, for the dense mass of humanity, augmented by refugees from the northeast, taxed the capacity of the land to sustain them in their primitive pastoral-agricultural economy. Hemmed in by the Europeans to the west and pressed from the east by other tribes, the Xosa, Tembu, and Mpondo peoples jostled one another in a land that seemed increasingly inadequate. Governor George Cathcart described the territory between the Keiskama and the Kei as the most favored part of South Africa in its fertility, abundance of water, and capability for improvement.[39] Officials uniformly observed, as successive portions of the Kaffirs' lands were detached and made available

---

[38] Kayser to Ellis, July 8, 1834, London Missionary Society, South Africa Folder (microfilm in UCLA Library).

[39] Cathcart to Secretary of State, May 20, 1852, C.O. 48/326, P.R.O.

for European settlement, that there was plenty of land for the tribesmen
if they would be more provident and industrious. The incongruity of
such assertions with the acceptance of the necessity of huge farms of
6,000 acres or more for European settlers was not recognized. The
density of the population inhabiting Kaffirland was usually underestimated. The missionary Dr. J. T. van der Kemp, at the beginning of
the nineteenth century, estimated the male Xosa population at 40,000,
but Lieutenant Colonel Richard Collins, who visited the area in 1809,
thought this number approximated the total of all inhabitants.[40]
Lieutenant Colonel Somerset, just before the Kaffir war of 1834, calculated the entire tribal population west of the Kei River as between
40,000 and 50,000, but Colonel Robert England in 1832 estimated the
total at approximately 75,000, distributed under the following chief-
tainships: [41]

Tyalie and Gaikas	13,500
Makomo	6,700
Botma	7,800
Eno	13,500
Pato and brothers	20,000
Kaffirs at a distance from the immediate frontier on the upper Keiskama	13,500

Twenty years later Governor George Grey estimated the total Bantu
population west of the Kei at 90,000, including 8,000 Fingoes. The
territory in which this mass of population resided in 1834 had been
slightly more than 3,000 square miles, but by 1852, exclusive of the
reserve assigned to the Fingoes, the entire population had been compressed into nine locations totaling only 2,450 square miles.[42] As the
population continued to grow in a dwindling territory in which the
soil was progressively exhausted by overstocking and "Kaffir farming,"
the consequences were inexorable. After a tour of the country in the
1850's, Governor Grey described it as "densely inhabited," with as
many as thirty-two natives to the square mile in some sectors; this was
a heavy utilization of land for a people with a low level of technology.
Several kraals were always in sight of one another, and when the war
cry was raised at one, it spread in every direction with "wonderful

[40] "Journal of a Tour . . . to the North-Eastern Boundary, the Orange River,
and the Storm Mountains (1809)," in Theal, op. cit., VII, 37.

[41] Memorandum by Lt. Col. Wade, Dec. 17, 1835, C.O. 48/164, P.R.O.

[42] Grey to Labouchere, Oct. 18, 1856, C.O. 48/377, P.R.O.

rapidity." [43] Such concentration, even of a people less warlike than the Xosa, would have produced turbulence. The European government, the chiefs were convinced, had "stolen the land with the pen," [44] and war was the only means by which they could regain it.

The white settlers naturally did not see the problem in the same terms. The Kaffirs they regarded as a race of cattle thieves, whose depredations were the sole cause of wars upon the frontier. From the bush which covered their movements, they emerged in small parties to steal the farmer's cattle and kill his sheep and disappeared with their booty into their lair in Kaffirland. The chiefs, while they made fair professions, did nothing to restrain their tribesmen and, in fact, were in connivance with them, for they received a share of the booty. The only effective recourse was prompt retribution; the robbers and those who protected them should be thoroughly chastised and the tribes driven away from the vicinity of the European farms which were so sore a temptation to their cupidity. It was infuriating that the British government, which restrained the settlers from inflicting condign punishment upon these black heathens by its prohibition of the commando system, should also fail to protect the settlers against their forays; instead the farmers, who wished only to be allowed to live in security, were condemned by English philanthropists who had never seen a Kaffir and consequently idealized the tribesmen as inoffensive children of nature, the victims of European rapacity rather than the aggressors.[45] The *Graaff Reinet Herald* expressed the usual settler viewpoint when it stated:

There is no question that if the frontier population alone had the right and power of making laws for the security of the border, there would be no more Kaffir wars; but we doubt much if the shortsighted friends of the blacks will ever consent to give up their well-intentioned disastrous meddling, and allow of that system of humane severity which alone can keep our restless neighbours in order.[46]

The governors of the Cape, whatever their predilections with regard to the character of settlers and Kaffirs, saw the problems of the frontier

---

[43] *Ibid.*

[44] Fragment of a memorandum by C. L. Stretch, undated [1848], in South Africa, Odds 2, LMS Archives. The expression was used by Chief Makomo in an interview with Sir George Napier.

[45] For an extreme statement of this settler viewpoint see John M. Bowker, *Speeches, Letters, and Selections from Important Papers* (Grahamstown: Godlonton and Richards, 1864). The Bowker family was prominent in the affairs of the eastern frontier.

[46] *Graaff Reinet Herald,* Feb. 9, 1853.

from the standpoint of military security. Until 1834 one of the elements in frontier defense had been the use of commandos of armed burghers who could be called out by magistrates and landdrosts to take the field against depredators and disturbers of the peace. This traditional means of dealing summarily with Bushmen, Hottentots, and Bantu had been accepted by the British in their first occupation of the Cape and given legal status by Lord Macartney's Ordinance of 1797, but it had fallen increasingly into disuse, and greater reliance had been placed on regular forces. In June, 1833, Governor Sir Galbraith Lowry Cole had proposed to stiffen the Ordinance of 1797 and revitalize the system to deal more effectively with cattle thieves. But stories of the excesses of the commando system had filtered back to England, where it was represented, with a high degree of justification, as being conducted with little regard for human life and accompanied by acts of atrocious cruelty. This "frightful scourge of the native population," the British government decided, could not be reconciled with law and justice, and consequently it disallowed the commando ordinances.[47] For the policing of the frontier, governors after 1834 were consequently forced to rely primarily upon regular military forces, which were inadequate to perform the task. As military men they naturally were concerned that the lines they had to defend would be as advantageous as possible. The country between the Fish River and the Keiskama was a general's nightmare, for the tangled underbrush provided ideal cover for a lurking adversary while it rendered cavalry practically useless and reduced the infantry to a blinded, cursing mass of humanity. In mountain retreats within this area the tribal enemy could conceal itself from the troopers, occasionally venturing forth to ambush an unwary pack train. The ideal frontier was one that was clearly delineated, such as a large unfordable river running through the country with unlimited visibility and no prospects for concealment. Neither the Fish River nor the Keiskama fulfilled these specifications; the Kei, though not a large stream, was much more satisfactory, as it flowed through relatively open country.

These were the considerations that guided the governors of the Cape after each war; each new line of demarcation was designed to enhance security. But each new boundary further compressed the territory of the tribes and contributed to a sense of acute frustration and resentment which led to further wars. Though expelled from their lands, the chiefs and their tribes would not relinquish the determination to

---

[47] Stanley to D'Urban, Nov. 27, 1833, C.O. 48/151, P.R.O.

return, if not by consent, then by force. This irredentism was rocking the frontier in 1834. Governor Lord Charles Somerset had allowed the Xosa, on condition of their good behavior, to return to certain locations between the Keiskama and the Fish rivers to graze their cattle. But in 1829 Makomo's tribe had become involved in an encounter with the Tembu and had pursued them across the border into the colony. They were consequently expelled from the Kat River Basin, and a colony of Hottentots was settled in their place; in 1833 the tribes of Tyalie and Botma were also expelled for failure to keep the peace. But they persisted in returning despite all the efforts of military patrols, who burned their huts and drove them back across the Keiskama. In October, 1833, Lieutenant Colonel Thomas Francis Wade, the acting governor, visited the frontier where he found to his amazement that the whole countryside east of the Fish was ablaze with burning huts, and that hundreds of Bantu were carrying off their belongings and driving their cattle in the direction of the fords of the Keiskama. While observing this spectacle he was approached by Makomo, who complained bitterly that the tribesmen were being driven from their lands without cause. The conversation that ensued revealed the thought processes of the Bantu and of British officials. Makomo asked, "When am I to have my country again?" Wade said, "What country?" and Makomo replied, "This country where we are, and that country," pointing to the Hottentot settlement in the Kat River Valley. Wade lectured the chief on the sins of his tribe for which the loss of land had been appropriate punishment, but, riding away, Makomo, "in a very marked and peculiar manner," called back, "But we are to have the land again." [48]

There was an unbridgeable chasm between the two viewpoints. To the chief, the land belonged to his tribe, and remained their patrimony though they might be ejected from it by superior force. To the governor, his obligation, which transcended all tribal rights, was the maintenance of peace; the tribes might stay only if they remained peaceful and inoffensive. The issue between Makomo and Wade was essentially the same as that between other border chiefs and other governors. An independent Bantu society was incompatible with order; such stability could be achieved only by reducing the tribes to impotence, and in the process much of the tribal land was destined to be torn away.

The Kat River settlement, which was the object of Makomo's ire, was established by Governor Cole in 1829 on the advice of Andries Stocken-

---

[48] Memorandum by Wade, Dec. 17, 1835, C.O. 48/164, P.R.O.

strom, who was at the time commissioner-general of the eastern districts. Its principal purpose was to interpose a compact barrier of settlement against the Bantu in a sector that military men considered the
most vulnerable and dangerous on the entire frontier. Thus was fulfilled in a somewhat different form the plan, originally projected at
the time of the 1820 settlement, to colonize this area with a body of
Scottish highlanders as a protection for the left flank of the frontier.
At first Stockenstrom contemplated mixing the Hottentots, who were
taken chiefly from missionary stations, with English and Dutch settlers,
but the idea was abandoned on the assumption that no white man
would accept a grant so small as those being allotted to the Hottentots.
The original settlement comprised about 900 people, including 250
to 300 men available for defense. They were assigned allotments of
three morgen (approximately six acres) each. The Hottentots made
remarkable progress. In 1833 the settlement, now numbering 2,114,
possessed a stock of 250 horses, 2,444 head of cattle, and 4,996 sheep;
it had reaped 2,300 muids (6,900 bushels) of wheat and barley. Besides
temporary cottages of wattle and daub, they had built 12 substantial
stone houses, planted 13 orchards, and completed 55 irrigation canals.
The rest of the ceded territory west of the settlement was divided into
approximately 100 farms "of extensive size" for exclusively European
occupation.[49]

Beyond the mountains the character of the border was very different
from that of the coast. On the interior plateau the pastoral frontier had
already been extended across the Orange River, well beyond the official
boundary, where the cattle Boers had come into contact, but not yet
into conflict, with the Griquas. The Griquas were a mere handful of
people in comparison with the Xosa; and the number of Boers across
the Orange in 1834 was small.[50] In the vast spaces of the trans-Orange
country, there might have seemed land in abundance for all; but land
was useless without water, and in the dry plateau area water holes were
not plentiful. Huge acreages were required for pasture because of the
scarcity of herbage and the uncertainties of the seasons. Conflict be-

---

[49] James Read, Jr., *The Kat River Settlement in 1851* (Cape Town: Robertson,
1852), p. 6.

[50] The estimate of the missionary at Philippolis, Mr. Kolbe, was that there were
1,100 families (P. J. van der Merwe, *Die Noordwaartse Beweging van die Boere voor
die Groot Trek (1770–1842)* [The Hague: van Stockum, 1937], p. 290). John Philip
stated that there were 1,500 Boers beyond the Orange in 1834, meaning apparently
that number of heads of families (Philip's testimony in *Report from the Select
Committee on Aborigines*, 1836, p. 626).

tween Boers and Griquas for control of the land was ultimately inevitable, but in 1834 their relationship was still one of peaceful coexistence. The Orange River frontier settlement was not yet a military problem as was that on the coast.

The Boers had been acquainted with the character of the trans-Orange region for many years. As early as 1817, when Governor Somerset visited Graaff Reinet, a deputation of field cornets had requested him to allow farmers to graze their cattle beyond the border in times of severe drought. Somerset gave his consent to such temporary relief. But there was no means to ensure that temporary absences did not become permanent. To superintend a frontier line of more than 700 miles there were only five magistrates, the nearest not less than 20 miles from the frontier and one approximately 200 miles away. The field cornets, cattle farmers themselves, serving with no compensation from the government, could not be expected to attempt to enforce quarantine measures against their fellow Boers, even if they had had the power.

The 1820's were a decade of unusual drought and pestilence for the northern districts of Cape Colony. The little vegetation that survived the droughts was further ravaged by locusts and trek buck. In these years of pestilence the alternatives for the farmers of the Albany, Somerset, and Graaff Reinet districts were to trek in search of pastures or passively to accept ruination. In such seasons, the civil commissioner of Albany said, it was "just as practicable for them to graze their cattle in the streets of Cape Town as on their own farms." [51] Consequently, within a few years of Somerset's authorization for temporary migration beyond the border, a number of farmers had established permanent residences between the district border and the banks of the Orange River. In 1822, with a view to bringing these migrants again under the control of colonial law and preventing further advances, the boundary of the district of Graaff Reinet was extended to the Orange River,[52] but already some of the Boers had moved beyond the river to seek new pasturage for their cattle.[53]

In the midst of severe drought no official, however resolute, could enforce an interdict on the driving of cattle across the river. On several occasions Andries Stockenstrom, as commissioner-general for the eastern districts, rode beyond the Orange to order parties of emigrants back

---

[51] D. Campbell to Acting Colonial Secretary, June 27, 1834, in Philip Papers, LMS Archives.

[52] Stockenstrom to Spring-Rice, Nov. 5, 1834, C.O. 48/159, P.R.O.

[53] Van der Merwe, *Die Noordwaartse Beweging*, p. 207.

to the colony. His edict was obeyed, but he recognized that occasional sorties were useless in preventing or even restricting the trans-Orange migration. The impulse to move was far too strong and the powers of government were far too weak for any interdict to be effective. In the last years of Stockenstrom's commissionership another significant change had occurred. Until about 1830 it was customary for the inhabitants of border districts to solicit permission from government before crossing the boundary. Local officials, if they were unauthorized to grant such permission, usually let the applicants know that they would not oppose their pasturing cattle beyond the boundary, and in some instances gave distinct authorization. But by the end of the 1820's the emigration had assumed a different character. Frontier farmers left their homes without seeking the formality of governmental approval and with no intention of returning at the end of the drought. The civil commissioner of Albany admitted that if the means at his disposal were increased tenfold they would still be inadequate to restrain the migration.[54] When Stockenstrom left office in 1833 there were far more farmers beyond the Orange than when his term began.[55] Again the migration of the trek Boer had extended beyond even the formal control of government.

The territory across the Orange River from the settled districts of the colony was called Bushmanland until the 1830's. Thereafter for a time it became Griqualand. The change of designation reflected that displacement of the weak by the stronger which to many nineteenth-century observers seemed to have the fatality of natural law. The Bushmen's powers of resistance could not prevail against whites, Hottentots, or Bantu. Some had been absorbed by their Hottentot conquerors; many had been slaughtered by white and African foes who had ousted them from their hunting grounds. When they sought to survive by preying on the herds of the whites or the Bantu they were treated as vermin. A remnant of these people had sought sanctuary beyond the Orange River, but by the 1820's their tormentors had again caught up with them. Their only prospect for survival was protection by a humanely disposed government. In the 1820's such a hope had appeared when the British government, in response to evangelical pressure, had sent John T. Bigge and William Colebrooke to investigate conditions in Cape Colony. The commissioners found the Bushmen in the colony in a deplorable condition, and promised to offer as one of their major recommendations "the redemption of these unfortunate

[54] *Ibid.*

[55] Stockenstrom to Spring-Rice, Nov. 5, 1834, C.O. 48/149, P.R.O.

people from the state of misery and servile dependence to which they are reduced, and their settlement in kraals or villages in favourable situations." [56]

These were humane intentions, but reservation of land for Bushmen was not expected to be at the expense of the claims of settlers, and south of the Orange there was no more unoccupied land with adequate water which could be made available for a Bushman colony. Andries Stockenstrom, whose humanitarian instincts were aroused by the misery of these hapless people, proposed while he was landdrost of the border district of Graaff Reinet that they be settled in colonies north of the Orange River, where they would live under the supervision of missionaries whose influence with the Griquas, the Koranas, and other trans-Orange peoples could protect them. Partly in response to Stockenstrom's representations, the London Missionary Society in 1823 established a missionary station north of the Orange River, which was called Philippolis in honor of the society's South African superintendent, Dr. John Philip. But within three years this haven of refuge for Bushmen had become a residence for a section of the Griqua people, and the Bushmen again were forced to withdraw. Concerning the background of this displacement there is general agreement, but also an important area of controversy.

The Griquas were among the peoples who had withdrawn before the advance of European settlement. Their name seems to have been derived from a clan of the Hottentots variously called the Chariguriqua or the Grigriqua. In the latter part of the eighteenth century many of these people, a mixed breed of white and Hottentot, established themselves beyond the Orange River under the leadership of Adam Kok. Associated with the Griquas and eventually amalgamated with them [57] were the Bastaards, also descendants of white men and Hottentot women. Having fled from the colony to escape the oppression that was the lot of the colonial Hottentots, they were understandably suspicious of any gestures by the government at Cape Town to reimpose control over them,[58] but they could not entirely escape the environment from which they had fled. Dr. John Philip later declared that when the mis-

---

[56] Bigge and Colebrooke to Bourke, July 3, 1826, cited in van der Merwe, *Die Noordwaartse Beweging,* p. 242.

[57] The differentiation, however, was not obliterated by the mid-nineteenth century. Montague Johnstone, who observed them in 1843, wrote of them as distinct peoples (Johnstone to D'Urban, Jan. 11, 1843, D'Urban Papers, X). For a fuller description of the Griquas, see J. S. Marais, *The Cape Coloured People, 1652–1937* (London: Longmans, Green, 1939), pp. 32 ff.

[58] Andrew Smith, "Northern Frontier," n.d. [1834], G.H. 19/4, Cape Archives.

sionary John Anderson had first arrived among them in 1800 they were "a herd of wandering and naked savages, subsisting by plunder and the chase. Their bodies were daubed with red paint, their heads loaded with grease and shining powder, with no covering but the filthy kaross over their shoulders" [59]—a characterization applicable at most to only some of these people. When Stockenstrom observed them twenty years later, the majority were expert horsemen and marksmen with the musket and "as well mounted and armed as the generality of colonists." Many wore European clothes.[60] Their borrowing from colonial society undoubtedly was not entirely the result of missionary influence.

The missionaries soon gained an ascendancy over the main body of the Griqua tribes, with the power to make and unmake chiefs. They induced them to accept a relatively settled life in the present Griqualand West. Klaarwater, later renamed Griquatown, became the capital city. The name of Bastaard, offensive to the ears of the devout, ceased to be employed in polite usage.[61] When the leadership of Adam Kok II became unsatisfactory to the missionaries, they prevailed upon him in 1819 to abdicate his "captaincy" and procured the election of their protégé, Andries Waterboer, a recent arrival from the colony, in his stead. Waterboer thereafter vindicated the confidence of his benefactors by accepting not only their spiritual but their political guidance. He became the model of the Christian chief, a bulwark of order, the defender of the weak. This client kingdom of the missionaries became the instrument of John Philip's policy of interposing "belts of civilized natives between the colonists and their less civilized neighbours" as a means of stabilizing the border.[62]

A number of the Griquas refused to accept the new order of a missionary-dominated state and left the realm of Andries Waterboer. Some of them swelled the numbers of the banditti who infested the islands and the banks of the Orange River. Others followed Kok into exile. For three years Kok lived with his brother Cornelis at the village of Campbell (named for a missionary); later he lived near Backhouse (named for another missionary) on the Vaal River. But Philip, on his tour of the interior in 1825, found Kok's band, calling themselves "Bergenaars," wandering in the Modder Valley. Kok asked permission

[59] Philip's testimony, July 4, 1836, in *Report from the Select Committee on Aborigines, 1836*, p. 608.

[60] Stockenstrom to Spring-Rice, Nov. 5, 1834, C.O. 48/159, P.R.O.

[61] Samuel J. Halford, *The Griquas of Griqualand*, (Cape Town: Juta, n.d.), p. 42.

[62] Philip's testimony, July 4, 1836, in *Report from the Select Committee on Aborigines, 1836*, p. 625.

to settle at the Bushman station, and Philip consented. Kok migrated
to Philippolis in 1826. By 1829 the Bushmen had been removed from
their erstwhile home to another station on the Caledon River, and
Bushmanland became Griqualand.

Philip contended that the relationship between Bushmen and Griquas was friendly and that the Griquas were in fact protectors, but
one Griqua later testified that "we exterminated the Bushmen and Dr.
Philip gave us the country." [63] Both versions are exaggerations; certainly the Griquas did not exterminate the Bushmen of Philippolis, but
neither did they become their benefactors.

Andries Stockenstrom averred that Philip, in establishing a second
Griqua community at Philippolis, had, without a shadow of right to
alienate the land, ceded possession of the soil from the Bushmen to the
new owners, and that he had seen a paper to that effect in the possession
of the agent at Griquatown.[64] Philip retorted that Stockenstrom had
twisted the facts. He stated that because there had been some differences
of opinion between the Bushman mission and the Griquas, the former
had decided to leave and that Kok and his followers were left in possession of the site of the mission and the buildings on it. The transaction
to which Kok alluded referred only to the buildings and improvements,
for which the Griquas were required to pay, and had no reference to
the land at all; but Kok and his advisers had mistakenly assumed that
they had purchased the country as well.[65]

Whichever version was correct the consequences were the same; the
Bushmen were displaced by the Griquas. This second Griqua "state,"
however, was less satisfactory to the missionaries as a model native
society than Waterboer's was. Captain Adam Kok and his advisers were
much less subject to missionary influence than was the Christian chief
of Griquatown. Kok, in his dotage by 1834, was much under the influence of his son-in-law, Hendrik Hendriks, a man of independent
viewpoint, and consequently unpopular with the spiritual overseers of
the people.[66]

Philippolis was directly in the path of the migration of the colonial
farmers and consequently was destined to become an area of conflict
long before the remote territory of Griquatown. The military power of

[63] J. A. I. Agar-Hamilton, *The Road to the North, 1852–1886* (London, Longmans,
Green, [1937], p. 3).

[64] Stockenstrom's testimony, Feb. 19, 1836, in *Report from the Select Committee on
Aborigines*, 1836, p. 216.

[65] Philip's testimony, July 4, 1836, *ibid.*, p. 622.

[66] Philip to Wade, Oct. 10, 1833, *ibid.*, 1837, p. 237.

the Griquas, though impressive against tribesmen unschooled in the use of firearms, was inadequate to resist unaided the encroachments of the Europeans. Their numbers were few and their powers of resistance were undermined by the demoralizing effects of European influences. Debauched by liquor, seduced by the enticements of ready money for gaudy trinkets, the Griquas lost their powers of resistance. The liquor bottle again was the advance agent of European expansion at the expense of an unsophisticated people. In 1834 the process of demoralization had only just begun, but the shape of the future was already evident. Griquas had begun leasing their land to Boers and the canteens were doing a thriving brandy trade, with the impotent government of Adam Kok helpless to restrain the processes of destruction. The farms were usually technically leased rather than sold, but for terms of twenty, forty, sixty, and even ninety-nine years; in fact, they were alienated forever, and the Griquas had acquired in exchange little more than a craving for strong drink. In the eyes of the missionaries who sought to protect them not only against the Boers but against themselves, the Griquas of Philippolis had inherited the worst characteristics of their mixed ancestry. A representative of the Paris Evangelical Missionary Society, who observed them in 1836, described them as being phlegmatic like the Boer and slothful like the Hottentot, habitually sluggish until angered but, when aroused, "a true Hottentot, treacherous, malicious, and passionate, living in the present with no thought of the future." [67]

Both Griquatown and Philippolis, however, owing in large part to the missionary influence, were relatively orderly and settled societies. Stockenstrom, far from an unqualified admirer of missionaries, admitted that had it not been for the influence of the London missionaries over these communities the colonial border would have been infested with freebooters.[68] A few bands of Griquas and Korana Hottentots who had resisted the missionary influence lived a predatory life. From their kraals on large islands in the Orange River and in the bush on the right bank, these raiders, well armed and mounted, would descend suddenly upon isolated farms of the border districts of Clanwilliam, Beaufort, and Graaff Reinet, looting, killing those who resisted, and

---

[67] J. T. Arbousset, *Narrative of an Exploratory Tour to the North-East of the Colony of the Cape of Good Hope* (London: Bishop, 1852), p. 30. Descriptions of Kok's Griquas this time are also provided in Smith to D'Urban, Sept. 17, 1834, G.H. 19/4, Cape Archives; and Schreiner to Freeman, Aug. 8, 1841, South Africa 18-2, LMS Archives. Schreiner was a missionary at Philippolis.

[68] Testimony of Stockenstrom, Aug. 21, 1835, in *Report from the Select Committee on Aborigines*, 1836, p. 96.

disappearing with their booty. Also they terrorized the inoffensive and defenseless Bechuana tribes beyond the border. With each appearance of these Tartar bands, hundreds of Bechuana fled to the colony for refuge; and the colony, instead of driving them back to their death, permitted them to stay. As these Bechuana people refused to work for the farmers, they became during the period of their asylum a charge upon public funds. Obviously this lawlessness on the border could not be ignored; but the government had no available resources to deal with it. Even when the commando system had been legal it had been difficult to recruit burghers to hunt down the banditti. Farmers in more protected areas showed extreme reluctance to leave their families and their property; and the expenses of men and horses were paid from the public purse.[69] As a means of providing security for the frontier at no expense to the colonial government, the missionary-dominated republic of Andries Waterboer appeared to be a heaven-sent ally. By a treaty in 1834, Waterboer became a bulwark of order, particularly as a protection for the Bechuana.

Eastward of Kok's Philippolis lived the Basuto of Moshesh, a people destined to become one of the most powerful adversaries of the land-hungry white settlers but as yet largely insulated from conflict with the trekking farmers. It was a tribe born of disaster, transformed into a unified people by a masterly leader from the shattered remnants of tribes broken by the *Mfecane*. Moshesh's feat of organizing the resistance of this unpromising human material, first against tribal adversaries, and then against the Europeans, was one of the outstanding accomplishments of South African history. So impressive was his achievement that European observers found it difficult to believe that any mere native could have been responsible. Moshesh had grown to manhood as a minor tribal chief in the mountains of the northern part of present-day Basutoland; he and his followers, when attacked by the Mantatees and other tribes set in motion by the war of Chaka, had retreated to the flat-topped mountain of Thaba Bosiu, where he had resisted all efforts to dislodge him and had steadily grown in power as other refugees had accepted him as their leader.

Moshesh was no mere war chief; he was a most astute diplomat. He knew how to temporize to advantage, to play off potential adversaries against one another, to utilize every opening to protect the interests of

---

[69] Cole to Hay, Nov. 15, 1833, C.O. 48/150; Wade to Stanley, Dec. 10, 1833, C.O. 48/151; Wade to Stanley, Jan. 14, 1834, C.O. 48/154; Stockenstrom to Spring-Rice, Nov. 5, 1834, C.O. 48/159, all in P.R.O.; Melville to Editor, *South African Chronicle*, n.d. [1824], in Philip Papers 3-1, LMS Archives.

the people, preferably without the necessity of war. The mind of Moshesh, Europeans were forced to admit, was the equal of their own. They noted that his features were regular, his profile was aquiline, and his forehead was well developed, as befitted a man of great intellectual powers. In fact, except for his dark skin, he had the "look of a European." [70]

Hordes of Zulus, Fingoes, Griquas, and other attackers had beset Moshesh's strongholds and had been beaten back or had retired in frustration at being unable to come to grips with the defenders. When the raiders withdrew they left the open lands to the west of the mountains scoured of inhabitants. Over these territories Moshesh now asserted his claim, on the justification that the remnants of tribes that had resided there now lived under his chieftainship. The Basuto left their mountain sanctuaries to return to the corn lands of the Caledon River Valley, favored with rain from the mountains to the east which made possible agriculture without irrigation. By 1834 Basuto families had already resettled forty to fifty miles west of the Caledon.

Moshesh's claims did not go uncontested. An old enemy, the Batlokua chief, Sikonyela, son of that fierce queen who had given her name to the terrible Mantatees, resided with his followers in the upper Caledon. A recent arrival in the lands claimed by Moshesh, the Barolong of Moroko, had settled around Thaba Nchu with the Basuto chief's consent; but dispute over the nature of the Barolong's relationship to Moshesh was soon to produce conflict. Scattered throughout the Caledon also were villages of Korana Hottentots and Newlanders, the latter a half-caste people. Even before the arrival of the Europeans, therefore, the possession of the valley of the Caledon and the plateau to the west was already in dispute among a number of claimants. Further complicating the relationship of these peoples was a collision of the vested interests of two missionary societies. The Paris Evangelical Missionary Society, closely allied to the London Missionary Society, had begun work in 1833 among the Basuto, and its representatives were soon to become not only spiritual counselors of the Basuto but political advisers of Moshesh. Representatives of the Wesleyan Missionary Society had established themselves in a similar capacity among Moshesh's enemies.

In 1834, with the arrival of Sir Benjamin D'Urban, the Cape received

---

[70] Nearly every European visitor commented upon these features of Moshesh as setting him apart from the generality of his countrymen. The *South African Commercial Observer*, March 4, 1843, commented specifically on his "European" appearance.

a new constitution providing for the establishment of an executive council consisting of the governor and four officials, and a legislative council including these same officials, the attorney general, and from five to seven appointed citizens of the Cape. The consent of the Legislative Council was required for legislation, which could be nullified only by the action of the King in Council. But in the primary problems with which the governor had to deal, he remained as his predecessors had been, the virtual dictator of the colony. He was, however, a dictator with little power, for the British government had decreed that he must maintain order at the Cape with a handful of officials and a few hundred troops, and without recourse to the armed citizenry whose slaughter of the natives had provoked the indignation of British society. Further, D'Urban was required in 1834 to supervise the transition of Cape Colony from a system of slavery to a new "free society"; in fact, he was to preside over a social revolution which had begun with the passage in 1828 of the celebrated Fiftieth Ordinance, freeing the Hottentots from legal disabilities. To carry out this immense undertaking, the governor had at his disposal a few paid magistrates, whose districts averaged between 7,000 and 8,000 square miles.[71]

The prospects for a governor under such circumstances were not promising, and even a salary of £6,000 per year and perquisites offered small compensation. If he was fortunate a governor could hope to leave the colony in no worse state than he found it, but he ran a grave risk that his career would be ruined. In either event he could expect his policies to be attacked by a Cape population which he despised, "composed of all that is Vulgar, and worthless, and consisting of no conversation but the Gossip and slander of everyone's neighbour or friend, all alike, friend or foe." [72] He was sent by an economy-minded government to battle against cosmic forces; the result was predetermined.

---

[71] Napier to Russell, March 14, 1841, C.O. 48/211, P.R.O.

[72] The words are Sir George Napier's but the sentiments were expressed by virtually every governor of the Cape (George Napier to Richard Napier, Feb. 25, 1843, Napier Papers, Add. MSS 49168, British Museum.

Chapter IV

FINANCIAL AND HUMANITARIAN INFLUENCES ON SOUTH AFRICAN POLICY

THE CONVENTIONAL DICHOTOMY of economics versus humanitarianism, implying a conflict of material and spiritual impulses, is far too simple a framework within which to appraise British policy in southern Africa. Those who participated in the great missionary movements of the nineteenth century were no doubt convinced that their zeal to preach the gospel throughout the world was generated by a deep spirituality. Certainly this was the emphasis in the impassioned sermons delivered from the platform of Exeter Hall, but the character and the purposes of the humanitarian movement are not so easily explained. Men supported benevolent causes and men became missionaries for a wide variety of reasons. Missionary organizations were concerned not only with saving souls from imminent damnation; they sought to win them for themselves. In the conflict among the various societies for converts, Heaven and Hell seemed at times to be identified with the societies concerned. This clash of temporal interests influenced the policies of these organizations in South Africa.

Governors appointed to preserve tranquillity on the borders also appraised virtue and vice in finite terms. Men and movements were good when they advanced the governor's interests; they were evil to the extent that they frustrated his objectives. Missionary enterprises and governors, however, were not exclusively dedicated to self-interest; both might and frequently did seek to advance noble ends, but self-interest must not be excluded as an influencing factor.

British policy toward South Africa was dominated by financial considerations which, compared with the humanitarian impulse, seem sharp and clear; but judged on a purely economic basis, the actions of British governments and their representatives at the Cape sometimes seem little short of lunacy. Gladstone in 1852 told the House of Commons:

The tales of our frontier policy at the Cape, and the losses which that policy has brought upon this country, when they are recounted to those who come after us, will appear all but fabulous. It will appear the height of extravagance that this country should have gone a hunting, as it were, to the uttermost ends of the earth to find means and opportunities of squandering its treasure and the lives of its subjects for no conceivable purpose of policy.[1]

The balance sheets seemed to provide Gladstone's words with abundant documentation. Sir William Molesworth estimated that the average annual expenditure of Britain at the Cape in the three years ending in 1850 was £500,000, five times the expenditure in 1832–1834. This meant a cost of about £5 a year for every European colonist in South Africa, and approximately equaled the total value of British exports to South Africa. These were years of relative peace; the wars that broke out with increasing frequency after 1834 involved vast extraordinary drains on the Treasury. The war of 1834–1835 cost an additional £500,000; that of 1846–1847, almost £2,000,000; and the wars of 1851–1852, about £3,000,000.[2]

Before the commando system was abolished in 1834, the size of the British military establishment at the Cape had steadily declined. The force left for defense of the colony after its capture in 1806 was approximately 4,000 men, but was steadily reduced until in 1834 it was only about 1,800, of whom 1,000 were stationed at Cape Town and 800 on the frontier.[3] Thereafter the establishment steadily rose until in 1852 during the Kaffir war it totaled 7,614, and was yet deemed by

[1] Speech in House of Commons, April 5, 1852, *Parliamentary Debates*, 3d series, CXX, 745.

[2] *Ibid.*, 735. Accounting procedures made difficult precise calculations of South African expenditures, and Molesworth may have been overly generous in his estimates, but the official calculations were impressive enough. The Treasury estimated the expenditures of Great Britain in South Africa between 1843 and 1850 as follows:

	Net military	Civil	Naval	Total net expenditure
1843–44	£338,894.12.2	£ 4,902. 4.5	£2,279.12.2	£346,076. 8.9
1844–45	238,495. 1	11,602.12.8	2,543.14.8	252,641. 8.4
1845–46	237,823. 6.7	6,425. 6.4	1,990. 1.6	246,238.14.5
1846–47	689,515. 8.7	257,207.13.9	1,576. 1.1	948,299. 3.5
1847–48	714,986.18.6	52,056. 4.5	2,558. 1.9	769,601. 4.8
1848–49	396,765. 6.9	79,589. 2.7	2,443. 8.9	478,797.18.1
1849–50	280,679. 9.4	9,530. 8.3	2,609. 7	292,819. 4.7

"Civil" includes passage allowances for officials. "Naval" includes miscellaneous dockyard expenses—medical care, food, repairs of buildings. See "Abstract of Expenditure by Great Britain on Account of South Africa for Each Year since 1843," return to address of House of Commons, June 23, 1851, W.O. 1/449, P.R.O.

[3] Memo [1834], unsigned, on Cape defenses, C.O. 537/145, P.R.O.

the commander scarcely adequate. After the war some units were returned home, but the peacetime force at the end of 1854 was still 5,076, almost three times that of twenty years before.[4] In the two Kaffir wars between 1803 and 1834, armed burghers had supplied a substantial part of the force; in the three wars of the next twenty years, field commanders had to depend primarily upon regular troops, at consequent great expense to the British taxpayer. To Molesworth, Hume, Gladstone, and other advocates of rigid economy, two conclusions seemed inescapable: dependence on regular troops did not lessen the prospects of war, but rather increased them, for war became profitable for colonial merchants; the abolition of the commando system had sapped the self-reliance of the colonists, undermining their ability and inclination to defend themselves. To the economy-minded the Cape was a horrible example of all the fundamental errors of British colonial policy. Paternalism, expansionism, and misplaced humanitarianism had saddled Britain with great financial responsibilities with no perceptible benefit to anyone except perhaps a few moneygrubbing speculators in the colony.

Attacks on unwarranted expenditures at the Cape reflected the passion for economy which gripped British society after the Napoleonic Wars. All departments of government were dominated by the knowledge that their expenditures would be subjected to the most rigorous scrutiny by Parliament, and that evidence of waste would be pounced upon by members not only of the opposition but of the government party. In 1815 the national debt, which before the war had been less than £250 million, had ascended to £861 million. Payment of the interest on this massive obligation could be made only by the most rigid economy in governmental expenditures or by an increase in taxes, or both. Manufacturers were naturally opposed to levies upon the increasing production of British industry or to the resumption of an income tax, and other politically influential elements of the population shared their abhorrence of increased taxes. Consequently Parliaments were zealous to eliminate all unnecessary spending. This dedication to retrenchment was shared by Whigs and Tories alike, but it was applied with particular enthusiasm after the Whig government came into office in 1830. The Whigs had pledged themselves to retrenchment as well as to reform, and they took both promises seriously. Their successors in both the Liberal and Conservative parties also manifested a devotion to the goddess Economy which was both fervent and sincere.

The disasters that beset British agriculture in the 1830's and 1840's

---

[4] These figures are taken from the War Office returns, W.O. 17, P.R.O.

added to the urgency of demands for economy. In the early nineteenth century bad harvests were of far greater moment to British society than they were to be in later generations. Crop failures could and did have disastrous effects on the society and upon the public revenue. In the hungry 'forties bad harvests in England and Ireland produced not only misery for the people but a financial crisis for the government. The government in 1846 and 1847 spent approximately £10 million for famine relief in Ireland, in addition to the contributions made by private donors.

Other expenditures also were unavoidable. Strained international relations in the 1840's necessitated increases in military budgets. The cost of the army and navy, which had been pared in 1835 to £11.5 million, the low point in the century, rose to £18.5 million in 1847. The total gross expenditure of the country grew correspondingly, from £48,350,000 in 1835 to £57,130,000 in 1847, dropping slightly thereafter.[5]

These fluctuations in the national balance sheets were matters of concern in time of peace and might be considered the ultimate test of a government's effectiveness. The prevailing temper of Parliament was reflected in the deliberations of the Select Committe on Colonial Military Expenditure, which met in 1834 and 1835. The committee was dominated by advocates of retrenchment—Gladstone, Stanley, Spring-Rice, Edward (Bear) Ellice, and Joseph Hume—and they conducted a searching investigation into every conceivable aspect of military expenditure, including pay of officers and men, rations, and relative costs of regular forces versus native levies. Among their recommendations were the reduction of the size of the regular forces overseas and the substitution, when practicable, of less expensive native units, and the improvement of accounting procedures to reduce leakage.[6] Not all the specific proposals of the committee were carried out, but their emphasis was reflected in the policies of every government. No minister would consider additional expense without the most convincing of justifications. Sir Robert Peel, besieged by military and naval men to meet the French threat, wrote the Duke of Wellington in 1845 that his power to make provisions for defense was seriously limited by the country's financial condition. Despite the fact that Great Britain had not participated in a European war for thirty years, the national debt

---

[5] Sydney Buxton, *Finance and Politics* (2 vols.; London: Murray, 1888), I, 92–93.
[6] *Report from the Select Committee on Colonial Military Expenditure*, 1835. Information used by the committee is included in C.O. 323/220, P.R.O.

had declined only slightly, being yet at the astronomical figure of £787 million. The annual interest on that debt alone was £28 million. Under these conditions, he said, "We have to make the painful choice between two evils—the incurring of considerable risk in some part or other of our Extended Empire in the Event of War—or the rapid accumulation of more Debt if we are to be prepared at all points." [7] To Peel the state of the budget necessitated taking calculated risks with secondary British interests. Where some great national purpose was served, he, like other statesmen, was prepared to take a strong line. Immediate economy must be sacrificed for national security, or a major commercial interest. Peel would have gone to war with the French, if necessary, to prevent their taking possession of Chusan Island, which controlled access to southern China.[8] But neither Peel nor any other minister would countenance levies on the national treasury for territorial aggrandizement. With the exception of India, which paid for its own conquest, colonial wars were indefensible by any rational standard of national interest. Wars at the Cape were a catastrophe. To the government so unfortunate as to be involved, a Kaffir war was an awful visitation, like a plague of locusts, devouring the nation's wealth. When it was over, no problems were solved, no material compensations gained, and the ministry would have suffered embarrassment or even defeat for its alleged incompetence in having allowed the war to occur.

Colonial defense was not only a financial drain but a possible threat to the security of the home island. During the years of crisis in relations with France, military men were alarmed at the dispersal of military strength throughout the world for the protection of British possessions. The bulk of the army was stationed overseas where it was virtually useless for home defense, and the cost of maintaining troops in the colonies was far higher than in Britain itself, considering the expense of transports, the larger expenditures for rations in many areas, and the need to replace men who died or were hospitalized.[9] The following statistics produced only dismay for those charged with security: [10]

---

[7] Peel to Wellington, Aug. 9, 1845, Peel Papers, Add. MSS 40461, British Museum.

[8] Secret memo by Peel, April 22, 1845; memo by Aberdeen, April 22, 1845, Peel Papers, Add. MSS 40565, British Museum.

[9] Confidential Print by Grey, "The Army," printed at Foreign Office, Jan. 30, 1852, Russell Papers, PRO 30/22/10, P.R.O.

[10] Minute by Grey, Oct. 9, 1846, Grey Papers, Prior's Kitchen, University of Durham.

Army Strength (Rank and File)

Jan. 1	At home	Abroad	On passage or ordered home	Total
1836	35,716	49,495	1,311	86,522
1837	37,762	47,995	1,291	86,048
1839	36,586	53,953	849	91,388
1842	41,621	67,331	1,375	110,028
1843	44,017	68,868	1,285	114,170
1844	52,378	63,207	938	116,523
1845	50,598	62,980	1,480	115,058
1846	50,133	64,728	1,573	116,434

Colonial defense, therefore, created problems not only of economy but of national security. Likewise the expense of civil administration of the colonies made it subject to careful scrutiny. In the first British Empire, colonies had paid the costs of their own governments; after the American Revolution, Britain had sought to establish a degree of independence for its colonial governors from the taxing power of local legislatures. It seemed to most British politicians that the corollary of the principle that Britain would not tax the colonies for imperial purposes was that colonies should pay for their own administration. Colonial legislatures in turn asserted their right to control the spending of funds derived from taxes they had voted, and the eventual result was responsible government.

Representative government was not inaugurated in Cape Colony until 1854. Before that time local revenues and expenditures were subject to the restrictions generally in force in crown colonies. In the administration of the second Earl Grey, Goderich as secretary of state for colonies laid down a new system for the expenditure of public money in such colonies. He required the governor each year, before the month of June, to submit to his legislative council his estimates for expenditures not already fixed by the sanction of the home government which were to be chargeable to colonial revenue for the forthcoming year. If this estimate received the assent of the majority of the council, he would then transmit it to the home government for approval. If the majority dissented, the governor would request it to provide its own estimates and would then send the two proposed budgets to the British government for final decision. With the proposed expenditures the governor was required to submit the draft of an ordinance providing for the necessary revenues. Once a colony's budget was confirmed by the home government, no additional disbursements could be made unless an unforeseen emergency occurred, and then only after similar approval. Before authorizing colonial budgets the Colonial Office had to submit the estimates to the Lords Commissioners of the Treasury for approval.[11]

The intention of this procedure was to ensure maximum economy in colonial government in recognition of the fact that colonial and imperial expenditures could not be entirely disassociated. Thus the British taxpayer would be relieved of providing assistance to colonies in financial distress because of inefficiency or extravagance. Goderich's memorandum theoretically plugged the last remaining gap in the system for restriction of colonial expenditures, for all extraordinary disbursements already required approval of the Treasury and ultimately of Parliament.

In dispatch after dispatch Goderich preached to the governor the necessity of austerity at the Cape, continuing an emphasis that had begun under his Tory predecessor, Sir George Murray. Because public works sopped up more revenue than any other single function of government, the discretion of the governor to undertake any such projects was limited to £200; all programs of greater magnitude required approval from London. Goderich also abolished a number of minor offices with the object of bringing the budget into balance. "His Majesty's Government," he told Governor Lowry Cole, "will not listen to any representations having the tendency to arrest the progress of measures which, while they reflect no injustice on individuals, are called for by the necessities of the Empire at large." [12] Every penny must be accounted for, and the colonial government could not expect Parliament to subsidize it. If there was a deficit, the solution was to reduce the number and the salaries of governmental officers and to eliminate all but the most essential functions of government. This was the creed of Goderich and of his successors. Consequently the civil establishment at the Cape was reduced to a handful of officials, most of whom received inadequate compensation. But even with the most rigid economy the Cape government was barely able to meet its obligations, and a slight dip in the revenue would produce a deficit. The Cape was a poor country; a declining wine export and an infant wool industry were insufficient to support efficient government. The alternatives for Britain at the Cape were to subsidize its administration or to enforce economy at the expense of governmental efficiency. But in fact there was no choice; economy was forced upon the government by the mandate of British society, with fateful results.

[11] Circular, Goderich to Crown Colonies, Dec. 8, 1831, C.O. 854/1, P.R.O.

[12] Goderich to Cole, May 27, 1831, 49/23, P.R.O.

So far as mechanisms would accomplish the purpose, economical administration of the colonial empire seemed to be assured by the beginning of the 1830's. The personnel of the Colonial Office were acutely aware that all their financial actions would be given sharp scrutiny, and that Parliament was constitutionally hostile to extraordinary expenditures. Likewise, colonial governors were well indoctrinated with the gospel of economy. Peace and economy were the watchwords at the Cape as elsewhere. But in Cape Colony Britain was forced to fight wars requiring vast expenditures.

For this paradox, several alternative explanations were offered. Some argued that policy was frustrated by the wrongheadedness or the incompetence of colonial governors. Because officials at the Cape and other remote colonial stations were months removed from Westminster, they necessarily exercised considerable discretion. Consequently a governor who was inept, or who had ambitions for military glory, might embroil the imperial government in conflict he had been counseled to avoid. At the Cape, critics alleged, governors were both incompetent and ambitious. Between 1834 and 1854 all the governors, aside from Sir Henry Pottinger whose term of office was so short as scarcely to constitute an exception, were military men, veterans of the Napoleonic Wars, most of them old comrades of the Duke of Wellington or Fitzroy Somerset of the Horse Guards. Old soldiers never died; they were appointed governors of Cape Colony, where they sought in their last years to win military glory which had earlier eluded them. To send superannuated generals to a colony with a turbulent frontier seemed the height of folly. The critics were correct in their complaint that influence at the Horse Guards was often decisive in appointments to Cape governorships. But the level of ability of appointees was usually high, and with the exception of Sir Peregrine Maitland, who was sixty-seven at the time of his appointment, they were relatively young men for the ranks they held. Nor was the contention justified that disturbances were provoked by a governor's hunger for military glory; inaction rather than action of governors contributed to the wars of 1834–1835 and 1846–1847. But whether King Stork or King Log reigned at Cape Town, the consequences were the same.

The most powerful criticism of government policy in South Africa was more broadly based: it was not the man on the spot himself who caused disasters, but the system he represented. Paternalism stifled the self-reliance of the colonists and subjected them to control by a distant government which could not possibly understand their problems or act with efficiency and dispatch, and which was represented by irresponsible governors who, resident at Cape Town, were also remote from the frontier they were supposed to control. Such a system guaranteed that when wars broke out, they would be major conflicts burdening the British taxpayer with heavy expense, for Great Britain was constitutionally unable to fight a little war. The only solution was to assign to the colonists themselves the obligations of their own defense, which meant colonial self-government. It was, said Gladstone, "no question of British or Imperial interests whether the frontier of the Cape Colony should be the Fish River, the Orange River, or the Keiskamma," nor should Britain be required to maintain the peace of the border. The colonists of South Africa, like the frontiersmen of North America and indeed like their own forebears, should deal with the aborigines in their own way without recourse to any imperial assistance. Control by an alien authority "confers upon South Africa no benefit whatever, but ensures the perpetual recurrence of wars with a regularity which is perfectly astounding." [13] Molesworth expressed essentially the same viewpoint in a speech to Parliament in 1848:

> In fact, the Colonial Government of the country is an ever-changing, frequently well-intentioned, but invariably weak and ignorant despotism. Its policy varies incessantly, swayed about by opposite influences; at one time directed, perhaps, by the West India body, the next instant by the Anti-Slavery Society, then by Canadian merchants, or by a New Zealand Company or by a Missionary Society: it is everything by turns, and nothing long; Saint, Protectionist, Freetrader, in rapid succession; one day it originates a project, the next day it abandons it, therefore all its schemes are abortions, and all its measures are unsuccessful; witness the economical condition of the West Indies, the frontier relations of the Cape of Good Hope, the immoral state of Van Diemen's Land, and the pseudo-systematic colonization and revoked constitution of New Zealand.[14]

To Molesworth, Gladstone, and all others who believed that colonial self-government was the only means by which the Empire could be self-supporting, paternalism was inherently bad not only because it was expensive but because it could not accomplish its avowed objectives. Colonial problems could be dealt with effectively only by those who were intimately affected, whose vital interests were concerned in their solution. Consequently the imperial government in its own interests should delegate to the colonies all powers of self-government except those inconsistent with the imperial connection or injurious to the interests of other parts of the Empire. This was enlightened

---

[13] Speech on April 5, 1852, *Parliamentary Debates,* 3d series, CXX, 746–747.

[14] Speech on July 25, 1848, *ibid.,* C, 849.

doctrine for colonies of European settlement. The men who advocated such views have been honored as farseeing statesmen who recognized that the strength of the imperial connection depended ultimately upon the forces of self-interest and sentiment, binding free societies in an association advancing common purposes and common ideals.

The British, a pragmatic rather than a logical people, did not succumb to the logic of the argument until the experience of Canadian government demonstrated that no alternative would work. Responsible government in Canada was a precedent for other colonies, but the problem was more complicated in "plural societies." Did Britain retain responsibilities transcending mere economics toward native peoples within or on the borders of imperial jurisdiction? Was the treatment of these peoples a local or an imperial problem? This issue might be ignored in North America or Australia, where the aborigines had been reduced to insignificance; it could not be ignored in southern Africa where the aborigines were more numerous and where powerful missionary societies were active. Lord Stanley as colonial secretary raised one aspect of the problem in 1842 when, in response to resolutions from the Cape advocating representative government, he asked how, in a society embracing a diversity of races at varying stages of development, the principle of legal equality for all subjects of the Queen could be reconciled with free institutions.[15]

No one denied the existence of a moral issue. Those who believed that Britain should withdraw from native-settler conflicts did not contend that humanitarian considerations were irrelevant; they asserted that justice and morality could not be imposed in interracial relations by a government far removed from the problem, and that in the face of irresistible laws governing human relations such intervention not only did not accomplish its purpose but in fact prolonged the misery of the people it sought to protect. The effect of the intervention of the imperial authority had been uniformly harmful to both white and black. The *Edinburgh Review* in 1846 expressed this viewpoint in somewhat extreme form when it argued that slavery had been possible only because the white aristocracy had been supported by British garrisons, and that the slave trade had originally been fastened by Britain on its dependencies. Consequently the abolition of slavery and the slave trade stemmed from a belated revulsion against a system that Britain itself had imposed. Slavery was repugnant to Christian morality and could not be tolerated in the British Empire; the Emancipation Act was, therefore, a legitimate exercise of imperial power, but continual

[15] Stanley to Napier, April 15, 1842, C.O. 48/214, P.R.O.

intervention in the internal relationships of a colony degraded the stronger elements without benefiting the weaker.[16] Gladstone maintained that Britain should withdraw from the internal affairs of colonies faced with racial issues; the result would be improvement in the relationships of the peoples concerned: ". . . with reference to their relations with Aborigines or with Asiatics, it should rest with them to arrange for their security at any rate as soon as they are planted in the country and it is I confess my belief that if they had this duty to perform, the wars which we so often had to deplore would be both shorter and by far more rare." [17]

Few white settlers agreed that the withdrawal of British soldiers from the colonies would reduce wars, but they enthusiastically endorsed Gladstone's opinion that Britain's intervention in race relations had been disastrous. The *Grahamstown Journal* expressed a common settler viewpoint when it wrote:

Nothing in modern days has been productive of more widespread mischief than those measures which have been adopted professedly with the view of benefitting the condition of the natives or servile classes in the various British Colonies. . . . In almost every case the very opposite results have been produced to those intended, and thus, instead of order and harmony, we hear from every British Colony, where a majority of the servile classes consists of colored natives, of the disorganization of society, of frightful demoralization among the natives themselves, and of embarrassment, poverty and ruin, among their employers.[18]

The editors of the *Edinburgh Review,* convinced of the "weakness of abstract philanthropy when opposed to interest," [19] were acid in their contempt for the arrogant self-righteousness of those who assumed the title of evangelicals "or even other designations more flattering to themselves and disparaging to the rest of the Christian world." They abhorred these Saints who claimed a monopoly of religious zeal, who prided themselves on regular church attendance, stricter observance of the Sabbath, abstinence from ungodly amusements, and greater energy in promoting missions, forming religious societies, and circulating tracts. But, said the *Review,* "common sense will ultimately prevail." [20]

[16] *Edinburgh Review,* CLXVIII (April, 1846), 532–551.

[17] W. E. Gladstone, Memorandum on Colonies [1851?], Gladstone Papers, Add. MSS 44738, British Museum.

[18] *Grahamstown Journal,* May 6, 1848.

[19] *Edinburgh Review,* CXXVIII (July, 1836), 394.

[20] *Ibid.,* CXXX (Jan., 1837), 428–452.

The "Saints" were detested by men who prided themselves on their balanced judgments, their tolerance, and their "realistic" view of life, but they deeply affected the character of British society. Some have suggested that the humanitarian movement was a product of the changing structure of the British economy, that the abolition of slavery was the triumph of the East Indian commercial interest over the West Indian planters,[21] and that the preoccupation with the souls of the heathen was a purgation of a guilt-ridden social conscience. Such explanations are more revealing of the expositor than of the phenomenon. Humanitarianism did not, it is true, imply a reordering of the British social and economic hierarchy; it did not attack the "immutable laws of economics," but to conclude from this that it was the servant of vested interests would be unjustified. The humanitarians of the first half of the nineteenth century awakened the British conscience; their influence on subsequent social reform was substantial. Nor were they as ineffectual as their detractors alleged in guarding native interests in distant dependencies. Exeter Hall and the great missionary societies aroused the British public to injustices committed against native peoples in the colonies who otherwise would have been maltreated or even obliterated. They represented a tremendous moral force; their spokesmen were dedicated to a noble cause. It is true that the middle class, which was the primary source of support for Exeter Hall, was dedicated to profits as well as to the saving of souls. Commerce and civilization were frequently coupled with Christianity in exhortations to the faithful. The Committee on the Aborigines, presided over by the great emancipator Thomas Fowell Buxton, gave as one of the primary reasons for missionary activity the fact that "savages are dangerous neighbours and unprofitable customers, and if they remain as degraded denizens of our colonies, they become a burthen upon the State." [22] Appraisals of evangelicalism and humanitarianism in terms of "common sense," however, offer no insight into the character of a movement that transcended the rational. The character of a Wesley, a Wilberforce, or a Buxton is not reducible to a simple formula or a symmetrical analysis. Correspondingly, the movement to which they contributed and the forces they represented are not susceptible to simple explanation. Thackeray, in *The Newcomes,* could sneer that "in Egypt itself there were not more savoury fleshpots than at Clapham," but the Evangelical Revival of which the Clapham Sect was an

---

[21] See, for example, Eric Williams, *Capitalism and Slavery* (Chapel Hill: University of North Carolina Press, 1944).

[22] *Report from the Select Committee on Aborigines,* 1837, p. 45.

early expression [23] contributed to the Victorian ethic, to which Thackeray himself subscribed.[24] While it contained an element of cant, it also included an element of nobility.

The antecedents of evangelicalism were likewise paradoxical; the movement owed much to Wesley but it also absorbed influences from the *Aufklärung* and from the French Revolution. The great missionary societies, in their concern for the soul of the heathen asserted a recognition of the importance of the individual.[25]

The abolition of the slave trade and of slavery in the British Empire was a triumph over mundane interests; the response of British society and, ultimately, of Parliament was a testament to the sensitivity of the British conscience. In the years after 1834, however, there was no longer any clearly defined focus for humanitarian zeal. An outburst of popular indignation in response to reports of maltreatment of the recently manumitted slaves, now called apprentices, in Jamaica, did produce more than 3,000 petitions containing, it was said, more than a million signatures for the liberation of praedial as well as non-praedial apprentices in 1838.[26] But in general the humanitarian movement in the overseas dependencies became identified after 1834 with the missionary crusade.

As Clapham had been identified with the campaigns against the slave trade and slavery, Exeter Hall became the symbol of the post-emancipation humanitarian movement. The power of "Exeter Hall" was merely the summation of the energies of the great missionary societies which each May held their annual meetings within its walls. The public meeting was a means of demonstrating solidarity and power, stimulating fervor, and opening pocketbooks; and the hall, which could accommodate 5,000 people, offered the facilities for impressive mass demonstrations.

The May meetings at Exeter Hall transformed the character of the Strand and the West End of London. On foot and by cab, hackney coach, and omnibus, the faithful poured in by the thousands. Forests of placards surrounded the building advertising meetings, or religious newspapers. The unity and the diversity of the Christian faith was

---

[23] Ernest M. Howse, *Saints in Politics* (Toronto: University of Toronto Press, 1952), p. 117.

[24] H. F. Lovell Cocks, *The Nonconformist Conscience* (London: Independent Press, 1943).

[25] For an exposition of this view, see Cyril J. Davey, "Two Hundred Years of Methodism Overseas," *London Quarterly and Holborn Review* (Jan., 1960), pp. 3–8.

[26] Spencer Walpole, *History of England* (6 vols.; London: Longmans, Green, 1879–1880), IV, 165.

visibly represented. Impelled by a common sense of high purpose, the devotees of the various missionary societies participated in the May rites of rededication to their common cause of saving the heathen, but always with a degree of reserve toward one another as competing sects. Like rival orders in the Roman Catholic Church, the London, Wesleyan, Church, and Baptist societies fought with Satan while keeping a jealous eye on one another. But the evidence of the combined power of the "Sanhedrin of Exeter Hall" impressed even the worldly-minded habitués of nearby Whitehall and Westminster.[27]

The combination of huge crowds and noble thoughts produced a high degree of emotionalism in the sermons delivered at Exeter Hall, and the interaction of speaker and audience contributed to a fervor that excited the disgust of many observers. The *Times,* consistently critical of the unreality of the missionary societies, found in the May meetings of 1854 unhappy evidence of the divorcement of the British population from the stern realities. In the midst of a war, Exeter Hall was again crowded with the old faces, listening to the same old stories of the plight of the black heathen:

The reader of future history may learn perhaps with surprise that at a period when the nation was gathering up all its energies for a desperate struggle the chief public meetings in the metropolis concerned neither the Turks nor the Russians, the English nor the French, but were addressed particularly to the aborigines of Polynesia or the politics of Timbuctoo. . . .
. . . There is undoubtedly a species of sympathy which requires some unreality in its objects, or, if not unreality, at any rate that degree of enchantment which distance and doubt may contribute to them. It is of no use to say that there is misery enough in Bethnal-green, and ignorance enough within a mile of St. Paul's, to occupy all the energies of philanthropy or charity. It is to no purpose that Mr. Dickens writes so affectingly about the "quiet poor" and the sufferings upon sufferings which war must have in store for them. This is not the kind of wretchedness to be purveyed every May for the Exeter-hall sympathisers. . . . Occasionally, indeed, the romance is exchanged for reality, as when Lord Shaftesbury advocates ragged schools, or city missions come in place of Abyssinian seminaries. But this is not the true Exeter-hall style. The genuine May meeting is essentially charged with the foreign affairs of religion. Its sphere, to say the least, must be beyond the Line. It must receive its missionaries on return from abroad, and be presented with converts black and living from the latest settlement of the society.[28]

[27] *The Spectator,* quoted by the *Grahamstown Journal,* Oct. 5, 1843.
[28] *Times,* May 10, 1854.

This thrust at the preoccupation of the Saints with "black Quashee" was particularly telling because it was so uncomfortably close to the truth. The focus of missionary vision was beyond the seas; the degraded British poor might elicit revulsion or sympathy, but could not excite the imagination. The characteristics of Exeter Hall against which the *Times* inveighed were epitomized in a meeting of the London Missionary Society in August, 1836. The purpose of the gathering was to hear Dr. John Philip and to gaze on two native converts whom he had brought with him from South Africa, a Kaffir chief, Jan Tzatzoe, and the Hottentot Andries Stoffels. The *Missionary Magazine* reported:

Feelings, joyous and sacred in no ordinary degree, seemed to pervade the large assemblage. The object which brought together so many of the friends of the society was certainly one of more than usual interest. Those who watch with particular solicitude the long-benighted children of Ethiopia, struggling from their chains of spiritual darkness into the light and liberty of the gospel, must have listened with deep and blended emotions to the several speeches and statements that were delivered; but other sources of holy gratification appeared, in which all could equally share. There were men upon the platform, on whom, although differing from ourselves in colour, every eye was fixed with hallowed and intense delight—men who came amongst us as harbingers of a brighter day for Africa—earnests of an abundant harvest yet to come, and representatives of thousands of their countrymen who have embraced the truths of Divine revelation.[29]

In the years after emancipation there was a flowering of organizations dedicated to advancement or protection of the welfare of uncivilized peoples. The British and Foreign Aborigines Protection Society was founded in 1837 as a direct outgrowth of Thomas Fowell Buxton's Parliamentary Committee on the Aborigines, and in 1839 the Anti-Slavery Society was organized. Buxton was a prominent member of both. When he retired from Parliament in 1837 he devoted much of his energy to the organization of the African Civilization Society, which was to continue and extend the work of the African Institution for the extinction of the slave trade and the civilization of Africa. There was a plethora of societies with noble objectives, each boasting impressive names on its directorship and in its list of members. It had become fashionable to be associated with such causes. Fashionable bodies, however, rarely possess an intense moral fire. The new societies were not able to maintain the pitch of passion that had characterized the antislavery movement, nor could public opinion again be so profoundly stirred. The Aborigines Protection Society could not arouse

---

[29] *Missionary Magazine* (Sept., 1836), p. 54.

the terror in politicians which the Clapham Sect had inspired. Nor could Buxton, after his retirement in 1837, recapture the power he had exerted as a member of Parliament. After his death in 1845 there was no heir apparent.

It would be erroneous to conclude that after 1834 the power of the humanitarian societies was dead. Judged in terms of their financial support, the missionary societies were somewhat more prosperous in 1854 than twenty years earlier. In 1832–1834 the receipts of the London Missionary Society were £53,726; in 1845–1846, £79,745; but by 1853–1854, had slipped slightly to £76,781.[30] The Methodists, somewhat more affluent, had an income of £111,730 in 1851–1852, and the Church Missionary Society, £107,699 from the United Kingdom and £10,975 from other parts of the world.[31] The *Missionary Magazine* estimated that in 1850 the Protestant missionary societies of Europe and America spent about £700,000, and the Roman Catholics, £140,000. The total amount of receipts reported at the May meetings in Exeter Hall in 1847 was £548,955, divided as follows: Established Church in England and Ireland, £190,291; English Dissenters, £199,490; Protestants of Scotland and Ireland, £159,174.[32] The importance of these statistics should not be overstated, but they do indicate that the societies, measured by the number of missionaries in the field and the extent of financial support, were making as substantial an effort in 1854 as they had at the time of emancipation. The May meetings continued to overflow Exeter Hall, and huge audiences also were attracted at other times of the year for special meetings of the societies.

In the first fifty years of their existence missionary societies were undoubtedly overly preoccupied with spectacular results and with numbers of conversions. When it became evident that these conversions were largely superficial and that the numbers were exaggerated, an inevitable reaction set in, and support for the missionary societies sagged for a time, about mid-century.[33]

Amidst all the vagaries in its fortunes the missionary movement always retained the characteristics of a crusade. No outrages against the aborigines in the British Empire escaped their notice and, if government did not always heed the pleas of their deputations, neither did it ignore them.

---

[30] For the financial statements of this and other societies, see the *Missionary Magazine* for the appropriate years.

[31] *South African Commercial Advertiser*, July 21, 1852.

[32] *Missionary Magazine* (Jan., 1852), pp. 12–13.

[33] Davey, *op. cit.*, pp. 3–8.

The power of British humanitarianism was restricted not only by the limited resources of the societies but by the dominance of economic considerations in the formulation of imperial policy. Governments were usually sympathetic to appeals on behalf of "backward peoples," provided that intervention required no financial sacrifice. The consequence too often was vigorous pronouncements unsupported by substantial force.

Chapter V

THE MISSIONARY INFLUENCE
IN SOUTHERN AFRICA

SOUTHERN AFRICA was one of the earliest fields for missionary endeavor. Long before the Evangelical Revival in England, the United Brethren, more commonly known as the Moravians, had selected the Cape as a mission field. In 1737 Georg Schmidt arrived to minister to the Hottentots. He established a missionary institution at a place then called Sergeant River, later known as Baviaans kloof and Genadendaal. Schmidt's baptism of several Hottentots produced an outcry among the white settlers, and he was haled before the governor and council, who ordered him to desist from any further baptisms or the administering of Holy Communion, asserting that his church had no right to ordain him as a minister of the gospel. An additional cause of this interdict was the jealousy of the Dutch Reformed Church at the intervention of a rival sect. Schmidt was recalled by his church in 1743, and almost fifty years passed before the Moravians made another effort. In November, 1792, three missionaries reopened Schimdt's old station at Baviaans kloof.

Despite early difficulties with settlers and government the Moravians were a relatively conservative body. They devoted themselves to instructing their Hottentot followers in the principles of Christian life, and refrained from intervention in the political and social conflicts of the colony. Consequently they soon enjoyed the favor of the government and the colonists, who contrasted them with the meddling political missionaries of the British societies.[1] By 1834 the Moravians had established six stations, five among the Hottentots and one among the Tembu, with thirty-eight missionaries, and claimed 3,099 native converts, all except eight of whom were Hottentots.[2]

The most influential societies in southern Africa, in terms of political force, were the London and Wesleyan Missionary societies, and

[1] Johannes Du Plessis, *A History of Christian Missions in South Africa* (London: Longmans, Green, 1911), p. 257.
[2] *Missionary Register* (Jan., 1835), pp. 23–26.

the rivalry of the missionaries of these two groups had important social consequences. The London society, like the Methodists, was the child of the Evangelical Revival, of the passion of Wesley and White-field. The fervor of its founders was expressed by the Reverend George Burder in his call to the faithful in 1795 to form the society:

> It is now almost eighteen hundred years since the Friend of Sinners left our world, and left it with this gracious charge to His disciples,—"Go ye forth, and teach *all nations*." At the same time He assured them that, thus employed, they should, in all ages, and in all places enjoy His Presence.
>
> Let us do something *immediately*. Life is short. Let us work while it is called today; the night of death approaches; and our opportunities for being useful will close for ever.[3]

The constitution of the society stipulated that the sole object was "to spread the knowledge of Christ among heathen and other unen-lightened nations."[4] The society's first missionary efforts were directed to the South Seas, where the initial reverses might have destroyed the enthusiasm of a less dedicated leadership. But in 1799 the society ex-panded its missionary field to southern Africa when it sent two ordained ministers, Dr. J. T. van der Kemp and J. J. Kicherer, with two assist-ants, to the Cape on board a convict ship bound for Botany Bay. The missionaries received a warm welcome from residents in Cape Town, and the South African Missionary Society was formed to assist in the conversion of the heathen. But this beginning, though auspicious, was misleading, for the society was destined to become the bane of the settler population. Van der Kemp attempted to form a missionary station among the Xosa, but found them unreceptive. Consequently, after more than a year's residence in Kaffirland, he withdrew to the frontier settlement of Graaff Reinet. The government, anxious to stabi-lize the vagrant Hottentots, induced him to establish an institution where Hottentots might reside, learning habits of industry while they received religious instruction. From the establishment near Algoa Bay of that institution, named Bethelsdorp, the primary effort of the Lon-don Missionary Society for the next generation was among the Hot-tentots.

This identification of the London Missionary Society with the wel-fare of the Hottentots led early to conflict with the settlers over alleged ill-treatment of Hottentot "apprentices," and van der Kemp and James Read, the missionary in charge of Bethelsdorp, became anathema to

---

[3] Richard Lovett, *The History of the London Missionary Society, 1795–1895* (2 vols.; London: Frowde, 1899), I, 18, 23.

[4] *Ibid.*, I, 30.

the Cape government, as to the Boers, by their allegations to the British government that numerous atrocities had been committed which had been ignored by local authorities. Governor Sir George Yonge, who prided himself on his enlightened, humanitarian views, was at odds with van der Kemp within two years of the latter's arrival. The missionary, he averred, used "the Canting Phrases of Godliness" to mask ulterior objectives. Van der Kemp and the society he represented grasped at great power, commercial and political. They sold European goods to their proselytes at huge profits and they were politically subversive —they were, in fact, Jacobins.[5] As the missionaries became more energetic and more vocal in their espousal of the Hottentot cause, condemnation of their activities grew more strident. The fact that van der Kemp and Read lived with nonwhite wives merely documented the settlers' conviction of the Negrophilia of the London missionaries.

The conflicts of van der Kemp and Read were mere skirmishes; the battle between the missionaries and the settler community achieved its highest intensity during the tenure of Dr. John Philip as superintendent of the London Missionary Society in South Africa. The bitterness engendered during these years has indelibly marked South African society, and John Philip has become a permanent symbol: to his admirers he represents the triumph, albeit temporary, of the forces of virtue; to his enemies, he was the agent of the Devil. The causes of Philip's notoriety are in part personal, in part institutional. It is scarcely an exaggeration to say that Philip during his lifetime created a myth of South African history which ensnared not only himself and his admirers but their most violent opponents.

All shades of opinion agree that Philip was an able politician, but the moral conclusions are antithetical. Cory wrote that though Philip was never a declared politician, "he was par excellence a political intriguer who could even overshadow a Machiavelli";[6] a textbook for Afrikaner students described this "clever propagandist and political missionary" as "a sort of uncrowned king" of Cape Colony.[7] But Macmillan, the first historian to use Philip's own correspondence,[8] presented a portrait of Philip as a statesman, disinclined to intervene in

[5] Yonge to Henry Dundas, April 17, 1800, most secret; Yonge to Dundas, Oct. 22, 1800, both in George M. Theal, *Records of the Cape Colony* (36 vols.; Cape Town: G.P.O., 1899–1907), III, 113–119, 338–340.

[6] George E. Cory, *The Rise of South Africa* (5 vols.; London: Longmans, Green, 1921–1930), II, 403.

[7] A. J. H. van der Walt, J. A. Wiid, and A. L. Geyer, *Geskiedenis van Suid-Afrika* (2 vols.; Cape Town: Nasionale Boekhandel, 1955), II, 396.

[8] The personal papers of Philip, deposited in the University of the Witwatersrand

political questions until the gravity of the moral crisis forced him to act, but when so compelled, moving powerfully and effectively. This was Philip's conception of himself. During his vendetta with the colonial government of Lord Charles Somerset, he wrote that as an individual he was prepared to undergo vilification without complaint, but "when the cause of mankind and the cause of God come to be in danger—I can be silent no longer and it is my duty to speak out." [9] Philip's view of life was simple. The cause he represented was the cause of God; those who opposed him were the powers of evil. They persecuted him because he sought justice for the aborigines,[10] but he was prepared to endure abuse, even to suffer death: "I have many sins and infirmities to be humbled before God, but the prosperity of the cause of God in Africa has always been dearer to me than my own temporal interests, than the concerns of my family and than life itself; and no one in my situation less interested in its prosperity will ever be able to endure what I have endured and to carry on the work of God in that country to a successful issue." [11]

Philip's statements of facts were not always reliable; he was sometimes guilty of exaggeration and outright misstatements. His critics in his lifetime and since have called him a deliberate liar, unscrupulous in his use of evidence. This conclusion misapprehends his character and contributes to misinterpretation of his role in South African history. Philip was a zealot; his tremendous vitality was channeled into the advancement of the aborigines with which he identified himself and the society he represented. Like most zealots, he was a moral totalitarian. Philip lived in a world of intrigue infested with diabolical forces; an appraisal of such a man by the standards of cold rationality and objective fact is irrelevant.

The London Missionary Society was basically of the Congregational persuasion; Philip's assertion of authority irritated those of the London missionaries who believed in a high degree of independence rather than centralized authority. Robert Moffat, whose temperament was

---

Library, were destroyed by fire in 1931. Fortunately, Professor W. M. Macmillan had already published his two books based upon these documents, *The Cape Colour Question* (London: Faber and Gwyer, 1927), and *Bantu, Boer, and Briton* (London: Faber and Gwyer, 1929). But Philip's letters to the directors of society are preserved in the LMS Archives in London.

[9] "A Commentary Addressed to the Secretary, LMS, on his [Philip's] Dealings with the Colonial Government since his going to Africa," March, 1825 (microfilm from LMS Archives deposited in UCLA Library, reel 1).

[10] See his letter to his mother, Sept. 13, 1824, *ibid.*

[11] Philip to Directors, Oct. 6, 1837, SAF 15-3, LMS Archives.

akin to Philip's, called him "the Pope." The designation was apt; not only was Philip an autocrat but he assumed infallibility in matters of faith and doctrine. Philip's exaggerated opinion of his power was enhanced by the restricted environment in which he lived. He not unnaturally assumed that when he advocated a line of policy and that policy was adopted, he was the cause of the adoption—*post hoc, ergo propter hoc.* Historians who have evaluated his work have with less excuse fallen into the same error.

In the 1820's, when Philip's objectives were frustrated by the government in Cape Town, he appealed to the British public and to Westminster. His accounts of the plight of the Hottentots in his reports to the directors of the London Missionary Society contributed to the appointment of a commission of inquiry to investigate conditions at the Cape, especially the treatment of the colored population. In 1826, convinced that there was no hope for improvement in the status of the Hottentots through local action, he sailed for England, intent on presenting their case to Parliament and the ministry. But the great men of England, with the exception of Thomas Fowell Buxton, were generally uninterested in granting him an audience. By the publication of his book, *Researches in South Africa,* in April, 1828, he sought to evoke a response from the public which would stir the politicians to action. The book created considerable discussion, and Buxton availed himself of this aroused interest to announce his intention to bring forward a parliamentary motion calling on the government to use its authority to secure freedom and legal equality for the Hottentots. Sir George Murray, secretary of state for colonies, after an unsuccessful effort to induce Buxton to delay the motion, promised to introduce it as a government measure if Buxton would agree to make or encourage no speeches on the subject. Meanwhile, independently, the object had been achieved at the Cape by the passage of the Fiftieth Ordinance by Governor Richard Bourke on the advice of Andries Stockenstrom.[12] By Philip's account, when the ordinance reached England the government sought his advice, and he counseled them to reinforce it with an order in council that would prevent future alteration of the provisions of the ordinance by colonial action alone.[13]

---

[12] The Bourke Papers contain information on the background of the Fiftieth Ordinance. Among the important letters are Stockenstrom to Bourke, private, June 21, 1828, and W. W. Burton to Bourke, private, June 22, 1828, both in Bourke Papers, t 7/7, Rhodes House, Oxford.

[13] Philip presents his version of these events in detail in a memorandum, "Voyage to England—the success and bearing of the Hottentot question on the great slavery question," apparently written in 1846 (Philip 3-5, LMS Archives).

Philip's description of his experiences in London implied that Sir George Murray had been guided by his advice in appraising the Fiftieth Ordinance. This impression of direct influence gave him status at the Cape, but it was almost certainly untrue, for by the testimony of the staff he had had only one interview with the Colonial Secretary, and that was at the solicitation of the directors of the London Missionary Society, whose secretary also was present on that occasion.[14] Such deviations from facts subject him to the charge of deliberate falsehood. The allegation is unduly harsh, but he possessed a conveniently unreliable memory.

Philip's experience in England from 1826 to 1829 established the pattern of his life. He had helped to plan strategy and tactics in a noble cause and had been consulted by men of power, and his advice had led to governmental action. Buxton himself relied upon him not only for information but for advice with regard to great issues. The taste of power was sweet. Essentially a politician, Philip loved disputation and the sense of participation in momentous decisions. Other politicians professed to be the servants of the people; Philip believed himself to be the servant of God.

Certainly Philip was devoted to the welfare of the Hottentots in the sense of protecting them from maltreatment by the settlers, but there is no evidence that he, any more than the settlers, respected them as individuals. His attitude was that of a benevolent despot. The inhabitants of the missionary institutions remained in a state of tutelage to their spiritual overseers; and so long as they were decent, industrious, and docile they were entitled to remain.[15] Philip made and unmade chiefs of the Griqua tribes. Andries Waterboer was his creature; he followed Philip's advice. In turn Philip praised him as a devoted Christian and a great leader of his people.

After his apparent success in 1828 Philip continued to seek to influence British policy through correspondence with the London directors and with his friend Buxton. Buxton was in fact the only British politician with whom Philip could communicate on intimate terms. But Philip did not adequately recognize that he supplied only the fuel

---

[14] See C.O. memo, "Missionary Institutions at the Cape of Good Hope," Oct. 15, 1831, C.O. 48/144, P.R.O.

[15] W. Elliott, who was sent by the LMS to assist Philip at Cape Town in the late 1840's, when the old man's powers were failing, dared to suggest in 1849 that the missionary institutions did not contribute to the progress of the Hottentot people. After Philip's outburst in response, Elliott complained that Philip did not fight fair. This was a familiar complaint of those whom Philip attacked. For this correspondence see SAF 24, LMS Archives.

and Buxton the power. So long as Buxton was a force, Philip was a man to be reckoned with. Governors feared Philip because they believed that he had influence with Buxton, and they dreaded the power of the Saints in Parliament. Buxton's influence declined rapidly after the passage of the Abolition Act and was of little consequence with governments after his retirement from Parliament in 1837. Yet Philip continued to correspond with him thereafter as if he could still perform the miracles of the 1820's.

Philip's restricted knowledge of the bases for government policy led him to unwarranted conclusions. When Governor D'Urban consulted him on frontier policy, Philip assumed that he possessed great influence; he did not know that D'Urban also consulted with representatives of the Wesleyan Missionary Society and with governmental officials, some of whom gave advice similar to Philip's, before arriving at a decision.

Philip contributed to the negotiation of Governor Napier's treaties with Adam Kok and with Moshesh in 1843, and these agreements were in accordance with Philip's design of encouraging independent native "states" on the borders of the Cape to maintain order beyond the Orange. But it would be unwarranted to conclude from this that Napier was under Philip's influence. In the absence of a British agent in the trans-Orange territories, Philip's information was of great value. Napier sought to promote tranquillity in the region at minimum expense; treaties such as Philip suggested seemed a promising expedient, and the missionaries of the London society at Philippolis and the allied Paris society at Thaba Bosiu were useful intermediaries.

Philip has been drawn larger than life; he has been credited with greater political influence than he possessed. He first contributed to this exaggeration, and his enemies have helped to perpetuate it. He was a man of great ability and energy, and a courageous advocate of the rights of the oppressed; but, like many other men of courage and conviction, he lacked discrimination and was devoid of a sense of charity toward those who opposed him. These qualities made him the best-hated man of his day. Perhaps as fair an evaluation of Philip as any has been made by Johannes Du Plessis: "Philip has been made in turn the subject of the most extravagant laudation and the most unmeasured vituperation. Neither one nor the other is wholly deserved." [16]

Though other missionary associations maintained stations in southern Africa, the principal rival of the London Missionary Society in its work of evangelizing the nonwhite peoples was the Wesleyan Mission-

---

[16] Du Plessis, *op. cit.*, p. 152.

ary Society, and the conflicts between Philip and the Wesleyans were conducted with an intensity comparable to his battles with the Cape government and the settlers. The official establishment of the Wesleyan Missionary Society in 1813 was formal recognition of a missionary emphasis that had long existed, and was indeed implicit in Wesley's conception of the world as his parish and of the obligation of Christians to minister to the heathen. The first Wesleyan missionary at the Cape, like those of the London society, experienced difficulties with the local government. Somerset forbade the Reverend John McKenny to preach in Cape Town, but on instructions from the Colonial Office Somerset accepted McKenny's replacement, Barnabas Shaw.[17] The reasons for this initial governmental antipathy were different from those involving the London society. The Methodists were suspect because they were dissenters; the London missionaries were in disfavor with Somerset and other governors because they were turbulent priests, subversive of quiet and order.

The main theaters of missionary conflict were Kaffirland and, particularly after 1834, the trans-Orange country. Before the Kaffir war in 1834 the Wesleyans maintained six stations among the Kaffirs and three among the Bechuana and Korana tribes beyond the Orange. The principal endeavors of the London society continued to be among the Hottentots and the Griquas. In 1834 it maintained twelve Hottentot stations and institutions within Cape Colony, a mission among the Hottentots settled in the neutral territory on the borders of Kaffraria, and four stations among the Griquas. By contrast, the London missionaries in 1834 had only one station among the Kaffirs,[18] though subsequently they increased the number to four. Kaffir wars destroyed mission stations of the various societies and the official number of stations consequently fluctuated, but the missionaries soon returned to begin again.

The Wesleyan missionaries were unlike their London counterparts and the representatives of most other societies in one important respect. They conceived their mission to be to minister to white settlers as well as to the black heathens. Their circuits included both colonists and tribesmen, and their missionaries were consequently far more intimately connected with Europeans than were those of the London society. This association with the settler community unquestionably influenced the viewpoint of Wesleyan missionaries and contributed

---

[17] Wesleyan Missionary Society (hereafter cited as WMS) to Bathurst, Oct. 30, 1815; Bathurst to Somerset, Nov. 9, 1815, both in Theal, *op. cit.*, X, 365–368.

[18] *Missionary Register* (Jan., 1835), pp. 28–39.

to the clash between the South African spokesmen of the two great societies.

The contrast between the two bodies is illustrated by the career of William Shaw, who became the principal spokesman for the Wesleyans. Shaw came to South Africa to minister to the Albany settlers of 1820, but within three years he extended the Wesleyan missionary influence into adjacent Kaffirland by founding Wesleyville near the kraal of the Gcaleka chief Pato. But the expansion was an extension of a corporate enterprise, not a divorcement from an earlier emphasis. Shaw and his fellow missionaries retained their association with the Albany settlement. Philip, with headquarters in Cape Town, had no communication with the mind of the frontier settlers; nor did his missionary informants among the Hottentots, the Griquas, and the Bantu. Shaw, with headquarters in Grahamstown, and his fellow Methodist missionaries could not separate themselves from the settler viewpoint.

The missionary conflicts in South Africa were in part the product of the personal characters of the missionaries and the aggravations of combative tendencies by environment. There has been no adequate analysis of the missionary character, of the motives that led men and women to enlist in the cause of Christianizing the heathens. Certainly the avowed purpose explains little of the nature of the missionary psyche. Educational backgrounds varied widely. At one extreme, van der Kemp had studied philosophy and religion at Leyden and medicine at Edinburgh; at the other, Joseph Williams of the same society had little formal education, and wrote English with noticeable difficulty.[19] Some, such as William Shaw, were stable, well-balanced personalities. But many were beset by mental afflictions, ranging from pettiness and querulousness to pathological conditions of morbid introspectiveness and delusions of persecution. For personalities highly susceptible to emotional illness, the transition from the urban British society to the wilderness of South Africa was a traumatic experience which sometimes proved too intense. Whatever the background of the missionary and his mental characteristics, the loneliness of life among an alien people imposed tremendous strains.

Further complicating the lives of some missionaries were wives who were either emotionally unbalanced or highly contentious; for others, difficulties arose from the absence of wives. One who suffered from

---

[19] Donovan Williams, "The Missionaries on the Eastern Frontiers of the Cape Colony, 1799–1853" (unpublished Ph.D. dissertation, University of the Witwatersrand, 1960). Williams has made an intensive study of the backgrounds and the characteristics of South African missionaries.

having a wife was W. B. Boyce. When Boyce was at Wesleyville, he was harassed by a quarrel between his wife and Nonube, a great lady of the Xosa tribe. Mrs. Boyce, highly impressed with the dignity of her station, was revolted by the filth of the Kaffir women; when Nonube came to visit her, she professed to be ill and consequently unavailable. Nonube uttered some rude remarks and frightened Mrs. Boyce, who complained to her husband; he demanded an apology from the tribe. Harry Smith, at the time administrator of the territory, witnessed this feud with great amusement. He wrote that Boyce "is the most fiery little devil earth, heaven or hell ever produced when his wife is in the way, but when cool a very clear fellow." [20]

In their isolated environments, missionaries communicated with one another primarily through the medium of letters, often delivered months after they were written. Men so cut off from a normal intercourse were likely to read and reread their correspondence. Lifetime grievances frequently erupted from misinterpretations of language to imply insults that were unintended, followed by insults back and forth which were intended.

The wonder is not that so many missionaries were excessively sensitive and introspective, but that so many bore their burdens with courage and resolution. Life for the missionary among the Kaffirs was characterized by acute frustration, for the Xosa seemed virtually immune to the doctrines of Christianity and clung to their pagan ways, their dirt, and their "abominable" practices with a tenacity that must have shaken the resolution of the most dedicated emissary of Christianity and bourgeois Victorian morality.

The quarrels of the London and Wesleyan societies are not entirely to be explained by the mental characteristics of individual missionaries. Rather, they arose largely from the essential characteristics of organizations. All the missionary societies sought to transmit to the heathen the word of God as communicated through Jesus Christ, but the objectives for which they were formed came in time to be overlaid with the vested interests of the society itself.

Charles Booth in his study of the condition of the poor in London observed that the zeal of charity workers often had little or no relationship to the improvement of the condition of those they avowedly sought to serve; the poor became the objects of much "ignoble competition," which did not benefit them but swelled the sense of importance of the competing organizations: "Highly coloured appeals bring in a golden return, treats and blankets swell the lists of mothers and chil-

---

[20] Smith to D'Urban, July 16, 1836, confidential, G.H. 34/8, Cape Archives.

dren on the books of the undertaking, and, above all, the sectarian spirit binds and braces together the energies of the band of workers." [21]

This characteristic of organizations, that a body formed as a means to an objective also becomes an objective in itself, is, of course, not peculiar to religious groups. The phenomenon of "expediters" who become additional echelons of obstruction is sadly familiar. The generalization should not be overstated to imply that the organization becomes utterly divorced from its avowed objects. Missionaries in South Africa did seek to instill in the heathen knowledge of the word of God, and many were dedicated men. But when the London, or the Wesleyan, or the Glasgow Missionary Society spoke of Christianizing the natives, somehow Christianity was identified with the advancement of the society. Missionary enterprises, all avowedly dedicated to the same objective, took on the characteristics of rival organizations, even of deadly enemies, and their relations with one another were often akin to the jungle world of international relations rather than to a community of believers. The differences among these societies were not theological but organizational. Of course, there was an added zest when there were theological differences. At the annual meeting of the London Missionary Society in Exeter Hall in 1846, the directors reported that wherever the London missionaries were laboring, the emissaries of Rome were intruding. The directors assured the faithful they were fully cognizant of the nature of the menace:

If we had never committed ourselves to the work of converting the heathen, we might then have been comparatively innocent in leaving the Romanist to do it; but having taken our stand in this work, to allow ourselves to be driven from it by such antagonists, who can hear of it for a moment. Better never to have planted our foot on the shores of heathen lands, than allow it to be supplanted by those old corrupters of the truth of God.[22]

Attacks on Roman Catholics might be explained in terms of a deepseated hostility attached to Popery. The rivalry between the London and Wesleyan societies could not be explained in such doctrinal terms, but their conflict was intense. They were like rival imperialist states fighting over colonial territories. Toward chiefs and tribes with whom they resided they felt a proprietary interest; other chiefs and tribes, particularly those associated with other societies, they tended to regard

---

[21] Charles Booth, *Life and Labour of the People in London*, 3d series (8 vols.; London: Macmillan, 1902), VII, 417–421.

[22] *Missionary Magazine*, CXXI (June, 1846), 83.

with hostility or distrust. The Quaker James Backhouse commented, after a tour of South African missions, that "almost every Missionary we met with entertained a favourable opinion of the people among whom he was labouring; but very few were clear of strong prejudice against those who were distant from them." [23]

An early illustration of the characteristic of South African missionaries was a violent controversy over the control of an insignificant fountain at Daniel's Kuil in Bechuanaland, between Griquatown and Robert Moffat's station at Kuruman. James Archbell, a Wesleyan missionary stationed with the Bastaard chief Barent Barends, discovered while reading the missionary journals from England that the London Missionary Society had listed Daniel's Kuil as a field of itineration for its Griquatown mission. Archbell immediately dispatched an inflammatory letter to Peter Wright, the missionary at Griquatown, informing him that this assertion of control was a violation of the rights of the Wesleyan society, as Barends was a Wesleyan chief and claimed jurisdiction over the fountain. Archbell admitted that he had not been engaged in missionary work at Daniel's Kuil, but stated that now that two additional missionaries had arrived to help him, he expected to begin regular itineration there. Further, he told Wright, he highly disapproved of Wright's conduct in having without warrant invaded this territory.[24] Wright replied with asperity that Daniel's Kuil had been a field of itineration from Griquatown for many years and had appeared in the London society's lists for fifteen years before Archbell had discovered the fact.[25]

The correspondence became increasingly violent, with both sides indulging in personal insults of a most unchristian character. The issue eventually involved Philip and Shaw and ultimately had to be submitted to the London headquarters of the two societies for decision. What was at stake was not the "soul of the heathen," as Daniel's Kuil was frequented only by a few wandering savages. The conflict was over territorial jurisdictions. Archbell contended that Barends was an independent chief and that his alleged political control of Daniel's Kuil established an ecclesiastical claim.[26] Philip sought to demolish Archbell's case by the assertion that the various Griqua and Bastaard chiefs were mere creatures of the London Missionary Society. London mis-

---

[23] James Backhouse, *A Narrative of a Visit to Mauritius and South Africa* (London: Hamilton, Adams, 1844), p. 318.

[24] Archbell to Wright, Aug. 17, 1832, Philip 3-1, LMS Archives.

[25] Wright to Archbell, Sept. 5, 1832, *ibid.*

[26] Archbell to Wright and Hughes, Oct. 31, 1832, *ibid.*

sionaries had found them wandering in a savage state and had prevailed
on them to settle down and engage in agricultural pursuits. They had
not opened a country for the missionaries but the missionaries had
found a country for them. This country they did not possess in their
own names but in the name of the London Missionary Society, and
the colonial government had sanctioned the deed. The London society
had recommended that certain chiefs be recognized by the Cape government, and its recommendations had been approved by the governor.
Philip asserted that Barends had never been recognized as a chief and
had never held a higher office than that of deputy chief of Griquatown.
He was consequently a subject of Waterboer, and the London Missionary Society therefore had jurisdiction over Daniel's Kuil.[27] The
correspondence, leaving aside the invective, was essentially concerned
with spheres of influence.

The Wesleyan missionary W. B. Boyce reacted in the same terms
to reports in 1838 that the British government was about to annex
Natal. His principal concern was that unless his society moved rapidly,
the London missionaries by stealth would appropriate the territory for
themselves. He wrote to the London directors:

> I have no doubt but that eventually it will turn out that Dr. Philip &
> Buxton are scheming to help the Natal scheme & monopolize the country for
> the London Society's mission. Do not imagine that these gentlemen I mean
> Dr. P. & Stocken[strom] care one farthing for the rights of the natives, or
> any provision for the future religious instruction of these natives near Natal.
> . . . Would it not be a masterly step to strike the first blow? . . .
> The great battle of Armageddon is only just beginning: When Gog and
> Magog are discomfited then I will become a member of the Peace society, but
> until then "war to the knife." [28]

At about the same time that Boyce was warning his society of the
malevolent intentions of their London rivals, John Philip was informing his directors of the aggressive policies of the Methodists. He
wrote the secretary that the Methodists cared not one whit for the
welfare of the colored inhabitants of the Cape. "Their object is not
to attack the strongholds of Satan but the flourishing stations of all
other divisions of the army of Christ"; they sought, in fact, "universal
empire." [29]

The rivalry of the two societies had political consequences north

---

[27] Notes by Philip on Wright to Archbell, Dec. 1, 1832, *ibid.*

[28] Boyce to Beecham, Nov. 10, 1838, Albany MSS, Methodist Missionary Society
(hereafter cited as MMS) Archives.

[29] Philip to Ellis, March 6, 1840, SAF 17-1; Philip to Freeman July 8, 1840, SAF
17-2, both in LMS Archives.

of the Orange River in the environs of the Basuto Chief Moshesh. In 1833 missionaries of the Paris Evangelical Missionary Society, with the blessings of Philip and the London society, began missionary work among the Basuto. In effect, the two societies agreed that the land of the "mountain king" would be the special preserve of the French missionaries, who might look for advice and counsel to their London brethren. From the beginning Eugene Casalis and his fellow French missionaries accepted John Philip as their diplomatic representative with the Cape government and sought his advice on all "political questions." At about the same time that the Paris missionaries arrived among the Basuto, three Wesleyan missionaries, including the redoubtable James Archbell, led a portion of the Barolong people southward from the trans-Vaal country. In December, 1833, they negotiated an agreement with the Basuto chief and Mosemi, one of his vassals, to allocate land around Thaba Nchu to the Wesleyan society for the mission station for the Barolong. This agreement, like so many other arrangements with native chiefs, was interpreted in widely different ways. The document which the Wesleyan produced as evidence provided that Moshesh and Mosemi agreed to the "absolute sale" of this country to the Wesleyan society for the price of seven young oxen, one heifer, one sheep, and one goat.[30] Moshesh admitted that he had made an arrangement with the Methodists but, of course, contended that he had merely granted the use of the land to the society.

Whatever the nature of the agreement, the Wesleyan and Paris missionaries soon became spokesmen for rival chiefs, and the rivalry was accentuated by the sponsorship of the two societies. Moroko, chief of the Barolong, and Sikonyela, chief of the Mantatees, became protégés of the Wesleyans, and Moshesh became the client of the Paris missionaries. Shortly after Casalis arrived, he wrote to Philip asking for advice as to how he should act toward the Wesleyans. Philip counseled moderation:

> With regard to the conduct you should pursue to the Wesleyan Missionaries I have but one advice to give, in so far as possible live peaceably with them, and with all men. You move in separate orbits, and . . . you may each of you share in your respective spheres, spreading your light and influence around you, without coming into collision, and to the mutual advantage of each other. I shall always be glad to hear from you and your brethren and to advise you in all your difficulties.[31]

---

[30] "Agreement entered into by Kaffir Chiefs and the Missionaries," Dec. 7, 1833, in Cathcart to Newcastle, March 28, 1854, C.O. 48/364, P.R.O.

[31] Philip to Casalis, March 23, 1834, Philip Box I, Folder 1, LMS Archives.

Amity was not of long duration. Within a few years the Paris and Wesleyan missionaries were locked in bitter conflict over the territorial claims of their tribal protégés. The immediate cause of this missionary battle was the spread of Boer settlement north and northeast from the Orange River, a movement that menaced the interests of both societies. But instead of drawing together to fight the intrusion of the trekkers into the lands of the tribes, the representatives of the two societies fought with each other. Early in 1842, in describing to Lieutenant Governor Hare his impressions of the Basuto country which he had recently visited, Philip took the opportunity to broach a favorite proposal. Ever since he had induced Governor D'Urban to negotiate a treaty with Waterboer in 1834, Philip had envisioned a cordon of native principalities under London missionary influence which would control the "marches" of the Cape's inland borders. When he had first conceived this dream, the threat to security had come from a handful of banditti; but now, with the migration of the emigrant Boers across the Orange, a far greater menace had arisen to the tribes north of the river and to the peace of the frontier. To Philip, the need for treaties of mutual defense was now urgent and imperative. He pressed on Hare the desirability of making Waterboer-type alliances with Adam Kok and with Moshesh.[32] Hare, oppressed with the impossible task of maintaining order on a boundary of hundreds of miles with only a few hundred troops, was receptive to the suggestion. Perhaps Philip was right in believing that well-armed Griquas and the powerful chief Moshesh could hold the Boers in check without the necessity of support from British troops. Waterboer, for a trifling gift of £150 per year, had been a bulwark of order within the area of his influence; perhaps Kok and Moshesh could perform a similar function at little or no expense to the British government. Governor Napier, likewise preoccupied with the problem of maintaining tranquillity "on the cheap," agreed that the expedient was worth trying. Consequently, with Philip acting as an intermediary, the Cape government at the end of 1843 negotiated treaties with Kok and with Moshesh; Philip argued that these two chiefs controlled the frontier territory and that arrangements with other chiefs were unnecessary and undesirable, for to negotiate treaties with minor chieftains would reduce the value of those with the great border lords.[33] Philip also defined the limits of Moshesh's territory and assured the government that "his missionaries" would obtain the

[32] Philip to Hare, July 12, 1842, SAF 18-1, LMS Archives.
[33] Philip to Napier, Aug. 25, 1842, C.O. 48/224, P.R.O.

signatures of chiefs Kok and Moshesh to the completed treaties.[34]

When the messenger from Cape Colony arrived at Moshesh's mountain, the Paris missionaries were surprised to find that he brought not
a draft but a completed treaty ready for signature. But they were
gratified at its enlightened provisions.[35] Casalis told Philip that if his
work was not appreciated by the ungrateful world, he could look
forward to the heavenly prospect of the gratitude of "poor Africa's
children" who had benefited by his exertions. But one provision of
the completed treaty caused Moshesh and his missionary advisers to
have misgivings. The clause that Philip had written defining Moshesh's
territory was unduly restrictive, and the boundaries did not include
the district occupied by Moshesh's vassal Moroko and the Barolong
tribe, which remained largely outside the delimited area and consequently at the mercy of the Boers.[36]

The news of the government's treaty with Moshesh was received by
the Wesleyans with very different reactions. William Shaw was visiting
the society's trans-Orange missions when he heard of the projected
alliances. He immediately sent off a communication to Hare that "the
chiefs of tribes connected with the Wesleyan missions"—Moroko and
the Bastaard captains, Piet David, Gert Taaibosch, and Carolus Baatje
—were anxious to enter into similar agreements. Their tribes, he said,
had long been in close association with one another, and their combined force was stronger than that of the Basuto nation. It was clear
to Shaw that the treaty with Moshesh, formulated in secret without
even the slightest intimation of its contents to the Wesleyan Missionary
Society, was a blatant grasping for power by the London Missionary
Society's Paris allies. The boundaries laid down for Moshesh's tribe
extended far beyond his rightful jurisdiction and over the territories
of the independent Barolong, Bastaard, and Mantatee peoples. The
confirmation of so iniquitous a document would mean war.[37]

The issues were not basically the conflicts of Moroko and Moshesh,
but those of the Wesleyan and Paris Missionary societies. Casalis was
no doubt correct when he alleged that Moroko, Carolus Baatje, and
Gert Taaibosch would have made no protest against Moshesh's para-
mountcy had the Wesleyans not insisted on their asserting their inde-

[34] Note by Montagu, Sept. 8, [1843], G.H. 19/4, Cape Archives.
[35] Casalis to Philip, Dec. 14, 1843, SAF 19-4, LMS Archives.
[36] Ibid.
[37] Shaw to Hudson, Dec. 15, 1843, in J. W. Sauer and G. M. Theal, eds., Basutoland
Records (3 vols.; Cape Town: Richard, 1883), I, 57–60.

pendence; [38] and certainly the document on which Moroko's claims to independence rested was a missionary document, alien to tribal concepts of land tenure.

In 1843 the great menace to the trans-Orange tribes was not the pretensions of Moshesh or of Sikonyela but the encroachments of the emigrant Boers. The Napier treaties with Kok and Moshesh were an anachronism; it was unrealistic to expect these chiefs to maintain order in territories in the path of the land-hungry Europeans; rather than providing a substitute for British military protection, they made British intervention necessary. In proposing such alliances as a bulwark of order, Philip was a victim of his delusions. The Methodists, in opposing them, were prisoners of their narrow sectarian interests. At a time when the tribes in common faced the threat of expulsion from their lands by a steadily growing European menace, the missionaries accentuated tribal differences and thus contributed to the ruination of those they sought to protect. To assert this is to cast no reflection on the motives of individual missionaries or of their societies. In the circumstances it was perhaps inevitable that the missionaries should become in fact the diplomatic agents of the tribes with whom they resided. Chiefs received missionaries for a variety of reasons, the least significant of which were theological. They were useful as teachers of agriculture and of methods of irrigation; their presence gave the tribe a voice in the councils of the governor at Cape Town, and their advice was valuable in the hazardous diplomatic negotiations that might determine a tribe's destruction or survival.[39] Moshesh could not accept Casalis' religious doctrines, but he was guided by his secular advice. Conversely, the missionaries could not divorce themselves, even if they would, from being identified with the tribe among whom they labored. James Allison, a missionary to Moroko, wrote the secretary of his society that "the natives are apt to look with an evil eye" on missionaries resident with their enemies, and that when there were conflicts over territorial rights, the missionaries were forced, however reluctantly, to act as the spokesmen of their chiefs in negotiations with the British government.[40] After Governor Sir Harry Smith proclaimed British sovereignty over the trans-Orange country in February, 1848, the position of the missionaries became even more complicated, because the

---

[38] Casalis to Philip, April 11, 1844, SAF 19-4, LMS Archives.

[39] See Williams, *op. cit.*, pp. 64 ff., for a discussion of the chiefs' motives in accepting missionaries.

[40] Allison to Secretaries, WMS, Jan. 31, 1850, Bechuanaland Letters, MMS Archives.

British government provided no political agents to deal with the tribes over whom Smith now professed to exercise jurisdiction. In 1851 Major William Hogge and Charles Owen, sent by Downing Street to report on the state of affairs beyond the Orange River, said that the wars of the territory had been as much among the missionaries as among the rival chiefs,[41] and that each society "supported the pretensions of its particular chief, whether friendly or hostile to the Government." [42] In particular, they condemned the Reverend James Cameron, a Wesleyan missionary with Moroko, whom they asserted had acted more like a politician than a missionary.[43] Cameron replied that when two parties requiring to communicate lacked other means of communication, the missionaries had no alternative but to act as diplomatic agents.[44]

From a combination of their own vested interests and environmental circumstances, the missionaries were forced to accept a political role in southern Africa. But a political role is not identical with political "influence." It is true that governors of the Cape were inclined to be deferential, if possible, to the missionary interest, in part because they believed that open conflict would subject them to attack by humanitarian organizations at home which sustained substantial force in Parliament and could bend governments to their will.[45] Every governor between 1834 and 1854 displayed his concern over censure by references to possible attacks by humanitarian groups on his policies. The tone might be defiant, as was Sir Henry Pottinger's, or apprehensive, as was Sir Harry Smith's, but in each instance the governor manifested awareness.

Governors sometimes assumed that missionaries had more political influence than they in fact possessed. D'Urban in 1836 ascribed the defeat of his policies to the power of the Saints, but he was misinformed. When Sir Harry Smith in 1851 expressed to Earl Grey his alarm that he might be pilloried in Parliament for alleged "tyranny and despotism," he was in danger of recall not for despotism but for ineffectuality. Earl Grey assured him that he had no cause for worry about

---

[41] Hogge to Grey, Dec. 19, 1851, Grey Papers, Prior's Kitchen, University of Durham.

[42] Asst. Commissioners to High Commissioner, Dec. 8, 1851, Sauer and Theal, *op. cit.*, I, 477.

[43] Hogge and Owen to Cameron, Dec. 3, 1851, *ibid.*, I, 474.

[44] Cameron to Hogge and Owen, Nov. 25, 1851, Bechuanaland Letters, MMS Archives.

[45] See, for example, Bird to D'Urban, private, March 4, 1839, D'Urban Papers, VII, Cape Archives.

attacks by Sir Edward Buxton and others, for the public did not really "sympathize with this false & sickly humanity," but that he was subject to criticism for excessive leniency when "greater severity in the beginning would have stopped much mischief." [46]

As Grey's counsel made clear, the ultimate test of a governor was not his conformity to humanitarian ideals but his effectiveness in maintaining order at minimum expense. Governors sought the advice of missionaries on frontier problems largely because they were the most knowledgeable white men on such matters. They sometimes followed missionary advice when it seemed to promote their own objectives. The missionary was used by the governor rather than the governor by the missionary. But each governor, assuming that his predecessor had been overly influenced by missionary spokesmen, dedicated himself to demonstrating his independence. Sir Henry Pottinger wrote Earl Grey in 1847 that he was determined to prevent missionary interference in politics.[47] What he meant was that he was determined to prevent missionary activity in opposition to his policies.

The nature of missionary influence on Cape policy between 1834 and 1854 has been misunderstood; by the perpetuation of the Philip legend, its power has been overstated. The great tragedy of the missionary movement was that this manifestation of a great spiritual awakening could evoke so little positive response within South Africa, either among whites or blacks. It remained a foreign importation. The settlers hated the meddling intrusion that subjected them to obloquy from Britons who could not understand South African problems. The tribesmen and their chiefs, while they recognized certain temporal advantages in the residence of missionaries among them, rejected the alien doctrines of Victorian Christianity.

---

[46] Grey to Smith, Sept. 15, 1851, private, Grey Papers.
[47] Pottinger to Grey, private, Oct. 30, 1847, *ibid.*

Chapter VI

WAR AND ANNEXATION, 1834–1836

SOME MEN are remembered for great deeds, others for identification with great events. Had Sir Benjamin D'Urban died in 1833 his name would soon have passed into oblivion. He had been a gallant soldier in the Peninsular campaign and his rise to high rank in the British Army was a testament to ability rather than family connections. As governor for thirteen years in slave-owning colonies of the West Indies and Guiana he had administered the affairs of their vexed societies with ability and tact. He died at the age of seventy-two. But the events that cause him to be remembered occurred in a period of less than two years; the remainder of his life was an anticlimax.

D'Urban, like Philip, had become a symbol. To the white settlers of his day and since he has been a martyr to the misguided humanitarianism of the British Colonial Office. At his death in 1849 the *Grahamstown Journal* wrote that the colony had lost "one of the best and warmest friends." His name, "associated as it is with all that is good and honorable and generous, will ever live in the memory and be dear to the affections of the people of this colony." [1] Historians partisan to the white colonists have continued and developed the legend of Sir Benjamin D'Urban "the Good," victimized "to support a philanthropic Eidolon." [2] Liberal writers condemn him for the policies his partisans admire. In the ideological battle, the character and the policies of D'Urban have been obscured.

D'Urban was sent to South Africa to achieve objectives that were contrary, with resources that were inadequate. He was predestined to fail. He was to preside over the legal emancipation of the slaves; execute revolutionary changes in the administration of justice; introduce

---

[1] *Grahamstown Journal,* Sept. 1, 1849.

[2] The quotation is from A. Wilmot and J. C. Chase, *History of the Colony of the Cape of Good Hope* (Cape Town: Juta, 1869), p. 335, but the sentiments are expressed by George M. Theal, George E. Cory, and most Afrikaner historians.

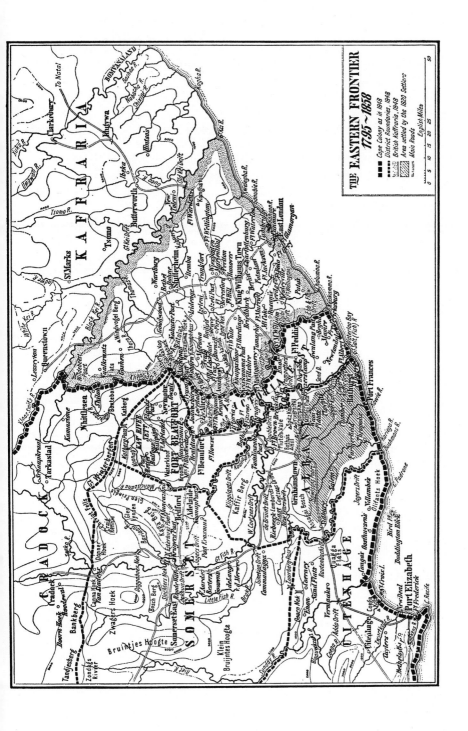

THE EASTERN FRONTIER
1795~1858

Cape Colony as in 1848
District Boundaries, 1848
British Kaffraria, 1848
Area settled by the 1820 Settlers
Main Roads

English Miles
0 5 10 15 20 25   50

a new system of government, including the institution of a legislative council and eventually of municipal institutions to replace the old burgher senate; and stabilize the frontier by a system of alliances with native chiefs. And, of course, all these ends were to be achieved with the most rigid economy.

Word of the passage of the Emancipation Act had reached the Cape just before D'Urban's arrival. His predecessor, Acting Governor Francis Wade, had reported a month earlier that news of impending abolition had been greeted by the settlers with "a dogged, gloomy silence." The white population, while not likely to rise in open hostilities against the British government, was generally disaffected not only by the decree on slavery but by a series of actions by the British government which convinced them of its bad faith. The colonists had muttered at the alleged manipulation of the Dutch rix-dollar and the conversion of the old currency to British pounds sterling on unfavorable rates. Now the British government proposed to remove their slave property on confiscatory terms. Payment for slaves was made in London at low valuations and with deductions even from these inadequate payments. Slaves in the West Indian colonies were in most instances mortgaged to capitalists in London, but those of the Cape were mortgaged to merchants and others resident in the colony.[3] Contributing to the Boers' antipathy was a severe depression in the wine industry for which the growers held Britain responsible, as the government had encouraged capitalists to invest in increasing cultivation of wine grapes and then had provided no protection for their product in competition with foreign wines for the English market.[4]

The administration of the internal affairs of Cape Colony in this difficult transitional phase was in itself enough to tax the abilities of any governor. The sullen antagonism against which Wade had warned might at any time erupt in violence; the institution of a new system of colonial government required the governor's time and attention. But D'Urban also was charged with the stabilization of the frontier between the colony and the Kaffirs. Before his appointment the Colonial Office had exercised little control over the border policies of Cape governors. The character of relations with the tribes varied with the character of the governor. Somerset had been vacillating and inconsistent. Richard Bourke had pursued a mild line, endeavoring to con-

---

[3] Wade to Stanley, Dec. 6, 1833, C.O. 48/151, P.R.O.

[4] Extracts from the diary of C. L. Stretch, in Anti-Slavery Papers, G. 10, Rhodes House, Oxford.

ciliate frontier chiefs by negotiation of grievances and by presents. Bourke's successor, Lowry Cole, finding the border disturbed, had pursued a vigorous policy against the tribesmen. In May, 1829, he ousted Makomo, son of Gaika, from land on the Kat River which he had been permitted to reoccupy.

Cole planned to follow the colonization of Hottentots at Kat River with other settlements of Hottentots and English settlers, and the British government approved.[5] Bourke had allowed the Kaffirs to enter the colony freely; Cole prohibited them from doing so. Wade, during his short tenure as acting governor, continued Cole's policies. Though expelled from Kat River, Makomo, Botma, and Tyalie had been allowed to graze their cattle in the "neutral belt" on the west bank of the Keiskama, in the vicinity of the Chumie River, on condition of their good behavior. In November, 1833, Wade, under the impression that they had abused this indulgence, ordered their immediate expulsion beyond the Keiskama. His troops drove men, women, and cattle across the river and burned the huts the Kaffirs had erected. This summary eviction occurred at a time of severe drought; consequently the tribes suffered heavy losses of cattle.[6]

While the policies of the government fluctuated with what must have been to the Kaffir a bewildering and infuriating inconsistency, the frontier was left inadequately protected. Cole's attempt to revive the old commando system as a means of frontier defense was disallowed by Lord Stanley on humanitarian grounds, but without providing an alternative system of defense adequate to maintain order.[7]

The British government before 1834 had totally misapprehended the nature of the South African frontier problem. It accepted the stereotype of the frontier Boers as cruel savages who visited atrocities on defenseless people, but expressed no objection to the settlement of English settlers in territories wrested from the Kaffirs. At a time when the tribes of southeastern Africa were in disorder as a result of the wars of Chaka, and fleeing tribes and fragments of tribes poured into the Xosa lands seeking protection, further increasing the pressure on land already restricted by the advance of the settlers, the government

---

[5] Goderich to Cole, May 29, 1831, C.O. 49/23, P.R.O. Goderich's only restrictions were that no Boers were to be permitted to settle in the neutral territory and that slavery was to be prohibited.

[6] A most perceptive analysis of British policy at the Cape is contained in a paper presented by John Beecham of the WMS to Buxton in 1835 (C.O. 48/165, P.R.O.).

[7] Stanley to D'Urban, Nov. 27, 1833, C.O. 48/151, P.R.O.

neither recognized the magnitude of the problems developing across
the border nor took appropriate measures to meet the military threat.
Powerful chiefs were aggrieved at the loss of lands they considered
their own; across the border in the colony grazed the fat cattle of the
settlers, wandering virtually unguarded over vast acreages, an irresistible temptation to the Bantu. The Cape government at the time
of D'Urban's arrival had insufficient power to preserve order; it had
the power only to retaliate and thus to invite war.

The Colonial Office under Lord Stanley conceived a new approach
to border policy. Clearly peace could not be maintained by British
military power without a substantial increase in force and in cost;
clearly also, the interests of Britain dictated a reduction in expenditures for the defense of the South African frontier. The objectives of
peace and retrenchment might be promoted by a system of alliances
with Kaffir chiefs by which, in exchange for small annual gifts of mer-
chandise, they would accept responsibility for the peaceful conduct
of their followers. To assist them in this task, the colonial government
would station among these native allies "prudent and intelligent"
residents. To replace the commando system, the governor was to organize the inhabitants of the frontier districts into a *posse comitatus* to
protect themselves against native attacks. Such an organization would
provide a more effective defense and would also prevent the settlers
from acting on their own initiative to perpetuate deeds of violence
against their tribal neighbors. Before D'Urban left London, Stanley
appears to have sketched out for him this new border system. Here,
in embryo form at least, was the policy that has since been variously
attributed to Lord Glenelg, to John Philip, or to D'Urban himself.[8]

Superficially, Stanley's conception seemed to be akin to the system
of alliances with Indian princely states. But there was no real resem-
blance. South Africa provided no parallel to the great Sepoy armies
maintained at Indian expense which could overpower enemies and
overawe refractory allies. A few hundred British troops along an extended colonial border could not perform a similar function. D'Urban
was thus sent to execute a task that was beyond the powers of any

---

[8] From D'Urban's correspondence it seems clear that he was aware that in annexing Kaffir territory he was contravening Stanley's instructions. John Bell, the
Cape colonial secretary, in expressing his approval of D'Urban's annexation, wrote
that he had never "been able to comprehend how any treaty such as that contemplated by the home authorities" could have been carried into effect (Bell to D'Urban,
May 29, 1835, in D'Urban Papers, VII, Cape Archives; see also D'Urban to Bird,
private, July 20, 1835, D'Urban Papers, P-C 2).

man. To attribute to him the disasters that followed is as just as to blame Herbert Hoover for the Great Depression.

D'Urban was an able governor. His successor, Sir George Napier, relied upon his advice, and Earl Grey fifteen years after D'Urban's dismissal wrote that his "opinion on Cape affairs weighs with me far more than that of any man who has been there." [9] These estimates of D'Urban by his contemporaries clash with his indictment by later writers for excessive dilatoriness. It is true that D'Urban did not leave Cape Town for the frontier until January 8, 1835, one year after his arrival in the colony, and then only after a war had already broken out. A partial explanation of the delay is his preoccupation with the internal problems of the colony. From the dispatches of his predecessors which he undoubtedly read on his assumption of office, he must have concluded that the serious danger in the first months of his administration would be the reaction of the settler population to the abolition of slavery. His experiences in the slave colonies of the West Indies must have given him additional reason to expect unrest. From the perspective of Cape Town, the emancipation issue seemed paramount. Petitions by slave proprietors, while couched in moderate terms, clearly demonstrated that this was a potentially explosive issue.

Reports from the frontier, on the other hand, were contradictory and in general conveyed no sense of imminent disaster. When Colonel Henry Somerset, commandant on the frontier, upon whom D'Urban perforce relied for intelligence, reported in October that the tribes of Makomo, Tyalie, and Botma were suffering from lack of grass for their cattle, D'Urban gave him permission to allow them provisionally to pasture their herds again in the Chumie area. But Somerset, if he had any forebodings of imminent war, did not communicate them to his chief. Somerset's reports on frontier conditions in fact supplied no precise information. D'Urban reminded him that the great changes in process within the colony demanded the governor's personal superintendence, and that he could not leave Cape Town unless there was some tangible danger of war. If such a danger existed, he told the commandant, he would immediately leave for the frontier,[10] but he received no such intelligence until the Kaffirs poured into the colony.

While the frontier seemingly remained peaceful, D'Urban busied

---

[9] Grey to Smith, private, Aug. 14, 1851, Grey Papers, Prior's Kitchen, University of Durham.

[10] D'Urban to Somerset, private and confidential, June 13, 1834, D'Urban Papers, VII.

himself with preparations for emancipation. His problems were complicated by the failure of the British government to give him clear instructions as the basis for his actions. Because the bulk of the slaves were in the West Indies, the Colonial Office had based its plans for the execution of the Abolition Act on conditions in that area; it had made no specific provisions for the Cape, where the situation was in many respects utterly dissimilar. Repeatedly D'Urban requested his superiors for instructions tailoring the West Indian regulations to Cape Colony, but it was not until the beginning of November, 1834, that he finally received the order in council on the basis of which emancipation was to be carried out.[11]

The other important issue D'Urban had to face during his first months at the Cape was a proposed ordinance for the suppression of vagrancy, which had the support of the slave proprietors and a majority of his legislative council, including Lieutenant Governor Wade. D'Urban successfully opposed the measure as discriminatory against the liberties of one section of the population, but it was the end of October before he was able to assemble the dossier on this vexed subject for submission to the Secretary of State.[12]

On the basis of the evidence before him, D'Urban acted intelligently in remaining at Cape Town rather than proceeding with dispatch to the frontier. The charge that his dilatoriness brought on a Kaffir war is based primarily upon wisdom after the fact.

D'Urban was not unconcerned over the frontier problem during his residence in Cape Town. He devoted scrupulous attention to acquiring information on the character of the border problem and suggestions as to its solution. Contrary to Philip's assumptions, D'Urban did not rely upon him as his principal adviser. He sought advice from, among others, Thomas Philipps, one of the Grahamstown settlers, from William B. Boyce, the Wesleyan missionary, and from members of his executive council. Philipps, who had a long interview with the governor in the first week in February, found him "most pacifically inclined" toward the Kaffirs.[13] This was the state of mind in which D'Urban had left London. His conversations with Lord Stanley and

---

[11] D'Urban wrote to Stanley on May 31, 1834, that he had not yet received the draft Order in Council on Slavery. His letter was not answered until September 12 (C.O. 38/155, P.R.O.). John Bell, while in London in the spring of 1834, was employed to suggest modifications of the order in council so as to make it applicable to the Cape (C.O. 48/159 P.R.O.).

[12] D'Urban to Spring-Rice, Oct. 27, 1834, C.O. 48/156, P.R.O.

[13] Philipps to Godlonton, private, Feb. 14, 1834, Cape Colony Letters I, Rhodes House.

with William Ellis of the London Missionary Society had given him the impression that much of the turbulence on the frontier was caused by disorderly elements among the settlers, in particular the Boers, and that tranquillity might be restored to the borders by treaties with native chiefs based on mutual respect and mutual responsibility for the maintenance of order on each side of the line.[14]

D'Urban's conception of the nature of the frontier problem may have been influenced indirectly by Philip before the two men met, for Stanley was a friend of Philip's friend Buxton, and Ellis derived much of his information on Cape affairs from the society's South African superintendent. But it appears to have been D'Urban who suggested the desirability of a treaty system to Philip, rather than vice versa. Philip was an imperialist. He would have preferred the extension of British sovereignty over tribal Africa as far away as Delagoa Bay "on the plan adopted by the ancient Romans which led them to spread themselves and their institutions over the countries which submitted to their government," [15] with Britain acting as the benevolent protector of the Bantu against the rapacity of the white frontiersmen. Philip was aware, however, that his dream, which would have required a substantial augmentation of British military force, was not likely to be realized in an economy-minded era.[16] As an alternative, he supported the treaty system.

Boyce also supported the negotiation of treaties with the chiefs, by which they would hold themselves responsible for cattle stolen from the colony when the spoor was traced into their country; the establishment of a clearly defined colonial boundary; and clarification to the chiefs and tribes in the neutral territory of the nature of their tenure. Boyce's emphasis was somewhat more severe than Philip's, but in most respects his proposals were identical.[17] Thomas Philipps ad-

---

[14] This conception is strongly implied in D'Urban to Philip, private, May 31, 1834, D'Urban Papers, VI, and D'Urban to Somerset, private and confidential, June 13, 1834, *ibid.*, VII.

[15] Philip to D'Urban, March 13, 1834, in *Report from the Select Committee on Aborigines*, 1836, App., p. 693.

[16] In a letter to Fairbairn, May 9, 1837, Philip wrote: "I am quite aware that my plans would have required an advance of the military, and it is a question whether such an advance would have been acceded to by the Home Government, but could it have been obtained my plan would have been cheapest in the end" (Philip Transcripts, University of Cape Town Library).

[17] Boyce to D'Urban, March 31, 1834, in *Report from the Select Committee on Aborigines*, 1836, pp. 179–183; a copy of this letter is also in the Methodist Missionary Society Archives.

vised D'Urban along the same general lines.[18] These similarities indicate that D'Urban had suggested the broad outlines of a new frontier policy and that his consultants were proposing the mechanisms by which it might be made effective. This impression is strengthened by the governor's statement to the Executive Council that the policy he intended to pursue had been laid down within "a comparatively narrow compass by His Majesty's commands," conveyed in Stanley's dispatch of November 27, 1833.[19]

In accordance with Stanley's desire for the establishment of a defensive burgher force, D'Urban requested the civil commissioners of border districts to provide him with information on the numbers of men capable of bearing arms and of officials available to make the scheme effective. The testimony of the civil commissioner of Worcester indicated something of the difficulty the government would face in the organization of frontier farmers. In his district, which stretched over a distance of approximately 240 miles from east to west, there were about 1,300 men capable of bearing arms. The only public officials were the field cornets and one field commandant, and there were few persons he considered adequate to the responsibilities of a justice of the peace. Nevertheless, the governor persevered; he requested the attorney general to frame an ordinance for the assembly and control of the new defense force.[20]

By the end of June, 1834, D'Urban's plans were clearly delineated. In a formal communication he had notified the assembled chiefs of Kaffirland of his friendly intentions, but warned them that he expected them to restrain their followers from acts of thievery. He had instructed officials on the frontier to repress all violence on the part of the settlers, but to afford them protection against marauders; [21] he had made preliminary inquiries into the feasibility of the border force; and he had expressed the intention to come to the frontier to make a general settlement as soon as affairs at Cape Town permitted.

D'Urban had at first hoped to visit the border before midyear, but was forced continually to defer his plans as a succession of pressing problems commanded his attention at the capital. Philip, about to set out in mid-August on a journey to his society's missionary stations, offered to herald the governor's impending arrival to the Kaffir chiefs

---

[18] Philipps, "A concise Narrative of events . . . ," enclosure in Maitland to Gladstone, Oct. 1, 1846, C.O. 48/264, P.R.O.

[19] Minutes of Executive Council, June 20, 1834, C.O. 51/35, P.R.O.

[20] Minutes of Executive Council, June 21, 1834, *ibid.*

[21] D'Urban to Philip, private and confidential, July 14, 1834, D'Urban Papers, VI.

and to use his good offices to promote a pacific border settlement. D'Urban, assuming that Philip had great influence with the chiefs, accepted, and further agreed to meet Philip at the Hottentot settlement of Kat River, where he would negotiate a treaty of alliance with the Griqua captain Adam Kok.

Philip traveled to the society's mission at Buffalo River, where he had conferences with Kaffir chiefs, and then proceeded to Kat River to meet the governor. Adam Kok and his missionary adviser at Philippolis were there in expectation of signing a treaty with the governor, but went home after waiting in vain for several weeks.

Andries Waterboer, who had also been invited to meet Philip and the governor at Kat River, on hearing at Graaff Reinet that the governor was detained at Cape Town, decided on the advice of his missionary companion Peter Wright to proceed directly to Cape Town. The governor gave them a most gracious reception. Waterboer dined with D'Urban, rode in the viceregal carriage, and was treated with the utmost respect by government officials. Then the chief and the governor signed a treaty by which Waterboer was to keep order within his jurisdiction in exchange for an annual salary of £100 and an additional subsidy of £50 for the education of his people.[22] This alliance was intended to be the first of a series; it was the only one D'Urban was able to negotiate. Within less than two weeks after its signature, a Kaffir war had begun.

Philip, before he set out on his mission as the emissary of a liberal governor and an intermediary with the chiefs, wrote to his society expressing his hopes and his fears with regard to a prospective border settlement:

I am the only person in the Colony who knows the Governor's mind on the subject, but this is a circumstance that must be known here, and I must not anticipate too much till I see how he will be able to stand in the midst of all his civil and military authorities on the frontier who will do everything in their power to shake his personal resolution, and who will, should any new and pacific system be introduced to supersede the old system, do everything possible to defeat us in our object.[23]

The tone of this letter is characteristic of Philip; the impression it conveys is that the governor had embraced Philip's enlightened philosophy but might be seduced by the military and civil authorities. His statement also suggests that he was the bearer of intelligence which

---

[22] Philip to Ellis, Jan. 2, 1835, SAF 14-3, LMS Archives.
[23] Philip to Wilson, Aug. 13, 1834, SAF 14-2, LMS Archives.

only he and the governor possessed. The first of these implications contains the core of the legend that the governor accepted Philip's views on border policy until after he reached the frontier and fell under the insidious influence of the frontier mind; the second relates to a dispute as to precisely what mission Philip was to perform for the governor.

It is untrue that D'Urban was seduced from humanitarian principles in the environment of Grahamstown. D'Urban's conceptions of border policy were never identical with Philip's, and in some respects were antithetical. By the middle of 1834 he had formulated his frontier policy, and the outbreak of war and his associations with frontier settlers and military men merely accentuated its harsher tones. D'Urban considered the "neutral territory" between the Fish and Keiskama rivers to be under the jurisdiction of the governor. Tribes who lived in this area existed on sufferance; they could be ousted for bad behavior. Reports from border districts of widespread thefts [24] led him to consider summary action. He suggested to Somerset in August that Eno's tribe, allegedly the worst offenders, be ousted from the neutral territory, and their lands given to Pato, Kobus Congo, and Kama, who had been "well-conducted." [25] In September he told Somerset that, as a preliminary to his own negotiations with the chiefs, he hoped "some tolerable restitution of plunder" would be arranged by the commandant.[26] In October he wrote Somerset from Cape Town of his suspicion that the nonattendance of the Slambie tribe at a conference called by Somerset suggested that they were guilty of concealing stolen cattle and wished to avoid being confronted with the accusation. But he advised Somerset to defer forcible measures until he could arrive for personal consultation.[27] In December, his departure yet delayed, D'Urban received news that a patrol under a young ensign had been ambushed and its leader wounded by an assagai while returning with cattle allegedly stolen from the colony. He drew up a memorandum for Somerset's guidance which contained essentially the principles he later carried out and for which he was condemned by the humanitarians. He told the commandant that he entirely approved of the

---

[24] In July D'Urban expressed to Philip his deep concern over reports of stolen cattle; in the six months preceding mid-June, he said, there had been thefts of 900 head of cattle and 100 horses (D'Urban to Philip, private and confidential, July 14, 1834, D'Urban Papers, VI).

[25] D'Urban to Somerset, private and confidential, Aug. 15, 1834, D'Urban Papers, VII.

[26] D'Urban to Somerset, private and confidential, Sept. 12, 1834, *ibid.*

[27] D'Urban to Somerset, private, Oct. 17, 1834, *ibid.*

imposition of a heavy fine of cattle on Eno's tribe and that it should be "inflexibly enforced." In addition, Eno must produce the culprit who had wounded the young officer, either to be punished by the Kaffirs themselves for intent to commit murder, or given over to the colonial authorities. If there was any hesitation in complying, Eno himself or the chief of the delinquent kraal should be seized and held as a hostage, and if the aggressions of the tribe did not immediately cease, D'Urban also authorized the expulsion of Eno's tribe beyond the border. But on December 23, before Somerset could act on these instructions, the Kaffirs had invaded the colony.

Undoubtedly Somerset in his zeal to round up cattle was unnecessarily provocative. In a situation requiring the utmost delicacy and mature judgment Somerset was gauche and impetuous.[28] The chiefs found him completely unpredictable. Makomo told Sir Harry Smith that "Somerset was good to us one day, cross another, we had no dependence on him." [29] Somerset's conduct may have accelerated a war but his policies were the policies of his superior in Cape Town. His deficiency was not insubordination but incompetence.

After the alienation between Philip and D'Urban over the latter's war policy, partisans of the governor sought to make Philip a scapegoat. They alleged that D'Urban had commissioned Philip to deliver a message explaining the elements of the new border policy which the governor hoped to introduce and to use the influence it was assumed he possessed to convince them of the governor's benevolent intentions, and that Philip on his return from the frontier had told the governor that he had carried out his mission and that the chiefs had expressed satisfaction at the proposed new arrangements. Instead of acting as an agent of government, his detractors alleged, Philip had in fact, though perhaps unwittingly, acted as an *agent provocateur*. On his visits to the frontier in 1830 and 1832, they said, he had stirred the chiefs' dissatisfaction by sympathizing with them as victims of injustice in the loss of their lands, and that his counsel on his visit in October, 1834, to "shed no blood" pending the arrival of the governor

[28] Governor Bourke chastised Somerset for bad judgment on more than one occasion (see, for example, Bourke to Somerset, confidential, Sept. 5, 1828, Bourke Papers, t 7/12, Rhodes House, Oxford). D'Urban, after several months' observation, referred to "the imbecility of the Instruments I am obliged to work with" (he meant in particular Somerset and Civil Commissioner Campbell; D'Urban to Bell, June 2, 1835, D'Urban Papers, VII). Somerset's survival so long in a position of responsibility is a testament to the importance of good family connections.

[29] Smith to D'Urban, private and confidential, Jan. 28, 1836, G.H. 34/7, Cape Archives.

had done nothing to quiet their agitation.[30] Philip, on the other hand, denied that he had ever agreed to act as D'Urban's agent and that he had ever communicated any message to the chiefs in the capacity of D'Urban's emissary.[31]

Philip's denial is difficult to reconcile with statements he made in his private correspondence before his departure, but the accusation that he contributed to the outbreak of war by indiscreet statements to Kaffir chiefs is fantastic. Not even Sir Harry Smith, who detested Philip as a meddler, would make such a charge. Makomo, Tyalie, and other Kaffir chiefs told Smith that they were pleased when Philip had come among them to tell of the peaceful intentions of the governor; that they had laid their complaints before him, assuming him to be the "mouth" of the governor; and that he had told them to be patient in awaiting the redress of their grievances.[32]

The causes of the war were far more deeply rooted than the incitement of a meddling missionary or the dilatoriness of a governor. It originated in the competition of European settlers and tribal Africans for land, in the incompatibility of European settlement and tribal society, and in the lamentable inability of governmental authority to control the forces on either side of the border by any means short of war. Makomo probably described its immediate background as well as any one when he told of his deep resentment at his expulsion from the Kat and Chumie basins and of subsequent harrying of the tribes by patrols in search of stolen cattle. In October, 1834, Somerset had given Tyalie leave to graze the royal cattle west of the Keiskama, and soon afterward these cattle had been rounded up by a patrol and some of them taken into the colony. When the Kaffirs had resisted, the troops had fired on them, wounding several tribesmen, including chief Xo-Xo.[33] Jan Tzatzoe told the select committee of Parliament in 1836 that every Kaffir who saw Xo-Xo's wound went back to his hut, took up his assagai and shield, and set out to fight, as it was "better that we die than be treated thus." [34] In the view of the settlers the war was begun by an unprovoked attack upon peaceful frontier farmers, and this treachery should be repaid by ruthless measures including not

---

[30] Beresford's testimony, March 14, 1836, *Report from the Select Committee on Aborigines*, 1836, p. 265.

[31] Philip's testimony, Aug. 1, 1836, *ibid.*, p. 679.

[32] Smith to D'Urban, private and confidential, Jan. 28, 1836, G.H. 34/7, Cape Archives.

[33] Smith to D'Urban, private and confidential, Jan. 28, 1836, *ibid.*

[34] Testimony of Jan Tzatzoe, June 20, 1836, *Report from the Select Committee on Aborigines*, 1836, p. 564.

only the destruction of the aggressors but the expulsion of all the tribes from the vicinity of the colony.

At first Philip, the Wesleyan missionaries, and the governor were in essential agreement that the war was attributable primarily to an unjust and ineffective system rather than to the rapacity or the wickedness of tribesmen or settlers. But as the war progressed and as reports of the slaughter of Kaffirs and the burning of their crops and habitations filtered out of Kaffirland, Philip became more and more a partisan of the Kaffirs against the governor. The Wesleyan missionaries, some of whom were at first inclined to be judicious in their appraisal of the causes of the war,[35] supported the policies of the governor and eventually termed the war "unprovoked aggression." The course of the war and its antecedents thus became inextricably mixed in the minds of these partisans, and in passion they used expressions more extreme than their actual viewpoints. D'Urban, after four months of chasing an elusive enemy, was so injudicious as to refer to the Kaffirs as "treacherous and irreclaimable savages," [36] and being a stubborn man he felt compelled to defend such language thereafter against the outcry of the humanitarians in England. In July, 1835, in a petition to D'Urban, the Wesleyan missionaries expressed their sympathy with the colonists and their condemnation of the Kaffirs as aggressors who had "most wantonly, cruelly, and ungratefully commenced this war with a people who sought and desired their welfare and prosperity." [37] Such high-toned words, given even more extreme coloration by Philip's selective emphasis in his communications to London, became part of the picture of South Africa as seen from Downing Street and thus were of great political consequence.

For the transformation of the benevolent governor of 1834 to the advocate of extermination in 1835, Philip blamed the influence of Grahamstown and the Wesleyan missionaries. But D'Urban was not enamored of the environment of Grahamstown, which he found "charged with Panic," exploding "in every sort of improbable Fancy from time to time," [38] and he used the Wesleyan missionaries only to the extent

---

[35] William Boyce and William Shaw attributed the war primarily to the defects of the border system. But other missionaries were not so detached or restrained. Three of them wrote to London headquarters that "a more wanton aggression upon a peaceful People—who were desirous of promoting their best interests—has never been committed" (Shrewsbury, Young, and Haddy to Secretaries, WMS, Jan. 1, 1835, MMS Archives).

[36] General Orders, May 11, 1835, D'Urban Papers, V.

[37] W. B. Boyce, *Notes on South-African Affairs* (London: Mason, 1839), App., p. 1.

[38] D'Urban to Thomson, March 24, 1835, Private Letter Book 1, D'Urban Papers.

that they served his own objectives. When he called the Kaffirs "irre-claimable savages" or described them as "wolves," [39] he was indulging a penchant for hyperbole which he shared with his subordinate Harry Smith, but the expressions were his, not responses to the influence of others. This compulsion to write in extreme language cost dearly, for the words of D'Urban and Smith obscured their actions, and gave an impression of carnage which had no relation to fact. Philip recorded his horror at Smith's boasts of the large quantities of corn he had destroyed, the cattle he had captured, the huts he had burned, and the Kaffirs he had slaughtered—it was not a war, but a massacre.[40] Although it is true that the strategy against an elusive enemy who refused to stand and be killed was to lay waste his lands and starve him into submission, Smith's accounts of his destructive accomplish-ments were greatly exaggerated. William Boyce estimated that the total losses of the Kaffirs in cattle were not more than 30,000 head, whereas they had swept up from the colony several times that num-ber.[41] Boyce may have understated Kaffir losses, but no observer sup-ported Smith's inflated claims. Andries Stockenstrom, who made in-quiries in 1836, concluded that not more than 2,000 warriors had been killed, rather than the 4,000 reported by D'Urban and Smith.[42]

D'Urban's prosecution of the war and his plans for the peace were not dominated by his choler against treacherous savages. He was a military man; his task was to destroy the enemy's powers of resistance and to impose terms of peace which would make the recurrence of hostilities unlikely and, if war did recur, would ensure that the colony would enjoy a maximum strategic advantage. Even before he left Cape Town he had become convinced that the tribes in the neutral territory should remain only during good behavior; the bulk of the Kaffirs by making war on the colony had forfeited any claims to con-sideration. But beyond that there was the larger question of postwar security which included, among other considerations, the future boundary. Within three weeks of the outbreak of hostilities D'Urban's second-in-command, Harry Smith, had broached this issue. The prox-imity of the Kaffirs to the Fish River bush had given them the oppor-tunity to burst into the colony. The new boundary must be drawn through open country which would prevent the enemy from moving

---

[39] D'Urban to Bell, May 24, 1835, D'Urban Papers, IX.

[40] Philip to Ellis, June 29, 1835, SAF 14-4, LMS Archives.

[41] Boyce, op. cit., p. xii. Boyce admitted that the tribes did not gain so much as the disproportion implied, as they were obliged to subsist on animal food and thus slaughtered huge herds.

[42] C. W. Hutton, ed., The Autobiography of the Late Sir Andries Stockenstrom (Cape Town: Juta, 1887), pp. 327–328.

without being observed by patrols. Smith suggested that D'Urban might consider the Buffalo River, the next major stream beyond the Keiskama, as a possible boundary because it met these specifications.[43]

It is not clear from D'Urban's correspondence when he made the decision to push the boundary forward to the Kei. The Reverend Mr. Boyce, who was on terms of intimacy with the governor during the war, stated that D'Urban's intention to make the Kei the boundary was known in the colony as early as the end of January, 1835, and before his arrival on the frontier. Thus, said Boyce, the measure could not be attributed to the influence of settlers and frontier officials; rather the decision was purely military, calculated to reduce the possibilities of future collisions and to establish a secure frontier for the colony.[44] But D'Urban maintained that no one had been aware of his plans until two days before they were executed.[45]

It is possible that the decision to extend the frontier to the Kei River was based on the conclusion that the "chief instigator of all the mischief" was Hintza, a Transkeian chief who was assumed to be the paramount chief of all the Xosas. D'Urban had been convinced from the outbreak of the war that this was no spontaneous explosion, but a well-organized invasion which was the product of long planning.[46] Hintza's alleged connivance, not only in providing refuge for cattle stolen by the Gaika tribes from the colony, but in provoking them to war, convinced D'Urban that the conspiracy was far more widespread than he had at first imagined. Consequently, even before he had reduced the Gaikas to submission, he sent his forces beyond the Kei to humble Hintza. On the banks of the Kei on May 10, 1835, he proclaimed that he had "defeated, chastised and dispersed" the aggressor Gaika and Slambie chiefs, had conquered their country, and had compelled Hintza to accept terms of peace. To protect the colony "against such unprovoked aggressions which can only be done by removing these treacherous and irreclaimable savages to a safer distance," the offending chiefs and their tribes were to be "forever expelled" beyond the Kei River, which was hereafter to be the boundary of Cape Colony.[47]

The implication of this general order was that whole tribes were

---

[43] Smith to D'Urban, Jan. 14, 1835, D'Urban Papers, VII. The letter is printed in George M. Theal, *Documents Relating to the Kaffir War of 1835* (London: Clowes, 1912), pp. 11–14.

[44] Theal, *op. cit.*, p. 31.

[45] D'Urban to Bird, private, July 20, 1835, D'Urban P-C 2, Cape Archives.

[46] D'Urban to Spring-Rice, Jan. 5, 1835, C.O. 48/161, P.R.O.; D'Urban to Hay, private, March 24, 1835, D'Urban Papers, IV, printed in Theal, *op. cit.*, pp. 112–113.

[47] General Orders, May 11, 1835, D'Urban Papers, V.

to be uprooted. Within two days D'Urban clarified his intentions with the explanation that he had meant to banish only the offending chiefs and those members of the tribes who had actually invaded the colony or had been implicated in the murders of British subjects.[48] In this conquered territory, which he denominated Queen Adelaide Province, he would settle in assigned locations tribes that had not been engaged in hostilities, members of the "aggressor tribes" who had disowned their chiefs, and the Fingoes whom he believed he had released from the "bondage" of Hintza. Approximately 17,000 Fingoes with more than 22,000 cattle were escorted by Colonel Somerset from Hintza's territory for resettlement between the Fish and Keiskama rivers.[49] The "liberation" of the Fingoes "from the most wretched slavery" [50] D'Urban regarded as a major coup which might make his annexation more palatable to the humanitarians in England. The remainder of the conquered territory was to be made available for occupation by white settlers.

D'Urban was uneasy about the reactions of the British government to his abrupt decision, so greatly at variance with the policy he had been instructed to carry out. Bravely he assured John Bell that he was "tranquil as to the results at home," [51] but his preoccupation with the theme belied his avowals. He assumed that "the Buxton party" would condemn his measures because the *South African Commercial Advertiser,* edited by Philip's son-in-law, had already begun the attack. But it was not only the Saints who caused him trepidation; he visualized a negative response by the advocates of economy. He had been sent to carry out a policy of retrenchment which included the stabilization of the frontier at the Keiskama River. Now he had added several thousand square miles to Cape Colony and had assumed responsibility for many thousands of Kaffirs who had previously been beyond the border. He and his colonial secretary feared violent attacks on him for incurring needless expense. Bell wrote to D'Urban in June, 1835: "If Joseph Hume is at the helm in Downing Street by the time your dispatch reaches it the game is up, and the colony ruined." But whoever was secretary of state, warned Bell, James Stephen was a "fixture" at the Colonial Office, and no minister would dare to oppose him and his

---

[48] "Memorandum for the Information and Guidance of Major Cox . . . ," May 12, 1835, *ibid.,* VII.

[49] Instructions for Colonel Somerset, May 5, 1835, Private Letter Book 1, D'Urban Papers; D'Urban to Aberdeen, June 19, 1835, C.O. 48/161, P.R.O.

[50] D'Urban to Gordon, June 26, 1835, D'Urban Papers, IX.

[51] D'Urban to Bell, June 2, 1835, *ibid.,* VII.

supporters.[52] By the end of July D'Urban, brooding over his annexation, which he assured himself was not only expedient but necessary, had concluded that Bell's forebodings were likely to be realized and that his measures would probably be disallowed.[53]

Two forces that had nothing in common beyond their opposition would thus crush D'Urban between them: the humanitarians would condemn him for the unjust character of his annexation; the economy-minded, for making any annexation at all. John Philip did not oppose D'Urban's May policy because it was expansionist, for Philip was an expansionist himself. He would have supported the extension of the colonial boundary to the Kei River provided that the land between the Keiskama and the Kei was reserved for the Kaffirs and they were recognized as British subjects. But he was indignant at the "extermination of the Kaffirs" to gratify the land lust of the colonists.[54] Although the London and Wesleyan societies, in common with their South African missionaries, differed over the causes of the war, they were united in opposing the allocation of any lands in the annexed territory to white settlers.[55]

Neither the extermination of the Kaffirs nor their expulsion was within the powers of D'Urban, even had he so wished. His assumption, when he announced the annexation of Queen Adelaide Province, had been that only "a few straggling robbers" still lurked in the bush and that his Boer auxiliaries would soon eliminate them.[56] It was not long before he was disillusioned. Instead of a few hunted refugees he had to contend with thousands of warriors who had retired to the mountains between the headwaters of the Chumie and Buffalo rivers, from which they could not be dislodged. The ebullient Smith, who had boasted of his prowess as the scourge of the Kaffirs, had to confess that he was unable to oust them from these natural fortresses or even to prevent their making occasional raids into the colony. Ironically, he blamed his impotence on the paralysis of his cavalry from a shortage of corn for their horses.[57] The British army and its auxiliaries, which in May had seemed all-conquering, were reduced two months later to

---

[52] Bell to D'Urban, June 25, 1835, *ibid.*, IX.

[53] D'Urban to Bird, private, July 20, 1835, D'Urban P-C 2, Cape Archives.

[54] Notes by Philip on Campbell to Philip, June 19, 1835, SAF 14-4, LMS Archives; [Philip] to [Ellis?], May 26, 1835, C.O. 48/165, P.R.O. This latter letter was sent to the Colonial Office by the London Missionary Society.

[55] For the Wesleyan position, see Beecham to Glenelg, Nov. 3, 1835, C.O. 48/163, P.R.O.

[56] D'Urban to Bell, May 24, 1835, D'Urban Papers, IX.

[57] Smith to D'Urban, July 25, 1835, G.H. 34/7, Cape Archives.

protecting its posts in the "conquered territory" and maintaining its line of communication to the rear, and D'Urban was forced to conclude that he could not hold the province without substantial reinforcements.[58]

Smith, while continuing to profess that his savage enemies possessed few of the attributes of human nature, admitted that even if he was able to clear the Amatola Mountains, the war would be far from over, as large numbers of hostile Slambies would continue to roam the area between the Buffalo and the Kei. He suggested two alternatives, either to attempt to detach the Slambies from the Gaikas by coming to terms with the former and assigning them lands, or to conclude a general peace:

> If these savages are to be treated as men and rational beings, there exists much matter for discussion as to the justness of their final expulsion . . . [for] history affords few examples of the direct banishment of the people of the nation. . . . I candidly avow that I am one of those "wicked Christians" who do not look upon these unfortunate savages in the light of a nation, but from their continual incursions on the Colony in time of peace, for their late treachery, for their merciless murders of everyone who falls into their hands, I view them as irreclaimable savages (after all the exertions of the missionaries) whose extermination would be a blessing, altho if circumstances hereafter should identify me with them, my study and exertions should be for their reformation, improvement and consequent happiness.[59]

These comments reveal, beyond an insight into the mentality of Harry Smith, an ambivalence in distinct contrast to his earlier self-confidence. D'Urban faced the unpleasant reality that his power was not adequate to his commitments. It was not merely the tenacity of the Kaffirs which disturbed him; eventually they could be ground into submission. But the governor and Smith were not entirely free agents; continuation of the war might further jeopardize the annexation of the new province, for the Saints were "in power." Peace based on humane terms might win over even "old Buxton himself." [60]

In May D'Urban had dictated the terms of peace; he now sought an accommodation with an as yet undefeated enemy which would not involve an obvious loss of face. When the chiefs, suspicious of a trap, would not come out of hiding to treat with a British officer,[61]

---

[58] D'Urban to Smith, confidential, July 31, 1835, Private Letter Book 2, D'Urban Papers.

[59] Smith to D'Urban, confidential, Aug. 16, 1835, Smith Papers, VI, Cape Archives.

[60] Smith to D'Urban, most private, Sept. 1, 1835, G.H. 34/7, Cape Archives.

[61] Warden to D'Urban, received Aug. 16, 1835, D'Urban Papers, VII.

D'Urban turned to the Wesleyan missionaries as intermediaries. At the beginning of August, William Shepstone, Samuel Palmer, and William Boyce set out from Grahamstown for the kraal of Pato, one of the "loyal" chiefs. When they explained to him and his brothers their errand of peace, Pato suggested that they send their message to Makomo and the Gaika tribe through four women, one of whom had married into the tribe and had returned from the mountain hide-out a few days before. The message the emissaries asked the women to deliver was a combination of warnings and promises: Makomo had been a friend to the missionaries, and now they sought to repay his kindness by warning him that a storm was growing which would soon overwhelm his tribe unless he sued for peace immediately. Already a large body of troops had arrived and another was expected momentarily. The Boers had finished ploughing and were ready again to ride into Kaffirland. The governor had said that if he entered Kaffirland again, he would sweep the country clean, but the missionaries knew that he was merciful and that if the chiefs asked for forgiveness and told him they were tired of the war, he would give them land for their tribes. The women returned with the word that Makomo and Tyalie would take the missionaries' advice and say "mercy, great chief, but we will not at first ask for a place to sit in, nor will we mention our not going over the Kei, we will merely ask for mercy." [62] Stripped of threats and bombast on the one side and abject phraseology on the other, the meaning of the interchange was clear: peace could be arranged if D'Urban would abandon his May policy of expulsion. D'Urban for a time dallied with the idea of making a separate peace with Makomo and the Gaikas, which would be "well regarded in England," and then turning his full force on the Slambies,[63] but he finally decided to conclude a peace with all the hostile tribes. The terms of the treaties of September 17, 1835, were vastly different from those D'Urban had sought to impose in May.

The September settlement marked a revolutionary new approach to South African native policy. For the first time since Europeans had landed at Table Bay, a still virile tribal society was brought under the direct jurisdiction of European authority, with the status of subjects of the Crown. Not only were the chiefs and their people assigned

---

[62] Journal of Shepstone, Palmer, and Boyce, Aug. 3–17, 1835 [written at Grahamstown, Aug. 21, 1835], *ibid.*, IV. For a detailed account of the negotiations, see George M. Theal, *History of South Africa since September, 1795* (5 vols.; London: Swan Sonnenschein, 1907–1910), II, 123–124.

[63] D'Urban to Smith, Sept. 2, 1835, D'Urban P-C 2, Cape Archives.

locations within the colony, but they were to be under the control of British magistrates and British law. The areas not allocated to the new subjects were to be available for occupation by Europeans. In their broad outlines, D'Urban's plans were not dissimilar to those of Sir George Grey twenty years later. Tribalism was the enemy of order and civilization; so long as the Kaffirs were under the power of their chiefs and their witch doctors, they would continue to be a pestilence to the border. Under the influence of British law and British magistrates and of missionaries "of a mild and instructive persuasion," [64] these "irreclaimable savages" might yet be reclaimed and transformed into docile subjects of the Crown. It was a noble experiment, wrote D'Urban; if it failed the only alternative was the bayonet and the musket.[65] The process must be a long one, and it must be "gradual and gentle"; it must be so subtle in its working that the power of the chiefs would be drained away before they were aware of the implications of the new order. They must not "be startled at the outset,— or their eyes opened to the future consequences of the process,—until by its advancing force,—when they do, at length, discover all its influence,—they shall have no longer any power to be effectually restive." [66]

The conception was highly imaginative; the intellectual and physical resources to execute it were sadly deficient. Neither D'Urban nor his subordinates had any understanding of the nature of tribal society. Conceivably the governor's plans to transform pagan tribesmen into civilized Christians might have been achieved by the expenditure of great resources and much human energy in education in its broadest sense, while the objects of conversion were held in awe by overwhelming force. Such a program was out of the question. D'Urban's power had been insufficient even to impose a dictated peace upon the tribes, and, even had he conceived of schemes of social reform, a penurious British government would not have provided him with the means to execute them. In his hopes that he might steal the authority of the

---

[64] The phrase is Smith's (Smith to D'Urban, confidential, Oct. 6, 1835, G.H. 34/7, Cape Archives).

[65] D'Urban to Hare, confidential, Sept. 19, 1835, D'Urban P-C 2, Cape Archives.

[66] Confidential memo by D'Urban, Sept. 30, 1835, on notes by D'Urban of Sept. 17, 1835, G.H. 34/5, Cape Archives. Further to promote the security of the new province, D'Urban and Smith arranged with Kreli, son and successor of Hintza, who had been killed while trying to escape from protective custody, to cede a strip of land beyond the Kei as far as the missionary station at Butterworth in exchange for remission of part of the fine of cattle imposed upon his father (D'Urban to Glenelg, March 16, 1836, C.O. 48/166, P.R.O.).

chiefs before they were aware of the theft, he greatly underestimated the mental powers of his opponents; in selecting Harry Smith to administer the new province, his justification could only be the paucity of alternatives.

During his lifetime and since, a variety of adjectives have been applied to Smith. He was "impulsive," "mercuric," "brave," "warm-hearted," but he was never described as "subtle." He believed that savages were impressed by the dramatic and considered himself an accomplished thespian before such an audience. Pridefully he told the governor how he had cowed Makomo by "acting a storming passion," holding the treaty in his hands and threatening to tear it up unless the chief prevented his followers from committing acts of thievery, and then winning his gratitude by assigning him a small additional piece of land. Makomo's response to this performance is not recorded.[67]

Smith's displays were not entirely contrived. A passionate man, Smith could fluctuate wildly in his estimates of men and matters, and his emotional range was most impressive. At the time of the war he described the Kaffirs as wild beasts who should be exterminated; with the peace he argued successfully that the locations proposed for them were inadequate to sustain their population.[68] As administrator of the province he devoted as much energy to winning their good will and protecting their interests, as he saw them, as he had to hunting them during the war. With all his virtues, however, Smith was not well suited to the functions of administrator of Queen Adelaide Province. His proneness to emotional judgments and his ultrasensitivity strained his relationships with his associates. When he was at odds with the Reverend Mr. Boyce, in whom D'Urban had reposed confidence as an adviser on frontier affairs, Smith described him as "fanatical and more full of Dragooning our New Subjects into this and that than a hundred soldiers." [69] When he and the missionary became reconciled he wrote, "Would to God I had only a few *such men*—he is a most excellent man of business, honest, frank, and energetic." [70] Smith had not been in office a month before he was threatening to resign unless the home government gave him the dignity of a lieutenant-governorship, and he complained bitterly that the Horse Guards had not given his services the recognition they deserved.[71] His tenure in office was interspersed

[67] Smith to D'Urban, Sept. 27, 1835, G.H. 34/7, Cape Archives.
[68] Smith to D'Urban, Sept. 1, 1835, in Theal, *Documents Relating to the Kaffir War*, pp. 366–367.
[69] Smith to D'Urban, Oct. 27, 1835, G.H. 34/7, Cape Archives.
[70] Smith to D'Urban, Nov. 10, 1835, *ibid*.
[71] Smith to D'Urban, private, Oct. 11, 1835, *ibid*.

with frequent requests for release from office. D'Urban, bombarded by dispatches from his unpredictable subordinate, finally delivered him a lecture which contained as sound an evaluation of Smith as has been made. After paying tribute to Smith's courage and ability as a soldier, D'Urban went on:

> But—will you have the truth—I have now and then cause for apprehension on account of your *Discretion,* as in danger of being thrown overboard by your vivacity—by your imbibing hasty & extreme opinions, & acting upon them hastily & extremely—lose sight for the moment of all but the object in your view—regardless of its collateral bearings upon others of equal or perhaps greater importance—& forgetting that all we do must be combining parts of a general system if we would do well at all. Hence too, my instructions must sometimes be overlooked. I am aware that they may appear tame & languid to your more vivid imagination—& for aught I know they may often be foolish enough—but if they be so *I* am responsible for them. This apprehension & the reflections to which it necessarily leads (I am bound to tell you in all candour . . .) have suggested to me serious doubts as to the safety of trusting very large & extreme power in your hands.[72]

Smith was able to convince himself that in less than three months he had transformed the outlook of his Kaffir subjects and that, by a combination of sternness and humanity expressed in theatrical terms, he had established an ascendancy over the tribesmen stronger than that of any chief. He wrote to D'Urban on November 30, 1835, that the "people of all tribes look up to me as the Great Chief under Your Excellency—so pray Your Excellency, let me go on *play acting.*" [73]

In his more sober moments, however, even Smith was compelled to admit that the condition of Queen Adelaide Province was far from satisfactory. He ruled by military force over a collection of tribes whom his census takers had reported as totaling 72,700.[74] His subordinates, with few exceptions, he regarded as incompetent, and the magistrates who were requisite to the operation of the new system were not appointed. At a time when he was boasting of his complete control over the new subjects, he reported that he had burned seven hundred huts in one week, but that "the poor devils" came back to their old lands outside the location; [75] and in seizing the cattle of two chiefs for alleged thefts of their followers he stirred up disturbances that, if the

---

[72] D'Urban to Smith, very private, Dec. 8, 1835, D'Urban Military, Cape Archives.

[73] Smith to D'Urban, confidential, Nov. 30, 1835, *ibid.*

[74] The distribution of tribes in Queen Adelaide Providence, according to the census of 1835, was as follows: Congo, 7,500; Gaikas, 56,500; Slambies, 9,200 (D'Urban to Glenelg, Feb. 6, 1836, C.O. 48/166, P.R.O.).

[75] Smith to D'Urban, Nov. 3, 1835, D'Urban Military, Cape Archives.

tribes had not been exhausted by the recent war, might have led to another outbreak. Makomo, whom Smith believed he had reduced to complete docility, sent messengers to tell other chiefs that "the Bull cannot eat, when he puts down his head to graze, he is seized by force of arms—let us go to another country where he can do so in safety." [76]

The state of Queen Adelaide Province was thus in the nature of a lull rather than a peace. Order depended upon the force at Smith's disposal and the exhaustion of the tribes, rather than upon the enlightened character of Smith's measures or the power of his personality. Even during his brief tenure thefts of stock from the colony again began to rise, and evidence of disaffection among the chiefs led D'Urban to caution Smith to be on the alert against another outbreak.[77] Gaikas jostled Tembu, and the Xosa tribes generally fumed at the assignment of part of their country to Fingo dogs and the remainder to white settlers. As Smith's quarrels with D'Urban became more frequent and more intense, the asperity of his criticisms of his superior for alleged lack of support elicited from D'Urban the frosty comment that Smith's language was not appropriate to that of a subordinate.[78] In particular Smith bitterly protested D'Urban's appointment of Somerset, "whose imbecility in war is equal to his vacillation and love of intrigue in peace," as magistrate in charge of the Tembu, without consultation, thus contributing to the undermining of Smith's over-all authority.[79]

D'Urban's policy of direct rule over the Ciskeian tribes had been in operation only about six months before he received word that his arrangements were likely to be reversed by the British government, and Smith had served less than a year before he was succeeded by Stockenstrom. So brief a span may seem scarcely adequate to sustain a judgment of the system's prospects of success, but, judging the system's merits solely upon the testimony of its protagonists, the conclusion seems inescapable that it was foredoomed to failure. Smith deluded himself by the assumption that he could separate the tribesmen from their chiefs and impose a new morality through the application of stern measures backed by military power. The system eliminated none of the circumstances that had produced the war of 1834; it solved no problems. It was simply a rule of force destined to maintain a degree of order only so long as that force was adequate.

---

[76] Smith to D'Urban, confidential, April 10, 1836, G.H. 34/8, Cape Archives.

[77] D'Urban to Smith, confidential, March 15, 1836, D'Urban Military, Cape Archives.

[78] Memorandum, D'Urban to Smith, July 2, 1836, *ibid.*

[79] Smith to D'Urban, very private, July 2, 1836, G.H. 34/8, Cape Archives.

D'Urban's September policy did not conciliate the Kaffirs, nor did it entirely satisfy the frontier colonists. He had hoped that the assignment of lands in the conquered territory to white settlers might serve the dual purpose of tranquilizing the frontier by interposing a belt of Fingoes and European farmers between the Kaffirs and the old colony and appeasing the land hunger of the settlers. When it was announced that applications would be entertained for farms in the territory between the Fish and the Kei, there was a rush to register claims. There were nearly four hundred applicants, the majority of whom were Boers; but there were a large number of English settlers. Among these were the numerous members of the Bowker family.[80] D'Urban assured John Mitford Bowker that his own grant and those of his family, the Southeys,[81] and that of Theophilus Shepstone would receive precedence over all others in the event that the British government approved his measures.[82] Those who expected land grants might be expected to approve D'Urban's policy, but many others complained that his system did not promote genuine security. The Kaffir menace remained, and available military forces could not provide protection against marauders. The Boer pastoralists of the Somerset district, already embittered by a succession of grievances against the British government, were in motion in the first stages of the Great Trek long before the news reached the Cape of the disapproval of D'Urban's measures.

After the reversal of his annexation, D'Urban devoted the remainder of his life to the vindication of his policy. Like a magpie he collected every scrap of evidence that seemed to support his contention that his measures had been a success. Carefully he filed them away for future reference. But after examining this mass of clippings, notes, and letters, the impression remains that perhaps it was best for D'Urban's subsequent reputation that he was so soon repudiated. The early termination of his system made it possible for him to argue that had it been given a fair trial, it might have solved the frontier problem. If it had continued, it would almost certainly have proved bankrupt, as bankrupt as all other efforts to achieve order in southern Africa in an era of penurious government.

---

[80] William Smith to D'Urban, July 1, 1840, D'Urban Papers, IX. A list of applications for farms is to be found in B-K 32, Cape Archives.

[81] The Bowkers and the Southeys, prominent families of the eastern border, were much involved with the politics of the area.

[82] D'Urban to Bowker, confidential, June 10, 1836, D'Urban P-C, 1835–1837, Cape Archives.

Chapter VII

THE GLENELG DISPATCH AND THE TREATY SYSTEM, 1835–1839

WHEN Sir Benjamin D'Urban annexed Queen Adelaide Province in May, 1835, he was aware that he had violated his instructions. He could not know that one month previously a new secretary of state for colonies had been appointed who would achieve notoriety because he repudiated this expansion. D'Urban and Glenelg have become symbols in the South African society of the antithesis between liberal humanitarianism and the "settler viewpoint." Their actions and their assumptions have become obscured by the roles assigned them. Proponents of the settlers' case argue that Glenelg's "infamous dispatch," the product of a bigoted, misguided pseudo philanthropy, was a disaster for both whites and Africans because it overturned a sound and orderly system of government and restored the frontier to a state of anarchy.[1] Humanitarians have praised the "golden dispatch" as a triumph of morality over greed. John Philip was jubilant at this further demonstration of the enlightenment of British policy,[2] and subsequent writers who have admired Philip have praised Glenelg. W. M. Macmillan wrote that it was "to Glenelg's credit, and to the honour of British imperialism that annexation was not to be lightly and greedily sanctioned for the sake of acquiring territory."[3]

Both D'Urban and Glenelg are miscast. Although D'Urban sympathized with the settlers, whom he felt had been the innocent victims

---

[1] A. J. H. van der Walt, J. A. Wiid, and A. L. Geyer, *Geskiedenis van Suid-Afrika* (2 vols.; Cape Town: Nasionale Boekhandel, 1955), II, 400.

[2] Philip wrote of the Glenelg dispatch: "It not only does honor to Lord Glenelg as a Statesman and a Christian, but to the country of which he is one of its highest ornaments" ("Estimate of Sir Fowell Buxton's success in the cause of humanity" [written in 1846], Philip 3–5, LMS Archives).

[3] W. M. Macmillan, *Bantu, Boer, and Briton* (London: Faber and Gwyer, 1929), p. 141.

of an unprovoked Kaffir attack, he was no admirer of the settler mentality. He was a military man concerned with the establishment of a
more adequate system of security. In 1835 his decision to promote this
objective seemed to coincide with the interests of the frontier community, and consequently he was lionized, particularly after his policy was
repudiated by Downing Street.

Charles Grant, Baron Glenelg, was an evangelical, a member of the
committee of the Church Missionary Society, and the son of a prominent member of the Clapham Sect, and his reversal of D'Urban's
annexation was applauded by the great missionary societies. But it is
unwarranted to conclude from these facts that his action was simply
an expression of humanitarianism. Glenelg could have approved
D'Urban's policy of September, 1835, and still have been called a
humanitarian had he insisted on an interdict against European settlement. Such a decision would in fact have been in accordance with the
recommendations of John Philip. But approval of D'Urban's measures
would have meant the extension of British authority, creating additional responsibility and expense. There has been too much preoccupation with Glenelg, too little with the policy of the government of
which he was a member. Peculiarly, Glenelg, described by his detractors as indolent, has been assigned sole responsibility for a voluminous
dispatch containing an enormous amount of information and based
upon a number of previous drafts. The Glenelg dispatch cannot be
understood by an analysis of Glenelg's antecedents and of his personal
predilections. It was a product of long consultation within the Colonial
Office and reflected the collective decision of a cabinet that certainly
was not dominated by "humanitarian" inclinations.

D'Urban's policy instructions from Stanley, confirmed by those of
Spring-Rice,[4] were to avoid political interference beyond the borders
of the colony and to seek frontier tranquillity without undertaking
greater responsibilities or incurring additional expense. The outbreak
of war transformed the character of the border problem but it did not
provide D'Urban with carte blanche. In June, 1835, before he had
received word that Lord Aberdeen had been replaced by Charles Grant,
D'Urban privately expressed the opinion that his action would be
severely criticized at home, particularly by "the Buxton party," [5] and
in July he predicted that the annexation of the province would probably be disallowed by the British government.[6] In D'Urban's view the

[4] Spring-Rice to D'Urban, Oct. 14, 1834, C.O. 49/26, P.R.O.

[5] D'Urban to Bell, June 2, 1835, D'Urban Papers, VII, Cape Archives; D'Urban to
Willoughby Gordon, June 26, 1835, ibid., IX.

[6] D'Urban to Bird, private, July 20, 1835, D'Urban P-C 2, Cape Archives.

gravest threat to his policy came from Thomas Fowell Buxton, whose power had been demonstrated by passage of the Abolition Act. D'Urban assumed that Buxton's attitude would be determined largely by Philip and that Philip's hostility was revealed by the virulence of the editorials in the *South African Commercial Advertiser*, edited by his son-in-law, John Fairbairn.

D'Urban was not inclined to wait passively for the verdict. He too had powerful friends at home whom he proposed to enlist in his cause, among them Sir Willoughby Gordon, the quartermaster general, and Sir Herbert Taylor, private secretary to William IV. Through them and old associates at the Horse Guards he hoped to counteract the influence of Buxton on the Colonial Office. Slow and uncertain written comunication was not sufficient; he needed representatives in London who intimately understood the problems of the Cape and the basis for his decision. For this purpose he employed two of his officers, his aide-de-camp, Captain G. de la Poer Beresford, and Major A. J. Cloete. Each had great assets for the task. Cloete was an able and ambitious officer who hoped that D'Urban's favor would advance his career,[7] and Beresford was a scion of one of the most influential families in Britain. Beresford had had the reputation of being a ne'er-do-well, and his service under D'Urban was intended by his family to be a means to his rehabilitation. His early indiscretions plagued him at the Cape—his friends in England heard that he was operating a faro bank —but D'Urban's assurances of his good conduct contributed to a reconciliation with his father.[8] D'Urban's support cemented the young man's loyalty; his associations gave him unusual opportunities to present his case; and he had the ability to act as a persuasive advocate. In Beresford, D'Urban had a most useful assistant.

Cloete arrived in England in August, Beresford in September, and each independently began an active campaign in behalf of D'Urban's annexation of Queen Adelaide Province. Cloete interviewed Sir Herbert Taylor; Fitzroy Somerset; R. W. Hay, the permanent undersecretary for colonies; and Lord Glenelg. Beresford through Taylor was granted an interview with the King, who inquired minutely into the details of D'Urban's decision and indicated in words and gestures that he believed the May measures of the Cape governor to have been not only wise but necessary. Beresford also presented D'Urban's case to Sir George Grey, the parliamentary undersecretary, and in at least two discussions to Lord Glenelg. With the exception of Grey and Glenelg, who were noncommittal, all agreed that D'Urban had acted wisely.

[7] Cloete to D'Urban, Feb. 22, 1835, D'Urban Papers, V.
[8] Beresford to D'Urban, [June], 1835, received July 2, 1835, *ibid.*

Beresford reported general agreement at the Horse Guards that "it has been right well done," and he was told on "good authority" that Wellington had said, "Leave D'Urban alone, it is in good hands, he will soon put that all to right for you." [9]

D'Urban's emissaries in London saw two great hazards that could contribute to the repudiation of his policy. The Whig government might fall, to be succeeded by a weak Tory regime which might have to lean upon the Saints to stay in office; and Buxton's recently appointed Committee on the Aborigines might become a sounding board for the philanthropists and intimidate even a Whig government.

Certainly any committee with Buxton as chairman could not be treated with indifference by the cabinet. Buxton's autocratic temper was evident in the proceedings of the select committee. The questions he asked witnesses reflected his assumption that the white colonists and the Cape government had been the aggressors in the Kaffir war. Even hostile witnesses like Colonel Wade were led to admit that the patrol system and the burning of native huts had been highly provocative, and the cumulative effect of testimony before the committee seemed to support the conclusion that the system before the war had been grievously unjust. Cloete, who attended many sessions of the committee, wrote D'Urban that Buxton completely dominated the committee and that none of the members dared to contest his "scandalously prejudiced" conduct of the hearings.[10] But the transcripts of the proceedings do not bear out the contention that Buxton dictated the committee's line of action. The membership included Sir Rufane Donkin, former acting governor of the Cape; Sir George Grey, parliamentary undersecretary; and William E. Gladstone, none of whom was overawed by the chairman. The record included much testimony in defense of the colonists and the Cape government; and the recommendations of the committee at the end of its deliberations were a damp squib, and provided no guide to governmental policy. The committee's proceedings, however, were significant, for the Colonial Office through the participation of the Parliamentary Undersecretary was informed on South African conditions through the evidence presented by the various witnesses.

A more direct influence of the Saints on the Colonial Office was

[9] Beresford to D'Urban, Sept. 12, [1835], *ibid.* Other letters on which this information is based include Cloete to D'Urban, private, Aug. 23, 1835; Cloete to D'Urban, private, Aug. 29, 1835; Cloete to D'Urban, Aug. 30, 1835; Beresford to D'Urban, Nov. 3 [1835]; Cloete to D'Urban, Nov. 12, 1835; Beresford to D'Urban, Dec. 8, [1835], all in *ibid.*

[10] Cloete to D'Urban, private, Aug. 29, 1835, *ibid.*

provided by interviews at the Colonial Office, most important of which was a conference on September 26, 1835, between Buxton and William Ellis of the London Missionary Society and the Colonial Secretary, which lasted several hours. At that meeting Ellis and Buxton presented Philip's version of the origin of the war and pleaded the injustice of expelling whole tribes from their territory when they had been the victims rather than the aggressors. Glenelg was by no means uncritical of this testimony; in rebuttal he expressed D'Urban's version that the war had resulted from a grand conspiracy for which Hintza was the inspiration and that the plunders and outrages of the Kaffirs had necessitated the military measures that had led to hostilities.[11] But against the mass of information from the Cape presented at that interview and by Ellis by letter and in conferences thereafter, the case for D'Urban rested essentially only on one dispatch and the evidence of Beresford and Cloete. Against the energetic Buxton-Ellis-Philip prosecution of the case for the Kaffirs, this defense was woefully inadequate. By the end of November Ellis could assure Philip that although the Colonial Office had given him no precise information on what its response to D'Urban's annexation would be, he was confident that the decision would be in accordance with humanity and justice.[12]

Buxton and the London Missionary Society certainly influenced the character of the Glenelg dispatch. Much of the information on which Glenelg depended was provided by Philip and other Cape informants sympathetic to the Kaffirs. The evidence seemed overwhelming both to the missionaries and to D'Urban and the colonists that the conclusions of the dispatch were also dictated by the Saints, whose view had been faithfully reproduced by a colonial secretary predisposed to accept their advice. But such an interpretation of the reversal of D'Urban's policy ignores certain inconvenient facts. Buxton, Ellis, and Philip did not condemn the annexation of the province as such; Philip, at least, favored extension of British authority, and the decision to withdraw to the Fish River was not based upon advice proffered by any spokesman of the humanitarian cause. On the other hand, R. W. Hay, never identified as a humanitarian, expressed doubts about the desirability of annexing additional territory and incurring new responsibilities in a colony already too large.[13] Further, the decision of Glenelg was arrived at after the most careful consideration with his parlia-

---

[11] Ellis to Philip, private, Sept. 26, 1835, Ellis Private; Ellis to Philip, Sept. 26, 1835, Letters Outgoing, both in LMS Archives.

[12] Ellis to Philip, Nov. 25, 1835, Ellis Private, LMS Archives.

[13] Cloete to D'Urban, Aug. 23, 1835; Beresford to D'Urban, Nov. 3, [1835], both in D'Urban Papers, V.

mentary undersecretary, Sir George Grey, and with Stephen, and had the approval of the entire cabinet. The instructions to D'Urban to disgorge Queen Adelaide Province cannot be adequately explained in terms of Buxton's influence or Glenelg's humanitarianism. Repudiation of D'Urban's annexation satisfied not only Exeter Hall but the Chancellor of the Exchequer; it was humanitarianism "on the cheap," designed to please both God and Mammon.

From the receipt of D'Urban's dispatch announcing his annexation, the Colonial Office staff under Stephen's direction had begun the task of distilling information from every available source on the causes of the Kaffir war. D'Urban's account of unprovoked aggression did not accord with the testimony of witnesses, pro-settler or pro-Kaffir, before Buxton's committee, with Philip's accounts from the Cape, or with earlier correspondence in the files of the Colonial Office.

While D'Urban awaited the response of his superiors to his momentous decisions of May, 1835, Glenelg delayed his reply in anticipation of further information from the governor. D'Urban, with some justification, cursed the Colonial Office for its failure to respond; Downing Street with equal justice considered D'Urban remiss for not providing adequate documentation on which to base its reaction to his decision. Certainly his failure to inform his superiors of the details of his September policy was not reconcilable with efficiency or intelligent self-interest.

However the responsibility for this stalemate may be assigned, D'Urban's failure to communicate promptly and fully the character of and the justifications for his policies eliminated any prospect that they would be approved. The lobbying of his representatives, Beresford and Cloete, could not be a substitute for a carefully written, detailed, and documented dispatch. But in all probability no action of D'Urban's could have prevented his reversal. His Draconian *diktat* to the Kaffirs in May aroused the indignation of the Saints; his policies of both May and September did violence to the Whig government's objectives of retrenchment.

A great deal of energy has been devoted to investigating the authorship of the Glenelg dispatch, principally by those who assumed that a somnolent secretary of state could not possibly have written it. It was a joint production of Glenelg and Sir George Grey with a great deal of assistance, principally of an editorial nature, from James Stephen; but its principal author was Glenelg himself, who devoted an enormous amount of time and reflection to the problem of the Cape frontier and whose exhaustive analysis was embodied in the various drafts of

the dispatch composed from the end of November until its final transmission on December 26.[14] But authorship of the dispatch is far less
important than its fundamental philosophy. The framework of the
Glenelg dispatch was dictated primarily not by the viewpoint of its
signator but by the policies of the government of which he was a
member. Stephen reflected the awareness of the Colonial Office of these
overriding considerations when he wrote Howick a summary of the
vexing problems of the Empire. Rebellion threatened to erupt in
Canada, the planters of Jamaica were disaffected, but the Cape was
perhaps the blackest spot of all. D'Urban, stated Stephen, had provided
little information, but what little he had reported caused acute apprehension. He had conquered several thousand square miles of worthless
territory and proposed that for the defense of an extended border Parliament provide approximately £300,000 per year, an increase of about
two-thirds over previous appropriations. This was intolerable, said
Stephen; "the fee simple of the whole Country would be dearly
bought at half a year's purchase at this rate." From the evidence of
missionaries and others, the war had been "a most foolish and wicked
business," and the annexation reflected the governor's ambition for
the title of "Africanus." [15]

Stephen's opinion that this was an unjust war resulting in an inex-
pedient annexation was shared by the Melbourne cabinet, which
carefully reviewed the dispatch in its various drafts before giving
approval to the final version. There were some criticisms of its style.
Howick objected to the irony with which one of the early drafts described the acts of D'Urban; but there was no dissent as to its substance—all agreed that Queen Adelaide Province must be given up.[16]

The major change in the character of the dispatch was the product
of intervention not of the cabinet but of the King. William IV, saddled
with a government he did not want, regarded most of the Melbourne
cabinet with unconcealed aversion and Lord Glenelg with particular
contempt. William's experience in the navy, particularly in the West
Indies squadron, had given him a special interest in colonial problems,

---

[14] Evidence on the authorship of the Glenelg dispatch is to be found in two series
in the Public Record Office, C.O. 537 and C.O. 48, principally C.O. 537/145 and
C.O. 48/192. A detailed analysis of the dispatch, with which I am in general agreement, is made by James Roxborough, "Colonial Policy on the Northern and Eastern
Frontiers of the Cape of Good Hope, 1834-45" (unpublished Ph.D. dissertation, Oxford University, 1953).

[15] Stephen to Howick, Oct. 26, 1835, Grey Papers, Prior's Kitchen, University of
Durham.

[16] Reports of these discussions are in Howick's Journal, Grey Papers.

and, he thought, a special knowledge. The King believed that the Empire could be maintained only if Britain vigorously asserted its authority. He considered Glenelg to be the protagonist of a timid and compromising colonial policy, particularly with regard to Canada, and he did not hesitate to express this opinion to the cabinet and to Glenelg himself.[17] But William was not content with mere purgation of his frustrations; he insisted that the King must be consulted and that consultation involved the right not only to object but to require revisions of policy. The Whig government, disinclined to resign for less than the most extreme provocation, on occasion modified its position rather than clash with William. One of these retreats changed the basic character of the Glenelg dispatch.

D'Urban's success in converting William was as complete as his failure to influence the Melbourne government. The King, already predisposed in favor of an aggressive policy, was easily converted by Sir Herbert Taylor and Beresford to unqualified support for D'Urban's measures.[18] Consequently, when he saw the draft of Glenelg's dispatch to D'Urban, he exploded. In tone and substance the dispatch was unacceptable to William. Glenelg argued that the policies of the Cape government had provoked the Kaffirs; William responded that their "ferocious and plundering" character was sufficient explanation for the war and that D'Urban was quite justified in considering them "irreclaimable savages," though perhaps it was impolitic to use that language in a local proclamation. Glenelg contended that extension of the frontier would require larger expenditures for administration and military defense; William asserted that by selecting a more advantageous line than the bush country of the Fish-Keiskama, expenditures would ultimately be reduced. In almost every respect William's views clashed with those of Glenelg, and on the character of the instructions to the governor the King was unyielding. The original version of the Glenelg dispatch was peremptory; it ordered D'Urban to retrocede the annexed territory and to enter into treaties with the Kaffir chiefs for mutual security. William refused to approve the disavowal of D'Urban's actions without giving the governor an opportunity to defend them. The governor was an able officer with special knowledge of the Cape frontier, William stated, and D'Urban's conclusions could not be lightly dismissed. Consequently the dispatch might convey only the observations of the Colonial Office on the evidence before it, and

---

[17] Henry Reeve, ed., *The Greville Memoirs* (3 vols.; Longmans, Green, 1874), III, 274–278.

[18] Beresford to D'Urban, Sept. 12, [1835], D'Urban Papers, V.

not orders. No final decision could be made until D'Urban had had time to submit his reply.[19]

William's refusal to approve instructions to relinquish the territory produced a spirited discussion in the cabinet on December 23. Glenelg, with support from his predecessor Spring-Rice, now Chancellor of the Exchequer, argued that the cabinet should stand firm. Other members of the cabinet, though they all expressed approval of the original version, were disposed to yield the point. But Howick strongly objected to surrender; he told his colleagues that he could not consent to the dispatch being emasculated, and that if the cabinet agreed to the alteration, he would join Buxton in denouncing the decision.[20] Confronted with this threat, the cabinet agreed to a compromise. In the final draft of the dispatch Glenelg wrote that he could not give fixed and unbending instructions until he had full information from D'Urban, and concluded with the statement that a final decision would not be made until D'Urban had had the opportunity to respond.[21] The compromise was not a success. D'Urban interpreted it to mean that his policies might yet be approved by the home government if he could demonstrate that they were working effectively, and the border policy of the British government remained for months in a state of uncertainty which was resolved with a maximum of unpleasantness after the arrival of Andries Stockenstrom to carry out Glenelg's policy.

Some historians have argued that the course of events would have been different had D'Urban been more prompt in reporting to the Colonial Office the details of his treaties with the Kaffir chiefs in September, 1835, which had withdrawn the harsh policy of expulsion. It is true that D'Urban's letter of November 7, announcing his conclusion of peace on liberal terms, did not arrive at the Colonial Office until after Glenelg's dispatch had left England. On September 24, however, the Cape colonial secretary, John Bell, had written the imperial permanent undersecretary, R. W. Hay, describing in general language the outlines of D'Urban's September policy, and Bell's letter was received in Downing Street on December 8. Through Bell's letter and newspapers from the Cape arriving in London before December 26, the staff of the Colonial Office should have been aware of the abandon-

---

[19] William's observations are written on a draft of the dispatch contained in C.O. 537/145, P.R.O.

[20] Howick's Journal, Dec. 23, 1835, Grey Papers.

[21] Substantial extracts from the final version of the Glenelg dispatch are printed in Kenneth N. Bell and W. P. Morrell, *Select Documents on British Colonial Policy, 1830–1860* (Oxford: Clarendon, 1928), pp. 463–477. The full text, marked "Approved William R," is contained in C.O. 537/145, P.R.O.

ment of the May policy of expulsion and extermination. By 1835 Hay had been excluded from any active part in colonial policy, and it is possible that Bell's letter did not come to Glenelg's attention.[22] But there is no reason to believe that if it had it would have altered the main outlines of the dispatch, as the September policy did not reverse the annexation of Queen Adelaide Province nor did it change the interpretation of the course of events leading to the outbreak of war. Glenelg's dispatch was dictated by humanitarian views on the antecedents of the war and by considerations of economy with regard to its consequences. As James Stephen said, "Lord Glenelg objected to the War as unjust in its origin, as cruel in its progress, and as expensive and impolitic in its results." [23] D'Urban, preoccupied with proving the morality of his actions, never understood this duality, nor did the humanitarians who hailed it as a triumph for their cause.

The policy laid down by the Glenelg dispatch was essentially that which D'Urban had been instructed to follow on his arrival at the Cape, with modifications based upon consultation between the Colonial Office and Captain Andries Stockenstrom. Few men had knowledge of the South African frontier comparable to Stockenstrom's. From his early youth he had lived on the frontier when his father had been landdrost of Graaff Reinet. He had become an assistant clerk in the landdrost's office in 1808. Since then he had served in a variety of frontier posts including the position his father had occupied, and on January 1, 1828, had been appointed commissioner-general of the eastern districts. But Stockenstrom was out of sympathy with the policies of Lowry Cole and of the military men on the frontier, and he resigned his position in 1833 with the intention of retiring to his father's native Sweden. He was in Stockholm when he received a letter from Spring-Rice asking him for information on the South African frontier problem and for suggestions for its solution. His response to that letter and, more importantly, his testimony before Buxton's select committee established him on Downing Street as that *rara avis*, a man with extensive experience on the Cape frontier who had retained a liberal viewpoint toward the Kaffir tribes.

Stockenstrom's condemnation of the reprisal system and of the seizure of Kaffir lands was as violent as that of John Philip. In 1834 Stockenstrom had seemed to be an advocate of the extension of British author-

---

[22] D'Urban's dispatch was received in the Colonial Office on January 30, 1836; that dispatch and Bell to Hay, Sept. 24, 1835, are in C.O. 48/162, P.R.O.

[23] Minute, Dec. 14, 1836, by Stephen, C.O. 325/38, P.R.O. This minute includes also the comments of Robert Smith on the expense of the war.

ity. He had pointed out that since 1828 the Boers had been migrating beyond the northern frontier and that this movement, which was likely to increase, could not be halted by fiat. The government, he had told Spring-Rice, had two alternatives. It might adopt a policy of *laissez faire,* allowing the trekkers to go further without control, dispossessing the natives, and reducing those who survived the slaughter to servitude. Eventually, past experience demonstrated, it would be forced to intervene after the mischief was irremediable. Far more intelligent would be government intervention beyond the border to prevent the trekkers from taking land without the consent of the natives, and to reserve extensive tracts for native occupation. There the chiefs would continue to rule under the benevolent guidance of British advisers. On the eastern frontier, where the tribes were able to maintain internal order and to defend themselves, he believed that the proper course was a treaty system by which the chiefs would be held responsible for restraining Kaffir marauders. As a means of maintaining order and preventing depredations, imperial troops on the Kaffir border were virtually useless. Such duties were harassing and degrading; the British Army should not be used to hunt every cow that a Boer fancied to be stolen, nor was it effective in the event of hostilities against the skulking, hit-and-run warfare which the Kaffirs had learned to fight since their repulse before Grahamstown in 1819.[24]

Stockenstrom argued that to impose a complicated and expensive administrative system upon the Kaffir tribes was undesirable; rather, they should continue to be independent, subject to no restrictions by alien authority. They would gradually be converted into peaceful neighbors through gentle contact with a superior civilization. In the meantime the colony must be protected by an efficient military force, supported by armed burghers subject to strict control to ensure that they would be used only for defense, and vulnerable areas along the frontier should be filled up by a dense population.[25] These views were in complete accord with Glenelg's own opinions, and the Secretary of State must have congratulated himself on finding a perfect instrument for the execution of his policy of retreat and retrenchment. Accordingly, in January, 1836, he appointed Stockenstrom lieutenant governor in charge of the eastern districts.[26]

[24] Stockenstrom to Spring-Rice, Nov. 5, 1834, C.O. 48/159, P.R.O.

[25] Stockenstrom to Glenelg, Jan. 7, 1836, C.O. 48/167, P.R.O.

[26] The suggestion that a lieutenant governor be appointed had been made by Thomas Philipps. John Philip was opposed to such an appointment on the ground that a local official would be subject to stronger pressure from the frontiersmen (Philip to Ellis, Dec. 19, 1835, SAF 14-5, LMS Archives).

Stockenstrom was a poor choice. Before he arrived at the Cape he was already *persona non grata* among the frontier settlers because in his testimony before Buxton's committee he had condemned the reprisal system, had ascribed much of the cattle thievery on the border to the carelessness of the owners, and had implied that in many instances reports of stolen cattle had been fraudulent.[27] This testimony caused many of his fellow colonists to consider him a traitor to his people who had sold himself for a few pieces of silver. Had this odium been Stockenstrom's only liability, one might conclude that he suffered for his virtues as an official with liberal principles in an environment hostile to liberalism, but Stockenstrom's personality compounded his troubles. Like many other forceful men he had tunnel vision; he saw only his own objectives and accepted only his own means. He was unable to grasp a viewpoint contrary to his own, quick to take offense, and incapable of restraint when aroused. None could question the courage of Andries Stockenstrom, but for this position of responsibility, courage was not enough. No official carrying out the Glenelg policies could have been popular with the settlers on the border, but Stockenstrom was certain to be peculiarly unpopular.

The Glenelg dispatch of December 26, 1835, arrived in Cape Town in March, 1836,[28] while Stockenstrom was yet in London. For months D'Urban had been living in suspense, his hopes fluctuating with each succeeding mail, soaring with favorable reports from his agents and plummeting when the intelligence was gloomy. As late as November 3 Beresford reported that he had no doubt of the government's ultimately confirming all that D'Urban had done. D'Urban could not know that the source for Beresford's confident prophecy, R. W. Hay, had no influence whatsoever in the formulation of policy.[29] Three days after the date of the Glenelg dispatch, Beresford wrote the governor that he had had two interviews in the past week with Glenelg and three with Sir George Grey, and that he had gathered the impression that nothing would be finally settled until the government had had further correspondence with D'Urban.[30] Against Beresford's assurances, however, D'Urban saw an accumulation of gloomy evidence. By the end of January, 1836, gossip was circulating around Cape Town that the country beyond the Fish River was to be returned to the Kaffirs.

[27] See George E. Cory, *The Rise of South Africa* (5 vols.; London: Longmans, Green, 1921–1930), II, 286–289, for a summary of Stockenstrom's testimony.

[28] D'Urban received the dispatch on March 21 (D'Urban to Glenelg, March 23, 1836, C.O. 48/166, P.R.O.).

[29] Beresford to D'Urban, Nov. 3, [1835], D'Urban Papers, V.

[30] Beresford to D'Urban, Dec. 29, [1835], *ibid.*

D'Urban assumed the source of the rumor to be Philip's son-in-law, John Fairbairn, editor of the *South African Commercial Advertiser*.[31] In February, 1836, Philip sailed for England accompanied by a minor Kaffir chief, Jan Tzatzoe, and a Hottentot, Andries Stoffels, who could be used to whip up humanitarian fervor.[32] But the decision had been reached long before Philip left South Africa.

When the dispatch from Downing Street finally arrived on March 21, D'Urban boiled with indignation at the evident triumph of the philanthropists. Obviously the government had decided to sacrifice him to the expediencies of English politics; for the votes of the Saints they had repudiated a policy that was sound and right.[33] On more sober reëxamination of the dispatch, however, and undoubtedly after consultation with his capable colonial secretary, John Bell, D'Urban saw a possibility that he might yet confound his enemies. The less importunate language upon which William IV had insisted conveyed the implication that the final decision would not be made until after D'Urban had had the opportunity to defend his decisions. It was evident that the policies Glenelg condemned were the abortive decisions of May, 1835. The treaties of September, D'Urban was convinced, were in accordance with true humanitarianism, and until he received a decision on his dispatch announcing the liberal arrangements with the chiefs, there was yet hope, though, he recognized, a forlorn one.

Accordingly, though his reply expressed "deep regret" at the Secretary of State's decision and the foreboding that it would mean the ruination of the colony and the consignment of the Kaffirs to barbarism, his language was respectful and restrained.[34] He confided to Smith that he intended to take full advantage of the discretionary authority the minister allowed him and to continue the administration of Queen Adelaide Province. In the meantime he would prepare a resounding rebuttal against the unjust aspersions on his conduct which a credulous Colonial Office had accepted on the authority of Philip and the "anticolonial Party." [35] Meanwhile his spirits were raised by

---

[31] D'Urban to Smith, confidential, Feb. 19, 1836, D'Urban Military, Cape Archives.

[32] Philip would have wished Makomo to accompany him. Tzatzoe was a second choice, and Philip was doubtful that the Cape government would allow him to leave the country (Philip to Ellis, Dec. 19, 1835, SAF 14-5, LMS Archives).

[33] This estimate of D'Urban reaction is based on Smith's response on April 3, 1836, very private, G.H. 34/8, Cape Archives. Due allowance has been made for Smith's reaction being more explosive than his chief's.

[34] D'Urban to Glenelg, March 23, 1836, C.O. 48/116, P.R.O.

[35] D'Urban to Smith, very secret and confidential, April 8, 1836, D'Urban Military, Cape Archives.

rumors from England through Cape merchants that his dispatches announcing his September policy, received at the end of January, had convinced the government and that his measures had been approved.[36] Surely the final decision, favorable or unfavorable, would come soon.

Consequently relations between the Colonial Office and D'Urban were for months at dead center, each misapprehending the other's intentions. Glenelg expected the governor to provide a fully documented defense of his policies. D'Urban assumed that the arrangements of September superseded those of May and that he should take no further action until the Colonial Office responded to his dispatch of November. Each found the silence of the other unaccountable.

While they awaited further communications from Downing Street, D'Urban and Smith were far from inactive. Not only were they busy in the preparation of their defense against the slanders of the "Philippine party," but they were in active correspondence with their military associates at home. Smith, with D'Urban's approval, chose to regard the indictments contained in the Glenelg dispatch as a direct affront to his own honor and integrity, and he wrote Wellington, Lord Hill, and Fitzroy Somerset a justification of his conduct which was in fact a defense of D'Urban's policy and an appeal for intervention with king and cabinet to uphold the decisions of September, 1835. To Wellington, Smith recalled his old commander's last general orders at Cambrai expressing continuing interest in the honor and welfare of his subordinates, and his subsequent favors, and asked the Duke, if he considered the conduct of the Kaffir war to be in accordance with civilized usages, to say so to William IV.[37] Smith sent similar letters to Sir James Kempt, Sir John Lambert, and others.[38]

At the end of May D'Urban at last had word from Glenelg in response to his dispatch of November. The minister's comments further excited the governor's resentment: the Kaffirs could not be made British subjects by a treaty, as that status could be conferred only by the King himself; no European could be allowed to settle in the annexed territory; Hottentot auxiliaries had been unduly detained and should be returned immediately to their families.[39] But with indomitable determination, D'Urban professed to see in the Secretary of State's strictures a basis for hope. In all of this denunciatory dispatch,

---

[36] D'Urban to Smith, confidential, April 15, 1836, *ibid.*

[37] Smith to Wellington, private and confidential, May 14, 1836, G.H. 34/8, Cape Archives.

[38] Copies of these letters are in *ibid.*

[39] Glenelg to D'Urban, Feb. 17, 1836, C.O. 48/162, P.R.O.

there was no explicit instruction to abandon Queen Adelaide Province. The dispatch, D'Urban concluded, was a further manifestation of Glenelg's spinelessness. In this "most Jesuitical and mystifying" communication, "a Delphic sort of oracle in truth," Glenelg might be seeking to shift the onus to his governor, leaving the Colonial Office free if anything went wrong to explain that the governor had mistaken his instructions.[40]

At the beginning of June the governor unburdened himself in a long denunciatory dispatch to Glenelg, written in language rarely used by a subordinate to his superior officer.[41] All the pent-up emotions flooded out; D'Urban's purpose was no longer vindication but the wounding of a minister whom he regarded with manifest contempt. For this attack he expected to be immediately recalled. Even William IV, when he read this mass of invective, was appalled by the language, and Sir Herbert Taylor wrote to D'Urban:

I must freely own to you my dear D'Urban with the candour of an old and sincere friend that the tone and expressions of that Dispatch surprised me and I could with difficulty believe that you could have been persuaded to adopt such in *any* Communication, much less in one addressed to such high official authority, . . . I had never agreed with the Authorities at home in the view they took of the measures you had pursued, and I think they judged very unwisely in not confirming them but the objections or prejudices of the Government had been confined to the Measures and never extended to the man.[42]

The tone of the dispatch suggested that D'Urban had concluded that all hope for his vindication had evaporated, but remarkably he professed to believe for several months thereafter that a miracle might yet occur. He was not prepared to abandon his annexation without explicit orders from Downing Street. The final decision, for good or ill, he expected would be transmitted to him by the newly appointed lieutenant governor.[43]

Stockenstrom arrived in Table Bay on July 3, 1836, but because of an outbreak of smallpox on the voyage he and his family, with the

[40] D'Urban to Smith, confidential, May 27, 1836, D'Urban Military, Cape Archives.

[41] D'Urban to Glenelg, June 9, 1836, C.O. 48/167, P.R.O. The dispatch was apparently composed by D'Urban personally without consultation with his colonial secretary, John Bell. Bell later insisted that he had not seen Glenelg's dispatch of December 26 until months after it arrived in Cape Town, and that he did not know of the contents of D'Urban's reply until it had already been copied by a clerk (Napier to Glenelg, private, Jan. 22, 1838, C.O. 48/188, P.R.O.).

[42] Taylor to D'Urban, private, Aug. 16, 1837, D'Urban Papers, V.

[43] D'Urban to Smith, confidential, May 27, 1836, D'Urban Military, Cape Archives.

other passengers disembarking at Cape Town, were placed in quarantine for the next three weeks. This was an ominous introduction for the new lieutenant governor.

Stockenstrom's forthright comments to the Aborigines Committee had preceded him and many of the settler population in the frontier regarded him with loathing. Harry Smith, on learning of Stockenstrom's appointment, reported that the news had been received with "universal dissatisfaction"; he was "very unpopular" with all the English, the Boers detested him, and the Kaffirs held him responsible for the location of the Hottentots at Kat River in territory from which Makomo had been evicted.[44] Smith was not entirely an objective observer, for Stockenstrom's appointment as lieutenant governor frustrated his own ambitions, but his assertion of settler hostility to Stockenstrom was not greatly exaggerated.

In Cape Town, however, Stockenstrom's reception was friendly enough. D'Urban received him not only with the honors appropriate to the dignity of a lieutenant governor but with warm hospitality. While in quarantine Stockenstrom had forwarded to the governor copies of his instructions; they were a blow to D'Urban's hopes, for they contained no new information beyond what had already been received, but despite his disappointment D'Urban's first impressions of Stockenstrom were favorable. The lieutenant governor seemed a "straight forward man of business," not at all the thorny character D'Urban had been led to expect. Stockenstrom assured D'Urban that he was prepared to support the governor's policies until the receipt of final instructions from the Secretary of State,[45] and the two parted amicably. But within twenty-four hours of Stockenstrom's departure from Cape Town, a vendetta began between the two which equaled in virulence that between D'Urban and Glenelg.

The immediate cause of the breach between D'Urban and Stockenstrom was the governor's decision, without any intimation to his subordinate, to revoke martial law in Queen Adelaide Province. When Stockenstrom heard the news on his arrival in Swellendam, he was justifiably shocked, for without martial law the D'Urban policy in the new territory would collapse. As Smith had admitted, without martial law the executive officer in the province had "no more power or authority to repress evil than any ordinary person by the slow and

---

[44] Smith to D'Urban, confidential, May 1, 1836, G.H. 34/8, Cape Archives.

[45] D'Urban to Smith, private and confidential, Aug. 5, 1836, D'Urban Military, Cape Archives.

common Process of the Law." [46] Stockenstrom naturally assumed bad faith. In this judgment he was overly harsh, but clearly the governor had been guilty of excessive reticence. For months before Stockenstrom's arrival D'Urban and Smith had been aware that the system of martial law in Queen Adelaide Province rested on shaky legal foundations. The annexed territory was part of the Cape, the Kaffirs were British subjects, and the authority of the Cape Supreme Court extended over the new acquisition. While Stockenstrom was still in Cape Town, D'Urban had several discussions with Chief Justice Sir John Wylde, concluding on August 17, the day of Stockenstrom's departure, with the decision that martial law must be revoked.[47] The coincidence caused Stockenstrom erroneously to believe that he had been duped.

No official could have succeeded in the circumstances in which the lieutenant governor was placed. Though Stockenstrom's orders were to coöperate with the governor until the final decision by the Colonial Office, it was evident to D'Urban that Stockenstrom had been sent to preside over the liquidation of his policies. Coöperation between the two would have been impossible even if theirs had been tractable natures; the irascibility of Stockenstrom and the vindictiveness of D'Urban merely aggravated their hostility. The decision of the Colonial Office to send out an agent of a new policy as the subordinate of the spokesman of the old was a blunder. When Stockenstrom arrived at headquarters in Grahamstown he was at war with the governor, and most of the men on whom he had to depend for support were partisans of D'Urban. The military officers who greeted Stockenstrom on his arrival with professions of friendship and respect hoped for his early discomfiture and were prepared to hasten it. Harry Smith, who wrote private letters of good will to Stockenstrom while sending copies to D'Urban, withdrew shortly after the lieutenant governor's arrival, but other malcontents remained. Colonel Somerset, in charge of the military forces on the frontier, detested this crude colonial with whom he had had unpleasant associations on earlier occasions; and he enthusiastically coöperated with D'Urban's request to inform him of everything of importance which transpired on the frontier.[48] Major Charles Michell [49] and other officers in whom Stockenstrom confided

---

[46] Smith to D'Urban, confidential, July 30, 1836, D'Urban Papers, VI.

[47] D'Urban to Wylde, confidential, Aug. 17, 1836, D'Urban P-C 1835–1837, Cape Archives.

[48] D'Urban to Somerset, confidential, Sept. 23, 1836; D'Urban to Somerset, Dec. 30, 1836, both in D'Urban Military, Cape Archives.

[49] Michell to D'Urban, June 6, 1837, D'Urban Papers, V.

also felt it their duty to keep the governor fully informed. The English settlers of Grahamstown gave Stockenstrom a hostile reception, and he was soon plunged into the unpleasantness of a lawsuit against Captain Duncan Campbell, civil commissioner of Albany, who had circulated reports that he had been guilty of the cold-blooded murder of a Kaffir in 1812.

Before he left London Stockenstrom had secured full support from the Colonial Office for a new border policy, and as the first step toward carrying it out he almost immediately began the withdrawal of troops to the Fish River, where he proposed to concentrate them, on the justification that security forces should be strongest where the enemy was most powerful and the colony most exposed. Troops on the Kei River or on the Keiskama, he argued, would be of little use if the Kaffirs were to rush into the Fish River bush, from which they could descend on the colony.[50] This decision D'Urban chose to regard as eliminating any hope of effective government in Queen Adelaide Province. Convinced that the decision of the Colonial Office was in any event irrevocable, he ordered Stockenstrom to evacuate the province.[51] Released from any obligation to the D'Urban system, Stockenstrom renounced possession of the territory beyond the Keiskama in December, 1836, annulled the treaties of September, 1835, and negotiated new treaties with the Kaffir chiefs, who were to be permitted to return with their people to assigned locations between the Fish and Keiskama rivers. This system was fundamentally contrary to D'Urban's policy. D'Urban's objective had been to dissolve the authority of the chiefs. Stockenstrom recognized their authority and their responsibility for the conduct of their people, though they and the tribesmen inhabiting lands west of the Keiskama would remain British subjects. All Kaffirs entering the colony would be required to be unarmed and in possession of passes from one of the British agents stationed with the chiefs, and if found without passes would be punished by the chiefs. The chiefs would station responsible representatives of their tribes near the frontier to watch for stock thieves and to work in close coöperation with British commanders to prevent depredations, but the chiefs would be solely responsible for recovering stolen cattle driven across the Fish River; no longer would troops harass the tribes by patrols. On their part, the colonists were expected to exercise due vigilance in the protection of their herds and flocks, em-

[50] Stockenstrom to D'Urban, Oct. 3, 1836, C.O. 48/179, P.R.O.

[51] D'Urban to Stockenstrom, Oct. 13, 1836, enclosure in D'Urban to Glenelg, Dec. 2, 1836, C.O. 48/167, P.R.O.

ploying if necessary armed herdsmen. If thieves still evaded their vigilance, farmers were to notify the nearest field-cornet or military commander, and declare on oath that they had been plundered despite having exercised due precautions. The field-cornet or -officer would then take up the chase to the border and if the quarry nevertheless escaped would notify the Kaffir border sentries.[52]

D'Urban could not have been expected to approve the lieutenant governor's policies, which were "fraught with disastrous consequences to the colony." [53] He was powerless to repudiate the decisions but he felt no obligation to support them. Indeed he devoted his energies to discrediting Stockenstrom's measures. He had convinced himself that he had evolved a system that would have ensured the security of the frontier with progressively diminishing expense and would have promoted the civilization of the border tribes who in turn would have influenced their barbaric neighbors. Peace, Christianity, and commerce would have extended over southern Africa.[54] Now all these fair prospects were swept away by a muddled minister under the influence of bigots with no knowledge of South Africa. His preoccupation with the enormity of his reversal approached the psychotic. Through letters to his friends, including those who were charged with the execution of Stockenstrom's policies, through damnation of the treaties by an executive council sympathetic to his views, and in any way that might be damaging to those who had repudiated him, D'Urban expressed his sense of outrage. The Stockenstrom system was undermined by the hostility of the governor.

D'Urban encouraged the contempt of military officers for this "Boer" who had been placed in authority over them; offensive references to Stockenstrom's characteristics and his policies went unrebuked. Lieutenant Henry Warden reported that Makomo and Tyalie had told him that "Stockenstrom is not the Groot Baas, the Groot Baas sits at the other end of the colony. How can this Grahamstown Governor be a great man when he was born in this country and his father a Boer? We believe all other Governors came into the world Great men but a great man could not be born in this country." [55] These words, which Warden wrote he had heard with great amusement, perfectly expressed his own opinion and that of other officers.

---

[52] For the provisions of these treaties see proclamation by Stockenstrom, Dec. 5, 1836, and Stockenstrom to D'Urban, Feb. 13, 1837, and enclosures in D'Urban to Glenelg, June 24, 1837, all in C.O. 48/175, P.R.O.

[53] D'Urban to Somerset, Dec. 30, 1836, D'Urban Military, Cape Archives.

[54] Note by D'Urban, Sept., 1842, D'Urban Papers, X.

[55] Warden to D'Urban, May 26, 1837, *ibid.*, VI.

For almost two years after Stockenstrom's appointment the British government delayed the selection of a successor to a man whom the Colonial Office must have known was seething at the repudiation of his policies. It was not until October, 1837, that the decision was finally made that Sir George Napier should succeed D'Urban at the Cape, and he did not arrive at Cape Town until January, 1838. A partial explanation for the delay was the decision of the Colonial Office in December, 1835, to give D'Urban an opportunity to defend his actions before pronouncing final judgment, but any doubts Downing Street may have had as to the governor's reaction had been resolved at least a year before his dismissal; the truculence of his dispatches made it evident that his further role would be obstructionist. The choice of a successor also involved time, for the appointment had to be made by the cabinet after consultation with the Horse Guards. The Melbourne government proceeded with leisurely pace. Various candidates were considered, among them Sir George Arthur,[56] whom the cabinet eventually decided to appoint as lieutenant governor of Upper Canada. During the summer of 1837 the question was suspended while members of the government rested from their labors at their various retreats. Glenelg repeatedly pressed Melbourne to reach a decision. The Colonial Secretary's fault in this instance was not indolence but lack of force; the result, however, was the same. By its dilatoriness the Melbourne government ensured that Stockenstrom would inaugurate the new frontier policy under conditions of maximum frustration.[57]

Under the circumstances it is remarkable that Stockenstrom accomplished as much as he did. A few incidents marred the peace of the frontier; a small body of Kaffirs attacked some Fingoes, but, despite the governor's efforts to magnify the encounter, it was a minor skirmish. In general the eastern border remained quiet despite the migration of the Boers on their Great Trek into the interior. C. L. Stretch, in whom D'Urban and Smith had reposed great confidence and whom Stockenstrom appointed diplomatic agent to the Gaika tribe, was one of the few officials who resisted the temptation to act as the governor's agent. Stretch estimated that there were three times as many reports of depredations while the D'Urban system was in operation as there were during Stockenstrom's tenure, and that the chiefs, who had plotted

---

[56] In defense of the Melbourne government, it should be noted that they had offered the governorship to two persons before William's death in June, 1837, and each had refused to serve (Taylor to D'Urban, private, Aug. 16, 1837, D'Urban Papers, V; Arthur is mentioned in Melbourne to Howick, Aug. 22, 1837, Grey Papers).

[57] This statement is based on a mass of correspondence in C.O. 48/175, P.R.O.

an uprising against D'Urban's undermining of their power, welcomed Stockenstrom's treaties as "a wall," affording protection for their status and security for their people against the incursions of military patrols.[58]

Even Stretch admitted, however, that Stockenstrom, surrounded by a hostile community, was not able to devote his full energies to the administration of the new system, and that when he departed from the colony in 1838 to seek vindication in England after he lost a libel suit against a slur on his character, the spirit of his system departed with him. The relative peace on the frontier during Stockenstrom's brief tenure did not prove the soundness of his policies; he did not remain in control of the eastern province long enough to demonstrate the validity of his ideas. Even before he left South Africa, there were indications of impending trouble, symbolized by the theft of cattle from Stockenstrom's own herds. As Stretch and other border officials recognized, no system could be effective without a force sufficient to overawe the Kaffir chiefs.[59] Such a force the British government was unwilling to provide. Migration of the frontier Boers stripped the eastern district of much of the manpower from which armed levies could be drawn, but there was no effort to make good their loss either by provision of an effective border police force or by an increase in the military establishment. On the contrary, the British government sought to reduce still further its security force.[60]

The war had cost British taxpayers £154,000 beyond ordinary military expenses; now the stress was on retrenchment.[61] In November, 1837, Glenelg assured Howick that the Cape budget would "be reduced as speedily as the safety of the Colony may permit to the Establishment of 1834, and that this reduction will be made by diminishing the number of British Troops employed on the Station," substituting for them "as far as may be practicable levies to be made of the Natives of the Colony." [62] D'Urban had estimated that the minimum force necessary for the defense of the colony, including the ports as well as the frontier, would be approximately 2,300 men, including 450 Hottentots in the Cape Mounted Rifles; Stockenstrom proposed to protect it with only 1,500.[63] Of course Stockenstrom's plans were received with great favor

---

[58] Memorandum no. 1 [by Stretch], 1846, in Philip 2–6, LMS Archives.

[59] *Ibid.*

[60] See Russell's comments in a debate in the House of Commons, April 15, 1851, *Parliamentary Debates*, 3d series, CXVI, 241–242.

[61] Colonial Office minute, Nov., 1836, C.O. 325/38, P.R.O.

[62] Glenelg to Howick, Nov. 4, 1837, quoted by C. F. J. Muller, *Die Britse Owerheid en die Groot Trek* (Cape Town: Juta, [1948]), p. 86.

[63] D'Urban to Glenelg, June 20, 1837, C.O. 48/172, P.R.O.

by an economy-minded government, which was delighted to have their validity confirmed by the man whom it had appointed as D'Urban's successor, Sir George Napier.[64]

Napier was a member of that prolific family that seemed to dominate the British military and naval establishment during the first half of the nineteenth century. In an age where the range of acceptable eccentricity among members of the elite was comparatively wide, the Napier family had more than its share of unorthodoxy. George's elder brother Charles, conquerer of the Sind, would probably have been certified for treatment in a mental institution had he lived in the less tolerant twentieth century. Unlike his brilliant flamboyant brother, George was safe and sane; he was often described as honest, but never as brilliant. An unkind biographer has stated that he was a dunce at school.[65] He had been a brave but undistinguished soldier in the Napoleonic Wars, when he had lost his right arm at the assault on Ciudad Rodrigo.

George was like the other Napiers in his consuming ambition to achieve imperishable fame; the governorship of the Cape offered him his opportunity. It was his first important civil position, and he determined to make himself memorable as the governor who kept peace on the border.[66] During his tenure his devotion to peace at almost any price earned him the animosity of the Grahamstown community, which branded him as being soft on Kaffirs. Robert Godlonton, editor of the *Grahamstown Journal,* wrote that Napier "blundered through his term of office." [67] But to the Colonial Office Napier seemed at first an admirable selection, a military man who agreed wholeheartedly with the wisdom of the Glenelg-Stockenstrom policy that the Cape should be governed "upon the principles of peace, humanity, and impartial justice, both towards the colonists and native Tribes of all descriptions." [68] His manifest sympathy with these enlightened views [69] led both his admirers and his detractors to consider him "a convinced negrophilist." [70] They misunderstood his motivations.

---

[64] Napier to [Stephen?], Oct. 16, [1837], C.O. 48/174, P.R.O.

[65] *Dictionary of National Biography.*

[66] George Napier to William Napier, Nov. 23, 1851, Napier Papers, Add. MSS 49168, British Museum.

[67] Robert Godlonton, *Case of the Colonists of the Eastern Frontier of the Cape of Good Hope* . . . (Grahamstown: Richards, Slater, 1879), p. 32.

[68] Testimony, June 23, 1851, *Report of the Select Committee on the Kafir Tribes,* 1851, p. 202.

[69] Napier to [Stephen?], Oct. 16, [1837], C.O. 48/174, P.R.O.

[70] Eric A. Walker, *A History of Southern Africa* (London: Longmans, Green, 1957), p. 206, describes him in these terms.

The inhabitants of the colony, both white and black, Napier privately viewed with contempt, though unlike some other English governors he concealed his feelings. His servants were "beyond everything, & the *Devils* all coloured will not do a *single thing,* without you *stand over them,* turn yr. back one Instant, & they lay down & sleep—or else go off to drink, men & women are alike in this." [71] Cape society generally was "stupid" and "ignorant," embracing "all that is Vulgar, & worthless, and consisting on no conversation but the Gossip and slander of every one's neighbour or friend, all alike! friend or foe." [72] His philosophy of government was not dictated by his opinions of the character of Cape humanity. His preoccupation was with the maintenance of order at minimum expense. He later described his policy to a select committee of the House of Commons:

Taking the greatest amount of property lost by their [Kaffir] depredations to be £4000 per year, I thought to myself, Is it worth while for such an amount of loss to encounter all the damage that will be done by going to war? . . . looking at the amount stolen and at the nature of the people, I thought it was much better to submit to a loss than to incur the bloodshed and expense which would be caused by a war.[73]

Such a policy might be subject to serious question as a means to permanent peace; Napier was concerned only with "peace in his time." Whatever label may be appropriate to his views, he was not a "humanitarian." He had no patience with meddling missionaries, who did "more mischief than any other set of men," [74] and Philip, five months after Napier's arrival, admitted that "it is difficult to say how he will act, everyone puts his own construction on his words and apparent intimacies and his looks and he is claimed by both parties." [75] Napier relied for advice on the colonial secretary, John Bell, "the best fellow in the world, clearsighted, longheaded," and "as attached to me as if he was my brother." Bell made fraternity easier by disassociating himself from the previous administration, professing to have disapproved of much of D'Urban's policy and, in particular, of the annexation of Queen Adelaide Province.[76] But eventually Napier developed a close

[71] George Napier to Richard Napier, Feb. 2, 1839, Napier Papers, Add. MSS 49168.

[72] Same to same, Feb. 25, 1843, *ibid.*

[73] Testimony given June 23, 1851, *Report of the Select Committee on the Kafir Tribes,* p. 202.

[74] Napier to Yorke, June 8, 1839, C.O. 48/202, P.R.O.

[75] Philip to Ellis, June 1, 1838, SAF 16-1, LMS Archives.

[76] George Napier to Richard Napier, Feb. 2, 1839, Napier Papers, Add. MSS 49168.

connection with D'Urban as well, and the ex-governor, now living in retirement at nearby Wynberg, became his successor's principal adviser with regard to policy toward the Boer trekkers in Natal.

In 1842 Napier recalled that Cape Colony had been in a dismal state when he arrived in January, 1838. War was imminent, the population was in despair, property values had depreciated steeply, and the Boers were emigrating by the thousands, but "by perseverance and steadiness and an honest purpose (I am aware I am not a man of talent and cleverness)," he had accomplished a wonderful transformation.[77] The governor grossly exaggerated the contrast. When he arrived in the eastern districts on his first tour of inspection in the early months of 1838, he encountered expressions of dissatisfaction with the Stockenstrom system, which he met by the straightforward reply that he was determined to give unqualified support to the new policy, with which he was in entire agreement.[78] But apart from the migration of the Boers from the frontier, certainly a movement fraught with grave consequences, the eastern frontier was relatively placid. In May Napier met the chiefs of the Gaika and Slambie tribes. As was usual at such meetings, they complained about the boundaries of the colony having been extended into territory that was rightfully theirs, in particular the Kat River settlement, and their demeanor convinced the governor that irredentist sentiment would not soon die out. Like Harry Smith, Napier believed in flamboyant language when addressing Kaffirs, and he told the chiefs that if their people ever ventured over the boundaries he would "drive them far beyond the Kay River into distant parts, and that they never should behold the lands of their ancestors again!" This strong language had "the desired effect." [79]

At this May meeting Napier made one significant alteration in Stockenstrom's treaties. He told the chiefs that when cattle had been traced to their territories, if they did not give up the stolen animals or cattle equal in value within one month, he would order troops to enter the chiefs' kraals and take equivalent values in cattle by force. Resort to such measures of course was certain to be resented by the tribes. D'Urban had sought to promote security of property by conferring on the tribesmen the status of British subjects controlled by a system of martial law. Napier assumed that the chiefs had the power to restrain marauding by their tribesmen and to apprehend the thieves

---

[77] Same to same, Jan. 2, 1842, *ibid.*
[78] Cory, *op. cit.*, III, 443.
[79] Napier to Glenelg, May 25, 1838, C.O. 48/189, P.R.O.

and their booty, and that failure to do so demonstrated willful evasion. Napier showed no more understanding of the extent and the limitations of the chiefs' authority than had D'Urban.

With Stockenstrom as his adviser, Napier might have developed a clearer comprehension of the nature of the tribal society with which he had to deal; but Stockenstrom, besieged by a multitude of troubles, was unable to offer effective assistance. He had lost the suit for libel, he had been branded as a traitor to the settlers, his child had died, he was broken in health, and now the Secretary of State had seemed to lend credence to the slanders of his good name by ordering a full investigation of the charges. Glenelg's implied doubts as to his character deeply wounded Stockenstrom; he had been the victim of calumny "because he had espoused the cause, of which his Lordship is himself the Chief Champion," and for this Glenelg had rewarded him by suggesting that he might be suspended from office. Consequently he asked Napier for leave to go to London to clear his name.[80] Napier gave his approval with a sense of relief, for he recognized that Stockenstrom would be a difficult subordinate. In both private and public correspondence, Napier professed to admire Stockenstrom, and he was undoubtedly sincere. In a private letter to his family he appraised Stockenstrom as "manly, honest, upright, and honorable," the victim of the most vicious slanders,[81] and in endorsing Stockenstrom's decision to return to England he recorded his "most unqualified approbation" of his conduct and public service.[82] But he also knew that Stockenstrom's unpopularity had largely destroyed his effectiveness and that it was desirable that he be replaced. Consequently he encouraged Stockenstrom in his determination to go to England and resign his commission. From his conversations with Stockenstrom, Napier assumed that he would not return to Cape Colony, and that Napier's own selection, Colonel John Hare, would be appointed in his place. The change in the atmosphere of Grahamstown after Stockenstrom's departure confirmed the governor in the wisdom of his decision. Three weeks after the lieutenant governor had left for Cape Town, Napier wrote his sister-in-law that party feeling had calmed amazingly and "all come to me." Napier left the frontier with a sense of well-being: his own appointee was in office; the border was quiet; the Kaffirs were docile

---

[80] Stockenstrom to Napier, July 2, 1838, enclosure in Napier to Glenelg, July 2, 1838, *ibid.*

[81] George Napier to Anne Napier, "Private and only for our own family," Sept. 4, [1838], Napier Papers, Add. MSS 49168.

[82] Napier to Glenelg, July 2, 1838, C.O. 48/189, P.R.O.

—they say "the one armed Governor has made the Colony *too hot* for Thieves! but he is just, and treats us like men." [83]

Stockenstrom was not so easily exorcised as Napier had expected. When the lieutenant governor arrived at the Colonial Office he had worked himself up to a pitch of intense indignation. He intended to express his displeasure that Glenelg should have entertained any suspicion against his good name, and after throwing his vindication in the face of the Colonial Secretary, to resign his position. But his reception disarmed him. The staff of the office greeted him warmly; James Stephen assured him that his work had been highly approved. This cordiality somewhat mollified him, and an interview with Glenelg dissolved the last traces of his anger. The Colonial Secretary explained that an investigation had been ordered not because of lack of confidence, but because prejudging of the baselessness of the charges would have deprived Stockenstrom of the honorable acquittal that he had now received.[84]

Glenelg was not indulging merely in soothing rhetoric. To this cultivated Briton the blunt honesty of Stockenstrom was a refreshing contrast to the polished fraudulence he saw around him. Here was a tortured giant of a man who had suffered for his virtues; it was understandable that in the midst of his torments and suffering from ill-health, he should be unreasonably sensitive to imagined slights. Basking in the approval of his superiors, Stockenstrom forgot his decision to resign. After much discussion of the respective functions of the lieutenant governor and the governor, Glenelg decided to send Stockenstrom back to his position at the Cape, though he declined to entertain the latter's request that he be accorded "some special mark of Her Majesty's favor"—a knighthood or a baronetcy—to confound his opponents in the colony.[85]

This was a minor disappointment. The great blow, from which Stockenstrom would never completely recover, was soon to fall. For several years Glenelg had been under increasing attack for his alleged indecisiveness not only from the official opposition but from fellow members of the Melbourne cabinet. Stockenstrom's arrival in England coincided with a crisis in Glenelg's career, for Russell and Howick had delivered an ultimatum to Melbourne that unless Glenelg was replaced they would resign from the government.[86] Finally, in February, 1839,

---

[83] George Napier to Anne Napier, Sept. 4, [1838], Napier Papers, Add. MSS 49168.

[84] Glenelg to Napier, private, Oct. 3, 1838, Napier Papers, Add. MSS 49167.

[85] Glenelg to Stockenstrom, private, Jan. 26, 1839, C.O. 49/29, P.R.O.

[86] Russell to Melbourne, Feb. 2, 1839, in F. A. Rollo Russell, *Early Correspondence of Lord John Russell, 1805–40* (2 vols.; London: Unwin, 1913), II, 245.

Melbourne gave way and agreed to ask Glenelg for his resignation; in accordance with Russell's suggestion, Lord Normanby, who had been Lord Lieutenant of Ireland, was designated Glenelg's successor.[87] Glenelg, a sacrificial offering for cabinet unity and the release of pressure from the opposition, retired from public life. His successor would have been well advised to remain in Ireland, for as colonial secretary he was also made the target of criticisms of all the shortcomings of the colonial system. Howick, who had persisted in resigning even after Glenelg's dismissal, later admitted that the change had produced deterioration rather than an improvement in the management of colonial affairs.[88]

Shortly after Normanby replaced Glenelg, Major Samuel Charters, military secretary to Sir George Napier, arrived in England. Charters was devoted to his chief, whose mind he believed he knew as well as his own. He was appalled to hear that Stockenstrom was to return to the Cape, for he was certain from conversations with the governor that Napier not only did not expect his return, but did not wish it. Confident that he was acting in Napier's interest, Charters wrote the Colonial Office requesting that the lieutenant governor not be allowed to depart until Napier had responded to the news of the government's intentions.[89] This plea had particular force, as there were doubts within the office itself as to the expediency of Stockenstrom's return. Glenelg had hesitated for months before confirming his decision in January, 1839, and had kept Stockenstrom in London thereafter on the justification that the advice of the old frontiersman was essential in the formulation of policy toward the Boer trekkers [90]—a valid reason but also an excuse for delay. Charters' representations and pressure from London commercial men associated with the Cape increased the reluctance of the Colonial Office to act until it had received word from Napier. Lord Normanby, at first inclined to order Stockenstrom's return, vacillated, and finally in August, after reading Napier's dispatch manifesting a distinct lack of enthusiasm for Stockenstrom's resuming the lieutenant-governorship, decided to revoke the decision.[91]

For this action Normanby was condemned by the humanitarians.

[87] "Memorandum respecting the changes which were made in Lord Melbourne's Administration in 1839," by Grey, Jan. 14, 1884; Howick to Melbourne, Jan. 30, 183[9]; Russell to Howick, private, Feb. 3, 1839, all in Grey Papers.

[88] "Memorandum respecting the changes which were made in Lord Melbourne's Administration in 1839," Grey Papers.

[89] Charters to Secretary of State, June 4, 11, 1839, C.O. 48/205; Stephen to Charters, June 1, 1839, C.O. 49/30, all in P.R.O.

[90] Minute by Stephen on Napier to Russell, June 25, 1840, C.O. 48/208, P.R.O.

[91] Notes on Napier to Glenelg, June 1, 1839, C.O. 48/200, P.R.O.

The sacrifice of Stockenstrom was a surrender to settler agitation, "an announcement that the mere hostility of such a party shall have power to outweigh the deliberate approbation of the Government itself, as respects the conduct of its own officers, working out its own views to the best of its ability, and without other cause assigned to ensure his deprivation." [92] Glenelg had manfully supported his appointee, and as a special mark of his approbation had returned him to his position at an increased salary, and Normanby had jettisoned him to avoid unpleasantness—so ran the humanitarian theme. What they could not know, and what Normanby could not tell them, was that Glenelg himself had advised his successor that Stockenstrom should not return, as his usefulness was ended.[93]

As a consolation, Normanby's successor Lord John Russell offered Stockenstrom a knighthood and the lieutenant-governorship of St. Vincent in the West Indies,[94] thus fulfilling a prophecy of John Philip's.[95] Stockenstrom refused but accepted a baronetcy and a pension of £700 per year (he grumbled that the amount was inadequate) [96] and returned to the Cape, where as a private citizen he flayed the policies of governors for the next fifteen years.

The forced resignation of Glenelg and, following within six months, the replacement of Stockenstrom have been seen as marking an ebb in humanitarian influence. Such a conclusion is unwarranted. Glenelg was removed not because he was a humanitarian but because he was deemed to be excessively dilatory; Stockenstrom was replaced because he was a contentious personality, in ill-health, who did not enjoy the favor of the governor of the Cape. The criteria on which Glenelg and Stockenstrom were judged bore no relationship to "humanitarianism." The British government was preoccupied with the problem of maintaining order in the Empire; in 1839 neither Glenelg nor Stockenstrom seemed able to contribute to that objective.

---

[92] Herschel to Russell, Feb. 5, 1840, Napier Papers, Add. MSS 49167.

[93] Minute by Stephen on Napier to Russell, June 25, 1840, C.O. 48/208, P.R.O.

[94] Normanby to Russell, private, Sept. 22, 1839, Russell Papers, PRO 30/22/3, P.R.O.

[95] Philip to Ellis, July 29, 1839, SAF 16-1, LMS Archives.

[96] C. W. Hutton, ed., *The Autobiography of the Late Sir Andries Stockenstrom* (2 vols.; Cape Town: Juta, 1887), II, 203.

Chapter VIII

NAPIER, MAITLAND, AND THE EASTERN FRONTIER, 1839–1846

SHORTLY AFTER Andries Stockenstrom left for England in the summer of 1838, Sir George Napier wrote an appraisal of the man he assumed would never return as lieutenant governor. Stockenstrom, he concluded, was "one of the ablest fellows I ever knew," and if the colony was restored to tranquillity the credit should go mainly to him, for his knowledge and judgment of frontier conditions were unequaled.[1] Despite the alienation of the two after Stockenstrom's forced resignation, Napier never altered his opinion that Stockenstrom knew the Kaffir tribes as did no other white man.[2] This refusal to allow personal pique to influence his judgment reflected a basic virtue in Napier's character; he was a straightforward, honorable man.

Napier was not always discriminating in his judgment of associates. At the time of his appointment one of his closest friends, Sir John Herschel, had said that "the General will do well if he can be kept out of the hands of bad men." [3] Herschel implied no reflection on Napier's moral fiber or courage, but he recognized that the general, a "simple man with ambitions worthy of his family," could be duped by devious advisers. Certainly Napier was credulous, but the deficiencies of his governorship were not caused by sinister influences. Rather, they were the product of his applying to civilian responsibilities experience that was almost entirely military. Napier was ambitious to be remembered as the general who kept the peace. Stockenstrom's unpopularity contributed to unrest; further, he was a civilian and Napier considered it essential that the official in charge of the frontier combine the powers of civil authority and military command. The governor's selection for the lieutenant-governorship was Colonel John Hare, an officer of long

---

[1] George Napier to Richard Napier, July 13, 1838, Napier Papers, Add. MSS 49168, British Museum.

[2] See *Report of the Select Committee on the Kafir Tribes,* 1851, p. 204.

[3] Philip to Ellis, Sept. ——, 1838, SAF file, LMS Archives.

experience and little imagination, whose natural disinclination to action was accentuated by the physical infirmities of his declining years. Hare had "as great an abhorrence of war" as Napier himself. Napier wrote: "He has a gentle and peaceful disposition, high honour, fine temper, mild manners, but *firm as a rock,* in a righteous cause, and *solidly liberal* in all his ideas. . . . He like myself pretends to no cleverness of talent, only zeal, activity, good and temperate judgment, and no other wish but to do his duty." [4] Napier was correct in that Hare was not "clever," but he greatly overestimated his vitality.

The best that can be said of the appointment was that Napier might conceivably have made a worse one. Colonel Henry Somerset, whom both Bourke and D'Urban had singled out for recognition for his asininity, had applied for the position on the basis of his intimate knowledge of frontier conditions and his popularity with both Boers and Kaffirs.[5] Somerset's appointment would have been a disaster; Hare's was merely a blunder. Before his death in 1846 the lieutenant governor had achieved the rare distinction of uniting all elements of the white population, from the missionaries to the extreme settlers, in the belief that he was unqualified for the office he held. As successor to Stockenstrom, Hare at first had the sympathy of most of the Grahamstown community, but his inactivity soon produced an alienation, and during the War of the Axe he was generally regarded with contempt; one of the settlers, J. M. Bowker, in asking Napier to recall Hare, wrote that his want of judgment and foresight had brought ruin to the frontier, and "that his every act up to this moment is that of incompetency and imbecility." [6] Bowker, one of a family of "wild men," was incapable of speaking in measured language, and he was unfair to Hare, who was no imbecile but was simply invested with responsibilities beyond his powers.

Any official occupying Hare's position, however able, would have been subject to severe criticism, for the system he was required to administer was fundamentally unsound. Stockenstrom's treaties, in the eyes of the chiefs, were not only an agreement with the British government but a personal covenant with a man they respected. They assumed that the replacement of Stockenstrom indicated a change of policy which could only be for the worse. Had Stockenstrom remained in office in good health and undistracted by the barbs of his enemies,

---

[4] George Napier to Richard Napier, Jan. 18, 1839, Napier Papers, Add. MSS 49168.

[5] Somerset to Glenelg, July 13, 1838, C.O. 48/198, P.R.O.

[6] George E. Cory, *The Rise of South Africa* (5 vols.; London: Longmans, Green, 1921–1930), IV, 466.

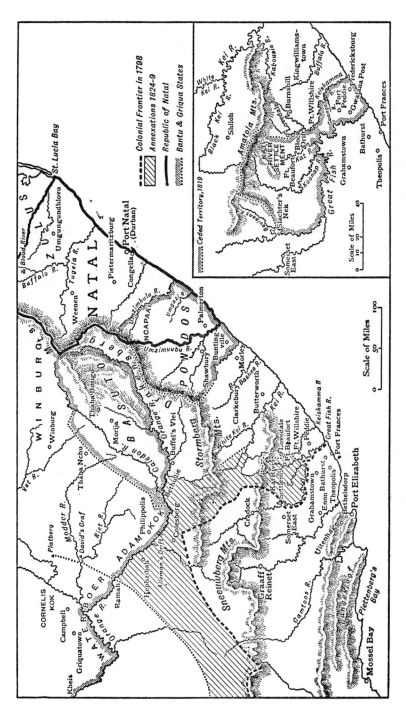

EASTERN AND NORTHEASTERN FRONTIERS OF CAPE COLONY, 1798–1844

his system would undoubtedly have worked more effectively. Stockenstrom would certainly have been more vigorous in the application of
the treaties.[7] Testifying before a parliamentary committee in 1851,
two wars later, Stockenstrom reiterated his conviction that the only
effective policy toward the Kaffirs was one that recognized them as
"barbarians who will plunder, and require to be kept tight," though
treated with strict justice and humanity.[8] The policy of Hare and
Napier was not one of keeping them "tight"; it was characterized by
strong words and lax measures.

Napier's determination to avoid war was reinforced by the inadequacy of his military resources. William Shaw of the Wesleyan Missionary Society assumed that the "soft" policy of Napier and Hare
toward the Gaikas reflected the governor's tendency to truckle to the
London Missionary Society, which favored the Gaikas, against the
Wesleyan chiefs.[9] At the same time John Philip was expressing his
"trembling anxiety" that unless Stockenstrom returned there would be
another war.[10] Napier's policy had nothing to do with sectarian jeal-
ousies; his creed was peace.

Occasionally, after much provocation, Napier and Hare used force
against offending chiefs, but their actions were sporadic and unpredictable. In September, 1838, Napier had exacted a promise from the
Tembu chiefs to return all the stolen cattle traced to their country,
but months passed without any action by the chiefs. Finally in April,
1839, Hare with a detachment of the Cape Corps entered their lands
to enforce payment. The chiefs promised to make restitution within
twenty-four hours, but did not do so. Hare heard that their cattle
were in fact being driven to uninhabited country beyond the mountains, and ordered his troops to seize the required number. They
carried out their orders enthusiastically, driving in 450 head of cattle,
considerably more than the Tembu tribes allegedly owed the colony,
at a cost of one tribesman shot in the operation. Hare ordered the

---

[7] Thomas Philipps stated that Stockenstrom told him that Napier had been too
lax in enforcement of the treaties and that Lord Glenelg's orders had been that the
Kaffirs should be treated humanely, but that if they "behaved ill," Stockenstrom was
to understand that the safety of the colonists was to be the primary object. On his
first meeting with Napier, Stockenstrom mentioned this order of Glenelg's, and the
governor replied that he had received similar instructions. See "A concise Narrative
of events . . . ," enclosed in Maitland to Gladstone, Oct. 1, 1846, C.O. 48/264, P.R.O.

[8] Testimony of Stockenstrom, June 19, 1851, *Report of the Select Committee on
the Kafir Tribes*, p. 167.

[9] Shaw to Beecham, Feb. 1, 1839, MMS Archives.

[10] Philip to Ellis, Feb. 22, 1839, SAF 16-3, LMS Achives.

resident agent to select the exact number owed at a fair valuation and to return the rest.[11]

This action was approved by the Colonial Office as a legitimate exercise of military force. But sporadic demonstrations by military parties, while they might accomplish the immediate objective, contributed to war. They were actions against a people and their chief and not against an individual thief, on the assumption that the depredations could be committed only with the tacit approval of the tribe. There was much justification for this belief if the depredators were members of the tribe, as was by no means certain in many instances, but whether "guilty" or "innocent" the tribe was embittered by invasions of its lands and confiscation of cattle.

The frontier system satisfied neither governor nor chief. Napier fumed at the failure of the chiefs to fulfill their obligations, and the chiefs resented the harangues of the lieutenant governor at their quarterly meetings and nourished one another's fears of impending measures. They saw an omen of evil in the appointment of the arrogant Colonel Hare who spoke to them in such high tones. The seizure of Tembu cattle increased their alarm. The Gaika tribes told their diplomatic agent that if armed parties entered their territories to seize cattle, they would regard this invasion as a declaration of war. Shortly thereafter the rumor circulated among them that the government intended to replace the agent, Captain C. L. Stretch, whom like Stockenstrom they had come to respect as a just man; they informed Hare that if Stretch left them, they would not accept another agent in his place. Hare, unaccustomed to being addressed by Kaffirs in such direct terms, concluded that agitators must have stirred up the chiefs. He told the chiefs that their language was unbecoming and that if he decided to replace Stretch, though he had no immediate intention of doing so, he would act without consulting them.[12] This response, of course, gave further substance to the fears of the chiefs. Far away in London the staff of the Colonial Office read the accounts of this conference with grave misgivings. The Parliamentary Undersecretary confessed that he did not admire the tone of Hare's or Napier's letters, and that it was "the mark of a feeble mind" to attribute every expression of Kaffir disaffection to agitators.[13] Had Hare and Napier seen

---

[11] Hare to Napier, April 24, 1839, enclosure in Napier to Glenelg, May 7, 1839, C.O. 48/200, P.R.O.

[12] Napier to Russell, Feb. 17, 1840, C.O. 48/207, P.R.O.

[13] Minutes on Napier to Russell, Feb. 17, 1840, *ibid.*

these observations they would undoubtedly have commented that officials in London did not know their Kaffirs.

By September, 1840, Napier had become convinced that the Stockenstrom treaty system could not be continued without major modifications. Border farmers were besieging Hare with complaints of plunder by Kaffirs and of the murder of armed herdsmen whom the settlers were required by the treaties to assign to watch their stock. The temper of the colonists, as reported by Hare, was dangerous; unless some action was taken to redress their grievances, they might take the law into their own hands and form a commando to enter Kaffirland to retake plundered cattle, and the result would certainly be another war.[14]

In Cape Town these reports were received as evidence of the imminent breakdown of the treaties and as proof of the necessity for drastic measures against offending tribes. Among those most prominent in advocating a stronger line was Judge William Menzies, whose characteristics often belied his judicial title. Menzies was essentially visceral rather than cerebral, a man of great courage and resolution, but inclined to act without full consideration of the facts. While Napier remained under Menzies' influence, he was inclined to agree with the judge's opinion, for he was overly subject to the influences of men whose wisdom he assumed to be greater than his own; but when the governor arrived on the frontier, he observed conditions utterly different from what he had been led to expect. Instead of imminent war he found "the most profound tranquillity." There had been few depredations for several weeks, and the chiefs had exerted themselves to recover colonial property.[15] Nevertheless, he referred Menzies' proposed changes to the Gaika agent, C. L. Stretch, whose knowledge of the Kaffirs he regarded as second only to Stockenstrom's. Stretch was appalled. The supplementary treaties that Menzies had drawn up would have gutted the Stockenstrom system by granting wide latitude to the colonists to enter Kaffirland in pursuit of stolen property.[16] If Napier attempted to reimpose the old order, there was certain to be war. Instead, Stretch suggested certain minor modifications to which he was certain the chiefs would agree provided that the implications were fully explained. Napier accepted this advice;

---

[14] Napier to Russell, confidential, Sept. 21, 1840, C.O. 48/208, P.R.O.

[15] Napier to Russell, Nov. 6, 1840, *ibid.*

[16] Napier to Russell, Dec. 11, 1840, *ibid.;* Memorandum no. 1, by Stretch, 1846, Philip 2–6, LMS Archives,

Stretch convinced the Gaika chiefs that they had nothing to fear from the changes; and Napier was able at conferences in December, 1840, conducted "in all good humour," to gain the consent of the chiefs of all the Kaffir tribes to Stretch's suggestions. The revised treaties eliminated the requirement of maintaining an armed herds- man, which had caused high casualties among herdsmen without increasing security for stock; gave unarmed colonists the right to pursue their property into Kaffir territory; and assigned to the chiefs responsibility for the apprehension of murderers and their trial and punishment according to Kaffir law.[17]

These revisions of the Stockenstrom treaties did not fundamentally change the frontier system. They were not imposed alterations. But another change, initiated by the colonists rather than the government, had unfortunate effects in stimulating the antagonism of the frontier farmers and contributing to the ruination of the treaty system. News- papers on the frontier began printing lists of stolen animals in two categories, "Reclaimable" and "Not Reclaimable." Those in the first category were animals lost to the colonists which could properly be reclaimed under the treaties. Those in the second were allegedly stolen but for various reasons could not be so claimed, as the spoor might have been lost or the animal might have wandered away; any animal that a farmer claimed to have lost by theft could appear on the "Not Reclaimable" list. The publication of this list in the *Grahamstown Journal* and other newspapers gave an impression of lawlessness which the facts did not justify. Animals lost or strayed as well as stolen appeared on the list, and any theft by white, Hottentot, Fingo, or Kaffir was attributed to the Kaffirs. This innovation developed by the press of the eastern district in coöperation with frontier officials was probably more destructive of Stockenstrom's measures than any mod- ification in the treaties themselves. It convinced the farmers, and eventually the Cape government as well, that the system was bankrupt; and it convinced the Kaffir chiefs of the malevolent intentions of the Europeans. Makomo expressed the chiefs' state of mind when he told Stretch that since Stockenstrom's departure the government seemed content "to take half the Treaties." [18]

Downing Street read Napier's reassuring dispatches with satisfaction, and expressed gratification that he and his lieutenant governor were imbued "with the spirit of justice and humanity" enjoined by the

[17] Cory, *op. cit.*, IV, 353.
[18] Memorandum no. 1, by Stretch, 1846, Philip 2–6, LMS Archives.

Glenelg dispatch of December, 1835.[19] These noble sentiments were not mere cant. Lord John Russell as colonial secretary, like his predecessors, accepted an imperial responsibility for the protection of primitive peoples against aggression by British colonists. The sense of higher obligation is evident in a note of Russell's in 1841: "It should be the policy of the Governor to draw closer the connexion between the Colony & the Caffre tribes, to influence them by means of the Missionaries and resident Agents, and to punish any colonist who may do them injury so that they may look up to the British Power as their friend & protector." [20]

Missionaries and resident agents, however, could not transform the Kaffir society into law-abiding Victorian Christians, and the punishment of colonists who "did the Kaffirs injury," while desirable as a manifestation of British justice, did not go to the heart of the matter. The problem was not that individual colonists maltreated Kaffirs— in the 1840's such incidents were infrequent—but that the two societies were fundamentally incompatible. The collisions between emigrant Boers and native tribes far beyond the frontier were a manifestation of the "natural" relationship between settlers and tribesmen; the interposition of the imperial authority on the Cape eastern frontier restrained these tendencies, but with inadequate resources. Whatever government was in office, the policy of London was to pare military expenditures, not to expand them, and Napier's requests for reinforcements were uniformly rejected. These "barren and unprofitable regions" were a morass which swallowed up large military expenditures without any prospect of ultimate returns.[21]

The emphasis on economy strengthened Napier's resolution to avoid provocative actions. Thus, when chiefs resisted demands for restitution of cattle, he did not press them to the point where war might become necessary. An illustration of the Napier policy was his treatment of the case of a farmer named Neiland who reported that Kaffirs had stolen forty-three of his cattle, valued at £322.10, and murdered his herdsman. The spoor was traced into Makomo's country and he thus became by the treaties responsible for recovery of the cattle. Through Makomo's exertions, fifteen head were recovered and it was proved

---

[19] Russell to Napier, Dec. 31, 1840, C.O. 49/34, P.R.O.

[20] Minute by Russell, [April, 1841], on Napier to Russell, Jan. 7, 1841, C.O. 48/211, P.R.O.

[21] These were Stephen's sentiments, and in this opinion he was in agreement with the views of the Secretary of State (see minutes on Napier to Russell, June 1, 1841, C.O. 48/212, P.R.O.).

to the satisfaction of the agent that the thieves had in fact been from Tyalie's tribe, not Makomo's. But Tyalie denied that more than twenty head had ever entered his country. In addition to the fifteen recovered by Makomo, Tyalie sent in twenty-five cattle, valued at £105, as payment for those still missing and as compensation for the murder. By the terms of the treaties Tyalie's refusal to make full restitution could have justified forcible measures by the government, but instead Hare paid Neiland from the colonial treasury, and the murderer went unpunished.[22] Russell approved this expenditure, but suggested that such use of colonial funds should be rare and, even when necessary, no more than half of the estimated loss should be paid to the aggrieved party, and concluded by reasserting his conviction that the best means of civilizing the Kaffirs was "to cultivate peace with them, and to keep up a constant intercourse with them by means of agents, missionaries, and merchants." [23] Russell's Tory successor, Lord Stanley, offered no more constructive advice.

By the end of 1842 it was evident to the Colonial Office, as it was to Napier, that the treaty system was ineffective. But they agreed that there was no practicable alternative. Stanley's parliamentary undersecretary hesitantly suggested that "if we have the power I must say that I think the removal from our frontier of those tribes who are what in Scotch law is called 'thieves by habit and repute' would be a good measure," [24] but his suggestion evoked no response.

Lieutenant Governor Hare, who had never understood the merits of Stockenstrom's treaties, had long since concluded that the system was worse than worthless. In August, 1842, he wrote Napier that four years of experience convinced him that the treaties were an invitation to plunder, that the Kaffirs, in particular the Gaika tribes, were "a nation of irreclaimable thieves," and that it had been a serious blunder to allow them to return to locations so close to the border. At his quarterly meetings with the chiefs he berated them for their faithlessness and threatened them with summary expulsion, fully cognizant that he was in no position to carry out his threats and that the chiefs were aware of his impotence.[25]

---

[22] Napier to Russell, June 1, 1841, *ibid.*
[23] Russell to Napier, Aug. 25, 1841, *ibid.*
[24] Minute by Hope, Jan. 25, 1843, on Napier to Stanley, Nov. 7, 1842, C.O. 48/222, P.R.O.
[25] Hare to Napier, Aug. 6, 1842, enclosure in Napier to Stanley, Nov. 7, 1842, *ibid.* A member of the Colonial Office staff commented on Hare's confession of the emptiness of his threats, "if so, the threats are best spared."

Hare did not understand that much of what he considered to be willfulness was symptomatic of disturbances within the Kaffir society, involving struggles for power among the chiefs and discontent among the tribes. The titular head of the Gaikas, Sandile, a feckless man without courage or ability, was anxious to justify the status heredity had conferred upon him. The ex-Regent Makomo, though debauched by liquor, was yet the giant of the Gaikas, to whom the petty chiefs usually looked for guidance; but he was stripped of the appurtenances of power when Sandile came of age. Both blacks and whites recognized the exceptional quality of Makomo. One officer on duty on the frontier wrote in April, 1843, that if the Kaffirs attacked the colony "one man and only one [Makomo] seems to me capable of producing and conducting so serious an evil," because he had "ability, boldness, energy, cunning—and the prestige of Rank." Makomo, this officer asserted, was "the hinge on which Caffre land turns"; he was "a powerful instrument for good or evil." [26]

In the early 1840's it seemed not at all unlikely that this influence would be for evil. The young men of the tribes were eager for war, and the British were evidently weak. Rumors circulated among the tribes at the end of 1842 that British troops had been defeated by the emigrant Boers, that the tribes beyond the Orange River had joined the Boers, and that the border was now virtually undefended. Theophilus Shepstone, assigned to the frontier post of Fort Peddie, reported that this erroneous information had transformed the character of the Kaffirs; they were now arrogant and "spoke in ecstasies of the success of the Boers and the destruction of the British," and exulted "at the downfall of those they now denominate their proud and haughty neighbors and late rulers." This language was coupled with the more practical demonstration of "making shoes," an ominous sign that the Kaffirs shortly intended to be in motion.[27] Shepstone's observation was significant; the only deterrent to a Kaffir rush into the colony was force, stronger force than was available.

Further evidence of the disturbed state of Kaffirland was the attempt to kill Sutu, mother of Sandile, as a witch. Chief Tyalie died in May, 1842, and Sutu was charged by a witch doctor with responsibility for his death. There was great excitement throughout Kaffirland, and reports reached the colony that the tribes might make a rush into the

[26] Johnstone to D'Urban, April 18, 1843, D'Urban Papers, X, Cape Archives.

[27] Shepstone to Hudson, Jan. 6, 1843, enclosure in Napier to Stanley, Jan. 6, 1843, C.O. 48/243, P.R.O. "Making shoes" was a sign of war, as the Kaffirs wore shoes only on long journeys.

colony. The Gaika agent C. L. Stretch believed that the "smelling out" of Sutu, who had exercised considerable influence among the Gaika clans, was connected with the political ambitions of Makomo and Umhala, who had favored her death by burning, but that the sentence was delayed pending the arrival of two of the principal chiefs, Eno and Botma, at the council. Meanwhile Sutu took refuge at the home of missionaries, and when the full council was convened, the object of the enemies was frustrated by the opposition of these two chiefs and Eno's son Stock. But for several weeks there was panic in the colony and Hare put the troops on an emergency footing.[28] The affair of Sutu illustrated how little officials in the colony knew of the currents affecting the tribes across the border; they saw disturbances but could not probe the causes.

While this agitation was at its height, Dr. John Philip was on his way back to Cape Town from a visit to the north. In the village of Somerset he and James Read, Senior, met the Wesleyan missionary, W. B. Boyce, at the home of a local minister. At this seemingly unpremeditated meeting, the conversation ranged for more than four hours over the affairs of the northern and eastern borders. According to Boyce's testimony, Philip, in commenting on the disturbed state of the tribes, expressed his regrets that the grand principles of the D'Urban treaties of September, 1835, had not been maintained, because only on such a basis could order and civilization be brought to the tribes, and he and Boyce agreed that they would combine their efforts to seek the restoration of the D'Urban system.[29] At first reading Boyce's report seems incredible, but his version of the conversation may well have been substantially correct. Philip had opposed D'Urban's seizure of Kaffir lands for purposes of colonial settlement, but he had long advocated the extension of British authority over the border tribes for their protection and as a means to the promotion of Christianity and civilization. D'Urban's September system avowedly sought these objectives. Napier's policy of drift offered no hope for the future, only the continuation of mutual exasperation, followed, sooner or later, by war.

The Napier luck held, and war came later rather than sooner. Napier was able to leave Cape Colony with his prophecy fulfilled that he would be a governor who kept the peace. But before his departure he came perilously close to bringing on the war that he had vowed to avoid at almost any cost. Even with due discount for the exaggera-

---

[28] Napier to Stanley, May 30, 1842, C.O. 48/219, P.R.O.
[29] Philipps to D'Urban, Aug. 24, 1842, D'Urban Papers, X.

tions of frontier farmers and of border officials, it had become evident
to the governor that serious trouble was imminent. Depredations were
again on the rise, and the chiefs met Hare's demands for restitution
with evasions or "insolence." Napier reluctantly concluded that unless
he demonstrated the power of the government, the chiefs might concert an invasion on the assumption that the colony was defenseless.
The troops at his disposal were few, and his available manpower had
been drained to a dangerously low level by commitments in Natal and
on the Orange River. The total force on the eastern frontier in June,
1843, was 1,209 rank and file, and from that number a substantial
proportion was needed to garrison Grahamstown, Fort Beaufort, Fort
Peddie, and nineteen other smaller posts. Hare estimated that the
maximum force available for a punitive expedition would be 700
men.[30] This military power was obviously insufficient to take action
against a major chief and to risk a general war. Hare found an appropriate object for punishment in a minor chief named Tola who
had the reputation of being an active thief. The lieutenant governor
instructed the diplomatic agents with the Gaika and Slambie tribes
to enlist the coöperation of Sandile and Umhala in Tola's expulsion,
the bait being the "eating up" of the culprit's cattle. These chiefs
agreed to join with the troops, and an elaborate plan was devised for
an invasion of troops, Kaffirs, and Fingoes to surround Tola and
prevent his escape. Not surprisingly, when the arrangements were
complete and the troops under Colonel Somerset had finally moved,
Tola and his followers had escaped with most of their cattle.[31]

The expedition was a spectacular failure. At a meeting of the Gaika
chiefs after Tola's expulsion, Hare announced the intention to assign
Tola's lands to Eno's son Stock and to reoccupy Fort Willshire, on
the Keiskama River, which had been unoccupied since Stockenstrom
had withdrawn the troops from it.[32] But, though Hare reported that
all the chiefs present, including Makomo and Sandile, "readily gave
their assent," [33] Eno and his sons suddenly lost interest after receiving
a message from Sandile, and no other chief would accept responsibility
for occupying the territory. Finally, in October, 1843, Hare reached
agreement with the chiefs at a meeting at which Tola himself was
present that Tola's lands would be assigned to Botma and that he would

[30] The correspondence is enclosed in Napier to Stanley, July 8, 1843, C.O. 48/230,
P.R.O.

[31] Johnstone to D'Urban, June, 1843, D'Urban Papers, X.

[32] Napier to Stanley, June 30, 1843, C.O. 48/230, P.R.O.

[33] Hare to Napier, June 29, 1843, enclosure in Napier to Stanley, July 8, 1843, *ibid.*

no longer be recognized as a chief. This agreement was in fact a victory for the chiefs, as Botma was the chief to whom Tola's land had been assigned by the Stockenstrom treaties, and who in fact had been assumed by the Cape government to be Tola's confederate in his marauding activities. Hare also won the consent of the chiefs to the construction of a military post in Tola's territory which was to be named Post Victoria.[34] But the troops were withdrawn from Fort Willshire within a month,[35] Post Victoria did not become an important military stronghold, and Napier was forced to admit that his venture in salutary punishment had not accomplished its purpose.

When petitioners from Grahamstown and other districts of the eastern province called for a return to the principles of the D'Urban treaties, Napier and Hare observed that even if it were practical to repudiate the existing system, the D'Urban measures would offer no greater hope for success. D'Urban himself had admitted that direct rule over the Kaffirs could not succeed without martial law, which the judges had declared illegal, and a sizable standing army larger than the present frontier force or than the British government was willing to provide. Even if the Kaffirs could be forcibly removed beyond the Keiskama, settlers would inevitably move into the vacated area and the old problems of European absorption of Kaffir land and Kaffir appropriation of European cattle would be reproduced. Napier and Hare agreed that the existing system encouraged the chiefs to connive in thievery, but they were directly opposed in their views of the alternative. Hare, whose patience with Kaffir evasion was exhausted, advocated reprisals by military force against any chief who did not fulfill his obligations. Napier suggested a gentler approach by which chiefs on the border would be paid annual allowances, contingent on the good behavior of their tribesmen.[36]

The Napier-Hare interchange was in effect a presentation to the Colonial Office of alternative programs that might be executed by Napier's successor, for Napier was aware that he was about to be replaced and was marking time pending the new governor's arrival. There was little in either proposal which seemed to Downing Street to promise a change for the better. Certainly a return to the D'Urban

[34] Hare to Napier, Oct. 3, 1843, enclosure in Napier to Stanley, Oct. 23, 1843, C.O. 48/232, P.R.O. For a description of Post Victoria, see Cory, *op. cit.*, IV, 370–371 and *passim*.

[35] Hare to Napier, June 29, 1843, enclosure in Napier to Stanley, July 8, 1843, C.O. 48/230, P.R.O.

[36] Napier to Stanley, Dec. 4, 1843, and enclosure, Hare to Napier, Nov. 13, 1843, C.O. 48/233, P.R.O.

policy of annexation was unthinkable. British authority could be reasserted only by war, which would be "ignominious if unsuccessful, inglorious if successful—and ultimately improvident whether successful or not." It would be incomparably cheaper to pay the farmers all their losses each year than to waste British revenues in such a bootless enterprise as the war of 1834–1835, when 5,000 men had crossed and recrossed Kaffirland, using up vast sums of money, laying waste the cornfields, killing cattle, and uprooting peoples, "military exploits" of which "one was ashamed to read," and accomplishing no constructive result. Hare's proposals for coercion by military force were likely to result in a return to the days of interminable border wars, and Napier's idea of paying the chiefs for good behavior, while perhaps worth an experiment, was at best a palliative. James Stephen, who considered any expenditures in the deserts of Cape Colony to be unjustified, had no sympathy for the plaints of the settlers. He wrote: "If men will settle in the neighbourhood of marauding Tribes, they cannot, I think, claim of their Government that at the National expence they shd. be rescued from the natural penalty of that improvidence any more than vine dressers and farmers at the foot of Vesuvius can expect indemnity against the effects of an irruption." [37]

Stanley was not willing to go so far as the Permanent Undersecretary in dismissing Kaffir depredations as an act of God for which the imperial government should assume no liability, but he would not endorse the use of force except as a last extremity. In effect the staff of the Colonial Office could agree only on the conclusion that they should await recommendations from Napier's successor, Sir Peregrine Maitland, on measures to remedy the evils of chronic border depredations.

Sir George Napier welcomed the new governor with more than usual warmth. For six years he had skirted the edge of disaster; and by caution, forbearance, and rare good luck he had ended his tenure without war. Through economy, good management, and a rising revenue, the Cape government was in a sounder financial state than it had been within living memory. When he transferred his authority to Sir Peregrine Maitland in May, 1844, Napier proudly informed his superiors that "the colony is in a very prosperous condition, and the most profound peace prevails beyond the borders." [38] This was the character of his governorship as he wished posterity to remember it— the Napiers were always abnormally anxious about the verdict of

[37] Minute by Stephen, Feb. 9, 1844, on Napier to Stanley, Dec. 4, 1843, *ibid.*
[38] Napier to Stanley, March 18, 1844, C.O. 48/239, P.R.O.

posterity—but Sir George was aware that the apparent affluence and tranquillity were deceptive. Catastrophe might befall the colony at any moment. Napier left before that moment struck; Maitland reaped the whirlwind.

Sir Peregrine Maitland was sixty-seven when he became governor of the Cape, but he seemed old beyond his years and the adversity that befell him within the next two years accelerated his physical and mental decline. In 1846 Earl Grey, who had known Maitland for many years, estimated that he was between seventy and eighty years of age, and concluded that Maitland, who had never been "a man of any great ability," should long since have been retired from office.[39] Others who were more kindly disposed spoke of Maitland's mildness and his "devoted piety"; [40] some suggested that ten or twenty years earlier he might have been an excellent governor.[41] But by 1846 none considered him to be equal to his responsibilities. Before the outbreak of a Kaffir war, Maitland's inadequacies were masked by the efficiency of his colonial secretary, John Montagu, who wrote many of the governor's dispatches,[42] but Montagu could not shield Maitland from the awful responsibilities of making decisions of "high policy."

The incompetence of Sir Peregrine Maitland was not primarily attributable to age. As lieutenant governor of Upper Canada between 1818 and 1828, he had displayed constitutional indolence and bigotry which provoked the reformers to fury. William Lyon Mackenzie wrote, in the *Colonial Advocate,* that Sir Peregrine was like the lilies of the field who toiled not, neither did they spin. Mackenzie described the governor's stately movements from his residence at Niagara to that at York in the social season as "the migration from the blue bed to the brown." Maitland's appointment to the Cape was a testament to the continuing influence of family connections in colonial appointments —his wife was the daughter of the Duke of Richmond—and a demonstration of the evils of such practices.

---

[39] Grey to Russell, Aug. 19, 1846, Russell Papers, P.R.O. 30/22/5, P.R.O.

[40] Stephen to Grey, Aug. 18, 1846, Grey Papers, Prior's Kitchen, University of Durham.

[41] C. W. Hutton, ed., *The Autobiography of the Late Sir Andries Stockenstrom* (2 vols.; Cape Town: Juta, 1887), I, 215. These views are expressed by Stockenstrom's editor.

[42] Stephen stated that some of Maitland's dispatches were "so very good as to reveal, just as clearly as if the signature were there, the agency of Mr. Montagu"; those that appeared to be Maitland's own work seemed "entirely wanting in that force of mind and will which the occasion required" (Stephen to Grey, Aug. 18, 1846, Grey Papers).

During the first months of his governorship, Maitland made a favorable impression upon all elements of colonial society. The heads of missionary associations were struck by his obvious Christian devoutness.[43] Philip again had entree to Government House, and the governor not only listened to him but followed his advice with regard to Boer-Griqua conflicts beyond the Orange River.[44] Before the end of the first year of his governorship Maitland had evoked enthusiastic applause from frontier settlers by revisions of the treaties with the Kaffir tribes. He seemed to have general support from the white population. But, as is so often true of a government that seeks to please everyone, Maitland's policies aggravated the basic problems that he confronted.

Maitland did not cause the disasters with which his administration is associated; no governor could have subdued the eruptions that rocked the border country from the Orange River to Natal. On the eastern border frontier settlers clamored for relief from depredations which they alleged were encouraged by the Stockenstrom system, while beyond the Fish River the structure of tribal society was being subjected to severe blows from within as well as without. A chief risked his authority if he tried to prevent his followers from plundering; the easy and popular course was to connive in their thievery. The internal politics of Kaffirland dictated that British demands for restitution be met with evasion, and encouraged open defiance if troops were sent into Kaffir territory to seize cattle. The danger was enhanced by the irresoluteness of Sandile, who was tempted to adopt a strong line to prove his power.

There were other more fundamental influences toward disorder. The chiefs, with good reason, saw in the white settlements across the border the enemy of tribal society. The Europeans threatened not only their lands but their very souls. Christian missionaries who sought to corrupt the people with strange doctrines hostile to the tribal mores were only one manifestation of this mortal danger that European society, in all its aspects, posed to tribal authority. It evidenced itself in manifold ways—in the arrogance of officials who dealt with Kaffir chiefs as if they were fractious children, in the contempt expressed by settlers' words and actions, in the insufferable haughtiness of the governors and their representatives when they lectured them for their sins or complimented them on their good behavior. With whatever degree of clarity the chiefs analyzed the threat of the Europeans, they understood that there would be no peaceful coexistence. Had Maitland

---

[43] William Shaw, *The Story of My Mission in South-Eastern Africa* (London: Hamilton, Adams, 1860), p. 171.

[44] Philip to Directors, LMS, June 24, 1844, SAF 20-2, LMS.

recognized the nature of the problems confronting him, he would still have been powerless to cope with them. The few hundred troops at his disposal might provoke a war; they could not prevent one.

Maitland had come to the colony with instructions to recommend alterations in a border system that the Colonial Office considered no longer effective, but he had received no guidance as to the direction of such changes. He was given almost complete discretion. Between March and September, 1844, Maitland remained in Cape Town, considering with leisurely reflection the nature of a new policy on which he received widely conflicting advice. The members of his executive council, however, agreed that the Stockenstrom treaties must be reinforced to give the colonial government power to apprehend and convict before colonial tribunals Kaffirs who had committed crimes within the colony. They suggested that rewards be offered to chiefs who apprehended such criminals and that annual presents be given to chiefs who restrained their followers from thievery in the colony.[45]

In September Maitland was impelled to action by a report from the frontier that a farmer named Jan de Lange had been killed in an encounter with Kaffir thieves near the Fish River. Hare professed to have proof that Makomo was shielding one of his principal councilors who was the grand instigator of the marauding expedition.[46] The evidence on which Hare based his conclusions was flimsy indeed,[47] and there was at least some question as to whether de Lange's party was not itself in violation of the treaties for having been armed. But Hare saw in the killing of de Lange an opportunity to apply the policy of condign chastisement from which Napier had restrained him. On the justification that Makomo and another chief, Sonto, had shielded some of the murderers, Hare sent a body of approximately 300 troops, dragoons, Cape Mounted Rifles, and infantry to occupy their territories until the culprits were given up. This display of force, Hare reported with satisfaction, "had all the effects I desired of striking terror into our troublesome and deceitful neighbours and forcing them to a compliance with my just and reasonable demands of surrendering to justice and for trial either before Colonial or Kaffir tribunals the murderers of the unfortunate Farmer De Lange." [48] Maitland's response to the

---

[45] Minutes, Executive Council, Sept. 2, 1844, C.O. 51/53, P.R.O.

[46] Hare to Maitland, July 31, 1844, enclosure in Maitland to Stanley, Sept. 6, 1844, C.O. 48/244, P.R.O.

[47] Cory, *op. cit.*, IV, 376.

[48] Hare to Maitland, Aug. 15, 1844, enclosure in Maitland to Stanley, Sept. 6, 1844, C.O. 48/244, P.R.O.

news of this precipitate action was to applaud the lieutenant governor's "judicious" conduct. After expressing confidence that Hare's prompt and decisive response to evasion would teach the neighboring chiefs and tribes that they could no longer "harass and plunder British subjects" with impunity,[49] Maitland set out for the frontier on board a Royal Navy steamer appropriately named *Thunderbolt*.

At the time of his departure from Cape Town Maitland was still reputed to be a man of deep humanitarian inclinations. John Philip's son found the governor "not merely a man of true piety but also of liberal principles and enlightened views," a true friend of the missions.[50] Within one week of his arrival in Grahamstown, Maitland had adopted policies that made him the darling of the eastern frontier. In September, 1844, Sir Peregrine, supported by the 27th Regiment, held a great meeting of the Slambie tribes, which had been guilty of relatively little thievery, and announced a new treaty system abrogating the agreements the chiefs had made with Stockenstrom. There was small pretense that these new treaties were negotiated; the chiefs were given an opportunity to thank the governor and to receive gifts of £10 in silver which they carried away in large cotton handkerchiefs which Maitland had thoughtfully provided.[51] This was an imposed system, backed by British bayonets; the backing unfortunately was inadequate.

The news of "liberation" from the Stockenstrom system brought jubilation throughout the eastern province. "The conflagration of tar barrels and bonfires turned night into day and all behaved as if suddenly released from some long-endured thraldom." [52] The *Grahamstown Journal* exulted that the enlightenment of Maitland's treaty had exceeded their wildest hopes; the "decision, far-sightedness, and independency" of the new administration had brought a bright new era to the frontier.[53] War was then only eighteen months away.

After an appropriate time, designed to show the governor's displeasure at their infamous conduct and to excite their alarm that he might be meditating further stern measures, Maitland admitted the Gaikas to his presence early in October. They were "very submissive." He had complimented the Slambies for their good behavior but he

---

[49] Maitland to Hare, Aug. 15, 1844, enclosure in Maitland to Stanley, Sept. 6, 1844, *ibid.*

[50] T. Durant Philip to Tidman, Sept. 28, 1844, SAF 20-3, LMS Archives.

[51] Cory, *op. cit.*, IV, 381.

[52] *Ibid.*, p. 380.

[53] *Grahamstown Journal*, Sept. 26, 1844.

castigated the Gaika chiefs for misconduct which had made it almost impossible to treat with them at all. The Gaika chiefs were appropriately humble and placed themselves at the governor's disposal, saying "we are your children, you must command us." Instead of announcing the provisions of the new treaties at this convocation, Maitland informed the Gaikas that he would communicate the terms of the new treaties through their diplomatic agent.[54]

Comparison of Maitland's treaties with Stockenstrom's does not at first glance reveal differences of such magnitude as to justify the settlers' hosannas. Chiefs were required to deliver thieves to the colonial authorities for punishment and received rewards for so doing, and colonists were to be indemnified not only for their losses but for the expenses of pursuit. The right of building forts and stationing troops in the ceded territory, provided for in the Stockenstrom treaties, was reaffirmed, but the provision forbidding patrolling of the territory was omitted. The governor guaranteed the chiefs annual presents ranging from £50 to £200 so long as they observed the terms of the treaties,[55] thus following a suggestion of Sir George Napier's. But the two treaties were fundamentally different. The Stockenstrom treaties had provided for the right to maintain forts; Maitland exercised the right. Stockenstrom had discontinued the hated patrol system; Maitland reinstituted it. The most significant distinction was in spirit. Stockenstrom had appeared to the chiefs as a liberator from the hated D'Urban era; they trusted him as a man of good will and freely consented to his arrangements. Maitland had none of Stockenstrom's credentials; he had unilaterally repudiated an agreement and imposed upon the tribes a new system, backed by the threat of military force. Maitland, the Xosa chiefs were convinced, was a man of war: "Did you not see the swords of the dragoons?" [56] Henry Calderwood, then a missionary but soon to leave his society to become a political agent, saw in the Maitland treaties an act of war against the Gaikas, and feared the consequences of the governor's injudicious conduct in suddenly breaking the Stockenstrom agreements.[57] Calderwood's forebodings were vindicated sooner than he expected.

---

[54] Maitland to Stanley, Dec. 7, 1844, C.O. 48/245, P.R.O. The Gaika treaties omitted the clause providing for rewards for good behavior.

[55] For an analysis of the differences, see C.O. minute on Maitland to Stanley, Dec. 7, 1844, C.O. 48/245, P.R.O.

[56] Eric A. Walker, *A History of Southern Africa* (London: Longmans, Green, 1957), p. 227.

[57] Calderwood to Directors, LMS, Nov. 14, 1844, SAF 20-3, LMS Archives.

The Gaika tribes, when finally presented with the drafts of Maitland's treaties, refused to accept unless two provisions were deleted. Their first objection was based upon a misunderstanding; they resisted the formation of a court to hear appeals from adjudication by government agents of claims for stolen cattle. But with regard to another provision of the treaty their resistance reflected keen comprehension. Article 20 provided that chiefs would not interfere with any of their subjects who became Christians and decided to reside near missionary villages, and would not molest them for refusing to comply with Kaffir customs. In introducing this article into the treaty Maitland had accepted the advice of missionaries, thus demonstrating his Christian piety. The staff of the Colonial Office found nothing disturbing in the article, which they doubtless considered an enlightened effort to eliminate barbarous customs, but the chiefs saw in its provisions a thrust at the vitals of the tribal system. They told Stretch: "This thing gives us pain, the person who advised the Governor to make this a subject of treaty loves blood [that is, is anxious for war]. It is a missionary who has complained and we want to know who he is—The Governor did not get this complaint in the Colony, it is a missionary." [58]

This direct attack on Kaffir society, coupled with the stationing of troops within tribal territories, confirmed the Gaikas in their suspicions of the hostile intentions of the British authorities, with whom the missionaries were now clearly in alliance. Relations with the colony entered a prewar phase; the question was no longer whether or not, but when, war would occur.

At this critical juncture Maitland's representative on the frontier was almost incapacitated. Colonel Hare, in ill-health and within months of death, burdened with an invalid wife and exhausted with the cares of office, in February, 1845, requested permission to retire.[59] Even before Hare's request the office of lieutenant governor had become subject to question. The position had been created for Stockenstrom; Hare had never been accorded the same responsibilities as his predecessor. In Grahamstown he had been the medium of transmission for reports from the frontier for decision by the government in Cape Town. On rare occasions he exercised independent judgment, as when he sent troops into Kaffirland without consulting the governor, but in general his function was to communicate reports from frontier

----

[58] Cory, *op. cit.*, IV, 385.
[59] Hare to Maitland, Feb. 13, 1845, enclosure in Maitland to Stanley, March 13, 1845, C.O. 48/251, P.R.O.

officials to Cape Town for decisions as to policy, thus adding another echelon and several days of delay to communication.[60]

Maitland does not seem to have recognized the hopelessness of his position. While the Gaika chiefs plotted war and the Slambies vacillated in their calculation of the consequences of joining, and while Boers and Griquas jostled each other beyond the Orange River, the governor professed to believe that he could control unrest along the entire colonial frontier with a total force of less than 2,800 men, including 293 cavalry and 2,477 infantry,[61] and a force immediately available on the Kaffir border of less than 1,600 men.[62]

> What I have to attempt is to act on the fear and sense of interest of the Chiefs; to overawe them into keeping good faith with the Government for their own sakes; to make it advantageous to them to discountenance inroads into the Colony, and to give up the thieves; and also to overawe their people into submission to the Chiefs when they endeavour to carry out the stipulations of the treaties, as otherwise the Chiefs who kept faith with the Government would be set at nought and deposed by the plundering part of their tribes.[63]

To speak of "overawing" with a few redcoats 70,000 warriors, 7,000 of whom were mounted and armed with muskets, was to demonstrate a total misapprehension of the potential adversary. The chiefs were not overawed; on the contrary, they were conscious of British weakness and confident of their own strength.

After Maitland's treaties there was a lull in thievery, but within eight months the border country was again infested with plunderers, bolder and more active than under the Stockenstrom system, and settlers were signing petitions condemning the government for its supineness. Maitland maintained that the fault was not lack of will but lack of power:

> So long as an uncivilized race, greedy of cattle, and equally unscrupulous and adroit as to the mode of obtaining them, lives along such a frontier as separates the Colony from Kafirland, nothing which the Government can do can be expected to prevent altogether the entrance of thieves into the Colony, or destroy their inclination to resist when pursued and attacked. Liability for occasional losses by Kafir depredators must, I fear, be for a long time to come inseparably attached to the position of the Frontier farmers.[64]

---

[60] Maitland to Stanley, Oct. 24, 1845, C.O. 48/253, P.R.O. The lieutenant-governorship was revived in 1847 with the appointment of Sir Henry Young.

[61] F. Somerset to Merivale, July 12, 1851, W.O. 1/447, P.R.O.

[62] Maitland to Stanley, Nov. 17, 1845, C.O. 48/254, P.R.O.

[63] *Ibid.*

[64] *Ibid.*

His treaties, Maitland admitted, had not restrained thievery; only fear of superior force could do so. Under these circumstances, provocative action by the colonial government was highly hazardous, but either through accident or design Hare issued orders that were a direct invitation to war.

Victoria Post, which Maitland had established in the ceded territory to watch for robbers, had not performed that function effectively, and its location was not suitable for a permanent installation, primarily because the water was both inadequate and unwholesome. Maitland recalled that at his first meeting with Sandile in 1844 the chief had expressed willingness to allow construction of a fort in his country, provided that the government paid him an annual rent and acknowledged his sovereignty. One site seemed particularly suitable, at Block Drift, just within the border of Kaffirland. This position in the midst of the Gaika tribes would have permitted observation of the routes into the Amatola Mountains likely to be taken by cattle thieves. Further, Maitland hoped that a fort might become a nucleus of civilization by giving employment to Sandile's people and providing protection for Christian converts who might settle at neighboring mission stations. Sandile may have agreed in 1844 to the erection of a fort, because at that time he feared that his territory might be seized if depredations continued, but in 1846 he was in a different mood. Influenced by the young men of the tribe who were eager for war, he sought to demonstrate his leadership by taking a resolute line. In January, 1846, when a party of five Royal Engineers arrived without notice at Block Drift and pitched their tent to begin a survey, Sandile adopted a high tone. He had recently slapped a white trader and helped himself to the contents of the trader's store. When Stretch sent a Kaffir policeman to protest this expropriation and some recent thefts of oxen, Sandile, surrounded by the young bloods of the tribe, replied that traders, missionaries, and any other white men in his territory were "under his feet," that he would do what he liked with them, and that if the governor had any complaints he should come to see Sandile in person. Further, he told Stretch that the surveyors' tent must be removed within a day.[65]

Such threatening language could not be ignored, and a detachment of troops was sent to Block Drift to protect the surveyors; but, having taken up the challenge, Hare then backed away. At a meeting with Sandile at Block Drift on January 29, 1846, the lieutenant governor, supported by a small detachment of British infantry and cavalry,

[65] Cory, *op. cit.*, IV, 412.

faced Sandile and a mass of armed warriors, estimated at between 4,000 and 5,000, who had assembled because of a rumor that the British planned to take their chief prisoner. Backed by such a force, Sandile was unrepentant. While he denied using offensive language, he repeated the substance of his demand that the British quit his territory. A few days later Hare withdrew the troops and the surveyors from Block Drift.[66] He justified this decision on the grounds that he had committed a blunder and should not let considerations of pride prevent his rectifying his mistake. Maitland, he said, had given orders that an engineering officer should inspect Block Drift, but he had misinterpreted these instructions and had called for a full survey. Sandile's resistance caused him to recognize that, not having secured the prior permission of the chief, he had been guilty of trespassing. Thus he withdrew.[67]

This explanation, whatever it may indicate as to Hare's nobility of character, suggests that the lieutenant governor was incompetent, for the withdrawal of the troops after Sandile's ultimatum was certain to be interpreted as a demonstration of weakness. Hare acted in this way when, by his own reports, Kaffirland was in turmoil and the young men were demanding war. Retreat at such a time brought war nearer.

Maitland's opinion was that Hare had lost an opportunity to humble the war party by taking a strong tone, insisting on the return of stolen cattle and a public apology by Sandile for his threatening language. Such resolution, the governor believed, would have strengthened the hand of the older chiefs who were opposed to war. Whatever the justification of this belief, there was no question that the war party was now in the ascendant. Makomo, aware that the ultimate consequences would be disaster for the tribes, asked asylum for himself and his people in the colony.[68] Across the border the mood was also martial. The Reverend William Shaw, always well informed on the undercurrents in Grahamstown society, in mid-February heard "whispers" that the lieutenant governor intended to test the war spirit of the Kaffirs by moving Victoria Post to the vicinity of Block Drift, but on the colonial side of the boundary. Confronted with troops within his location, Sandile would either submit to the challenge and be humbled, or resist; in either event an end would be made to this intolerable apprehension of Kaffir intentions.[69] In retirement at Wyn-

---

[66] Maitland to Stanley, March 21, 1846, C.O. 48/266, P.R.O.

[67] *Ibid.*

[68] *Ibid.*

[69] Shaw to Stretch, Feb. 18, 1846, SAF Odds 2, LMS Archives.

berg, D'Urban noted with gloomy satisfaction that the eruptions on
the frontier were "fast fulfilling" his predictions of ten years before
that the repudiation of his system would make another Kaffir war
inevitable.[70]

D'Urban's prophecies were soon fulfilled. Early in March, 1846,
a Kaffir appropriated an axe from Fort Beaufort store without paying
for it, and was arrested. His chief, Tola, who had weathered an earlier
storm when the troops had sought to hunt him down and was no
longer himself on the "wanted" list, demanded the man's release. The
frontier commissioner refused and sent the prisoner, handcuffed to a
Hottentot prisoner and under escort of four Hottentot policemen, to
Grahamstown for trial. The party did not arrive. Seven miles out of
Fort Beaufort they were ambushed by Kaffirs, allegedly of Tola's tribe,
and the escort was overpowered. The Hottentot prisoner was killed
and his hand hacked off, and the pilferer of the axe escaped with the
handcuffs dangling from his wrist. Hare interpreted Tola's refusal to
give up the murderers as a declaration of war by the Gaikas. In April
a mixed force of regulars, Cape Mounted Rifles, and colonial volunteers invaded Kaffirland, and within four days suffered a defeat in
which they lost half their baggage train. Thus, disastrously, began the
War of the Axe.[71]

There was no division of opinion in the colony or in Downing Street
that the Kaffirs were in fact the aggressors and must be humbled. Even
John Philip and his son-in-law John Fairbairn agreed. Fairbairn wrote
in the *Commercial Advertiser:*

> His Excellency now proceeds to undertake a work which any man may be
> proud to accomplish. A numerous bold and disorderly people are to be
> brought under the dominion of Law, and compelled to submit all their
> public affairs in the last resort to the final decision of the British Govern-
> ment. He goes, not to exterminate savages, but to subdue anarchy, and to
> establish the reign of justice on a foundation that no barbaric arm can
> shake.[72]

The reaction in London to the news of the outbreak of war was not
expressed in moral terms. Wellington attributed the war to "the in-
sufficiency of the force in the Colony to hold in awe the barbarian
Hordes on the borders of the Colony; owing to the unauthorized deten-
tion in LaPlata of the Troops sent by Her Majesty's Command to rein-

---

[70] D'Urban to Johnstone, private, Feb. 13, 1846, D'Urban Papers, VIII.

[71] For a detailed description see Cory, *op. cit.*, IV, 421 ff.

[72] *South African Commercial Advertiser*, April 1, 1846.

force and to relieve some of the troops at the Cape." [73] While the Colonial Office under the Tory Gladstone and the Whig Grey acknowledged Maitland's forbearance, its preoccupation was with the effective conduct of the war; and Parliament wrangled over expenditures of hundreds of thousands of pounds to subdue a band of savages inhabiting a territory of no conceivable importance to the British Empire.

Jan Tzatzoe, the "Christian chief" who had been feted at Exeter Hall when he appeared with Dr. Philip in 1836, protested that the British, not the Kaffirs, had torn up the Stockenstrom treaties, and that Hare, not Sandile, had committed an act of aggression when he sent troops to Block Drift without the chief's consent.[74] No one heard his plea; the humanitarians were preoccupied with other causes, and the politicians were concerned with the expense of the war and with its speedy conclusion, not with its antecedents.

[73] Wellington to Grey, Dec. 3, 1846, W.O. 1/440, P.R.O.

[74] Statement of Jan Tzatzoe about the commencement of the war of 1846–1847, [n.d.], SAF Odds 3–3, LMS Archives.

Chapter IX

THE GREAT TREK, TRANSORANGIA, AND NATAL, 1834–1846

MEMORY is a flexible instrument for rationalization and self-justification. In 1842 Sir Benjamin D'Urban, brooding over the evils that had befallen South Africa as a result of the reversal of his policies, noted that if his measures had been approved the Amaxosa would have become a nucleus for the civilization of tribes for hundreds of miles along the coast, wars would have ceased, and British commerce would have enjoyed profitable markets among erstwhile enemies. Further, the emigration of "a race of brave, obedient, industrious, and invaluable people" would have been averted, new lands under British jurisdiction would have been opened for the Boers, and the disasters to British arms in Natal would have been avoided.[1] D'Urban's fantasies about the transformation of tribal Africa to peaceful Christian communities may be dismissed as summer madness, and the implication that the Great Trek was a product of a revulsion against the Glenelg-Stockenstrom Negrophilia reflects a conveniently defective sense of chronology. Before the outbreak of the Kaffir war of 1834 the migration across the Orange River had already caused concern in Cape Town. D'Urban, who had at that time assumed that the flight of the malcontents had been caused by the Emancipation Act, would have directed the arrest of Louis Trigardt and several other *Voortrekkers* had his law officers not advised that he had no jurisdiction beyond the colonial boundary.[2]

Nations use the past similarly. In the Afrikaner mythology the trek of the 1830's has become the national epic, a manifestation of the ideals and the virtues that have preserved a people against forces that threat-

---

[1] Note by D'Urban, Sept., 1842, D'Urban Papers, X, Cape Archives.
[2] D'Urban to Somerset, private, Oct. 17, 1834, *ibid.*, VII.

ened to destroy their identity and even their physical existence. No mundane explanations would suffice; the hand of God was evident, and his people lived because they were worthy of his protection.

This was not the perspective from which the British government, in London or in Cape Town, viewed the migration. From the standpoint of imperial policy this eruption beyond the frontiers of the Cape was an extension of disorder. Prior to D'Urban's administration the primary annoyance on the Cape's northern frontiers had been the marauding activities of Bergenaar and Korana thieves who infested the islands of the Orange River, but this had been a minor matter from the distance of Cape Town and a pinprick from London. The intrusion of substantial numbers of Europeans into territories beyond the colony produced problems of far greater magnitude. Reports of the slaughter of natives by Boers were certain to evoke the indignation of humanitarians, and disorder beyond the borders was likely to spread to the colony itself. Sound policy dictated that this migration be controlled; expedient politics decreed that control be at minimum expense. Sir Benjamin D'Urban faced the responsibility of controlling a flood with a pail and a shovel.

The Great Trek is distinguished from previous expansion because of its magnitude, its motivations, and its consequences. There was no parallel in previous eras to the massive, organized movement of the middle 'thirties. In groups varying from a few wagons to as many as a hundred, approximately 10,000 men, women, and children left Cape Colony within the decade 1836–1846. Their motivations have been microscopically examined; and, while authorities vary in the weight they assign to various grievances, they generally agree that there was a higher proportion of "political" causes than in previous treks. From the testimony of the trekkers themselves, and more eloquently from their subsequent actions, the evidence is overwhelming that the movement was accelerated by revulsion against British rule and all that it implied. It is not within the province of this narrative to investigate again a movement that has been studied in such detail. But the Great Trek created problems for colonial policy as difficult as any that the imperial government had to face throughout the nineteenth century. Governors general in India employed far more extensive resources and manpower in support of their border policies; when expansion became necessary, as it often did, imperial disapproval was tempered by the knowledge that the annexation had been at no sacrifice to the British taxpayer and that the territories added to the Indian Empire might conceivably become profitable to the British economy.

South Africa, with the possible exception of Natal, seemed to have no such prospects.

South Africa was not the only dependency plagued by collision between settlers and tribesmen. New Zealand settlers were also embroiled in warfare with virile tribes. But nowhere else in the British Empire was there so much expended for so little purpose as in South Africa.

The Great Trek produced turbulence over thousands of square miles of wasteland on the borders of the Cape. There was no evident economic advantage in intervention—the sheep and the cattle of Boers, Griquas, and Bantu were not worth the bones of a single British grenadier; and there were imperative financial reasons for noninvolvement. Had Great Britain been able to insulate its conscience and the borders of the Cape from the struggles in Transorangia, there would have been no motive for intervention, but the evangelical conscience was sensitive and the Cape border was vulnerable. The Boer settlement of Natal was an additional complication, for it fronted on the sea and thus posed a potential threat to the lines of communication between Britain and India, not from the Boers but from a hostile maritime power with which the Boers might associate themselves. The British annexed the Orange River Territory and then, sick of turmoil and expense, regurgitated it. They annexed Natal and retained it. The difference in policy is significant. The landlocked Orange River Territory would always remain dependent on the good will of imperial Britain, whereas a Boer republic facing upon the sea would have had other alternatives.

Before 1834 the trek of farmers north of the Orange River was primarily a manifestation of land hunger accentuated by years of drought. Without such trekking, cattle could not have survived. But at about the time D'Urban arrived at the Cape, emigration beyond the Orange had begun to assume a different character. Duncan Campbell, civil commissioner of Somerset, observed in June, 1834, that a number of farmers had settled beyond the limits of the colony on the White Kei and to the north of Philippolis, and had no intention of returning. As few of these people had slaves, and the majority were young men from the western districts who had some stock and no land, he assumed that the migration was motivated largely by economic considerations. Whatever its antecedents, he admitted he could not prevent it even if the means at his disposal were increased tenfold.[3]

---

[3] D. Campbell to Acting Colonial Secretary, June 27, 1834, Philip 2–6, LMS Archives. Of the trekkers who settled temporarily near the White Kei, the most

At about the same time Kolbe, the missionary at Philippolis, was sending Philip alarming reports of the effects of the Boer migration upon
the Griquas. He recognized the intrusion of these European farmers as
a mortal danger to this dependency of the London Missionary Society,
but the feckless Griquas persisted in trafficking with the enemy. When
Kolbe remonstrated with Kok that his people were destroying themselves by leasing land to Boers, the chief acknowledged the danger but
took no action. Nor could he have done so even had he wished, for
his government was a "mere shade of authority." Kok seemed immune
to the missionary's exhortations. He had trekked before; he could trek
again. Instead of acting to rally his people to defend their society
against the Boers, the chief talked of leading a migration away from
Philippolis to a more remote area, perhaps in the vicinity of Moroko's
Barolong and the Wesleyan missionary Archbell. This combination
of cowardice and apostasy depressed Kolbe, and though he prevailed
upon Kok to stay, he feared that he had merely delayed the inevitable.[4]

From their different perspectives, Kolbe and Campbell saw the first
manifestations of the Great Trek as portentous of evil. Kolbe yearned
for the security of British law; Campbell saw that law without the
powers of enforcement was a mockery.

During Governor D'Urban's residence in Cape Town, the migration
of a few Boer families beyond the frontier seemed of relatively little
moment in comparison with the great issues of supervising emancipation and introducing a new system of government. But when he arrived
on the eastern frontier to direct the prosecution of a Kaffir war, reports
of Boer restlessness poured in to his headquarters. At the end of the
war he heard that farmers who had lost cattle and horses in the Kaffir
invasion were bitter because they had not been permitted to retake
them by the terms of peace, and because the authorities, though they
restrained the Boers from acting effectively in their own defense, were
unable to prevent the Kaffirs from infesting the colony's farms.[5] Colonel
Somerset, who toured the Somerset district in October, 1835, found the
Boers indignant and despondent at the impotence of the government.

In the absence of effective protection against plunderers, farmers

---

notable was Louis Trigardt, who left the Somerset district in June, 1834. Trigardt
took ten slaves, but the other thirty emigrant families near him had only five alto-
gether. By November, 1834, all Trigardt's slaves and all except one of the others
had run away to the colony. See G. M. Theal, *History of South Africa since September, 1795* (5 vols.; London: Swan Sonnenschein, 1907–1910), II, 274–275.

[4] Kolbe to Philip, July 14, 1834, G.H. 19/4, Cape Archives.

[5] Robson to D'Urban, Oct. 14, 1835, D'Urban Papers, IV.

had to defend themselves, but they complained that the government struck the weapons from their hands by imposing impossible restrictions. A thief could not be summarily shot; he must be taken to the nearest magistrate for trial, when the aggrieved farmer and supporting witnesses would be required to testify against him. Magistrates, however, were few and distances were great; sometimes a magistrate was as far away as forty hours' ride on horseback. A farmer who complied with the law took the risk of losing more property while he was attending the prosecution of a thief, and consequently many preferred to allow the culprit to escape rather than to prosecute.

There were other grievances—lack of title deeds, restrictions on gunpowder, and uncertainties about compensation for slaves—but the basic problem was the inability of the government to impose order, and, as D'Urban confessed, this was the one grievance beyond his power to remedy.[6] The government at home would not augment the forces at his disposal; on the contrary, it pressed him to reduce them, and the perverse Boers, while they complained of lack of protection, violently opposed the suggestion that they be enrolled in a militia.[7]

D'Urban expected that the migration of the Boers beyond the frontier would produce violence which could not be quarantined; he also knew that if such a migration occurred he would not be able to control it. He had issued a proclamation in September, 1834, prohibiting the migration of all colonists beyond the border without specific authorization by local officials. On the advice of Dr. Philip he had negotiated a treaty of alliance with Waterboer and would have made a similar agreement with Kok had war with the Kaffirs not intervened. But edicts were only as strong as the force behind them, and alliances with chiefs, while useful to control native banditti, were of little use against Europeans.

War interrupted the plans of many families to trek, and D'Urban's manifest desire to redress grievances contributed to further hesitation. Somerset told D'Urban in April, 1836, that Commandant Piet Retief had advised the farmers of the Winterberg district to wait for the final decisions on British policy, and that through his influence nearly all of them had given up their preparations to trek. Others, however, were not willing to wait, and were already on the move; Somerset heard rumors that many hundreds had already crossed the Orange River

---

[6] Somerset to D'Urban, Nov. 8, 1835, *ibid.*

[7] The fear of the Boers that the government planned to make soldiers of them was frequently cited as one of the important causes of disaffection (see, for example, James Collett to D'Urban, Dec. 15, 1835, *ibid.*).

bound for Natal, and that "a ship or two" had been dispatched from Cape Town to Natal with ammunition.[8]

The causes of the trek were too deep-seated to be met by any mere palliatives, and palliatives were all that D'Urban could provide. The objectives of government and the nature of the frontier Boers were basically antagonistic; the fact that the authority was British made the antagonism more intense. The Great Trek was a manifestation of a conflict that long antedated the British occupation, but the humanitarian influences which affected British policy gave to the trek a distinctive character. In the minds of many participants this was a migration of the children of God from a society dominated by strange and evil doctrines, "contrary to the laws of God and the natural distinction of race and religion, so that it was intolerable for any decent Christian to bow beneath such a yoke." [9] Such ideas were not mere rationalizations for a movement from the drought-ridden Cape frontier to the smiling lands of Natal. Natal became the promised land not only because it offered the prospect of well-watered pastures and fat cattle, but because it signified freedom.

By the middle of 1836 the fever had spread throughout the Somerset and Graaff Reinet districts, and was felt as far away as Swellendam. Stockenstrom's color-blind justice, the abolition of martial law in Queen Adelaide Province, and Glenelg's repudiation of the annexation added further impetus to the movement toward the new Eldorado.

Thus began a migration in a gigantic horseshoe movement over the Orange River drifts, across the high veld, skirting the Basuto country, and then flowing through the passes of the Drakensberg into Natal. Against the Boer cavalry the most redoubtable native tribes were almost helpless. The bravery and the discipline of the Matabele and the Zulus were of no avail against Boer muskets; nor could a few hundred Griquas, even though equipped with muskets, survive against Europeans who were more proficient in the art of war. Far beyond the colonial border there was now a new frontier of European-native conflict; without British intervention, that conflict was likely to be resolved by the slaughter of thousands of tribesmen and the subjugation of the survivors.[10] The British government could not

[8] Somerset to D'Urban, April 8, 1836, *ibid.*

[9] Anna Steenkamp, as quoted by Eric Walker, *The Great Trek* (London: Black, 1948), p. 91.

[10] The number of trekkers is uncertain. Walker, *op. cit.*, p. 6, estimates that 14,000 migrated in the first decade. Piet Uys, who journeyed beyond the Orange River in 1837, stated that he "met" more than 3,000 trekkers (Uys to D'Urban, Aug. 7, 1837, D'Urban Papers, III).

accept this "natural" resolution of conflict, but neither was it pre-pared to extend its responsibilities beyond the existing boundary.

Long before the Boer migration, Natal had fitfully engaged the attention of the Colonial Office. As early as 1824 a few British traders had settled at a place they called Port Natal, and merchants at Cape Town had sought to interest Downing Street in extending protection over them. The arguments employed had been the potential profits of trade with the Zulus and the prospect of American settlement unless Britain acted quickly. Neither the economic promise nor the political threat had moved the Colonial Office to action. In 1832 Lord Goderich authorized the appointment of a resident "of good sense and moderate pretensions" at a salary not to exceed £199 per year, to be paid from the Cape's finances, but this was the extent of the commitment. When D'Urban, in June, 1834, resubmitted the merchants' plea with essen-tially the same arguments, the government's response was the same: British intervention was out of the question, and the financial condi-tion of the Cape did not permit assumption of this additional respon-sibility by the colony.[11] In December, 1835, D'Urban pressed the Colonial Office to reconsider, putting forward the additional argument that the arrival of American missionaries presaged imminent annexa-tion by the United States, which might be averted by a company of infantry and a few guns. The response of Lord Palmerston, the foreign secretary, was that the United States was welcome to this territory which had no significance for any British interests.[12]

The Melbourne government was opposed to any annexation beyond the borders of Cape Colony. The attitudes that underlay the decision of the cabinet to order the retrocession of Queen Adelaide Province also applied to the lands into which the Boers had migrated. But the government could not dismiss entirely the consequences of the trek of British subjects beyond the frontier. The government sought a means of proving its concern for the welfare of the Africans without incurring additional liabilities.

There were a number of precedents which might serve as a model. By the India Act of 1784, courts both in the East India Company's territories and in Great Britain were empowered to try British sub-jects for offenses committed in territories of Indian native princes; [13]

---

[11] Hay to Cole, May 25, 1832, C.O. 49/25, P.R.O.

[12] D'Urban to Stanley, June 17, 1834, and minutes thereto, C.O. 48/155, P.R.O. American intentions to establish a settlement had been reported for several years (see John Bird, *The Annals of Natal* [2 vols.; Pietermaritzburg: Davis, 1888], I, 196, 197).

[13] 24 George III, cap. 25, sec. 44.

and by an amendment two years later, this jurisdiction was extended
to include "any of the country or parts of Asia, Africa, or America,
beyond the Cape of Good Hope, to the streights of Magellan, within
the limits of the exclusive trade of the said United Company." [14]
Parliament had passed similar legislation assigning extraterritorial
jurisdiction to courts in British North America and in Australia.[15]
The Cape of Good Hope Punishment Act of 1836 faithfully reproduced the spirit of the earlier legislation. It provided that all "crimes"
committed by British subjects south of 25° south latitude could be
punished in the Cape courts, but made no provision for the apprehension of offenders beyond the Cape borders. It was a manifestation
of noble ideals at no cost to the British taxpayer. This toothless statute
gave no pause to malefactors, and within two years of its passage all
pretense that it had force was stripped away by the Supreme Court
of Cape Colony. In 1838 the attorney general of the Cape, in a test of
the law, applied for a warrant to apprehend certain persons reported
to have committed thefts beyond the frontier. The majority of the
court held that the act was defective and could not be enforced in
the courts of the colony.[16] The significance of the act extended beyond
its immediate objective; it clearly implied that because the trekkers
could not unilaterally dissolve their allegiance, Great Britain could
legally assert its jurisdiction over them if and when it chose to do so.
But, for the time, the only restrictions on the trekkers were those they
themselves imposed; the only obstacles, the power of the native tribes
that opposed them. By the end of 1837 the Matabele had been driven
beyond the Limpopo, and a year later a commando, at a price of three
men wounded, avenged Piet Retief by the slaughter of 3,000 Zulus at
Blood River. On the grasslands of the high veld and the hills and
valleys of Natal the power of the Boers was supreme; only British intervention could prevent the consolidation of this ascendancy, and during the governorship of Sir Benjamin D'Urban Britain was quiescent.

This inactivity was much against D'Urban's inclination. Had he
had his way, the government would have availed itself of the activity
of Captain Allen F. Gardiner and announced the annexation of Natal

---

[14] 26 George III, cap. 57, sec. 29.

[15] By 9 George IV, cap. 31, sec. 7, any British subject charged in England with
murder or manslaughter committed anywhere could be tried in English courts.
In 9 George IV, cap. 83, sec. 4, the courts of New South Wales and Van Diemen's
Land were given power to try offenses committed in New Zealand and other Pacific
islands not subject to British or any other European sovereignty. These precedents
are summarized in C.O. 48/192, P.R.O.

[16] South African Commercial Advertiser, Feb. 28, 1838.

on the basis of the treaty Gardiner had made with Dingaan in June, 1835.[17] The Colonial Office, however, while professing admiration for Gardiner's zeal, was unequivocal in its opposition to any enlargement of British territory in southern Africa.[18] The limit to which Glenelg was willing to go was authorization of Gardiner's appointment as a justice of the peace under the Cape of Good Hope Punishment Act, though without any funds or executive power to support his jurisdiction. In Natal as in Kaffirland, Downing Street seemed to D'Urban to be demonstrating its incompetence, but he was forced to follow the line adopted by his superiors.[19]

The arrival of Sir George Napier coincided with the migration of the *Voortrekkers* into Natal. In an effort to stem the continuing exodus, Napier appealed to officials, ministers of religion, and other leaders of public opinion in the colony to use their influence to discourage intending emigrants, and he issued a circular notice to the Natal trekkers promising that no action would be taken against those who returned to the colony before January 1, 1839, but warning them that they were and would remain British subjects.[20] These paper measures had no effect.

In Cape Town and in London it was assumed that there must be a collision between the Boers and Dingaan's Zulus; whether this struggle would end with the extermination of the Boers or the subjugation of the Zulus was a subject of speculation in the early months of 1838. In May Napier, convinced that the Boers would smash the Zulus, urged the military occupation of Port Natal as a means of protecting the natives from extermination or slavery.[21] When reports filtered back to Cape Town of the murder of Retief and his followers and the annihilation of other Boer parties, John Philip saw in the disaster "the retributive hand of God." [22] Whatever the ultimate result, the British government could not ignore the turmoil. The Aborigines Protection Society in August petitioned Glenelg to occupy Port Natal to protect the native tribes against Boer atrocities.[23]

---

[17] D'Urban to Glenelg, confidential, Dec. 4, 1835, C.O. 48/162, P.R.O.; D'Urban to Glenelg, separate and confidential, Dec. 4, 1835, D'Urban Papers, IV.

[18] Glenelg to D'Urban, March 29, 1836, C.O. 49/28, P.R.O.

[19] D'Urban to Gardiner, private, Nov. 21, 1837, D'Urban, P.C. 1835–1837, Cape Archives.

[20] George E. Cory, *The Rise of South Africa* (5 vols.; London: Longmans, Green, 1921–1930), IV, 81–82.

[21] Napier to Glenelg, May 18, 1838, C.O. 48/189, P.R.O.

[22] Philip to Ellis, June 1, 1838, SAF 16–1, LMS Archives.

[23] Memorial of Aborigines Protection Society, Aug. 7, 1838, C.O. 48/197, P.R.O.

Under these pressures the Colonial Office gradually began to modify its position. Even James Stephen, who considered all territory in southern Africa worthless, began to have serious doubts that the policy of nonintervention could long continue. Reports of large migrations from Cape Colony and of traffic in provisions and ammunition from Cape Town to Natal caused Stephen to fear that the trek would not only drain the colony of its population but inflict upon the tribes terrible calamities which humanitarian feeling could not ignore. In view of these developments, he concluded that military control of Port Natal could not be long deferred. Sir George Grey, the parliamentary undersecretary, agreed that "a small force (& it need only be small)" would be indispensable at Port Natal.[24] Consequently, when Napier's announcement of his intention to occupy Port Natal was received in London in December, 1838, the mood of Downing Street was one of resignation. Glenelg noted that "there is no option but to approve what indeed N[apier] cd. not avoid doing—& to sanction what neither he nor we can avoid doing." [25]

By the time his letter reached London Napier had already acted. In November, 1838, to prevent the harbor from being seized by either Boers or Zulus, he authorized the occupation of Port Natal, with the express disclaimer of any assertion of British sovereignty over Natal.[26] In December a force of approximately 100 men under the command of Napier's military secretary, Major Charters, landed and began the construction of a fort. Charters arrived at a fortunate time. Two weeks later the Boers administered a crushing defeat to the Zulus at Blood River and were desirous of peace so that they could consolidate their position, and Dingaan, shaken by the disaster that had befallen his impis, welcomed the British as intercessors and possible allies.

This first occupation of Natal was motivated both by humanitarian sentiments and by the recognition that disorders in Natal affected the tribes bordering Cape Colony. Stockenstrom justified the action in humanitarian terms: the British government and nation could not "listen passively to the complaints on the one side, and the exulting boasts on the other of the extermination of whole tribes of blacks by Her Majesty's subjects which is now going on." [27] Napier instructed

---

[24] Notes by Stephen, Nov. 12, 1838, and Grey, Nov. 14, 1838, on Bell to Undersecretary of State, Sept. 3, 1838, C.O. 48/190, P.R.O.

[25] Note by Glenelg, Jan. 2, 1839, on Napier to Glenelg, Oct. 16, 1838, C.O. 48/191, P.R.O.

[26] Proclamation, Nov. 14, 1838, C.O. 48/190, P.R.O.

[27] Stockenstrom to Secretary of State, Jan. 12, 1839, Bird, op. cit., I, 498.

Charters not only to seek peace between Boers and Zulus but to investigate reports that Boer commandos had menaced the territory of the Pondo chief Faku, and Charters assured Faku of the governor's intention to protect the tribes from Boer aggression.[28] If Napier had ulterior objectives he carefully concealed them from the Colonial Office and from his most intimate associates. To his brother Richard he wrote that he did not "care a fig" about newspaper reports that he had deeper motives than the restoration of order: "Port Natal was occupied merely as a military post to prevent, if possible, the further effusion of blood." As to the desirability of eventual colonization, Napier was ambivalent. If the Crown assumed sovereignty there to control the Boers, it would have to face eventually the same necessity in more remote parts of Africa: ". . . so long as good grass and water are to be found in Africa, there will be found sooner or later the Dutch boer.—They idolize their flocks, they will brave hardships and death to procure the means of supporting these flocks, therefore if we follow them in all their wanderings & take possession as a colony of every foot of land which they seize the colony must extend to the verge of the habitable ground." [29]

In 1838 and for some years thereafter the British government had no interest in Natal as a field of colonization or a strategic base. The harbor of Port Natal was dangerous, guarded by sand bars and heavy surf, and was deemed adequate only for ships of 800 tons. Such a port held no attractions for the Admiralty, and the economic potentialities of Natal excited little interest in the government. As early as the 1830's, reports of the fertility of the soil and the benign climate attracted the attention of some merchants in the City of London, principally those engaged in the shipping trade to the Cape and the East Indies, but their first probings on Downing Street had a chilly reception.[30] Normanby, in acquainting his successor Lord John Russell with the problems he would have to meet at the Colonial Office, warned him that among his first visitors would be a deputation of merchants pressing for the colonization of Natal, and counseled him against giving them any aid and comfort, as there were no attractions in Natal which could outweigh the expense of adding to "the already overgrown settlements" of the British Empire.[31]

---

[28] Charters to Faku, Dec. 11, 1838, Bird, *op. cit.*, I, 436–437.

[29] George Napier to Richard Napier, Aug. 1, 1839, Napier Papers, Add. MSS 49168, British Museum.

[30] Grey to Borradale, May 29, 1838, C.O. 49/31, P.R.O.

[31] Normanby to Russell, private, Sept. 22, 1839, PRO 30/22/3, P.R.O.

The repeated expression of Colonial Office opposition to colonization or to permanent military occupation convinced Napier that the troops must be withdrawn at the first opportunity. Through the mediation of Charters' successor, Captain Henry Jarvis, Dingaan and the Boers accepted a peace by which the Zulu chief acknowledged the Boers' control over Natal from the Tugela to the Umzimvubu. Now that order was at least temporarily restored, Napier concluded that no useful purpose was being served by the British detachment at Port Natal. In September, 1839, he notified the Colonial Office of his intention to withdraw the force, and after waiting for several weeks for evidence of any change in policy, sent a transport to remove the troops.[32] On December 24 the British force evacuated Port Natal, and the Union Jack came down. As the boats carried the redcoats out to the waiting transport, the Boers raised the tricolor of the trekker republic. The symbolism was evident; the Boers considered themselves free men, divested of all obligations to the Crown. Even before the departure of the troops, the trekkers had reinforced their ascendancy. In October they had recognized Dingaan's older brother Panda as "Reigning Prince of the Emigrant Zulus," but as a vassal to the Boers. In February, 1840, Panda defeated Dingaan, who fled to Swaziland where he was killed. Boer rather than British order was imposed upon Natal.

Napier made his decision to evacuate Port Natal at a time when the resolution of the Colonial Office against colonization was beginning to weaken. Lord John Russell, who succeeded Normanby in September, 1839, had a less doctrinaire view of empire than his immediate predecessors. Russell's view of colonies was pragmatic. He was not in principle opposed to the expansion of the British Empire; colonies contributed to "the strength and wealth of the Empire" and annexation might "sometimes be inevitable, often advantageous." Under certain circumstances, however, annexation was neither necessary nor desirable. In Russell's opinion the two most important reasons for refusal to annex a territory were:

1. Where the occupation of territory hitherto held by aboriginal tribes must lead to flagrant injustice, and wars, & protracted misery—
2. Where the burthen of occupation is so great as to require a large expenditure for which there is no prospect of an adequate compensation. For

---

[32] Napier to Normanby, Sept. 30, 1839, C.O. 48/201; same to same, Nov. 11, 1839, C.O. 48/202, both in P.R.O.

an increase of troops cannot take place without an increase of establishments, nor an increase of expenditure without an increase of the burthens of this country.[33]

Though Russell was no doubt sincere in his concern for the welfare of the aborigines, his preoccupation was with the prospective balance sheets. Judged by such a criterion, the case for the annexation of Natal was not overwhelming. Russell was not immune to pressure from commercial interests, but he was aware that the only port was a poor one and he feared that settlers would be engaged in conflict with native tribes that would require reinforcements of British troops.[34] Whether or not the commercial prospects of Natal outweighed such liabilities was an issue for careful consideration. He first told the petitioning merchants that he would have to submit the problem to the entire cabinet, and then, on further consideration, he decided that the governor of Cape Colony might be able to provide more information; consequently he asked Napier for his "mature opinion." [35]

This deferral was a keen disappointment to the would-be colonizers. They had organized themselves into the South African Land and Emigration Association, and Russell's friendly reception to their initial overtures had encouraged them to hope for early and favorable action. Now they were forced to wait at least six months for a response from Cape Town. To prod the government to action, they expressed the intention of bringing the issue before Parliament and of pressing for the appointment of a select committee to report on the implications for Cape Colony and the Empire of the emigration of the Boers to Natal.[36] In so doing, they were careful to point out, their purpose was not to embarrass the government but to demonstrate that Natal could be developed into a profitable colony at no cost to the Exchequer; but the threat was still there. Russell consented to send out a questionnaire bearing upon the characteristics of Natal and its future prospects to a number of persons supposed to have special competence, including Charters, Stockenstrom, Sir James Alexander, Dr. Andrew Smith, ex-Commissioner Bigge, ex-Governors Donkin, Cole, and Bourke, ex-Lieutenant Governor Wade, and a number of others.[37] To this list

---

[33] Minute by Russell, Nov. 30, 1839, on Borradale to Secretary of State for Colonies, Nov. 18, 1839, C.O. 48/204, P.R.O.

[34] *Ibid.*

[35] Russell to Napier, Dec. 23, 1839, *ibid.*

[36] Redman to Russell, March 14, 1840, C.O. 48/209, P.R.O.

[37] Barber to Russell, March 14, 1840, *ibid.*

the Colonial Office added some referees of its own, including the Colonial Land and Emigration Board.

Further elaboration of the association's plans, however, cooled Colonial Office interest. It proposed to bring to Natal laborers from England on contracts not to exceed three years, their passages to be paid by the proceeds of land sales, with the government of the Cape advancing from £10,000 to £15,000 to finance the first shipment of from 1,000 to 1,500 emigrants. To make possible the indenturing of these laborers, the association requested the rescinding of an order in council of September, 1838, prohibiting such contracts.[38] The proposal to introduce indentured labor ignored the failure of similar plans in Australia and elsewhere, and a loan by Cape Colony, which was itself in debt, was out of the question.[39] Russell's interest in the colonization of Natal, however, was not tied to a specific scheme or a particular company. He had heard enough of the territory's fertility to believe that it held prospects for profitable British occupation; the longer occupation was delayed, the more formidable an undertaking it would become, as the Boers would in time become solidly entrenched in their trekker republic. Accordingly, in June, 1840, he instructed Napier to send a detachment to resume the occupation of Port Natal without awaiting a final decision on the future of the entire territory.[40]

Napier's thoughts ran along the same lines. Four days after Russell signed his dispatch, Napier was writing to advise the Colonial Secretary that delay was dangerous, as the longer the Boers were left without governmental authority, the more difficult it would be to restore them to obedience. If Britain decided to promote emigration, he deemed it wise to support this colonization with a force of from 1,200 to 1,500 troops. Napier thought it unlikely that the Boers, despite their threats of resistance to the reimposition of British authority, would fight regulars, but he considered it wise to be certain by employing an overwhelming force. After the military occupation some malcontents might trek again, but they would be locked in the interior of Africa where they would be less dangerous to British interests. If Great Britain was not prepared to annex Natal, Napier advised, it would be politic to recognize the Boers as an independent state and enter into a treaty of alliance. Otherwise, they would continue to cause commotions among the tribes on their southern border who in turn would collide

---

[38] Redman to Russell, May 4, 1840, *ibid.*

[39] Minutes on Redman to Russell, May 4, 1840, and C.O. to Redman, May 21, 1840, both in *ibid.*

[40] Russell to Napier, June 18, 1840, C.O. 49/34, P.R.O.

with the Kaffirs on the Cape's eastern frontier, bringing on another bloody war.[41]

Besides this intelligence from Napier, the Colonial Office received a report from two Quakers, James Backhouse and George W. Walker, who had been traveling throughout southern Africa for more than a year and a half. Backhouse and Walker reached a conclusion similar to Napier's but on the basis of different assumptions. They believed that the Boers of Natal would accept British authority provided it was benevolent to them, and that the introduction of an efficient government with a liberal land system might draw other Boers from the interior, where they were a menace to the native tribes, and make them useful subjects of the Crown. There was vacant land in abundance in Natal for all the emigrant farmers, and it would be unnecessary to dispossess any native inhabitants; but the British government must approach the Boers with delicacy, for if it acted rashly, many would trek into the interior.[42]

The reaction of the Colonial Office to Napier's and the Quakers' reports was illuminating. R. Vernon Smith, the parliamentary under-secretary, also expressed his chief's opinion when he stated that it was "a very good thing to have a settlement at Port Natal but a very difficult thing to pay for it." [43] But perhaps, as the Friends seemed to imply, Britain might be able to colonize the country with less force than Napier thought necessary.[44] Russell was impressed by the suggestions of Backhouse and Walker that annexation should be conciliatory and cheap rather than forcible and expensive. "On the general question," he told Napier, "I am favourable to the settlement of Natal as a British Colony but not prepared to expend large funds to conquer the territory from the Emigrant farmers." Thus he was inclined to support the suggestions of Backhouse and Walker that the Boers be conciliated and that the civil authority be left in their hands under the jurisdiction of their own president and council, reserving to a British officer the control of Her Majesty's troops, and with the clear understanding that the Crown could not tolerate slavery "in any form." [45]

Imperial policy in the 1830's, far from being the antithesis of that

---

[41] Napier to Russell, June 22, 1840, C.O. 48/208, P.R.O.

[42] "Extracts from Remarks of James Backhouse and George Washington Walker . . . ," enclosure in Napier to Russell, June 24, 1840, *ibid.*

[43] Note by Smith, Aug. 28, 1840, on Napier to Russell, June 22, 1840, *ibid.*

[44] *Ibid.*

[45] Russell to Napier, Sept. 5, 1840, *ibid.*

in the 1850's, was based on similar assumptions. True, Russell's policy was expansionist and the later policy was to retreat, but in both instances the ultimate basis for decision was that of profit and loss. Russell was prepared to annex Natal, provided there was no additional burden to the British taxpayer; twelve years later Grey decided to withdraw from the trans-Orange country because it had been demonstrated that continued control imposed financial burdens. This is not to imply that humanitarian sentiments were irrelevant; but, in 1840 as in the 1850's, they were not strong enough to dominate the Exchequer mentality.

Though Natal seemed to Russell to offer attractive prospects as a field of colonization and trade, he would not be rushed into an annexation that might expose the imperial government to hazard and expense. The proposals of the Land and Emigration Association were unacceptable because they required financial assistance from the Cape government. Also, the response of the Natalian Boers to British annexation remained doubtful. There was no need for haste. The one action that must be taken immediately was the reoccupation of Port Natal. With the harbor controlled, there would be no danger of foreign intervention, and the sea-borne trade of Natal would be in British hands. These considerations dictated Russell's instruction to Napier on June 18, 1840, to return a military detachment to Port Natal,[46] though Napier's suggestion of a force of 1,200 to 1,500 men he considered out of the question.[47]

With these instructions to guide him, Napier was prepared to act, but the form of his action was somewhat different from what Russell had intended. The governor found an opportunity for intervention when the Natal Boers sent a commando against a Baca chief, Ncapaai, who allegedly had been engaged in cattle stealing on a large scale. The Boers carried away 3,000 cattle and 17 child "apprentices." Ncapaai was a neighbor of Faku, to whom Napier had promised protection, and when Faku expressed alarm that the Boers would strike him next, Napier, in January, 1841, sent an expedition of 150 men under Captain Thomas Smith to the Umgazi River in Faku's territory. The avowed purpose of the movement was support for Faku, but Faku's territory was on the border of Natal, and thus was well situated as a base for the occupation of the territory when the decision was made to annex.[48] Russell was not convinced of the wisdom of this gambit. It seemed to

[46] Russell to Napier, June 18, 1840, C.O. 49/34, P.R.O.
[47] Russell to Napier, Sept. 5, 1840, C.O. 48/208, P.R.O.
[48] Napier to Russell, June 8, 1841, C.O. 48/212, P.R.O.

him hazardous to send a small detachment so far away from supporting
force to the border of what might become hostile territory; the results
might be disastrous rather than constructive. But with misgivings he
approved this demonstration of the Queen's support for friendly
tribes.[49]

The Umgazi expedition made the immediate reoccupation of Port
Natal even more pressing, for the port would be needed to provide
supplies for Smith's detachment. Consequently, in August, 1841, Russell again instructed the governor to send a military force to Port Natal,
with the injunction to avoid all interference with the Boers unless
they attacked the troops or friendly tribes.[50]

Again events outran instructions. By the time Russell's injunctions
reached Napier, the governor had made decisions based on further
developments in Natal. He had received reports of the plans of the
Volksraad to resettle thousands of "surplus" natives between the
Umtamvuna and Umzimvubu rivers, thus encroaching on territories
claimed by Faku and creating extreme danger of tribal warfare which
could spread throughout Kaffirland. Obviously the existence of an independent Boer government was a menace to peace; Napier therefore
decided to send Captain Smith and his detachment overland to Port
Natal as soon as the rainy season ended and the rivers became pass-
able.[51]

After numerous delays caused by swollen rivers, the troops finally
arrived in Port Natal in May, 1842, with no more serious opposition
from the Boers than verbal protests. Napier's prophecy that the farmers, despite the defiant language of their *Volksraad,* would not offer
resistance to the Queen's troops seemed to be vindicated. The illusion
was soon shattered when the Boers, under the leadership of Andries
Pretorius, beat back Smith's foray against their camp and laid siege
to the small British force, and were dispersed only when a relief force
arrived under Lieutenant Colonel Abraham Josias Cloete.

The defiance of Captain Smith by the Natal Boers dismayed Napier.
The place he coveted for himself as the governor who kept the peace
in South Africa had been threatened by a band of ruffians, and his
assurances to the Secretary of State had been proved optimistic. Seeking self-justification, he turned for counsel to Sir Benjamin D'Urban,
who gratified him by promising to write his friends at the War Office
endorsing everything Napier had done. He told the governor:

[49] Russell to Napier, April 24, 1841, C.O. 49/34, P.R.O.
[50] Russell to Napier, Aug. 21, 1841, C.O. 48/212, P.R.O.
[51] Napier to Russell, Dec. 6, 1841, C.O. 48/214, P.R.O.

Sir George, I have no hesitation in declaring to you that in my opinion you have not committed one single error from first to last, and if blame is to rest any where it cannot be with you, for you have been perfectly clear and open to the Secretary of State, and you have in my opinion full justification and authority for all the measures you have adopted, both Civil and Military and I repeat you could not have done otherwise and had I been in your Excellency's place, I should have acted precisely as you have.[52]

Napier carefully noted down these golden words. His spirits rose further with intelligence from Cloete, who by "pacific and merciful" measures, including an amnesty for all but four ringleaders, was reconciling the majority of the Boers to acceptance of peace.[53] The governor approved of these conciliatory measures, though he professed to hope that the archvillains might be captured: "I wish to God! that scoundrel Pretorious [sic] could be caught, as well as Bosoff [Boshof] old *Rose,* & *Breda*—but I fear they are as cunning as they are *cowardly,* and will never show their faces in any place where there is a chance of catching them." [54] In fact, he had no inclination to risk further disturbances. A disaster had been narrowly averted; he hoped now for tranquillity.

At this juncture a dispatch arrived in Cape Town which produced consternation. At the end of 1841 the Whig government had collapsed; Lord Stanley replaced Russell as secretary of state for colonies, and undertook a thoroughgoing review of the policies of his predecessor. As was so often true, the circumstances on which Downing Street had to base its judgments were obsolete. Stanley completed his analysis in March, 1842, on the basis of intelligence received as late as January. He knew that Napier intended to send Smith's force to Natal and he expected that it would occupy the port with no opposition from the resident population. But for what purpose? Stanley concluded that the resources of Natal, proved and prospective, were not worth any expenditure, and that the overstrained military resources of the British Empire should not be further dissipated. Napier had detained the 25th Regiment, which was needed in India; there must be no further delay in dispatching it. Stanley was not prepared to release the Boers from their allegiance, but neither was he inclined to assume the responsibility of governing them. He decided that the troops must be withdrawn and the trekkers informed that they must defend themselves against

---

[52] "Substance of what passed between Sir Benjamin D'Urban and myself . . . . at an Interview between us by my request at Government House on Saturday 18th [10th?] June 1842," Napier Papers, Add. MSS 49167.

[53] Cloete to Napier, July 8, 1842, *ibid.*

[54] Napier to Smith, private, July 18, 1842, *ibid.*

attack and that any attempt on their part to invade the territories of tribes friendly to Britain would be repelled by British forces. The most effective means to reduce the Boers to submission, he concluded, was to impose an interdict on trade with them. Denied provisions and ammunition, they might be impelled to return to Cape Colony.[55] Stanley's reasoning was unrealistic as applied to the circumstances of December, 1841; it bore no relationship to the conditions of June, 1842, when the dispatch embodying his views arrived at Cape Town.[56]

Napier, when he recovered from the shock, decided that the dispatch was an anachronism, and that he could use his discretionary authority to retain the troops at Port Natal pending Stanley's reaction to the events of May and June.[57] He gauged the prospective response correctly. By October Stanley acknowledged that altered circumstances had made his instructions inappropriate. Reports from Major Smith in Natal and from Napier had convinced him that there was no prospect whatever of removing the Boers from Natal. They would never return to the Cape voluntarily and they could not be evicted without using far larger military forces than the British government was willing to contemplate. The alternative of asserting British sovereignty while allowing the Boers to carry on their own government also possessed grave liabilities. While acceptance of Boer autonomy might in the short run avoid British expenditures for a civil and military establishment, eventually the bill presented to the Treasury could be enormous, for Great Britain would have to accept the consequences of embroilments involving British subjects over which it exercised no control. Gradually, and with manifest reluctance,[58] Stanley was forced to the decision that Natal must be annexed to the British Empire because all other alternatives were more objectionable, and in December, 1842, he authorized the annexation.[59]

In May Napier proclaimed the addition of the territory as a district of Cape Colony, and sent Henry Cloete, brother of Josias, as commissioner to establish the form of local self-government for the territory in consultation with the *Volksraad,* subject to certain conditions. There was to be no legal discrimination based on race, color, language,

---

[55] Minute by Stanley, March 18, [1842], C.O. 48/223, P.R.O.

[56] Stanley to Napier, April 10, 1842, C.O. 48/203, P.R.O.

[57] Napier to Stanley, confidential, July 24, 1842, C.O. 48/214, P.R.O.

[58] As late as December 2, 1842, Stanley had not yet made up his mind as to what course should be adopted (Stanley to Napier, private, Dec. 2, 1842, Napier Papers, Add. MSS 49167).

[59] Stanley to Napier, Dec. 13, 1842, C.O. 49/36, P.R.O.

or creed; no "aggression" against the natives would be tolerated; and slavery "in any shape or under any modification" was prohibited.[60] Cloete performed his mission with admirable tact and courage. He was greeted on his arrival at Pietermaritzburg by Dutch flags and demonstrations of violent feelings against British rule; but the majority of the *Volksraad*, if not the population at large, was willing to come to terms. Despite threats of armed resistance by some "bitter-enders," Natal came under British control without recourse to force. Those who could not tolerate the new order trekked again beyond the Drakensberg to join others who remained disaffected, but the large majority chose to remain in the hope that the new government would treat their claims to land with liberality and would not interfere significantly with their way of life.

There is no neat symmetrical explanation for the British annexation of Natal. Russell's interest in the commercial prospects of the colony were not shared by Stanley, who was convinced that the territory could never become prosperous because it lacked an adequate harbor and the Natal coast was dangerous for navigation.[61] Most historians agree that a compelling consideration was the desire to control the coast of southern Africa, thus holding the interior in a state of economic dependence and averting the possibility that Natal might fall into the hands of an unfriendly power, which might use it as a base against the British line of communication to India. There is undoubtedly substance in this interpretation, but the evidence on which it rests is scanty. Certainly the British government was concerned about reports that a Dutch adventurer, Johannes A. Smellekamp, supercargo on a merchant ship, had been encouraging the Boers to believe that the Netherlands was prepared to support them against Great Britain, and there was some suspicion that Smellekamp was supported by French interests that wished to embarrass Great Britain. But at the time Stanley decided upon annexation, the prospect of French intervention does not seem to have disturbed the Colonial Office, and it soon became clear in Downing Street that Smellekamp's assurances to the Boers were based on nothing more substantial than his own overactive imagination.[62]

Since the 1820's, when interests desirous of promoting annexation had first raised the specter of American annexation, British governments had manifested no alarm that a foreign power might establish

---

[60] Proclamation by Napier, May 12, 1843, Bird, *op. cit.*, II, 166–167.

[61] Stanley to Napier, Dec. 13, 1842, C.O. 49/36, P.R.O.

[62] Minutes on Napier to Stanley, Jan. 6, 1843, C.O. 48/234, P.R.O.

itself at Port Natal; and there is no evidence that in the 1840's the prospect of French intervention excited any more concern than had that of American action earlier. The harbor of Port Natal, in the opinion of the Royal Navy, was not suitable for a naval base, and had limited value for commercial purposes. The only good harbor on the southeastern coast, Delagoa Bay, seemed to be unusable because of the malarial swamps in its vicinity. Great Britain did not annex Natal to keep it out of the hands of the French or any other foreign power; the decision was influenced by the desire to make the coastal Boers subject to British economic control and isolate the remaining independent trekker territories in the interior of the continent. The last small loophole in this control of the coast was eliminated when Cloete negotiated the cession by Panda of St. Lucia Bay, which he had heard that Smellekamp might use as a harbor from which he could communicate with the Boers, but that inlet was of little use as a port because of a narrow and hazardous channel connecting it with the sea.[63]

Probably the greatest single consideration in the decision of the Peel government to annex Natal was the fact that the existence of an independent Boer society to the north and east of the Cape frontier was a menace to the Cape's border; so long as the trekkers remained uncontrolled, the government of the Cape could deal with only one side of a frontier problem which was bilateral in character. This problem was the dominant theme in Napier's appeals to the Colonial Office; and it appears to have been a dominant consideration in motivating Stanley to give his consent to the annexation. Reports that the Boers in the guise of apprenticeship had reintroduced a form of slavery provided a humanitarian justification for British intervention. Stanley annexed Natal largely because he was convinced that the independence of the Boers was reconcilable neither with order nor with humanity. Stephen, who, though not on friendly terms with Stanley, participated in the deliberations, stated that the object of the annexation was to overtake the Boers, to prevent their making wars on the natives, and to frustrate their designs to form a colony dependent on the Netherlands. But the occupation of Natal had not had the effect of containing the Boers; the virus had spread eastward into new territories, reproducing the evils that had caused British intervention in Natal. Where was it all to end? The reasons adduced for colonizing Natal, Stephen averred, applied with equal force to the whole southeastern coast of Africa, and the returns on the investment

[63] Cloete to Government Secretary, Oct. 28, 29, 1843, enclosures in Napier to Stanley, Jan. 22, 1844, C.O. 48/246, P.R.O.

would ever be the same—recurrent wars, mounting expense, and endless frustration. Benjamin Hawes, the parliamentary undersecretary under Earl Grey, admitted that Stephen's reasoning was impeccable, but Grey, impatient with arguments after the fact, dismissed the issue with the comment that "whether it were originally wise or otherwise to occupy the settlement of Natal, practically it is impossible now to abandon it, & the question is how it may be maintained at the smallest cost." [64]

The problem remained as to the policy of Great Britain toward British subjects of European origin beyond the borders of Cape Colony. By assertion of sovereignty over Natal, Britain made itself directly responsible for control of European-native relations between the coast and the Drakensberg, but this implied no acceptance of such responsibility west of the Drakensberg and the Orange River. There a different policy continued to be pursued. The Colonial Office did not develop a systematic policy toward the Great Trek. Its response was, in the best British tradition, *ad hoc*. Consequently British policy beyond the Cape frontier appeared uncertain, hesitant, and frequently contradictory. The one constant point of reference, the maintenance of maximum order at minimum expense, offered no clear indication as to what specific policy should be adopted.

In the trans-Orange country as in Natal, the interests of European farmers collided with those of nonwhite peoples, and the actions of Britain toward the Natal trekkers had repercussions throughout the entire area of Boer occupation. But in details the frontier problem north of the Orange River was unlike that in Natal. The missionary interest in the 1830's and 1840's was far more preoccupied with protection of the natives north of the Orange River than with the conflicts of Boers and Zulus. The London Missionary Society had made protégés of Andries Waterboer and of Kok's Griquas at Philippolis.[65] The Basuto of Moshesh were also in the favor of the London society through its fraternal relations with the Paris missionaries, whereas Moroko's Barolong were under the patronage of the Wesleyans. Waterboer's Griquas were somewhat isolated from the main stream of events, but Philippolis lay directly in the path of Boer expansion, and it was in response to Boer conflicts with Kok's Griquas that Britain first intervened beyond the Orange.

---

[64] Minutes on Maitland to Gladstone, May 26, 1846, C.O. 179/1, P.R.O.

[65] Adam Kok II died in 1835 and was succeeded as captain by his eldest son Abraham, whom the missionaries considered incompetent. Through missionary influence he was replaced in 1837 by his younger brother Adam Kok III.

The protection of the Griquas against the Boers was made more difficult, and ultimately impossible, by the fact that the Griquas themselves had admitted the enemy within the gates. The Griquas had leased much of their land to the Boers for twenty, forty, sixty, and even ninety-nine years for payments far below the value of the land.[66] John Philip could control the Griquas' choice of leaders, and he could dominate Adam Kok; [67] but he could not imbue Kok or the Griquas with resolution. The Griquas, he knew, could be saved only by the intervention of the colonial government. His dearest wish would have been to achieve the annexation of the Griqua country to the colony —"I would be contented to die to see this object accomplished"— and as early as 1832 he had urged the government to annex the Griquas,[68] but he recognized that the prospects of annexation were not bright. Consequently he had fallen back to support a policy of alliances, of which the agreement between Waterboer and D'Urban in 1834 was a model. Napier was not at first receptive to the extension of such alliances to other native chiefs. Despondently, Philip wrote home in 1841 that "we never had a government more deeply imbued with the *colonial* spirit than the present. Poor Sir George is anything the Boers and those around him choose to make him." [69] As always, Philip judged the character of others by their degree of coincidence with his own views.

Despite Napier's reluctance, Philip, on a trip to the Basuto and Griqua territories in 1842, discussed the prospect of alliances with Moshesh and Kok and found them receptive. After Philip left Moshesh's stronghold of Thaba Bosiu, the Basuto chief concluded that he could best promote the security of his tribe by a treaty with the colonial government, and in May, 1842, he authorized his French missionary advisers to write Lieutenant Governor Hare asking the conditions on which an alliance could be made.[70] In the discussions that followed Philip was able to resume his favorite role of the spokesman of native interests in negotiations with government.

Philip fancied himself as a missionary statesman; his earlier achievements through Buxton convinced him that he understood the mecha-

[66] Schreiner to Freeman, Aug. 8, 1841, SAF 18–2, LMS Archives.
[67] In a letter to the London headquarters, Philip wrote: "My influence with Adam Kok arises from the fact that no body but himself and his secretary knows of the letters I write him" (Philip to Tidman, Dec. 21, 1840, SAF 17–2, LMS Archives).
[68] Philip to [Tidman?], April 16, 1841, SAF 18–1, LMS Archives.
[69] *Ibid.*
[70] Casalis to [Philip], June 18, 1842, SAF 18–3, LMS Archives.

nisms of political action. Napier and Hare, he recognized, were not likely to be aroused by appeals solely to humanitarians. Their concern was with the problem of reducing the Boers of Natal to order and obedience. This analysis dictated the nature of his approach. At Grahamstown he explained to Hare that the land of the Basuto was strategically of great, perhaps of decisive, importance in the control both of Natal and Transorangia. It lay between the Boers of the Orange River country and those of Natal. Migrants to Natal passed through Moshesh's country, turning off to the north shortly before they reached Thaba Bosiu to a pass through the Drakensberg. Under British protection the Basuto country would be a wedge between two sections of disaffected Boers; in Boer hands it would be a means to the establishment of a united republic from the Orange River to the sea. Even if they were driven from Natal, the Boers could fall back into the mountains of the Basuto country from which it would be extremely difficult to dislodge them. Further, Moshesh's country was ideal for breeding horses, and was consequently especially coveted by the Boers. The stakes were high; the price to be paid for Moshesh's support, the negotiation of a treaty of alliance, was small.[71]

Philip presented the case for a Griqua alliance in similar terms. The Griquas, he told Napier, had been the guardians of order on the northern frontier. Under the guidance of London missionaries, they had maintained peace along the Orange River for more than twenty years, but now the intrusion of the Boers beyond the Orange and their settlement around the Griquas had disturbed the order of Transorangia. A collision between the two peoples was inevitable. Should the Griquas be destroyed, the colonial government would have lost a counterpoise, and order could be restored and maintained only by military force. Not only would the dissident Boers become a more serious menace to colonial security, but they would reintroduce the horrors of slavery and the slave trade throughout much of southern Africa. The colonial government in its own interest should act before it was too late. The most effective course would be the annexation of the territory around Philippolis to the colony; if that was deemed impractical, the interests of the colony as well as consideration of humanity dictated that treaties be negotiated with Kok as well as with Moshesh.[72]

---

[71] Philip to Hare, July 12, 1842, in J. W. Sauer and George M. Theal, eds., *Basutoland Records* (3 vols.; Cape Town: Richard, 1883), I, 45–46.

[72] Philip to Napier, Aug. 25, 1842, in SAF 18–1, LMS Archives; also in C.O. 48/224, P.R.O.

While Philip was pressing the governor to take action on the basis primarily of security, his correspondence with the London head-quarters of the society had quite a different emphasis. The stakes, he wrote the secretaries, were the existence of the missions and of the colored races; both would perish if the government did not act immediately and with vigor. The cause was one "in which every Christian, every Philanthropist, every statesman, and every friend of the human race must feel himself involved." The government of Sir George Napier would do nothing without instructions from Downing Street. Consequently the aid of Thomas Fowell Buxton as well as of the Aborigines Protection Society and other humanitarian bodies should be enlisted to stir the government to action; if it did not respond, great public meetings might produce the desired results. A treaty with Kok was merely an expedient for the present; the Griquas could be saved only if their country was eventually annexed to the colony.[73]

Philip's strategy revealed a curious combination of keen insight and divorcement from reality. He assumed that the Colonial Office continued to stand in awe of Buxton and he exaggerated the power of the Aborigines Protection Society and of the missionary organizations, but his approach to Hare and Napier, based upon the self-interest of the colonial government, was shrewd. Hare accepted the argument that an alliance would help to prevent a movement of armed Boers from the Orange River country in support of rebellious elements in Natal. Napier remained cautious. Alliances with chiefs like Kok and Moshesh might create the impression that the British government was in league with the colored people against the whites. Further, the price might not be so small as Philip's optimistic assurances indicated. An alliance might be the first step to British annexation and could embroil the colonial government in intertribal disputes in which it had no interest.[74] However, though Napier saw the flaws in Philip's arguments, he was pushed in the direction Philip recommended because the alternatives seemed even more hazardous. In September he issued a proclamation warning the Boers that if they encroached on territories possessed by Moshesh, Moroko, Kok, and other native chiefs, Her Majesty's government would regard their actions with "liveliest indignation" and that the offenders would subject themselves to penal consequences.[75]

---

[73] Philip to Secretaries, LMS, Aug. 30, 1842, SAF 18–4, LMS Archives.

[74] Napier to Stanley, July 26, 1842, and enclosure, Hare to Napier, June 24, 1842, C.O. 48/220, P.R.O.

[75] Proclamation by Napier, Sept. 7, 1842, Sauer and Theal, op. cit., I, 48.

This was essentially a restatement in more emphatic language of the ineffectual Punishment Act of 1836. Without delineation of the lands occupied by native tribes, "encroachment" could not be defined; without military force, it could not be punished. Beyond this reaffirmation Napier felt he could not go until he received further instructions from London. The case as he presented it to Stanley was that the majority of the farmers living near the Griquas and the Basuto, unlike those of Natal, had migrated for economic reasons rather than from a desire to throw off their allegiance to the Crown. Their land hunger would drive them into conflict with Kok and Moshesh unless Britain intervened. There were two ways of preventing this collision: to annex the territories occupied by Boers and natives and subject them both to British authority, or to make treaties as Philip had suggested. He did not presume to say which course would be preferable.[76] As Napier undoubtedly expected, Stanley's response was that annexation was out out of the question, but that where the Boers were favorably disposed, as they appeared to be in the vicinity of the Griqua territory, the British government might act as a mediator in disputes over lands while it protected the natives against aggression, if necessary by treaties.[77]

Before Stanley's response had reached Cape Town, Boer-native relations across the Orange River had gone beyond the stage on which London had based its decision. Despite Philip's efforts to portray the Griquas as a bulwark of order, their society was in mortal danger. Peter Wright, the missionary at Philippolis, who had tried for years to inoculate the Griquas with a spirit of resistance, wrote to Philip:

At the present crisis the Chief & people are not to be trusted with the care of their own affairs. The Chief is an excellent man, but very timid & wanting in energy. Hendriks [the secretary and Kok's son-in-law] you are aware can at any time place himself at the head of a strong & wreckless [sic] party & just do what may suit their purpose. This evil however may be corrected, but it will require time, caution, & the advantage of experience. . . . All parties I may say seem to throw themselves upon me & appear willing to follow my counsel.[78]

Wright's counsel, however, could not make an effective state of a collection of people with no will of their own. He could induce Kok to order away the brandy wagons, but the next day the brandy wagons

---

[76] Napier to Stanley, Sept. 15, 1842, C.O. 48/221, P.R.O.

[77] Minute by Stanley, Dec. 23, 1842, in Napier to Stanley, Sept. 15, 1842, C.O. 48/224, P.R.O.

[78] Wright to Philip, Oct. 7, 1842, SAF 19–1, LMS Archives.

would be back; and when Wright died in April, 1843, there was no one of comparable stature to replace him.

Against this confused and irresolute population, the power of the Boers was certain to prevail unless there was outside intervention, and in the last months of 1842 Boer power seemed to be mobilizing to destroy the Griquas. There was division among the Boers with regard to their relationships with Great Britain, but there was none in their attitude toward the natives. Michiel Oberholster might be willing to accept British sovereignty while Jan Mocke was defiant, but neither was prepared to accept the Griquas as equals, much less to accept Griqua sovereignty. They differed in that Mocke was eager to precipitate a collision while Oberholster was more cautious.

On one conclusion, however, Boers, missionaries, and officials were agreed: Boers and Griquas could not live quietly together without coercion by a superior force. When the inevitable clash occurred, it was not likely to be localized, for Boers living on the colonial side of the border would rush to the assistance of their comrades beyond the Orange. When the senior puisne judge of Cape Colony, the pugnacious William Menzies, arrived on circuit at the frontier village of Colesberg in October, he heard reports from the civil commissioner of that community which seemed to indicate that the crisis had arrived. Armed Boers led by Mocke were riding toward Alleman's Drift, the main ford of the Orange River, in territory claimed by the Griquas, intending to take formal possession of the entire territory beyond the river in the name of the Natal Republic. Menzies, with laudable courage but dubious wisdom, determined to forestall the Boer intentions. Accompanied by a few officials he proceeded to Alleman's Drift, where, on October 22, 1842, he erected a beacon and planted the Union Jack, and read a proclamation taking possession for the Crown of the territory south of 25° south latitude delineated in the Punishment Act of 1836. Two days later, when Mocke's party, totaling about 300 rather than the rumored 700, arrived, the judge delivered them a lecture on the law and the penalties to which they subjected themselves if they engaged in treasonable and seditious activities. It is doubtful that Menzies' discourse impressed the Boers with more than admiration for his bravery, though he reported that they had left the meeting much chastened.[79]

Menzies' avowed motive for this dramatic and, as he admitted, illegal performance was to assert the Queen's authority over dissident

---

[79] Menzies to Napier, Oct. 28, 1842, C.O. 48/224, P.R.O. A detailed account of this meeting is in Cory, *op. cit.*, IV, 287 ff.

British subjects. He must have recognized also that the effect of his action would be to embarrass the governor, and he undoubtedly welcomed the opportunity to expose the feebleness of Napier's policies by his own display of resolution. The *Grahamstown Journal*, like Menzies impatient at Napier's lack of aggressiveness, applauded the judge's decisiveness, which was in refreshing contrast to the "timorous hesitancy" of the executive branch.[80] Whatever his intentions, the effect was to complicate the frontier problem. Napier and his executive council were compelled to disavow an action so clearly contrary to the policy of the British government,[81] and the repudiation of Menzies gave support to the contention of Boer zealots who had argued that Britain would use no force more violent than words.

The annexation proclamation by Menzies was, as a Colonial Office spokesman noted, mere rodomontade, unless backed by more military force than could be provided.[82] But the disavowal of Menzies' action did not answer the question as to what policy the governor should pursue. Napier agreed with Menzies that the only course by which disastrous consequences for native tribes beyond the Orange River could be avoided was the assertion of British sovereignty,[83] but pending instructions from London he was unwilling to commit himself.

While Napier awaited word from London, the initiative was seized by Lieutenant Governor Hare. Reports from the civil commissioner at Colesberg convinced Hare that there was danger of an organized revolt of farmers in the colonial districts of Colesberg, Graaff Reinet, and Cradock in concert with the trans-Orange Boers, and, early in December, 1842, he sent from Grahamstown to Colesberg a force of approximately 850 men, gambling that the eastern frontier would remain quiet.[84] This display of power may have averted an attack on the Griquas by Mocke's supporters. Hare, who had followed his troops to Colesberg, had three interviews with representatives of the Boers and the Griquas. He told the Boers that he was determined to restore order and would hang all rebels. When the Boers pleaded that they had as much right to possess the country and to establish an independent government as did the Griquas, Hare dismissed these arguments and warned them that so long as the Griquas remained faithful allies, they would be supported by the full force of the British Empire. Fur-

---

[80] *Grahamstown Journal*, Oct. 27, 1842.

[81] Minutes of Executive Council, Oct. 27, 1842, C.O. 51/42, P.R.O.

[82] Minutes of Executive Council, Nov. 3, 1842, *ibid.*

[83] Napier to Stanley, Dec. 13, 1842, C.O. 48/224, P.R.O.

[84] Napier to Stanley, Dec. 16, 1842, *ibid.*

ther, he stated that the Boers by their rebellious spirit had forfeited
any rights to their leases of Griqua lands, but he would request Kok
to allow all Boers who received pardon to retain possession of their
lands.[85] His lecture was infuriating to the Boers, but the presence of
a substantial body of troops prevented open demonstrations. Hare
remained at Colesberg until the end of January, 1843, by which time
he decided that his demonstration had accomplished its effect, and then
returned to Grahamstown leaving more than 300 men at Colesberg
and another 100 at Cradock as insurance against further disturbances.[86]
The withdrawal of even so small a number of troops seriously weakened
the defense of the eastern frontier; and no troops could be spared from
Cape Town, where the garrison had been dangerously depleted.[87]

The crisis was somewhat relieved by reinforcements in the course of
the year, but the military manpower of the Cape was still meager for
the task of frontier defense. By March, 1843, instructions from London
had made it clear that the British government, though its policy
against expansion remained unchanged, was inclined to provide support for native tribes against Boer encroachments.[88] Accordingly
Napier decided to follow Philip's suggestion and to negotiate treaties
with Kok and Moshesh. At the beginning of October, after two months
of consultation with Philip on the specific terms, the government
secretary notified Napier that the treaties were ready for signature
and that Philip had agreed to write "his missionaries" to advise the
chiefs to agree to the terms.[89] Kok signed at the end of November and
Moshesh two weeks later. The terms of the agreements were similar to
those of the treaty with Waterboer in 1834. Each chief would preserve
order in his territory and assist the colonial authorities in apprehending criminals or fugitives from the colony. Moshesh was to receive not
less than £75 annually, either in money or in arms and ammunition,
as he should prefer, and Kok was to be paid £100 annually on the
same terms. Further, on information supplied by Philip, the boundaries of Moshesh's territory were described.[90] The French missionaries
at Thaba Bosiu hailed the treaty as "one of the most important events
which has to be recorded in the history of the Basutos," and Philip

---

[85] Wright to Philip, Jan. 2, 1843, SAF 19–1, LMS Archives.

[86] Hare to Napier, June 2, 1843, enclosure in Napier to Stanley, July 8, 1843, C.O.
48/230, P.R.O.

[87] Napier to Stanley, July 18, 1843, C.O. 48/130, P.R.O.

[88] Stanley to Napier, Jan. 26, 1843, C.O. 48/224, P.R.O.

[89] Montagu to Napier, Oct. 4, 1843, G.H. 19/4, Cape Archives.

[90] Sauer and Theal, *op. cit.*, I, 55.

as the great benefactor of Basuto people.[91] The Wesleyans were not so enamored; they considered the proceedings a power play on the part of the London Missionary Society to achieve a favored position for their protégés among those tribes associated with the Wesleyans.[92] The proposed boundaries of Basuto territory caused general dissatisfaction. Casalis wrote Philip that, although he was sure no dismemberment was intended, the stated limits of Moshesh's domain would exclude much of the district inhabited by Moroko's Barolong, who were subject to Moshesh's overlordship and thus would leave them at the mercy of the farmers.[93] William Shaw of the Methodist society protested that the boundaries embraced territories occupied by independent tribes including those of Moroko, Piet David, Carolus Baatje, and Sikonyela, who were determined to defend their territories against the pretensions of Moshesh.[94]

Confronted by directly contradictory testimony on an issue on which there was little objective evidence, the executive council decided that the statement of boundaries in the treaty should not be considered to imply governmental approval or disapproval of their accuracy, and that the contending parties should be encouraged to settle among themselves the limits of their respective territories. If this was not accomplished within nine months, a declaratory article would be appended to the treaty disclaiming any governmental endorsement of the specific boundaries. If the other chiefs settled their differences with Moshesh, the colonial government would be prepared to enter into treaties with them.[95]

The treaty with Moshesh, instead of being a means to order, had thus become a source of conflict, and the rivalry of missionary societies had encouraged divisions among tribes that it was imperative to unite. The issue of boundaries was destined to disturb the native territories of Transorangia for many years to come, but the primary contestants against the Basuto were to be the Boers, not the Barolong. Though he reflected a vested interest, Philip was correct that Moshesh was the strongest chief beyond the Orange and that the tribes should unite against a common menace.[96] Intertribal unity was undoubtedly impossible in any event, but Wesleyan-London conflict exacerbated disunity.

The treaty with Kok also contained ambiguities which accentuated

[91] Dyke to Philip, Dec. 13, 1843, SAF 19–4, LMS Archives.

[92] Shaw to Hudson, Dec. 15, 1843, Sauer and Theal, op. cit., I, 57–59.

[93] Casalis to Philip, Dec. 14, 1843, SAF 19–4, LMS Archives.

[94] Shaw to Hudson, Dec. 15, 1843, Sauer and Theal, op. cit., I, 57–59.

[95] Minutes of Executive Council, May 6, 1844, C.O. 51/52, P.R.O.

[96] Philip to Montagu, Jan. 16, 1844, SAF 19–4, LMS Archives.

tensions. Kok interpreted its terms to mean that the colonial government considered whites as well as Griquas to be subject to his authority, and that it was prepared to support him if there should be disorders. This was not the interpretation of the colonial government. While Napier and his council accepted Kok's authority over all inhabitants of his territory as a theoretical proposition, they rejected it as practical politics, for any attempt by Kok to punish an offending farmer was almost certain to cause bloodshed. Thus Napier advised Kok of the wisdom of pursuing a counciliatory policy toward the Boers. Nor did Napier interpret the treaty as imposing an obligation on him to send troops to support Kok's authority.[97]

Thus what Kok and Moshesh assumed to be a guarantee of mutual assistance was interpreted by the colonial government to be little more than an earnest of benevolent intentions. In expecting too much, Kok was encouraged to take a more determined line toward the Boers than he might otherwise have adopted, whereas the uncertain policy of the colonial government strengthened those Boers who wished to deal summarily with this contemptible bastard potentate. The consequence was a series of encounters culminating in a fire fight in April, 1845, with casualties on both sides, and the intervention of British troops. Proclamations and treaties backed by the threat of force made necessary the eventual exercise of force, and the sporadic intrusion and retreat of British power beyond the Orange River was no substitute for the imposition of a British administration.

Napier's successor, Maitland, in response to the intelligence that Boers and Griquas had collided, was forced to send troops to the Griqua territory. They dispersed the Boer commandos with relative ease, but such encounters in the field could not solve the basic problem. So long as Boers occupied lands intermingled with Griqua possessions there could be no peace in Griqualand. Wright's successor as missionary at Philippolis, William Thomson, had suggested as early as October, 1844, that the land be divided between Griquas and Boers, the Griquas to give up all claims to land and fountains beyond the Riet River, and the Boers to evacuate the land south of the river, the owners of unexpired leases to be compensated with amounts being fixed by arbitrators appointed by the governor. Thomson made this suggestion to Maitland at Colesberg, and the governor "seemed pleased and said it was a very equitable and reasonable suggestion." [98] When Maitland returned to the Griqua territory in June, 1845, to attempt

---

[97] Minutes of Executive Council, May 6, 1844, C.O. 51/52, P.R.O.

[98] Thomson to Philip, Oct. 17, 1844, SAF 21–2, LMS Archives.

a general pacification, however, the terms that he imposed were more unfavorable to the Griquas. Although Maitland's settlement recognized Kok's "absolute dominion" over all territories that he had previously controlled—a deliberately vague description, as no boundaries had ever been drawn—it divided the Griqua territory into two sections: "inalienable" lands where the Griquas were forbidden to grant any further leases or other rights of occupation to any white person, and an "alienable" area where such leases might continue to be made. The inalienable territory, which was less extensive than Thomson had proposed in October, 1844, was clearly defined.[99] No boundaries were drawn for the remainder. The maximum lease in the alienable territory was to be forty years. Lessees in the inalienable territory would continue to enjoy their rights until the expiration of the leases. Though Kok's sovereignty was affirmed, he was in fact subjected to the control of a British resident whose approval was requisite for all future leases, and who would preside over all litigation of conflicts between Griquas and British subjects. All payments of quitrents would be made to him; he would retain half for the expenses of his administration, and would remit the remainder to Adam Kok.[100]

Maitland endeavored to create a system that would pay for itself. To minimize conflict, he sought to draw a clear line of demarcation between Boers and Griquas. The influence of the resident was only moral; if it was defied, his only recourse was to call for military assistance, for he had no police power at his disposal to enforce the day-to-day decisions of government, except the tribesmen of Moshesh and Adam Kok whom by the treaties he might summon to his aid. But the most likely adversary against whom these warriors might be used was the Boers, and the employment of blacks against whites could embroil not only Transorangia but the frontier areas of the colony, for the colonial Boers could be expected to come to the assistance of their friends across the border.

The division of Griqua territory into inalienable and alienable sections did not separate the residents into clearly demarcated communities. Many Boers continued to reside on long-term leases within the inalienable territory, and in the alienable section, Griquas and Boers continued to be mixed. The mélange was charged with future conflict. Both Boers and Griquas expressed resentment at Maitland's intervention. The Boers smoldered at his treatment of them as rebel-

---

[99] For the boundaries, see Cory, *op. cit.*, IV, 316–317.
[100] Memorandum by Brownlow Maitland, June 25, 1845, SAF 21-2, LMS Archives. The agreement is summarized in Cory, *op. cit.*, IV, 315–316.

lious subjects and at his arrogant dismissal of their requests to be heard.
Kok protested that the governor, while recognizing his rights of sovereignty, had in effect stripped him of his powers by assigning authority over his people to a British magistrate.[101] The missionary Thomson
expressed the view that, if Maitland's decision to permit the Boers
to remain in the inalienable territory was allowed to stand, "there will
be a great breaking up among the people here." [102] On representations
from Kok through John Philip, Maitland agreed that Kok should have
criminal jurisdiction over his own people in all cases, but that the
British resident should be present at trials of Griquas accused of crimes
against British subjects.[103] But in all other respects the final treaty
of February, 1846, was essentially in accordance with Maitland's terms
of August, 1845.

The discussions with Moshesh and the "Wesleyan" chiefs were even
less productive. The claims of the contending chiefs were irreconcilable
and the governor decided to make no judgment at all. Nor could
Maitland deal effectively with the problem of Boer settlement in the
midst of the tribes. At the time of his visit more than 1,100 Boer families were already residing in tribal territories. Unlike those in the
Griqua area, most of them were there without any payment for the
use of the land and in many instances in open defiance of the chief.[104]
Around Moroko's Thaba Nchu there were more than 300 Boer families, of whom three had received permission to settle and fifteen
others had become permanently resident after receiving permission to
rest for a season. These Boers ignored the authority of a chief they
asserted had no more right to the country than they did. Practically
all had measured out their land without reference to Moroko, and
bought and sold land as if they held clear titles.[105] The same condition
obtained in other areas, and Moshesh's agreement to grant rights of
settlement to Boers in a tract of his country, provided they were removed from the remainder, was akin to attempting to channel a flood
when there were no dikes.

The Colonial Office recognized, as did Maitland, the defects of his
arrangements, and was even more pessimistic of their success.[106] But
as Stephen glumly admitted, it was vain to object without being able

[101] Memorandum by Kok, June 30, 1843, SAF 21–2, LMS Archives.

[102] Thomson to Philip, July 3, 1845, *ibid.*

[103] Maitland to Stanley, March 13, 1846, C.O. 48/261, P.R.O.

[104] Maitland to Stanley, Aug. 1, 1845, Sauer and Theal, *op. cit.*, I, 94.

[105] Cameron to Secretaries, WMS, June 16, 1845, Bechuanaland File, MMS Archives.

[106] Minutes on Maitland to Stanley, Aug. 1, 1845, C.O. 48/255; Stanley to Maitland,
Nov. 3, 1845, C.O. 49/38, both in P.R.O.

to suggest a better alternative.[107] Order could not be imposed without spending money, and the Colonial Office was proscribed from such expenditures. "I do not believe," wrote Stephen, "that it is possible that such a society as that of the Cape of Good Hope, occupying such a territory as theirs, should be well governed. . . . even if the arguments are almost conclusive to shew that what exists is bad . . . they may fail to show . . . that what is proposed is better." [108]

With the approval of Downing Street, Maitland appointed a British resident with jurisdiction over British subjects not only within the territories of Kok's Griquas, but within those of the Basuto and adjacent tribes as well. The first to accept the appointment, Captain Sutton of the Cape Mounted Rifles, resigned, fortunately for himself, after only two months in office, and Captain Henry D. Warden, in command of a detachment of that corps at Philippolis, who had previously been recommended for the position by D'Urban, accepted the impossible task.[109] He had been in office less than two months when he confided in Maitland's son Brownlow that the more he looked at the land problems of Moshesh and rival chiefs the more complicated they became.[110] His attempts to impose a solution eventually destroyed him.

Beyond the Orange as in Natal, Britain had been loath to extend its responsibilities. Eventual expansion was likely, but the day should be postponed as long as possible. When it became evident that proclamations had no effect in restraining the emigrant Boers, Britain was drawn inexorably into ever greater involvement, but, as James Stephen put it, "experimentally and doubtfully." [111]

---

[107] Minute by Stephen, n.d., on Maitland to Stanley, March 13, 1846, C.O. 48/261, P.R.O.

[108] Minute by Stephen on Smith to Grey, July 29, 1849, C.O. 48/289, P.R.O.

[109] Maitland to Stanley, Jan. 15, 1846, C.O. 48/260, P.R.O.

[110] Warden to B. Maitland, March 11, 1846, G.H. 14/1, Cape Archives.

[111] Minute by Stephen, n.d., on Maitland to Stanley, March 13, 1846, C.O. 48/261, P.R.O.

Chapter X

ADVANCE, 1846–1850

AMONG THE POLITICIANS and theorists of the day the significance of the repeal of the corn laws was variously assessed. Some foresaw the early death of British agriculture, with catastrophic social as well as economic consequences, while others prophesied that the era after repeal would be one of unparalleled prosperity. Those who thought about the Empire agreed that the abolition of the corn laws and, three years later, of the navigation acts, must necessarily produce a new relationship between Great Britain and the colonies. The nature of that relationship was uncertain—it must be developed pragmatically—but the general direction of change was evident. Whatever imperial system emerged, the colonies must accept responsibility for their own support. This was not a new doctrine, as governments since the early 1830's had been dominated by a passion for retrenchment in colonial expenditures; but from the 1840's the mandate of economy was rigorously imposed. The middle years of the nineteenth century were dominated by the Chancellors of the Exchequer, the high priests of economy, who could pronounce anathema on unnecessary spending. The greatest drain on the public was expenditure for the army and the navy, and a large proportion of the military establishment in the 1840's and the 1850's was employed in the defense of colonies.[1] The implication was clear that, if the colonies provided for their own internal security, the British budget could be pared substantially. A bête noire of economy advocates was the Cape. This colony, often deemed almost worthless except for strategic purposes, required for its domestic security a constant frontier force of several thousand imperial troops. Even with this protection, wars erupted with appalling frequency and cost millions of pounds, each war being more expensive than the last. Cape Colony presented one of the most critical imperial problems

---

[1] See memo by Grey, Oct. 17, 1846, enclosure in confidential print, "The Army," by Earl Grey, printed at the Foreign Office, Jan. 30, 1852, Russell Papers, PRO 30/22/10, P.R.O.

faced by British governments between 1846 and 1854. If it was true
that debates on colonial problems were usually conducted before a
nearly empty house, this was not so with the Cape, for appropriations
of millions of pounds engrossed the attention of the most insular of
politicians. In 1846–1847 the War of the Axe was disastrous to the
budget; three years later another and more expensive Kaffir war followed by a Basuto war produced further woes for the British Treasury.
Molesworth called the Cape "the Algeria of England," [2] and harassed
Chancellors of the Exchequer must have agreed that the comparison
was apt, for huge sums of money were poured into this maw without
producing any perceptible progress toward stability.

While the war of 1846–1847 was still in progress, the Peel government fell. In the new administration of Lord John Russell, the Colonial Office was assigned to the third Earl Grey. The appointment was
in tribute to his ability rather than to his popularity or his services
to the party. Grey was a difficult colleague. Since his entry into politics
as Viscount Howick he had displayed an independence of party
discipline which was most annoying to his fellow Whigs. Before Russell
had been invited to form a government, Grey had been tempted to
advocate a coalition government with Peel at the head because he believed a Whig government headed by Russell would be "sadly wanting
in weight." [3] But this wayward spirit had certain assets which convinced
the cabinet makers that he should, for all his deficiencies, be included
in the government. He had the confidence of the Anti-Corn Law
League, Cobden, and other supporters of free trade who were by no
means dedicated to the Whig party, and his support of the government in the House of Lords was of great importance in view of the
array of influence and talent which the opposition could muster there.
Last, no one could contest that his knowledge of the problems of
empire was unrivaled by any other politician.[4] C. B. Adderley, one
of Grey's most severe critics, admitted later that "the Colonial Administration of this Country never had an abler, or more high-minded
chief, or one whose every action was more completely dictated by pure
and generous motives." [5]

Grey's knowledge of colonies was not an unqualified asset; it might

---

[2] *Parliamentary Debates*, 3d series, C (July 25, 1848), 823.

[3] Grey's Journal, June 2, 1846, Grey Papers, Prior's Kitchen, University of Durham.

[4] These were the arguments of Charles Wood for including Grey (Wood to Russell,
private, [July, 1846?], Russell Papers, PRO 30/22/5, P.R.O.).

[5] C.B. Adderley Norton, *Review of "The Colonial Policy of Lord J. Russell's
Administration"* (London: Stanford, 1869), p. 1.

be argued that on balance it was a liability. The colonists' eternal complaint was that Downing Street could not possibly understand them through the media of dispatches, statistics, and blue books, and that deeper insights into colonial problems cŏuld come only from firsthand observation. This contention was greatly overstated; the Colonial Office often had keener perception of the characteristics of colonial societies than did the colonists themselves. But the mental characteristics that caused Grey to devour information on colonial problems also constituted his outstanding weakness as an imperial policy maker. The mind of Earl Grey inclined toward the grand scheme and the ultimate solution. In southern Africa there were no ultimate solutions, and the parallels that Grey could see between its problems and those in other areas, such as India and New Zealand, led him to make judgments that were unrealistic to the South African scene. Although Grey acknowledged that the Kaffirs were not identical with Indians or Maoris, he believed that "in the main, human nature is everywhere the same," and that the policy that had tamed "the wild predatory tribes of India" should also have prospects for success with the tribes on the borders of the Cape.[6]

Grey proposed to enlist the coöperation of the tribes in the process of creating order and promoting civilization. British troops would be required, at least at first, to police the frontier and to discourage all thoughts of aggression among the Kaffirs, but increasingly order would be maintained by the tribesmen themselves. The Kaffir chiefs would govern under the supervision of British officials, and the police force would be drawn from the tribes but would be under the command of European officers. The expense of this system would be largely, and eventually entirely, borne by revenue from the Kaffir territories. The policy, if successful, would convert the tribes from disorderly neighbors into a protection for the colony against "the fierce predatory tribes" beyond. The colony would thus achieve a stable frontier at little or no expense to the imperial government. Grey consciously modeled his policy on that pursued in India; he also drew inspiration from the testimony of Sir Benjamin D'Urban, whom he much admired and whose policy in 1835 and 1836 he considered to have been highly successful before it was repudiated by Glenelg.[7]

Indian policy, however, was not an appropriate model for South

---

[6] Earl Grey, *The Colonial Policy of Lord John Russell's Administration* (2 vols.; London: Bentley, 1853), II, 204.

[7] Memo by Grey on Kaffir War, n.d. [1851?], Grey Papers. This viewpoint is elaborated in Grey, *op. cit.*, II, 203–204.

Africa, and D'Urban's administration of Queen Adelaide Province had been far from the brilliant success that Grey imagined. The use of Kaffir troops to maintain order in southern Africa, as the Sepoy armies did in India, was a special enthusiasm of Grey's, shared neither by his colleagues nor by officers with experience both in India and at the Cape. Smith, with all his misconceptions of the Kaffir character, saw "neither affinity nor analogy between the Barbarians of India, however wild in the mountains, and the Savages of South Africa." Among other differences, he pointed out, the peoples of India had served in armies for centuries and could be relatively easily subjected to European discipline.[8] Grey would have instructed Sir Henry Pottinger to begin the organization of a native militia, but he was dissuaded by Russell who warned that it was dangerous to place weapons in the hands of "wild and savage tribes." The Prime Minister advised Grey to constitute only a small body of police under the command of English officers, and to give Pottinger complete discretion as to whether he could ever use armed Kaffirs at all.[9]

Grey's problems as colonial secretary were aggravated by a personality that roused his opponents to maximum hostility and antagonized even his associates. His frigid manner led most men erroneously to consider him arrogant; rather, he was impatient of slovenly thinking. He was deemed too rigid and doctrinaire; but he could change his mind when evidence warranted. Grey's basic weakness as a minister was that he was not a politician. He could not work effectively with others. In his zeal he frequently created the impression that he considered himself endowed with superior wisdom and virtue. He would not compromise for the sake of party advantage a position that he believed to be in the best interests of the country. These characteristics gave special zest to the attacks of his opponents, who by the end of the Russell government had made him their principal target, and cost him the good will of his colleagues. Though he lived for forty years after the Russell government fell, he was never again invited to hold a cabinet office.

By 1852 the high hopes Grey had entertained for himself had turned to ashes. The causes for his exclusion from high office were fundamentally in the character of the man; but the primary sources of his failure as colonial secretary were not personal but institutional. Any minister occupying the office between 1846 and 1852 was certain to be identified with catastrophe in southern Africa. He might accept the

---

[8] Smith to Grey, May 6, 1848, W.O. 1/443, P.R.O.

[9] Russell to Grey, Dec. 4, 1846, Grey Papers.

responsibility or seek to transfer it to a governor, but he could not significantly alter the course of events.

When Grey took charge of the Colonial Office the War of the Axe had been dragging on for several months, devoid of any exploits of valor or feats of arms which might relieve Parliament's preoccupation with the inordinate expenditures to support so many troops against a few thousand savages. It was a war without justification beyond the necessity for fighting it, for the land of the Kaffirs had no present or prospective value to Britain. Grey immediately concluded that Sir Peregrine Maitland had prolonged the war because he was unable to act with the necessary vigor, and that he was unfit for the responsibility of supervising a postwar settlement.

From Maitland's dispatches Grey gained the impression that the war was almost over, as the Kaffirs had been reduced to a state of extremity by the constant harrying of the troops, who had destroyed their crops and driven away their cattle. The imminent end of the war made urgent the appointment of a governor who would have the imagination and vitality to carry out Grey's plans for a new order on the Cape frontier. The ideal selection in Grey's opinion was Sir Henry Pottinger, who had distinguished himself as a political agent in India. Grey's prospective frontier system was modeled on that of the Indian feudatory states, which Pottinger understood as well as any man. By great good fortune Pottinger was in England in 1846, after three years of service as the first governor of Hong Kong, and had no immediate assignment. Grey in August consulted with Russell who agreed that every effort must be made to secure Pottinger's services.[10] Pottinger was not enthusiastic. His life had been in India, and it was to India that he wished to return. But after much coaxing and cajoling, culminating in appeals to his patriotism, Pottinger agreed to go to the Cape, with the proviso that he would be relieved when he had restored tranquillity, and with the understanding that for this sacrifice he would have strong claim to be appointed to a high post in India when one became available.[11]

Circumstances at the Cape, in Russell's and Grey's opinion, justified the use of such pressure and inducements. The war had presented the government with an opportunity to initiate a "new and bold" approach [12] to the problem of the frontier. The new policy was developed

---

[10] Russell to Grey, Aug. 20, 1846, *ibid.*

[11] Grey to Pottinger, Sept. 14, 1846, *ibid.*

[12] The adjectives are Hawes's, in a minute to Grey, Sept. 18, [1846], C.O. 48/264, P.R.O.

with great care. In September and October, 1846, the staff of the Colonial Office debated the details of Grey's instructions to Pottinger. When they had finally hammered out the elements of the revolutionary approach to Cape policy, however, there was surprisingly little that was distinctive from what had been tried and found wanting. The *sine qua non* was a defense system adequate to maintain the peace while the Kaffirs were led toward acceptance of British law and British order. Grey and his staff agreed that the commando system must never return, and that the core of the military defense of the colony must continue for some time to be regular troops, but immediate action should be taken to incorporate Kaffirs into the military system. These tribesmen, drawn initially from among the followers of the more friendly or trustworthy chiefs, might be employed instead of British troops in the western districts of the colony. Not only would these low-paid native levies reduce the cost of defense but they would be "real, though unavowed hostages for the tranquillity of their kindred." [13] A further supplement to the regular army, Benjamin Hawes suggested, might be provided by military settlements on the frontier, tenure being dependent on availability for immediate service at the call of the Cape commander.[14]

Though overwhelming military force was necessary while the Kaffirs remained restive, the eventual objective was self-discipline through voluntary acceptance of imperial authority. Service in the army was a useful method of indoctrination because it inculcated habits of unquestioning obedience. Education, with an emphasis on the practical arts, and religious instruction were also necessary elements in the process of civilization, and the missionaries should receive full moral, and perhaps some financial, support in this enterprise. Teachers should use the English language and any efforts to reduce the "Kaffir tongue" to writing as a medium of instruction should be strongly discouraged.[15]

These plans necessitated the extension of British authority into the Kaffir territories from which it had receded ten years before. Grey admitted that such expansion was contrary to the general principles of sound imperial policy: "Considered in themselves such acquisitions would be not merely worthless but pernicious—the source not of increased strength but of weakness—enlarging the range of our responsibilities while yielding no additional resources for properly sustaining

---

[13] This phrase appears in the draft instructions, but was deleted in the final form (*ibid.*).

[14] Minute, Hawes to Grey, Sept. 18, [1846], *ibid.*

[15] Draft instructions to Pottinger, [Sept.–Oct., 1846], *ibid.*

them." But he was required to deal with a condition, not with a theory. The security of the colony and the welfare of the Kaffirs themselves dictated that the Kaffirs be brought under control. Those tribes west of the Keiskama River who remained under colonial jurisdiction would lose all pretense of independence; henceforth they would be British subjects. Beyond the Keiskama the tribes would be subject to British authority, but with a government and laws adapted to their characteristics, subjecting them to firm but benign control, pruning away those elements that were abominating to civilized man but retaining the essential fabric of tribal society. The territory denominated British Kaffraria might include all or part of the lands between the colonial boundary and the Kei River—the exact extent was dependent on Pottinger's advice—and would be administered separately from Cape Colony. It would be primarily a native reserve; the governor should in no event permit intrusion of any cattle farmers of European origin, particularly Boers, though Grey believed that the settlement of Europeans with mechanical or agricultural skills would probably be advantageous.[16]

Grey's policy for British Kaffraria was essentially similar to that introduced by D'Urban in Queen Adelaide Province more than a decade earlier, and some of its features were like the schemes introduced by Sir George Grey among the Maoris of New Zealand. D'Urban was in London at the time discussions were taking place on Pottinger's instructions, and he probably consulted with Earl Grey and certainly conferred with Pottinger.[17] Despite the impressive combination of wisdom and experience brought to bear upon the problem, however, Grey's plans held no prospect for the solution of the Cape's frontier problems. Grey may have been deluded by Maitland's overly optimistic accounts of the course of the war or by D'Urban's assessment of Kaffir characteristics. Whatever the source of his misinformation, he underestimated the problem of permanently subduing the tribes beyond the colonial border. Fascinated by the spectacle of a few Europeans in India maintaining ascendancy over a population of millions without any burdens on England, he believed that similar techniques would have similar results in southern Africa. Not only could Kaffirs be trained to subdue Kaffirs on the southeastern frontier, but the tribes of Natal could be controlled similarly. The protection of the Crown might also be extended to chiefs beset by emigrant Boer cattle farmers, and their tribes could be taught by British officials to defend them-

---

[16] Grey to Pottinger, Nov. 2, 1846, *ibid.*
[17] Pottinger to Grey, Oct. 24, [1846], *ibid.*

selves. Thus, without any pecuniary outlay beyond the salaries of the
training officers, British protection could be extended over a huge area
of southern Africa.[18] The conception was highly imaginative, and, as
the events of the next four years demonstrated, totally unrealistic.

If the plans were defective, so also was the instrument. Pottinger had
no interest in the Cape. He accepted the governorship only because
of the assurance that his tenure would be short and his reward an appointment to a high post in India. His correspondence with Grey before his departure was more concerned with his emoluments than with
problems of administering the affairs of the Cape, and only a month
after he had accepted the appointment he expressed a preference for
the governorship of Bombay which had recently fallen vacant.[19] The
historian Theal, who thoroughly disapproved of Pottinger's amorous
adventures at the Cape, wrote that "he was much better adapted for
office in India than in South Africa." [20] The generalization was undoubtedly correct, though not perhaps in the sense intended. In fair-
ness to Pottinger it should be stressed that he gained little personal
advantage by going to the Cape. He would probably have been appointed to a position of responsibility in India in any event, and he
accepted office primarily because of considerations of duty. At his own
suggestion,[21] Pottinger was given a dual commission as governor and
as high commissioner to settle the affairs of territories adjacent to the
frontiers of the colony.[22] He expected that the war would be over or
in its terminal stages when he arrived at the Cape, and that his functions would be essentially those of an administrator rather than a
diplomat. He was speedily disillusioned.

When Pottinger landed in Cape Town at the end of January, 1847,
he found that the war was not over. Maitland's lifting of martial law
and disbandment of most of the burgher forces had been premature,
and it was left to Pottinger to complete the reduction of the Kaffirs to
submission. The new governor remained in Cape Town less than two
weeks before he sailed for the frontier to determine for himself the
true state of affairs. As usual, the reports were contradictory; like other
visitors to the eastern province, Pottinger was struck by the prevalence

---

[18] Grey to Pottinger, Dec. 4, 1846, C.O. 179/1, P.R.O.

[19] Hobhouse to Russell, confidential, Sept. 27, 1846, Russell Papers, PRO 30/22/5,
P.R.O.; Wood to Grey, Oct. 15, 1846, Grey Papers.

[20] George M. Theal, *History of South Africa since September, 1795* (5 vols.; London:
Swan Sonnenschein, 1907–1910), II, 56.

[21] Pottinger to Grey, Sept. 29, 1846; memo, Stephen to Grey, Oct. 3, [1846], both
in C.O. 48/264, P.R.O.

[22] Commission, Oct. 10, 1846, *ibid.*

of rumors and the avidity with which they were accepted and espoused.[23] But reports of political agents and officers in the field made
it evident that active resistance had not ended. Most of the principal
chiefs had offered their submission, and had registered themselves as
British subjects under Maitland's dispensation that all who did so
and delivered up a gun or, if they had no gun, six assagais, would be
immune from further attack; and several thousands of the tribesmen
had followed their example. But there could be no certainty that this
formal submission would be lasting. One of the chiefs, Pato, was still
in open resistance; if he was not broken, others might be encouraged
to follow his example.

The commander of the forces, Sir George Berkeley, had about 5,500
regular troops at his disposal, of whom more than 3,200 were on the
frontier.[24] This was a kind of war for which redcoats were ill-suited.
There was no opposing army; there were no pitched battles. European
conceptions of strategy and tactics were virtually useless. The objective
was to break the Kaffirs' will to resist by destroying their sources of
food and taking their cattle, while maintaining a constant alert for
ambushes against supply trains or isolated units. For this service colonial levies were superior to troops, and Hottentots were far superior
to either. The Cape Mounted Rifles and the Hottentot infantry were
unexcelled in tracking Kaffirs and their cattle and in guarding booty.[25]
Under the misapprehension that the Hottentots of Kat River held
their land on military tenure, Pottinger sought to conscript 400 men
from the settlement, and the failure of the villagers to respond created
in him a hostility that was not removed by his discovery of his error.
His success with the white burghers was no more impressive. It was
impolitic, he believed, to reimpose martial law; instead he appealed
for volunteers who would serve for a maximum of one month in the
field. Several thousand settlers responded, but, as so often happened,
they melted away when their services were urgently required. Berkeley,
like all regular army commanders before him, denounced the volunteers for their lack of devotion to the common cause. It was impossible,
he fumed, to carry on effective operations when troops worked when,
how, and where they pleased; if the men in the colony were unwilling
to defend it, the sooner the British army left them to their fate the
better.[26]

---

[23] Pottinger to Grey, March 13, 1847, C.O. 48/272, P.R.O.

[24] George E. Cory, *The Rise of South Africa* (5 vols.; London: Longmans, Green,
1921–1930), V, 33.

[25] Berkeley to Pottinger, secret, April 9, 1847, W.O. 1/441, P.R.O.

[26] Berkeley to Pottinger, April 12, 1847, *ibid.*

Pottinger had come to South Africa to establish a new frontier policy; his functions were to be civilian, not military. He was an administrator and a diplomat rather than a soldier, but his energies were almost entirely consumed by military problems and disputes with the commander in the field over the limits of their respective authority. Under the circumstances, Pottinger's special talents were largely wasted, though, in marked contrast to his predecessor, he devoted himself to his duties with zealous industry. He began his day, he wrote Grey, at 6 A.M. and worked invariably until midnight, sometimes later, with an intermission of two hours for dinner, comforting himself with the reflection that the high pressure could not last forever.[27] One is disposed to wonder when he had the time, much less the energy, for the licentiousness of which he has been accused.

Pottinger was able to give some attention to the purposes for which he had been sent. His predecessor had proposed that the Fish and the Kat rivers should be the limit of European occupation, but that the territory between the Fish and the Keiskama should be occupied by Hottentots who, supported by military posts, would be a buffer between Kaffirs and Europeans.[28] Pottinger disagreed. The mouth of the Buffalo River offered a better landing place for troops and stores than Waterloo Bay, which had hitherto been used. He was consequently inclined to advance the colonial boundary to the Buffalo River. He acknowledged that this extension would add further territory to a colony already overgrown, but he believed that the strategic advantages outweighed the liability. Between the Keiskama and the Buffalo he would locate those Kaffirs who were "the best disposed," but parts of the territory would be available for European settlement. Between the Buffalo and the Kei he would establish the protectorate of British Kaffraria. There he would carry out the system that Grey had enjoined upon him.[29] The major deviation from the policy on which he and Grey had agreed would be the extension of the colony's boundary from the Keiskama to the Buffalo, and the opening up of tracts in this annexed territory for white settlement. Thus, on the argument of strategic necessity, a governor again found justification for the advancement of European settlement and the further compression of territory allotted for occupation by the Bantu. Pottinger was superseded before he could consummate his project.

At about the same time that Pottinger arrived at the Cape, Sir Harry Smith returned to England to a hero's welcome for his exploits in

---

[27] Pottinger to Grey, private, May 16, 1847, Grey Papers.
[28] Cory, *op. cit.*, IV, 508.
[29] Pottinger to Berkeley, March 26, 1847, W.O. 1/441, P.R.O.

India, particularly his victory over the Sikhs which had won him a baronetcy and the distinction of appending "of Aliwal" to the title. Grey was entranced with Smith. Whether or not he had from the first thought of Sir Harry as a successor to Pottinger is not clear, but certainly he came to that conclusion after their first meeting. Smith, in Grey's opinion, was a perfect selection for the governorship of the Cape. He had known the Kaffirs both as adversaries and as subjects; he understood the problem of southern Africa as did no other prospective appointee; and he had distinguished himself in India, where basic lessons could be learned on the nature of frontier policy at the Cape. But the qualifications that Grey considered so impressive were in fact no qualifications at all. Smith was the most dangerous of men; an expert on the last war, he had formed his opinions on the basis of observations that were now obsolete, if they had ever been correct. Smith thought he "knew his Kaffirs"; he did not know them in 1835, and he knew them less in 1847, but he formulated his conclusions on the basis of the South Africa he remembered.

Much to Grey's gratification, Smith advised the minister that as soon as peace was restored, the number of British regulars at the Cape could be reduced by two-thirds; the security of the frontier could be established by augmentation of the Hottentot Cape Mounted Rifles. In the future, Smith said, he would never call out the burghers; instead he would require each burgher to send as a substitute a well-armed Hottentot or ex-slave. Under officers drawn from the young gentlemen of the colony, these troops would be superior to either regulars or white levies.[30] Further, Smith assured Grey that the frontier could be stabilized by 2,000 men, including colonial levies, whereas Pottinger had considered 5,000 soldiers scarcely adequate to defend Cape Colony and ensure the security of its borders.[31] Smith promised to be economical, whereas Pottinger had displayed a "truly Indian disregard of expense." [32] Before Pottinger was formally proposed for the governorship of Madras, Smith had already agreed to succeed him at the Cape.[33]

[30] Smith to Grey, May 7, 1847, Grey Papers.

[31] Grey to Russell, May 31, 1847, Russell Papers, PRO 30/22/6, P.R.O.

[32] This was an ill-kept secret. Lord Douro said to Smith at Apsley House, "So you are going to the Cape and Sir Henry Pottinger is to go to Madras?" (Smith to Grey, confidential, June 18, 1847, Grey Papers). There was then no official vacancy at Madras. In July, Russell thought of sending Cobden to Madras. Pottinger then would have stayed at the Cape, and Grey suggested to Russell that Smith be sent to Malta (Grey to Russell, private, July 6, 1847, Russell Papers, PRO 30/22/6, P.R.O.).

[33] Grey to Russell, July 13, 1847, Russell Papers, PRO 30/22/6, P.R.O.; same to same, private, July 14, 1847, Grey Papers.

Grey, who in the summer of 1846 had considered the appointment of Pottinger to the Cape as necessary to the national interest, a year later expressed impatience that he was still there. Smith was now the man of the hour,[34] enjoying the esteem of Russell and Grey. In July, 1847, arrangements were completed, and Grey was able formally to offer the governorship to Smith as "by far the fittest person" who could be selected.[35] Smith had been offered command of the troops of Bengal,[36] a more lucrative and less hazardous position. The interests of the Empire and the reputation of Smith would have been served had he returned to India.

Smith's temperament had not changed essentially since his previous stay at the Cape; if anything, his exploits in India had intensified his penchant for the dramatic. So long as this characteristic was confined to words and gestures or to emotional displays, it was relatively harmless, in fact endearing to his admirers. But it led to the illusion that order could be achieved by force of personality. Smith was by nature an expansionist. His Indian experience had convinced him that imperial expansion was inevitable; and from his association with Kaffirs and Boers he believed that he could extend British authority beyond the borders of Cape Colony with little expense to the Treasury. Both the emigrant Boers and the Kaffirs were like children, he thought. They could be managed if they were treated with firmness and justice. "Firmness," however, was more than the dramatic assertion that "I am now Governor. I WILL BE GOVERNOR!" [37] and "justice" was not possible where there was no accepted standard as to what justice was. Pottinger, when he heard that he had been appointed to Madras and that Smith would succeed him, expressed "great relief" to be going to a less nerve-racking and time-consuming post, and pleasure that Smith was to assume responsibility at the Cape, for "the very prestige of his name will awe the Kaffirs into instant submission." [38] Smith would have agreed; the events of the next few years would demonstrate that he was tragically wrong.

---

[34] Grey to Russell, July 13, 1847, Russell Papers, PRO 30/22/6, P.R.O.; fragment, Russell to Grey, July 14, 1847, Grey Papers.

[35] Grey to Smith, private, July 22, 1847, Grey Papers. Smith was appointed not only as governor and high commissioner but as commander in chief to avoid the conflict that had marred Pottinger's relations with Berkeley.

[36] Grey to Russell, July 29, 1847, Russell Papers, PRO 30/22/6, P.R.O.; Russell to Grey, July 31, 1847, Grey Papers.

[37] These were his words in response to an address of welcome in Cape Town (Cory, op. cit., V, 99–100).

[38] Pottinger to Grey, private, Sept. 28, 1847, Grey Papers.

During the first few months of his administration nothing occurred to disturb Smith's self-confidence. The colonists shared his optimism. The *Grahamstown Journal* considered his appointment as "one of the most graceful, as well as the most politic acts of the present administration," providing "a bright prospect of future tranquillity for this hitherto distracted country." [39] The contrast between this flamboyant, lovable military genius and his unpopular predecessor heightened the enthusiasm that greeted his arrival in December, 1847.

Smith took office at an auspicious moment. All resistance had ended, and Pato surrendered as soon as the new governor reached the frontier, thus lending further credence to the myth of Smith's charismatic powers. At King Williamstown, before a large assembly of Ciskeian chiefs and people, Smith staged a dramatic ceremony designed to impress the Kaffirs with the power and majesty of British authority. The tribesmen were congregated in a circle, with the great chiefs toward the center. Into this assemblage rode Sir Harry Smith and his staff, attired in dress uniforms. Smith carried in his right hand a sergeant's halberd, "well sharpened," the emblem of war, and in his left a staff resembling a broomstick with a brass knob at the end, the baton of peace. These symbols, he explained to Grey, had the qualities of magic among the Kaffirs. He told each chief to come forward and touch the stick he preferred—"it was immaterial to me"—and "they all cheerfully touched the symbol of Peace." He then read a proclamation establishing the Keiskama River as the boundary of the colony; abrogating all treaties with the tribes; and announcing the extension of the Queen's domain over British Kaffraria, the lands between the Keiskama and the Kei, where chiefs and people would live under British authority, subject to such rules as would best promote their progress toward Christianity and civilization. After reading these declarations "in a very impressive manner," accompanied by "various comments, threats and promises," he allowed each chief to come forward and kiss his foot, "a custom of their own in homage" and to acclaim him "Inkosi Inkulu (Great Chief)." [40] A few days earlier at Port Elizabeth, Smith had similarly humiliated Makomo. When the chief offered the governor his hand, Sir Harry forced him to the ground, put his foot on his neck, and brandished a sword over his head while he upbraided him for his misconduct.[41] By such performances, Smith believed that he reduced his "Black Children" [42] to awed but admiring submission. He

---

[39] *Grahamstown Journal*, Oct. 23, 1847.

[40] Smith to Grey, Dec. 23, 1847, C.O. 48/279, P.R.O.

[41] *South African Commercial Advertiser*, Dec. 22, 1847.

[42] Smith to Southey, Dec. 2, 1847, Southey Papers, Cape Archives.

reported to Grey that the enthusiasm of the Kaffirs at his return was "excessive." [43] The *South African Commercial Advertiser* caustically commented that while Oriental history abounded in instances of foot kissing, this was the first occasion when the Kaffir phrase "to come under the feet" had been interpreted in South Africa in anything but a metaphorical sense.[44] This old adversary was almost alone; Smith was not considered ridiculous until he ceased to be successful.

The attitude of Sir Harry Smith toward the Kaffir tribes was not unlike the attitude of master toward slave or of a member of the elite toward a social inferior. He was paternally benign so long as the Kaffirs were docile and respectful; he became violent when they frustrated him. At the beginning of his governorship, the Kaffirs were patently subdued and repentant and his heart warmed to them. Sandile, who alleged that his imprisonment by Berkeley was in violation of a promise of safe-conduct, was released. Smith reported that the chief and his counselors had displayed "great joy" in seeing their old master even though he spoke to them sternly, and that when he freed Sandile with the words, "Now go to your people," the chief had replied, "No—I will stay today near you, my former and best friend." [45]

Smith's penchant for hyperbole and dramatic display, and his naïve faith in the power of his personality to overawe a virile people, tempt one to dismiss him as a ludicrous caricature of an eccentric Victorian, but Sir Harry was in fact a man of considerable ability. In India, where he had achieved his glittering reputation, his substantial characteristics were demonstrated and his eccentricities were in consonance with the environment. Smith was a failure in Cape Colony for reasons beyond his own personal characteristics. The system that he initiated in British Kaffraria was in accordance with Earl Grey's conception that the Kaffirs, by a kind of indirect rule supported by their own taxes, could be reduced to order and led toward civilization. Within the old ceded territory, now designated the colonial district of Victoria, Smith established military villages where discharged soldiers would receive plots of land on condition that they be available for defense in an emergency; and he proposed to create a colonial militia which would likewise be available on call and would have the virtues of self-defense without the evils of the old commando system.[46] Neither of these schemes was successful. The military villages were wiped out in the

[43] Smith to Grey, Jan. 1, 1848, Grey Papers.

[44] *South African Commercial Advertiser,* Dec. 29, 1847.

[45] Smith to Grey, Dec. 18, 1847, C.O. 48/279, P.R.O.

[46] Government notices, Dec. 24, 1847, enclosures in Smith to Grey, Dec. 23, 1847, *ibid.*

first Kaffir onslaught in 1850, and the opposition of the settlers frustrated the establishment of a militia system. But in 1848 there were no doubts expressed on Downing Street with regard to these proposals; the only caveat was with regard to the expense of the military villages, which the Treasury had decreed must be borne by Cape Colony.[47]

In British Kaffraria a British commandant and chief commissioner was appointed over the new subjects with functions similar to those of Smith in 1835, to be assisted by civil commissioners who would supervise the conduct of the various tribes. These officials would not only act as advisers to the chiefs but would review their judicial actions to ensure that they were in accordance with "justice and humanity." The Kaffirs would be encouraged to send their children to missionary schools, and would receive seeds and ploughs and instruction in husbandry. Kaffir youths would be apprenticed to work in the colony in districts remote from the frontier, where under kind and humane employers they might learn habits of industry which would be useful to them and an example to their fellows on their return to Kaffraria.[48]

For the force to support the system, Smith proposed to rely increasingly on the Kaffir police, which his predecessor had expanded to two divisions totaling 400 men. Smith proposed to use these men, backed by the Hottentots of the Cape Mounted Rifles, as the primary means of preserving order. As habits of discipline were inculcated upon the tribes, the number of police would be increased and the British troops required as a reserve could be progressively reduced. Grey gave unqualified approval to these policies, which were "entirely in accordance with my own as explained in my instructions to Sir Henry Pottinger and yourself." [49]

Any prospect of success for the Grey-Smith policy was eliminated by the essential condition governing imperial policy, that colonial functions should be carried out at the expense of the colonials themselves. Liberals and Conservatives agreed that the War of the Axe had been a classic example of the evils of dependency. British soldiers supported by British money had had to fight a war to protect colonists

---

[47] Minute by Grey, April 18, 1848, on Smith to Grey, Jan. 1, 1848, C.O. 48/283, P.R.O. The Treasury agreed to allocate to the Cape the amount of the passage money saved by soldiers who were discharged in the colony rather than sent home.

[48] Smith to Grey, March 23, 1848, C.O. 48/284, P.R.O. The Colonial Office expressed doubts about the legality of the scheme but none concerning its humanity. Grey wrote, "I think substantially the arrangement a good one and I am somewhat afraid of suggesting legal difficulties" (minute by Grey, May 29, 1848, on Smith to Grey, March 23, 1848 *ibid.*).

[49] Grey to Smith, March 31, 1848, C.O. 49/41. P.R.O.

who were disinclined to defend themselves. Indeed, there was a suspicion that colonial commercial interests had hoped for the continuation of the hostilities which were so profitable for them. Hopefully, representative government in Cape Colony would bring a greater sense of responsibility, but in any event settlers and the governor must understand that the imperial government was no longer prepared to underwrite colonial internal security. "Our course," Russell told Grey, "must be to retrench in colonial defences." [50] The Colonial Secretary required no injunction. He had campaigned for economy and efficiency since the days when, as a junior minister, he had been the gadfly of the Melbourne administration, and he considered himself and his brother-in-law Charles Wood, the Chancellor of the Exchequer, as watchdogs in a cabinet sometimes susceptible to extravagance.[51] A serious commercial crisis in 1847 and 1848 reinforced Grey's determination to avoid immediate expenditures even though they might bring ultimate advantage to both Britain and the colonies. He wrote Smith in March, 1848, that "the tide of opinion both in the House of Commons and in the Country is running so strongly against expenditure and taxation, that it will be absolutely necessary for us to be very cautious in sanctioning any new expense." [52] When Grey had first sought Smith's advice on Cape affairs, Sir Harry had expressed confidence that he could substantially reduce the military forces in southern Africa without risk to security. Smith was under unremitting pressure from the time of his appointment to effect such reductions. When a Kaffir war broke out in 1850 and Grey was attacked for having compromised the safety of the colony, he replied that he had consistently emphasized to the governor that he should reduce the forces only so far as security permitted, and that Smith had been at fault for having set the level of safety too low. This defense was technically correct, but Grey called for economy with far stronger emphasis than he counseled caution.

Smith had a fundamental weakness which compounded his problems. He had the type of courage that wins immortality on the battlefield, but he lacked the iron will that a strong executive must possess. Sir Harry sought public approval, he luxuriated in an atmosphere of adulation, and he was inordinately ambitious. Confronted with hard decisions, he sought a course of action least hazardous to his popularity and to the favor of his superiors. This course, as was evident in the anti-

---

[50] Russell to Grey, March 30, 1848, Grey Papers.
[51] Grey's Journal, Oct. 18, 1847, Grey Papers.
[52] Grey to Smith, private, April 20, 1848, Grey Papers.

convict agitation of 1849, could be most hazardous of all. Smith un-doubtedly believed that he could control the Cape frontiers with a smaller British force than Pottinger had deemed minimal, but in his desire to please the ministry he acted recklessly. Grey desired economy; Smith was "strenuously opposed to any expenditure from the Imperial Treasury." [53] Grey wished to impose a system of government in Kaf-fraria which would uphold rather than undermine the authority of the chiefs; Smith, despite impressive evidence to the contrary, re-sponded that this was his philosophy as well. "When I administered the Government of Kaffirland in 1836, I opened the gates of a Flood which I could not stem, by undermining the power of the Chiefs—my error was soon apparent, and I was compelled to reëstablish that which it had before been my purpose to weaken." [54]

Smith, of course, did not deliberately court disaster for the sake of favor. His great blunder was that he underrated the menace of the Kaffir tribes, and overestimated the force of his own personality. His drastic reduction in the military forces at a time when he expanded British responsibilities was dangerous, and he lost the gamble.

Smith had been in Cape Colony less than three weeks when he in-formed the ministry that he was extending the northern boundary of the Cape to the Orange River. This was a logical action, for the Orange River was a far more reasonable boundary than the arbitrary line to the south which had been drawn in 1805, and reflected the reali-ties of British influence up to and beyond the river. Further, the barren land of approximately 50,000 square miles thus formally added to the colony imposed no additional burdens of administration, as it was frequented by only a few hundred wandering Boers and Bastaards.[55] The staff of the Colonial Office was alarmed at this unexpected annexa-tion, but Grey, while he regretted the necessity for Smith's extension of the boundary, accepted the superior judgment of the "man on the spot." He advised the governor, however, to do all in his power to dis-courage the extension of cattle and sheep farms into the annexed terri-tory, which could cause further collisions between natives and Euro-peans.[56] This advice was unrealistic, as cattle and sheep farmers had

[53] Smith to Grey, March 4, 1848, C.O. 48/264, P.R.O.

[54] Smith to Grey, March 4, 1848, C.O. 179/4, P.R.O.

[55] Michell to Smith, Dec. 8, 1847, enclosure in Smith to Grey, Dec. 18, 1847, C.O. 48/279, P.R.O.

[56] Minute by Grey, March 3, 1848, on Smith to Grey, Dec. 18, 1847, *ibid.*; Grey to Smith, March 31, 1848, C.O. 49/41, P.R.O.

moved in response to pasturage and water rather than to arbitrary lines of colonial jurisdiction, and there was no power in the colony to restrain them.

Smith's annexation of the territory between the colony and the Stormberg area up the Kraai River also had logical justification, for this area of about 700 square miles had been part of Queen Adelaide Province and was occupied by European settlers, some of whom had lived there since the 1830's, jostling the Tembu for possession of land.[57] This district Smith named Albert. Five days later he annexed to the colony the mouth of the Buffalo River. Again the reasoning was compelling. The estuary was the best harbor for many miles and had been used by the military during the recently concluded Kaffir war. Now that the war was over, it might well be used by smugglers attempting to evade the colonial revenue laws.[58]

News of these annexations following in rapid succession the extension of the colony to the Orange River caused further concern in Downing Street. Hawes expressed apprehension that a governor could annex a territory as large as an English county without even the formality of Colonial Office approval.[59] Still Grey's confidence in Smith remained unshaken.

Within a few weeks, however, even Grey was taken aback by the intelligence that the governor had annexed the lands between the Orange River and the Vaal. In his numerous discussions with the Secretary of State before going to the Cape, Smith had apparently given no hint of any plans for so dramatic a resolution of the trans-Orange problem. Probably the idea did not crystallize until after he arrived in Cape Colony. But on January 7, 1848, five weeks after he had landed at the Cape, and the day on which he held his theatrical meeting with the Kaffir chiefs, Smith's mind was already turning to the future status of the Boers beyond the Orange River. That night he wrote privately to Grey that he had received several friendly messages from Boers in the colony and across the Orange which indicated that, by visiting Transorangia, he could effect an amicable relationship between the emigrants and the colony. He could not decide until he had seen these "misguided people" what measures would be most effective in restoring them to obedience, but he had no doubt a solution could be found if the Boers were properly handled: "To deal with the honest but highly

[57] Smith to Grey, Jan. 9, 1848, and enclosures, C.O. 48/283, P.R.O.

[58] Smith to Grey, Jan. 14, 1848, *ibid.*

[59] Minute by Hawes, April 15, 1848, on Smith to Grey, Jan. 9, 1848, *ibid.*

prejudiced Boers, both patience and temper are required and if their case and supposed grievances are heard—reason will reestablish them in Good Faith toward the Government." [60]

The state of affairs beyond the Orange had deteriorated during 1847, partly because of weaknesses in the Maitland system, partly because of the personal deficiencies of the British resident, Captain Henry D. Warden. Maitland had tried to act as an honest broker, seeking a solution least provocative to the parties concerned. Thus he had drawn lines between Griqua and Boer settlements, but left Boers in possession of lands within the Griqua reserve. He had not attempted to delimit the lands of Moshesh and those of rival tribes or of the Boers in the vicinity, because their claims were in direct conflict. But the longer a decision was deferred the more these land conflicts festered. In anticipation that the governor would eventually draw a boundary, Moshesh sent Basuto into much of the disputed territory,[61] and the Boers continued to move where pasturage and water were available. But the governor did not come, for both Maitland and Pottinger had to direct their attention to the Kaffir war.

The position of the British resident was an unenviable one, as he was "a man of war without guns." He had the authority to try Europeans who violated the laws of the colony, but no power to apprehend them. He was to resolve intertribal disputes, but he had an insignificant force to support his dicta. The Maitland treaties were an invitation to disorder. Warden, unschooled for a diplomatic role and unfitted by temperament to play it, made disorder more likely. Where caution was imperative, Warden was impetuous; he was prone to rush into crises without first ascertaining the facts and assuring himself that he had the power to execute his mission. An example of the Warden touch was his foray against 400 families of Tembu who had fled from the hazards of the Kaffir war to Moshesh's country. This tribe was not at war with Great Britain and had committed no offense, but on the basis of a rumor that they were hostile Kaffirs who were in possession of stolen colonial cattle, Warden with a detachment of soldiers supported by a body of Boer volunteers seized 3,000 head of cattle. As they were driving the cattle toward Bloemfontein through mountainous country, followed by parties of outraged Tembu, most of the Boers deserted and Warden deemed it prudent to return all except forty-two head of cattle. Had Pottinger remained in office, he would probably have removed Warden for incompetence, but he left the problem for his

[60] Smith to Grey, Jan. 7, 1848, Grey Papers.
[61] Cameron to Secs, WMS, July 28, 1847, MMS Archives.

successor.[62] During his first months in office, however, Smith was concerned with a change of system rather than with personnel.

It was evident to Smith, as it had been to Napier and Maitland, that there was a fundamental inconsistency in the imperial government's asserting the accountability of British subjects for their actions against native tribes without providing a political system to support this objective. Napier and Maitland had believed annexation of Transorangia to be essential to maintain peace between Boers and natives, but had sought lesser alternatives in the face of Whitehall's opposition to expense.[63] Their half measures had not been successful. Smith's decision to annex was eminently reasonable and, as events demonstrated, completely ineffectual. In words that have become memorable, he announced to Grey the reasons for his action:

My position has been analogous to that of every Governor General who has proceeded to India. All have been fully impressed with the weakness of that Policy which extended the Company's possessions, and yet few, if any, especially the men of more gifted talents, have ever resigned their Government without having done that, which however greatly to be condemned by the Theory of Policy, circumstances demanded and imperatively imposed upon them. Such has been my case.

The security of all Countries *within* depends not only upon their sound internal condition but upon their security from without; and the existence of a relationship on the borders calculated to inspire confidence.[64]

This explanation belies the assumption of Smith's contemporaries that the annexation of the Orange River Territory was an impetuous act by a mercuric governor who interpreted the warm greetings of a few Boers as a vote for British sovereignty. Sir Harry's own words while he was touring the territory gave color to the misapprehension. He repeatedly declared that unless four-fifths of the Boers were in favor of annexation, he would not attempt it.[65] As he saw few settlers and talked to fewer still, an assessment of Boer attitudes would have required occult powers. Smith's decision was based not upon "public opinion" but upon a fundamental philosophy of empire. Like many other nonhistorians, he sought instruction in the lessons of history;

---

[62] Pottinger to Grey, Nov. 10, 1847, and enclosures, C.O. 48/276, P.R.O.

[63] C. W. de Kiewiet, *British Colonial Policy and the South African Republics, 1848–1872* (London: Longmans, Green, 1929), pp. 12–22.

[64] Smith to Grey, Feb. 3, 1848, C.O. 48/283, P.R.O. Printed in Kenneth N. Bell and William P. Morrell, *Select Documents on British Colonial Policy, 1830–1860* (Oxford: Clarendon, 1928), p. 509.

[65] Hogge to Grey, March 26, 1852, C.O. 48/333, P.R.O.

also he drew heavily on his Indian experience. Like the Indian governors general, he was confronted with the problem of security on the frontier. Smith would have endorsed the words of the *North British Review:* "It was necessary to advance our dominions farther and farther for the mere protection of what we already possessed. Feuds on the border must be subjugated as a safeguard against the infection of rebellion at home." [66]

Smith's fundamental objectives were neither to woo the Boers nor to protect the natives but to establish order beyond the Orange River, and to do so at no expense to the British taxpayer. His treatment of Boers, Griquas, and Basuto varied in accordance with that objective. Toward Adam Kok he was arrogant, berating him for his people's improvidence and bullying him into accepting an imposed settlement most disadvantageous to the Griquas. By Kok's account, Smith first informed him that the Boers now had permanent rights both in the "alienable" and the "inalienable" territory over lands they had leased. Further, in exchange for Kok's renouncing all rights to the alienable territory, Smith would make him "rich," with £200 per year for himself and £100 for his people. When Kok protested that he had no power to give away his people's lands, and preferred to keep the Maitland treaty, Sir Harry shouted, "Will you then kick my children out?" (getting up and acting out the sentence), "No, no, I am their oupa." After much further intimidation, including a threat to "hang the black fellow" (Kok) from the beam of the room, Kok was finally browbeaten into submission.[67] Smith's original ultimatum was modified in one respect, that at the expiration of their leases in the inalienable territory the Boers would leave if the Griquas paid them for their improvements; if the Griquas were not able to do so, the tenant would have a right to continue in occupancy, paying a small annual quitrent. As the Griquas were not likely to change their ways and save money for such purposes, the effect of the change was negligible. By Smith's terms, the Boers in fact gained perpetual ownership in both the alienable and the inalienable territory.[68]

Toward the powerful chief Moshesh, on the other hand, Smith was most gracious and respectful. He described the Basuto chief as "a very superior man, possessing a strong mind adapted for government." At a conference in Winburg, Moshesh agreed to accept the sovereignty of Queen Victoria as a means of protecting his people against the

[66] *North British Review*, XVI (Nov., 1851), 230.
[67] Statement by Kok [1848] in SAF Odds, LMS Archives.
[68] De Kiewiet, *op. cit.*, pp. 20–21.

encroachments of the Boers, but no effort was made to define the boundaries of the Basuto nation.[69]

Smith treated the Boers with cordial paternalism, listening to complaints and promising to redress legitimate grievances. Crossing the Drakensberg he saw several hundred Boer families trekking from Natal with their flocks and herds because of dissatisfaction over land titles. Through "a Mr. Pretorius, a shrewd sensible man," the same Andries who in 1847 had visited the colony in an unsuccessful effort to present his people's grievances to Pottinger, Smith assembled three or four hundred heads of families. In answer to their complaints about lack of land titles, location of natives in the midst of white men, and the Natal government's requirement that they take an oath of allegiance, Smith on the spot issued a proclamation guaranteeing grants of not more than 3,000 morgen (approximately 6,000 acres) to occupants of land; he offered Pretorius appointment to the land commission, and promised to remove the native population from proximity to the whites.[70] Further, according to Pretorius, the governor told the trekkers that he had annexed the Orange River Territory to the British Empire in response to the desires of the overwhelming majority of the Boers in that region. Smith's promises induced some farmers to return to Natal in hope of a changed order; but others, Pretorius at their head, maintained their determination to leave. Pretorius stated subsequently that when he heard Smith's announcement of the annexation of the Orange River Territory and his confident assertion that the action was in accordance with the *volkswil*, he was at first confused, for this intelligence was in direct contradiction to his own impressions. As Smith had assured him that he would abandon the project unless four-fifths of the Boers supported it, he resolved to find out for himself.[71] The consequences of his survey were disastrous for Smith's hopes of establishing an effective government.

In announcing the annexation, Smith had assured Grey that the cost of government would be borne by the emigrants themselves. There would be no need for subsidies either from Cape Colony, except perhaps in the first year or so, or from the imperial government; on the contrary, the Treasury would benefit by increased revenue from commerce which would flourish now that order was restored.[72] The govern-

[69] Conference between Smith and Moshesh, Jan. 27, 1848, in J. W. Sauer and George M. Theal, eds., *Basutoland Records* (3 vols.; Cape Town: Richard, 1883), I, 158.

[70] Smith to Grey, Feb. 10, 1848, C.O. 179/4, P.R.O.

[71] Hogge to Grey, March 26, 1852, C.O. 48/333, P.R.O.

[72] Smith to Grey, Feb. 3, 1848, C.O. 48/283, P.R.O.

mental system established for the new colony invested supreme power
in the governor, represented by the resident, who would be assisted
by officials at Winburg and at Caledon River combining the functions
of civil commissioner and magistrate. A land commission was appointed
to register land claims and determine the amount of quitrents. The
conditions of tenure would be the payment of quitrent and availability
for commando duty. At first the burghers had no share in the government beyond the election of commandants and field cornets, but in
1849 a local council was established consisting of the resident, magistrates, and two appointees from each district. Its legislation was subject
to approval by the high commissioner and applied only to white settlers.[73] Smith calculated that the total annual expense of this government would be £4,344; this would easily be met by quitrents and
licenses to traders, which he expected would produce revenue of from
£5,000 to £10,000 a year.[74]

This handful of officials obviously could carry on their functions
only if they had support or at least passive acceptance from the settler
population; to this extent Smith was correct in alluding to the necessity
of four-fifths of the Boers being favorable to the new order. But once
Britain had asserted its sovereignty over the territory, it would be difficult to withdraw, and widespread disaffection would necessarily require
the dispatch of British troops from the colony, for Warden's tiny
detachment could not deal with a serious outbreak. In assuming that
the Boers would be loyal if they had security of land tenure, Sir Harry
Smith underestimated the depth and the extent of bitterness against
British rule. In the Winburg district, the seat of much of the disaffection, the population was so hostile that the new magistrate was
unable to carry on his functions and the old Boer landdrost continued
to perform his duties as before. These families had left British rule
to live in freedom; they had founded a new society and were confident
of their ability to maintain it without British interference; they would
fight if necessary against subjection to alien rule. Pretorius became the
leader of these bitter-enders. He later declared that at first he had no
hostile intent, but collected adherents in the hope of demonstrating
to Smith that he had been mistaken and that nine-tenths of the
burghers were opposed to British sovereignty. Finding the decision
irrevocable, he marched on Bloemfontein in July, 1848, with a commando of about 400 men.[75] Warden, with a total force of 57 men,

---

[73] De Kiewiet, *op. cit.*, pp. 22–23.

[74] Smith to Grey, March 11, 1848, C.O. 48/284, P.R.O.

[75] Hogge to Grey, March 26, 1852, C.O. 48/333, P.R.O.

prudently capitulated without a fight and retreated to the Orange River. Smith dramatically dashed north and in a sharp skirmish at Boomplaats dispersed the rebels. Pretorius fled across the Vaal River, and the uprising was over.

The sudden collapse of Pretorius' rebellion and the refusal of most of the burghers to join in armed resistance Smith offered as proof that at least 90 per cent of the white population were loyal. They failed to resist the rebels, he explained, because they were too scattered for effective action and because the "cunning traitor" Pretorius had collected around him a desperate band of men "of ruined circumstances" who intimidated the peaceful inhabitants and coerced the young men to join them.[76] This conclusion was baseless. Most of the burghers did not join in the rising because they were not prepared to risk their lives and security in a gamble with dubious prospects of success. Had Smith not acted so promptly and decisively, or if he had suffered an initial reverse, the consequences could have been a full-scale rebellion. What was demonstrated was that the bulk of the settlers would accept British jurisdiction provided they were left in quiet possession of their farms and without interference in their basic code. Although they did not join Pretorius in arms, they shared his convictions that a social order that granted rights to natives even theoretically equal to the rights of the white population was contrary to divine decree, and that where native interests conflicted with those of the whites, the blacks must give way. By Smith's proclamation, the white settlers were under British laws; the natives of the territory, though now under British jurisdiction, were subject to no control. The resident was responsible for maintaining intertribal order, but the only force he could call to support him beyond his detachment of troops must be drawn from the settlers. Smith's assurances of self-supporting government depended on tranquillity, but the Orange River Territory was pregnant with conflict.

Smith's announcement of his annexation arrived several months before the news of Pretorius' rising, and was accompanied by his assurances that the trans-Orange Boers were well disposed, but the decision aroused considerable controversy. Henry Merivale, who had replaced Sir James Stephen as permanent undersecretary, pointed out that if Smith's objective was to contain the Boers, British dominion would constantly be extended into the interior of Africa, as the United States had been drawn step by step from the Alleghenies to the Pacific: "Every additional annexation renders the next annexation more rea-

---

[76] Smith to Grey, Sept. 10, 1848, C.O. 48/287, P.R.O.

sonable and more plausible, unless a stand is taken at once the end seems at an indefinite distance." But Merivale was ambivalent. He acknowledged that Smith had given substance to a protectorate which Great Britain had already assumed and he accepted the possibility that in this instance the boldest policy might also be the cheapest, and that the expense of governing might be compensated by the increase in revenue.[77] Hawes, the parliamentary undersecretary, had no such hopes. He had been alarmed by Smith's previous annexations. This leap beyond the Orange, he warned, was likely to burden the imperial government with vast problems and great expense. There was no reason to believe that it contributed in the slightest to the security of Cape Colony; if this expansion was approved, the government should accept the prospect of indefinite future expansion, for the restless Boers would draw them even further into the interior of Africa.[78]

Grey's first impression was more favorable than Hawes's. Although he acknowledged that the governor's action was in violation of the policy of nonexpansion, he was prepared to give Smith an opportunity to demonstrate that he could govern the additional territory at no expense to the imperial government. British influence had already extended beyond the Orange. Smith had merely attempted to strengthen it.[79] Many years later, with the wisdom of hindsight, Grey asserted that the Maitland system had been infinitely superior to Sir Harry's "most unfortunate" measures.[80] But in 1848 he was optimistic that the vigorous and talented Smith would accomplish what his predecessors had been unable to do by halfway measures: establish order on the Cape frontiers at the expense of the inhabitants of southern Africa. Sir Henry Pottinger wrote from Madras to express his dismay at Smith's unwarranted extension of the Empire, which would certainly "require both money and men." [81] Grey responded that, although he and Smith agreed in principle that extension of territory in Africa was an evil, under the circumstances the measures adopted were "inevitable and Smith's judgment was correct." [82] This was not mere

---

[77] Minute by Merivale, n.d., on Smith to Grey, March 11, 1848, *et al.,* C.O. 48/284, P.R.O.

[78] Minutes by Hawes, n.d. and May 10, 1848, on Smith to Grey, March 11, 1848, *ibid.*

[79] Minute by Grey, May 12, 1848, on Smith to Grey, March 11, 1848, *ibid.*

[80] Grey to Molesworth, Dec. 30, 1855, C.O. 48/368, P.R.O.

[81] Pottinger to Grey, Nov. 22, 1848, Grey Papers.

[82] Grey to Pottinger, private, Jan. 5, 1849, *ibid.*

loyalty to a subordinate, for Grey believed the annexation had a prospect of success. Against Hawes's vigorous dissent, therefore, he authorized approval of Smith's action with the proviso that the new acquisition must pay for itself.[83]

In this caveat Grey reflected the temper of Parliament and the
country, which was emphatically demonstrated during the debates on
the budget in 1848. In a year of revolutions, the British middle class
was concerned over extravagance in government and excessive taxation; threats of social disturbance or of another French war aroused
little response. When the ministry proposed to balance its budget by
an increase in the income tax from seven pence to one shilling on the
pound, the opposition from both sides of the house was so overwhelming that the government had to give way. Russell, in defending the
budget, had said that the deficiency in the revenue must be met either
by increased taxes or by substantial reductions in the army and the
navy. Parliament made it evident that it supported neither alternative;
the government must provide for the national security without additional taxes.[84] This parliamentary mandate had important implications for the Cape, for it intensified Grey's pressure on Sir Harry Smith
to reduce the number of regular troops in the colony.

Pretorius' rising gave the cabinet a fright. The Chancellor of the
Exchequer wrote to Grey:

> May the————I won't say who, run away with some of your colonies—Here
> is a new insurrection at the Cape—pray write to Sir H. Smith as to expence
> —for I really do not know what is to be done.
> The H. of C. will run very rusty indeed at a new Kaffir war.[85]

The news of Boomplaats and the speedy restoration of tranquillity
brought a surge of relief, but in public and private letters to Smith,
Grey never failed to emphasize the necessity of economy. Smith was
well indoctrinated. While he was yet in Cape Town preparing to
move north against Pretorius, he was at pains to reassure the Secretary
of State on "the all engrossing subject—expense," that the Boers would
be made to pay every penny of the costs.[86]

Immediate expense was a dangerous criterion by which to judge

---

[83] Minute by Grey, May 12, 1848, on Smith to Grey, March 11, 1848; Grey to Smith,
June 21, 1848; Grey to Smith, confidential, June 21, 1848, all in C.O. 48/284, P.R.O.

[84] For a summary of the debate on the budget, see *The Annual Register . . . of
the Year 1848* (London: Woodfall, 1849), *passim*. Grey, in his journal (Feb. 21, 1848,
Grey Papers), notes the government's reaction to parliamentary revolt.

[85] Wood to Grey, Oct. 6, 1848, Grey Papers.

[86] Smith to Grey, July 27, 1848, *ibid.*

a policy, and the discussions in the Colonial Office revealed little under-standing of the gravity of the problems of the new colony. Grey appears to have deemed its government a reinforcement of the Boers' own "rude system of self-rule," and the resident a mediator between the burghers and the adjunct tribes in assisting them to settle their own disputes. This was a caricature of reality. The burghers did not enjoy "self-government," and the conflicts between Boers and natives and among the tribes themselves were beyond the powers of any mere resident to resolve. For the time being, however, Grey's assessment was not of decisive moment. He had given Smith his full confidence; now he must support the actions of the governor until events had demonstrated that his policies were invalid.

So far as Grey was concerned, that proof was not long in coming. By the end of 1849 Cape Colony had become an incubus. The anti-convict agitation of that year provoked him to an indignant and im-politic response that because the imperial government had spent more than £1,000,000 in defense of the colony in the recent Kaffir war, it had a right to expect that the colonists would be willing to be useful in return.[87] This observation did not diminish the intensity of colonial resistance. Smith's irresolute conduct in response to colonial defiance caused Grey to lose confidence in the governor. In 1847 Smith had seemed a paragon; two years later the Secretary of State had developed serious doubts as to his physical and mental abilities [88] and as to the reliance that could be placed upon his reports.

In 1849 it was evident that the governor's optimistic assurances with regard to the Orange River Territory were not being fulfilled. Smith, in his haste to inaugurate a new system, had assumed soverignty over Boers and natives without attempting to settle the basic issue which would lead to conflicting rival claims to land. The boundaries sepa-rating Basuto, Barolong, and Mantatees remained undefined; but, more important, Boers had staked claims far beyond the triangle assigned to them by Moshesh at Maitland's request. In the valleys of the Caledon River and its tributaries, well watered and fertile, the

---

[87] For a description of anticonvict agitation, see *The Cambridge History of the British Empire,* VIII (Cambridge: University Press, 1936), 369 ff. Grey expressed him-self emphatically on the ingratitude of the colonists in a letter to Smith, private, Jan. 20, 1849, Grey Papers.

[88] In April and May, 1849, Smith was seriously ill with what was described as severe inflammation at the back of his head; it affected his whole system and neces-sitated his being confined to bed for almost a month (John Hall, Deputy Inspector General of Hospitals, Cape Colony, to Grey, May 13, 1849; Smith to Grey, April 26, 1849, both in Grey Papers).

most favored lands of the high veld, Boers and tribesmen elbowed each other for occupancy. These collisions would eventually bring war. In his cordial interchanges with Moshesh and the burghers, Smith made no reference to the definition of limits; rather he assured them that both Boers and Basuto "should drink out of the same fountains and live in peace." [89] But Smith, despite his rhetoric, recognized that lines would have to be drawn, and for this mission he appointed Richard Southey, secretary to the high commissioner. Southey's proposed boundaries could not have been more favorable to the Boers had a commission of burghers been invited to draw them. They cut off a large portion of Moshesh's country, inhabited by thousands of Basuto but by only a few Boer families, and added it to the "white" districts of Bloemfontein and Smithfield.[90] Boundaries were drawn primarily in relation to European settlement; tribal needs received short shrift where they conflicted with Boer claims.[91]

Despite the protests of the chiefs and their missionary advisers, these were the boundaries that, with minor modifications, Warden laid down late in 1849 and the tribes were forced to accept. Moshesh, harassed by Mantatee and Korana raids which Warden assured him would end when he "proved his friendship," and convinced that the alternative to acceptance of Warden's boundary was war with Britain, gave way and accepted the surrender of territory he believed to be rightfully his own.[92] Perhaps he thought wryly of Pretorius' prophecy when the Boer leader had sought Basuto coöperation against the British: "You don't know the English. They are an odd people—remember my word. You will repent for having joined them." [93]

Warden's settlement was a failure. At the expense of embittering a most powerful chief, he had drawn lines of demarcation highly favorable to the Boers. Boers and tribesmen, however, remained intermingled as before; the major difference was that the Boers now had legal sanction for their occupancy, and natives living beyond the boundary were guilty of encroachment. It would require force to eject them.[94]

---

[89] Hogge to Grey, March 26, 1852, C.O. 48/333, P.R.O.

[90] Cory, *op. cit.*, V, 176; W. M. Macmillan, *Bantu, Boer, and Briton* (London: Faber and Gwyer, 1929), p. 274.

[91] De Kiewiet, *op. cit.*, pp. 50–51.

[92] Freeman to Grey, Aug. 2, 1850, C.O. 48/311, P.R.O.; Martier *et al.* to Smith, Oct. 1, 1849, SAF Odds, 4–2, LMS Archives.

[93] Freeman's Account of Visit to Basuto Country; Moshesh's statement (1849), both in SAF Odds 4–2, LMS Archives.

[94] De Kiewiet, *op. cit.*, pp. 51–52.

Warden had a choice of alternative routes to disaster. As Major William Hogge later observed, "Had an Angel from Heaven been the British Resident Sir Harry's system could not have succeeded." [95] But Warden was unqualified for the position, and part of the indictment against Sir Harry Smith is that he retained him as resident though he knew him to be unsuited for the responsibility.[96]

Perhaps influenced by his clerk, brother-in-law to Moroko's missionary, Warden adopted an increasingly hostile line toward Moshesh. Though he had earlier considered the Basuto chief the soul of honor,[97] he became convinced that in the frequent encounters between Moshesh and Sikonyela and Moroko the Basuto were the aggressors; and by August, 1849, he had become convinced that Moshesh must be humbled. When Moshesh showed reluctance to accept an imposed boundary, Warden recommended that Smith add 350 soldiers to the British force, which, with the support of a Boer commando, would bring him to reason. Smith, though cautioning Warden against precipitate action, agreed that Moshesh must be forced to submit, preferably without war but if necessary through combined action by troops, Boers, and rival native tribes.[98]

Though Moshesh eventually gave way before these threats, reports reaching Downing Street before he submitted suggested that a war with the Basuto was imminent. For Grey this prospect was further woe in a year filled with misery. He had been deeply wounded by attacks in Parliament and in the colonies. Unrest in the sugar colonies of the West Indies and disturbances in Canada and at the Cape caused him to contemplate resignation. Worst of all, since the retirement of Sir James Stephen in 1847, Grey had assumed a burden of responsibility beyond his strength to bear. He warned Russell that without additional assistance he would sink under the load. Ideally, he would have reconstituted the Colonial Office on more efficient lines in accordance with Stephen's advice, but, as this seemed impossible for political reasons, he requested that a committee of the Privy Council be con-

---

[95] Memorial by Warden, Dec. 24, 1855, enclosure in Grey to Molesworth, Dec. 30, 1855, C.O. 48/368, P.R.O.

[96] This judgment is not based entirely on Smith's later testimony. In September, 1848, Smith wrote to Southey: "Be sure to get on well with Warden, he is very easily managed—but like all weak men very soon affronted" (Smith to Southey, Sept. 29, 1848, Southey Papers, Cape Archives).

[97] Warden to Woosnam, Oct. 27, 1847, enclosure in Pottinger to Grey, Nov. 10, 1847, C.O. 48/276, P.R.O.

[98] Warden to Smith, Aug. 5, 1849; Smith to Warden, Aug. 16, 1849, enclosure in Smith to Grey, Aug. 21, 1849, both in C.O. 48/298, P.R.O.

stituted, with Stephen as a member, to give him counsel on difficult colonial problems.[99] After some demur from Russell, who did not share Grey's exalted opinion of the former permanent undersecretary, the committee was appointed, with Sir Edward Ryan as chairman and Stephen as one of the members.[100]

Among the first subjects submitted to the committee for consideration was the legal status of the Orange River Sovereignty. The committee interpreted its charge to include not only the legality but the wisdom of the annexation, and its conclusions were in accordance with Stephen's antiannexationist views. In a draft report submitted to Grey and Russell early in December, 1849, the committee proposed to disavow Smith's proclamation of British sovereignty and to acknowledge an independent Boer state within the limits assigned to white occupation. The British government would make treaties with the native tribes which would offer them protection against Boer aggressions.[101]

In another report the committee recommended the early establishment of representative government at the Cape. To Grey the two questions were intimately related, as the fate of the trans-Orange country should be decided before the Cape legislature was constituted. Grey, who had leaned toward approval of annexation in 1848, had now also shifted toward retreat. He acknowledged that British withdrawal would lead to "bloodshed ending in the extermination of the native race," but the same reasons that justified British sovereignty between the Orange and the Vaal would lead to intervention beyond the Vaal and eventually to "the very heart of Africa." Such a policy almost certainly would involve expense which the House of Commons would not tolerate. Therefore, "though with much doubt and reluctance," Grey supported the disavowal of the sovereignty.[102] Had it not been for the intervention of Russell, the sovereignty might well have been abandoned in 1850. Unlike Grey, Russell had no hesitation as to the proper course. The imperial government must confirm the annexation. The committee's recommendation, he wrote, risked disastrous consequences:

It involves a disclaimer of Sovereignty already assumed and thereby weakens authority, shakes the tenure of land, and exposes the friends of the British

---

[99] Grey to Russell, Sept. 22, 1849, Russell Papers, PRO 30/22/8, P.R.O.

[100] There is considerable correspondence between Russell and Grey on this subject in the Russell Papers, PRO 30/22/8, P.R.O., and in the Grey Papers.

[101] The draft report is summarized in a memorandum, "Orange River Sovereignty," by Russell, Dec. 7, 1849, PRO 30/22/8, P.R.O.

[102] Grey to Russell, Dec. 4, 1849, *ibid.*

connexion to injury and robbery—On the other hand it keeps alive every source of dissension and by taking away the master hand sets loose every passion of hatred, revenge, and plunder, which it is in contemplation afterwards to restrain by British force. It would almost to a certainty arm the Boers against the Natives, and the Natives against the Boers—Indeed anarchy and bloodshed, and ultimate extinction of the less civilized Race are predicted as the foreseen results of the policy.

. . . It seems to me that whatever may be the ultimate decision of the House of Commons we ought to take that course which is best for the subjects of the Queen—best for the native races—best for the British Empire.[103]

Grey's doubts were by no means resolved by Russell's ringing declaration. He replied that he had no objection if Russell wished to propose to Parliament a bill for annexation, which was almost certain to be rejected.[104] Eventually Russell prevailed. A revised report submitted by the committee, though condemning the principle of expansion, concluded that disavowal of a sovereignty already assumed would produce worse evils than giving legal sanction to an accomplished fact, however unwise the decision might have been. The committee, however, in most emphatic terms recommended that all officers in southern Africa be prohibited, "in terms as specific as can be employed, and under sanctions as grave as can be devised, for making any addition, whether permanent or provisional, of any territory, however small," to the existing dominions of the Crown.[105] The horrific prospect of parliamentary debate was avoided by the decision that because the territory had been ceded, not conquered, no legislative action was required.[106]

Government of the Orange River Sovereignty by a British resident could not maintain the peace. The resident and his nominated council did not command the loyalty of the Boer population. A large proportion, perhaps a majority, remained antagonistic to the *rooinekke* (the English), and sympathized with Pretorius' objectives if not with Pretorius himself. Many more manifested a distinct disinclination to turn out on commando against the Basuto at Warden's behest. But, despite Boer reluctance, Warden was determined to subdue the Basuto. This, as was soon demonstrated, meant war, and war meant the end of the Orange River sovereignty.

---

[103] Memorandum, "Orange River Sovereignty," by Russell, Dec. 7, 1849, *ibid.*

[104] Grey to Russell, Dec. 10, 1849, *ibid.*

[105] Report by Committee of Privy Council, adopted by Queen in Council, July 13, 1850, C.O. 48/310, P.R.O.

[106] The attorney general of the Cape had offered a contrary opinion, and was induced to change it.

British policy in southern Africa had been characterized by great ends and slight means. Since the British occupation of the Cape, British statesmen had acknowledged a responsibility for the protection of African tribes against white aggression, and since the 1830's that responsibility had been legally proclaimed. But law and order could not be maintained by moral influence nor, despite Earl Grey's infatuation with Sepoy armies, could Africans be organized effectively to defend themselves. British law could be imposed only with the backing of British arms and British money. Defense forces were always inadequate to the mission they were required to perform. Wars, leading to ever greater expense, were the result, and demands in Parliament became overwhelming to end this waste of money and manpower and to require the colony to defend itself. Some have interpreted events in British South Africa in the 1840's and the 1850's in terms of the decline of humanitarianism. This seems a misrepresentation. British troops and money were employed in southern Africa to maintain order. The huge expenditures that aroused the indignation of Parliament were occasioned by wars against natives, not for their protection. It was not so much that "humanitarianism" declined as that the costs of maintaining the peace of the borders grew ever higher, and that resistance to imperial expenditure for colonial purposes steadily increased. Massive bills presented for both a Kaffir war and a Basuto war at the beginning of the 1850's forced a reconsideration of imperial policy, not because its basic assumptions had changed but because the consequences of expansion had become painfully apparent.

Chapter XI
RETREAT, 1850–1854

WITH A GOVERNMENT as with an individual, virtue is not established simply by professions of good intentions. Throughout the nineteenth century, in India and elsewhere, the avowed policy of the imperial government was antiexpansionist. But governors had repeatedly transgressed and had rarely been reprimanded; on the contrary, if their annexations were consummated with a flair and at no expense to the British taxpayer, they might expect the plaudits of the population and some mark of favor from their ruler. Sir Harry Smith could hardly be expected to understand that, when the government absolutely prohibited any further expansion, the interdict was, unlike previous assertions, inviolable.

Such doubts must have been intensified by the character of the secretary of state, Earl Grey, which represented in exaggerated form the contradictions of imperial policy. Grey was dedicated to efficiency and economy and to the transfer of burdens of colonial defense to the colonists themselves, and he was opposed in principle to the addition of more square miles to the British Empire. This was the cerebral side of Grey's nature. But Grey was also a dreamer. His vision ranged far beyond the borders of the formal Empire; he was enamored with the prospect of tribal kingdoms living in security and progressing toward civilization under the supervision of British agents. This conception he was loath to give up. Even after he had issued imperative instructions against expansion, he was still tantalized by the prospect.

Within a few weeks after he dispatched strict orders against further imperial adventures, Grey demonstrated that he himself remained susceptible to seduction. The temptation admittedly was strong. Early in August, 1849, David Livingstone, William Oswell, and Mungo Murray had discovered Lake Ngami. Their reports of the surrounding country, colored by repetition, stirred imagination and cupidity. The country through which they had traveled, from the London Missionary Society station at Kolobeng to the lake, was described as fertile, well wooded, watered by rivers that abounded in fish, and inhabited by a numerous, friendly people. This intelligence stimulated interest, and a number of hunters, traders, and travelers started for the Ngami country to see for themselves.[1]

Situated athwart the road to the north was a community that regarded the movement with alarm. The cattle Boers beyond the Vaal saw this first trickle of intruders as the advance guard of British intervention. Among these Afrikaners were many who had journeyed to the far interior to escape a detested imperial authority; some had fought only a few months before at the side of Pretorius in an effort to dislodge this alien rule in Transorangia. Now they faced the prospect of another struggle to maintain their independence. Their greatest security was isolation; to safeguard it they resolved to blockade the route toward the Great Lake. A trader who owned a farm in the Transvaal, and was thus considered by the *Maatschappij* as subject to its laws, was fined 500 rix-dollars and detained under surveillance for twelve months for having published in a colonial newspaper an account of the best route to Lake Ngami, and his companion, an English artist, was turned back.[2]

Warden's immediate response to this news was a call for action. Though his resources were insufficient to support his authority in the sovereignty, he recommended that all lands occupied by British subjects be declared under British rule and that a proclamation be issued that all persons resisting the Queen's authority would forfeit their lands. If this was done, he insisted with a typical lack of perspicacity, half the emigrants would at once submit, the worst malcontents would undoubtedly trek, and the way to the Great Lake would be reopened. With Warden the issue was simple; "a handful of prejudiced and ignorant Boers" had challenged the British Empire, and British honor and British interest dictated that the obstruction be removed. He acknowledged that "a respectable force" would be required; somehow, despite his paucity of manpower, he had faith that force would be provided.[3]

Smith, more sophisticated in the nature of British politics, was more circumspect. Though he had not yet received the government's prohibition against further annexation, he understood the dictates of economy, and he knew that Warden's phantom force could never materialize. His executive council concurred with him that, as the use

---

[1] Smith to Grey, July 12, 1850, C.O. 48/306, P.R.O.

[2] *Ibid.*

[3] Warden to Smith, June 15, 1850, enclosure in Smith to Grey, July 12, 1850, *ibid.*

of military force was out of the question, the most feasible policy was
to befriend the tribes near the lake, to encourage them to defend
themselves, and to discourage the Boers from their lawless course by
extending the Punishment Act of 1836 to the equator.[4] Smith, still
awaiting the final decision of the home government on his recent
annexations, was not prepared to take further initiative. The problem
was "so intricate" that he referred it to Grey for decision.[5]

The response of the Colonial Office to Smith's request for guidance
demonstrated that it was not so much expansion of British influence
which was under an interdict as expenditure of British money. Sir
George Barrow thought it would be a calamity if the Boers gained
possession of this rich new country; the extension of the Punishment
Act to the equator might check their aggressiveness, and the tribes
could be reinforced by a few missionaries, one of whom could act as
a British agent.[6] Such a delusion in a clerk was merely ludicrous; if
accepted by the Secretary of State it could be highly dangerous. But
Grey clung to his conception of Sepoy armies with relentless tenacity;
the prospect of native tribes being organized for self-defense addled
his usually sound judgment.

In his imagination Grey conceived a confederacy of native tribes,
presided over by a council of the most eminent chiefs. The United
Tribes would maintain a small well-armed security force modeled on
the Kaffir police. It would be trained by British officers and supported
by annual taxes, either in money or in produce, levied upon each
tribesman. Nominally the government would be directed by the chiefs.
In fact, the directing genius would be a British resident who could
advise the council and in the first stages control the armed forces.
With the assistance of missionaries and the spread of commerce, the
system would speedily extend itself. Other tribes would see the advantage of joining the comity and would seek admission. Civilization and
trade would thus be diffused over a large area at no expense to the
imperial government. The Boers, the scourge of the native tribes,
would unwittingly have become the agency of deliverance for the
Africans by impelling the tribes to organize.[7]

These were no idle musings but serious policy proposals dispatched

---

[4] Minutes, Executive Council, July 3, 1850, C.O. 51/73, P.R.O.

[5] Smith to Grey, private, July 14, 1850, Grey Papers, Prior's Kitchen, University of Durham.

[6] Minute by Barrow, Sept. 18, [1850], on Smith to Grey, July 12, 1850, C.O. 48/306, P.R.O.

[7] Minute by Grey, Oct. 2, 1850, on Smith to Grey, July 12, 1850, ibid.

through official channels to a colonial executive. The scheme dismissed the enormously complicated problems of associating rival tribes in a coöperative system, and of their voluntarily subjecting themselves to discipline and accepting a European system of taxation. Even if the conception was feasible, the assumption that the imperial government could act merely as a benevolent adviser without any risk of involvement was pure fantasy. Grey's imagination far outran Sir Harry Smith's. By comparison with this cosmic vision, annexation of the Orange River Sovereignty seems modest and rational. But Smith annexed the sovereignty, and Grey's conception was never acted on.

During the last months of 1850 ferment from the sea to the Orange River Sovereignty belied Smith's assurances that all was well on the borders of the Cape. Stockenstrom noted with wry satisfaction that "dashing dispatches, flourishing speeches and newspaper puffs" could no longer conceal the fact that war was imminent.[8] In the Orange River Sovereignty, Warden in September had sent a mixed force of soldiers, Boers, and Barolong against Sikonyela and Moletsane for their breaches of the peace, and had confiscated 300 head of cattle from Sikonyela and about 3,500 from Moletsane. Both expeditions were "completely successful." Warden was encouraged to expect that similar measures would be equally effective in reducing Moletsane's paramount chief, Moshesh, to obedience. The result was disastrous for the sovereignty. Warden could not subdue Moshesh with a detachment of troops supported by ragtag native allies and a few Boers, and he could expect no assistance from Cape Town. Before Warden fought with Moshesh, the eastern frontier was ablaze with another Kaffir war which not only absorbed all available troops but necessitated substantial reinforcements from Britain.

Since his dramatic convocation of the chiefs shortly after his arrival in South Africa, Smith's reports to London had uniformly conveyed gratifying intelligence. The Kaffir police, he indicated, had almost eliminated cattle thefts, and chiefs and tribes had put aside all thought of war and were perfectly submissive. The system had succeeded "beyond the most sanguine expectations."[9] These glowing reports were not merely propaganda for home consumption; Smith believed that the awe his name inspired and the efficiency of his Kaffir police made another war, at least during his governorship, almost impossible. He felt safe in sending home several battalions of regular soldiers.

[8] Stockenstrom to Grey, Oct. 25, 1850, C.O. 48/311, P.R.O.

[9] Smith to Grey, Jan. 7, 1850, C.O. 48/304, P.R.O. This is the tone of nearly every dispatch on British Kaffraria between 1848 and 1850.

By the end of 1850 he had reduced the number of troops from the 5,600 that had served during the War of the Axe [10] to less than 3,700, including 850 in the Cape Mounted Rifles,[11] and he assured the Secretary of State that further reductions would be made as the system of Kaffir police developed.[12]

The measures on which Smith placed such reliance merely imposed a thin film of order over a seething society. Sir Harry at no time displayed the slightest comprehension of the frustrations that gripped the tribes of Kaffraria. Mission schools were no specific for the malaise of a tribal society inhabiting constricted locations and embittered by forcible ejection from lands it had long occupied; migratory labor to the colony, while it offered some relief for the pressure in the locations, was of dubious value as a civilizing influence. The chiefs recognized Smith and his commissioners as the mortal enemies of the power and dignity of the chieftainship, and Smith, despite his disclaimers to Grey, saw his objectives in essentially the same terms. By words and by actions Smith demonstrated his intention to undermine the authority of the chiefs. The Great Men were the governor and his agents; the chiefs listened, observed, and understood. To this unrest was added in 1850 the catalyst of drought. From the summer of 1849 throughout the following year the pasture land of the Kaffirs was parched; by September, 1850, the country was "dry as a bone." [13]

This was the background for the emergence of the prophet Umlanjeni whose Delphic utterances the chief commissioner, Colonel George Mackinnon, heard were unsettling the tribes. There was no direct evidence that Umlanjeni counseled war, but his prophecies allegedly had spread excitement throughout Kaffraria and beyond the Kei. In the colony Kaffir servants deserted their jobs, in many instances leaving in such haste that they did not even ask for their wages.[14]

Despite these evidences of impending war neither Smith nor his commissioners seemed alarmed until hostilities actually broke out. "I cannot conceive," Smith wrote his chief commissioner, "that the majority of the Kaffirs are not most happy under our rule; every report

---

[10] Monthly Return of Troops, Dec. 1, 1846, W.O. 17/1627, P.R.O. This included 450 Cape Mounted Rifles.

[11] Monthly Report, Dec. 31, 1850, W.O. 17/1631, P.R.O.

[12] Memo by Earl Grey, n.d. [1850], Russell Papers, PRO 30/22/8, P.R.O.

[13] Mackinnon to Smith, Sept. 30, 1850, enclosure in Smith to Grey, private, Oct. 8, 1850, C.O. 48/308, P.R.O.

[14] George E. Cory, *The Rise of South Africa* (5 vols.; London: Longmans, Green, 1921–1930), V, 294.

I receive proves it." [15] From this premise he concluded that the causes of disaffection were Umlanjeni and the drought. If the police would seize this "regenerate Mahomet," [16] disturbance would subside; with a copious rain it would disappear.[17] The authorities on the spot, however, delayed apprehending Umlanjeni until they had evidence that he was guilty of incitement; and when they decided he was dangerous, it became impolitic to seize him. Umlanjeni remained at large, and the rains did not come. But Smith had one resource in which he had complete confidence—himself. The executive council agreed with him that his presence on the frontier would "at once put a stop to such evil intentions as may secretly exist" and that no additional troops need be dispatched.[18]

When the governor arrived at the scene of disturbances and conferred with his chief commissioner, he gained a somewhat different impression of the character of the crisis from the one he had accepted in Cape Town. Mackinnon admitted that the chiefs had at no time coöperated with his authority and were greatly discontented at the loss of their influence and of their revenue. He suggested that this bitterness might be reduced if they were paid annual stipends ranging from £20 for the greater chiefs to £10 for the lesser; the total expenditure would be about £250 a year.[19] This was a suggestion that Smith himself had made to D'Urban in 1836, and he heartily endorsed it. Mackinnon also informed the governor that Sandile had been the principal instigator of the "Umlanjeni excitement." Smith called a meeting of the principal chiefs to "explain to them individually and collectively their true position." [20] When Sandile, in fear of arrest, failed to attend, the high commissioner issued a proclamation deposing the offending chief and appointing Charles Brownlee, the Gaika commissioner, his successor.[21] The governor carefully assured the other chiefs that the punishment was directed at Sandile alone and that they had nothing to fear.

Privately Smith admitted that the deposal of Sandile was a crucial test of the system he had constructed. It would determine whether the

---

[15] Smith to Mackinnon, Oct. 10, 1850, enclosure in Smith to Grey, Oct. 14, 1850, C.O. 48/308, P.R.O.

[16] Smith to Mackinnon, Oct. 7, 1850, enclosure in Smith to Grey, Oct. 8, 1850, *ibid.*

[17] Smith to Grey, Oct. 8, 1850, Grey Papers.

[18] Extract, Minutes of Executive Council, Oct. 14, 1850, enclosure in Smith to Grey, Oct. 14, 1850, C.O. 48/308, P.R.O.

[19] Mackinnon to High Commissioner, Oct. 21, 1850, B-K 371, Cape Archives.

[20] Smith to Grey, Oct. 21, 1850, C.O. 48/208, P.R.O.

[21] Cory, *op. cit.,* V, 300.

Kaffir population would be ruled by the former "tyranny" of their chiefs, or would continue to enjoy "the mild and equitable rule" of British commissioners. He had no doubt of the outcome, he said, for "every Kaffir who possessed anything" was a supporter of the present system.[22] Within eight weeks of this confident assertion the Kaffir war had begun. On Christmas Eve, 1850, an expedition sent to arrest Sandile was attacked; within twenty-four hours the military villages Smith had established to protect the colony were wiped out, and Smith was beleaguered at Fort Cox. The Kaffir police deserted him, and in a few days many of the Hottentots of Kat River joined the rebels. Smith had been guilty, he now conceded, of a miscalculation. The Gaikas in whom he had reposed confidence had repaid his kindness with "treachery and cunning"; they were in truth "irreclaimable savages." [23]

The report of Sandile's deposal reached Downing Street several weeks before the news of its consequences. Grey's response was that it was not only proper but in accordance with the policy of upholding the chiefs' authority. The government must exercise power to depose a refractory chief, he insisted, in order to ensure that the chieftainship was a safe agency of authority.[24] The Secretary of State also "entirely approved" of Smith's decision to call out volunteers, but warned him again that he must under no circumstances pay the police or the volunteers from the military chest. The colony must pay for its own protection.[25] Sir Harry Smith, as Grey's counsel made clear, was not responsible for the Kaffir war of 1850–1853; its causes lay far deeper. For the catastrophe, however, a culprit had to be found. The opposition naturally blamed the government; and the ministry found a scapegoat in Sir Harry Smith.

The gravamen of the opposition's charge against the Russell administration, and Grey in particular, was that by their interference in a colonial problem they had contributed to a war likely to cost millions of pounds. The imperial government, critics insisted, could not prevent Kaffir wars; on the contrary, its meddling ensured their recurrence. There could be no resolution of the basic conflict between settlers and Kaffirs short of the extermination of the tribes or their complete subjugation. There was no Indian problem in the United States be-

[22] Smith to Grey, Oct. 31, 1850, C.O. 48/308, P.R.O.

[23] Smith to Grey, Jan. 20, 1851, C.O. 48/312, P.R.O.

[24] Minute by Grey, 9 [Jan., 1851?], on Smith to Grey, Oct. 31, 1850, C.O. 48/308, P.R.O.

[25] Grey to Smith, private, Feb. 14, 1851, Grey Papers.

cause the whites were unrestrained by "Aborigines Protection Societies" backed by the power of the imperial government.[26] The withholding of self-government from the Cape sapped the vitality of the colonists and burdened the imperial treasury without achieving any constructive purpose. The "barbarous and sanguinary wretches" whom Britain had sought to shield were now at war with their protectors. They did not wish to be civilized; they could not be civilized.

At its core, agitation in Parliament and in the press was concerned with expense. The government had repeatedly warned the colonists that they would have to bear the cost of another war. The emptiness of that injunction was exposed when the Chancellor of the Exchequer in June, 1851, had to propose a vote of £300,000 for the expenses of the war. The request, as Sir Charles Adderley and other opponents of imperial paternalism pointed out, was merely a first installment; the colony could not be presented with the bills until it controlled its own internal affairs. Meanwhile the settlers would sit passively and allow imperial troops and imperial money to defend them.[27] Most infuriating of all, there was no discernible return for this sacrifice. It was much easier for the House of Commons to vote £300,000 than it was to make the public understand what benefits they were to receive in return for the enormous expense of "these remote and inglorious hostilities." [28] Grey, as the symbol of imperial involvement in colonial affairs, was the focus of opposition attacks which threatened the life of the Russell government and eventually were an important factor in bringing it down. The *Times,* an inveterate opponent of the Whig regime, made Grey a favorite target:

In no instance in our colonial history can the misfortunes which have occurred be more directly and fairly traced to the conduct of the Colonial Secretary than in the case of the Cape colony. The present disastrous condition of affairs there is the legitimate consequence of Lord Grey's conduct. To his mischievous meddling the outbreak of the Caffres is solely attributable. The unprepared state of the colony is the result of his policy. The discontent of the colonists was produced by his ill temper and unwarrantable conduct. From the first moment of his colonial rule he has in every colony resisted to the utmost every attempt on the part of the colonists to manage their own affairs, and in South Africa he has been especially successful in giving efficiency to this the cardinal principle of his policy.[29]

---

[26] *Times,* June 21, 1851.

[27] See *Parliamentary Debates,* 3d series, CXVII (June 13, 1851), 328 ff.

[28] *Times,* June 17, 1851.

[29] *Ibid.,* Nov. 12, 1851.

Though the only tangible result of the first outbursts at the news of another war was the appointment of the Select Committee on the Kaffir Tribes,[30] the government might well have been overturned had a vote of no confidence been introduced.[31] The cabinet recognized that a way must be found to disengage the imperial government from the quicksands of the South African frontier. Only Grey was not prepared to acknowledge that the prewar policies had been erroneous in principle. Rather, he concluded, the fault had been in the application; Smith had overoptimistically reduced the imperial troops too far and too fast. Nor did the defection of the Kaffir police shake his confidence in the wisdom of employing them. To Grey the lesson of their desertion was that inadequate precautions had been taken to ensure fidelity. Their wives and children ought to have been located in such a manner as to prevent easy escape, and the police should have been kept intermixed with regular troops when it appeared that hostilities were imminent.[32]

Grey was not given to panic. The Kaffir war was a great blow to his hopes—it threatened his political career—but he retained the glacial calm that was a great intellectual asset and a great political liability. Unlike Smith, he was not ready to consign the Kaffirs to damnation because they had rebelled against British authority. They must be subdued as quickly and as inexpensively as possible—to that end he sent out reinforcements before the governor asked for them—but the causes of the war must be coolly and carefully assessed. Smith, dominated by his passions, burned to avenge himself on the ungrateful savages who had humiliated him; Grey, concerned with policy, chastised the governor for vowing to "exterminate" the Kaffirs. No doubt, he wrote, a large percentage of the Boers and many English settlers ardently desired the enslavement or extermination of the native races, but it was the obligation of Great Britain, even in a war against Kaffirs, to restrain these passions, not to encourage them; if it failed to do so, it would be "an eternal disgrace to us as a Christian nation." [33]

First reports on the antecedents of the war caused the Colonial Secretary to conclude that the Kaffirs were not without provocation.

---

[30] *Report of the Select Committee on the Kafir Tribes* (no. 635), 1851.

[31] One reason that such a vote was not introduced was undoubtedly that some of the leading critics did not wish to overthrow the government, at least at that time (Russell to Grey, March 31, [1851], Grey Papers).

[32] Grey to Smith, private, March 8, 1851, *ibid.*

[33] Grey to Smith, private, March 15, 1851, *ibid.*

With the imminent introduction of representative institutions, they had reason to fear that the settler mentality would become ascendant in Cape policy; and the chiefs had cause for unrest in their loss of power and prestige. In the reconstruction after the war, special efforts must be made to give the chiefs a stake in supporting the administration. In the first months of the war, however, it was not the Kaffirs but the trans-Orange Boers who caused Grey deepest anxiety. In mid-March, 1851, he wrote Smith:

> I much fear that we shall find the Dutch much more formidable enemies than the Kafirs & I am expecting with much apprehension the news of what may have been the effect in the Orange River Sovereignty of the difficulties to wh. you are now exposed.—I greatly fear that the opportunity may be made use of by Pretorious & his friends to attack Major Warden & I shall be much relieved if by the next mail there is no bad news from that quarter.[34]

To meet the Boer menace Grey again suggested organizing the native tribes. There was no possibility, he insisted, that the Boers would ever be friendly; the natives, if properly led and taught to use their strength, could contain the Boers and could be tied to the British by bonds of interest and affection.[35]

This confidence in native allies was not shared by Lord John Russell. who considered Grey's faith in Sepoy armies a peculiar idiosyncrasy; but the Prime Minister, the Colonial Secretary, and the cabinet all sought a postwar policy that could eliminate further imperial expense. For advice in the formulation of such a policy, firsthand information was required. Smith, immersed in a war far more protracted than he had contemplated, could not devote the time and energy required, and events had raised serious doubts about his judgment. Consequently Grey decided to send to the Cape as assistant commissioners Major William S. Hogge and C. Mostyn Owen. Both had had experience in Kaffirland; Hogge had led a Hottentot unit in the War of the Axe, and Owen had been in charge of a detachment of the Kaffir police. As originally conceived, the functions of the commissioners were apparently to relieve Smith of some of his burdens while he prosecuted the war. This seems to have been Grey's intention in March, 1851, when he first sought out Hogge. Neither Hogge nor Owen was interested in such a prospect. But as more communications came in from the seat of war indicating widespread unrest among the Hottentots and revealing the governor's bewilderment as to the causes of this disaffection, Grey

---

[34] *Ibid.*
[35] *Ibid.*

decided that the powers of the assistant commissioners should be enlarged to encompass a wide range of frontier problems.[36] When Grey stipulated that they would not be mere subordinates of the high commissioner, but would have the right to make independent judgments, they accepted.[37]

Officially Hogge and Owen were to assist the high commissioner in establishing a system of government in territories adjacent to the colony which would maintain future security.[38] Grey carefully explained to Smith that they had been appointed to relieve him of excessive burdens [39] and that they were "completely subordinate" to him.[40] This was not quite true, and as Grey steadily lost confidence in the governor it became less so. The assistant commissioners became largely autonomous of their titular superior; and Hogge, who soon established himself as the stronger of the two, became Grey's confidant.

At the time the commissioners were appointed the center of disturbances was the eastern frontier. By the time they arrived at Cape Town, the Basuto country was also involved. With all available manpower committed against the Kaffirs, the expedient course for Major Warden would seem to have been the one least disturbing to the *status quo*. But Warden was a man of action; defiance must be punished instantaneously.[41] Though the circumstances in which he was placed might have drawn him into war, Warden went out to meet it.

The Basuto, rankling under what they considered unjust treatment by Warden's government, heard tales of the prophet who had promised to rescue the tribes from the whites if they would slaughter yellow cattle and undergo certain purifications.[42] Their hatred of the sovereignty government focused on Moroko, whose Barolong had served with Warden against Moletsane and who behind British protection preened himself as an independent chief. The Basuto-Barolong borders

[36] Somerset to Grey, March 17, 1851; Grey to Hogge, private, May 2, 1851; Grey to Owen, private, May 2, 1851, all in *ibid*.

[37] Hogge to Grey, May 6, 1851, *ibid*. Hogge had retired and was raising hounds in Bedfordshire, and he made it clear that he was disinclined to leave this life for a minor office. His appointment may have been suggested by the Duke of Bedford, with whom he was intimately associated.

[38] C.O. to Hogge and Owen, May 31, 1851, C.O. 48/321, P.R.O.

[39] Grey to Smith, May 13, 1851, C.O. 48/314, P.R.O.

[40] Grey to Smith, June 14, 1851, Grey Papers.

[41] For a relatively sympathetic description of Warden, see B. J. Barnard, '*n Lewensbeskrywing van Majoor Henry Douglas Warden*, in *Archives Year Book for South African History*, 11th Year, Part 1 (Pretoria: G.P.O., 1948).

[42] Extract, Casalis to Syme, March 27, 1851, SAF Odds 4-2, LMS Archives. Note the similarity to the "cattle Killing delusion" of 1857 in Kaffirland.

became the scene of murder and cattle thievery, with the more power-ful Basuto usually the aggressors, and Moroko's pleas for help grew more pressing. Warden decided to act when the Barolong chief ex-pressed the intention to migrate from Thaba Nchu to Bloemfontein to seek protection; and Smith encouraged the resident in this deter-mination.[43] When Moshesh failed to attend a meeting at Bloemfontein to settle his disputes with Moroko and other chiefs, Warden sent a force of 150 soldiers and 120 burghers against him. They with their Barolong allies attacked the Basuto at a table-topped mountain called Viervoet. When the engagement was over, 159 Barolong had been killed, and the soldiers, the Boers, and the surviving Barolong had fled.[44]

In desperation Warden called on the commandants and field cornets to rally the burghers to his assistance to put down "the com-mon enemy of the white man." This was a war of races; "the year 1851 must decide the mastery between the white and coloured race, both here and in the colony." As an additional inducement, he offered volunteers one-third of all cattle captured.[45] When the Boers did not respond to this combined appeal to race and avarice, Warden bitterly denounced them to Smith as secret rebels. Two-thirds of the white population of the sovereignty, he alleged, were opposed to the govern-ment and did all in their power to thwart it. Some plotted with Moshesh, assuring him of their support; others tried to intimidate Sikonyela from joining Warden against the Basuto; because of their obstruction of his authority, he was unable to cope with Moshesh.[46] These reports caused Smith to decide that the recently arrived Hogge and Owen should go to the Orange River Sovereignty to investigate the causes of the disturbed conditions; in the meantime, Warden should act on the defensive.[47]

The assistant commissioners were not able to set out for the Orange River country immediately, for they were occupied with investigations on the eastern frontier. While they were thus detained, reports arrived in London of the reverse at Viervoet and of the refusal of the Boers

---

[43] Smith to Warden, June 17, 1851, in J. W. Sauer and George M. Theal, eds., *Basutoland Records* (3 vols.; Cape Town: Richard, 1883), I, 411–412.

[44] Cory, *op. cit.*, V, 419–420.

[45] Warden to Smith, July 6, 1851, Sauer and Theal, *op. cit.*, I, 421–422.

[46] Warden to Garvock, July 14, 20, 1851, enclosures in Smith to Grey, Aug. 8, 1851, C.O. 48/317, P.R.O.; C. W. de Kiewiet, *British Colonial Policy and the South African Republics, 1848–1872* (London: Longmans, Green, 1929), p. 55.

[47] Memo by Smith, Aug. 6, 1851, enclosure in Smith to Grey, Aug. 8, 1851, C.O. 48/317, P.R.O.

to volunteer. This information demonstrated to Grey that Warden was a bungler and that Smith's promises with regard to the sovereignty were as bankrupt as his assurances of Kaffir docility. In mid-September he reminded Smith that annexation had been approved on the assumption that the majority of the burghers supported it, and that they were willing to bear the burdens of their own defense. If this assumption was false, as the evidence seemed to suggest, the imperial government should withdraw as soon as it could do so with safety and honor. Such a decision would be lamentable, as anarchy and bloodshed would probably ensue, but in justice to the people of the United Kingdom the government could not incur expense to maintain its authority over those who would not support it.[48] Abandonment was, however, a last resort. The inhabitants of the sovereignty, white and black, must be informed of the views of the imperial government; if, after such explanations, they were willing to give the government their support and it could be made self-sustaining, there would be no cause for abandonment. In September Grey still hoped that by reform the sovereignty could be retained; a month later, he had decided it must be abandoned. In part this shift was occasioned by a continuation of dreary reports from official and nonofficial sources. Major Hogge's letters had documented what Grey already suspected, that Smith's reports were unreliable. The Kaffirs were far from beaten; on the contrary, they were growing in strength, and as a result of Moshesh's victory, the British could look for "an enemy or doubtful friend in almost every black man between Grahamstown and Natal." While this menace developed, Hogge wrote Grey, Smith conjured up phantom victories. In one dispatch 250 men were reported killed, of whom 247 were still alive and fighting; in another the enemy was said to be defeated when he retired to attack on more favorable ground. General orders transformed reverses into paper triumphs. Hogge contended that additional military forces would be required in the sovereignty even if the Boers remained neutral, which was not at all certain.[49]

Smith's own letters bore out Hogge's gloomy predictions with regard to the sovereignty. On September 20 he wrote Grey privately that even

---

[48] Grey to Smith, Sept. 16, 1851, C.O. 48/316, P.R.O. This dispatch is based on a draft in Grey's hand, marked Sept. 15, 1851.

[49] Hogge to Hawes, Sept. 18, 1851, Grey Papers. This letter is characteristic of several Hogge wrote in this period. He gained his impressions of the sovereignty from private letters. Among his correspondents were Captain Parish, commander of the Natal reinforcements stationed at Winburg, and A. Fraser in Bloemfontein. These letters were also forwarded to Grey.

with reinforcements from Natal Warden could do little more than defend himself, because the Boers refused to coöperate; the Orange River Sovereignty, the "Sind of South Africa," was certain to be the cause of more woe.[50] These reports caused Grey to revise his earlier opinion, and to decide on withdrawal from the sovereignty as soon as possible.[51] He consulted with Russell, who emphatically agreed.[52] To a draft dispatch of Grey's, Russell added the decisive words, "The ultimate abandonment of the Orange River Sovereignty should be a settled point in our policy." [53]

Before these words of doom had left London, Hogge and Owen were on their way to Bloemfontein. Their departure had been hastened by the news that Andries Pretorius had intervened in the affairs of the sovereignty. In September, 1851, Pretorius had informed Warden that at Moshesh's request he intended to mediate between the Basuto and the resident and proposed to enter the sovereignty for that purpose. Warden, already overwhelmed by adversity, assumed this notice to mean that Pretorius was on the way with a commando; he knew he was helpless to resist. But at the beginning of October another letter with a very different tone arrived from the rebel leader. In respectful language, Pretorius stated that he had been appointed head of a delegation to seek a treaty of peace with the British government. As Moshesh and some of the Boer inhabitants had requested his intervention to end the war, he hoped for an early and favorable answer. Beneath the polite language the meaning was cold and clear. The price of Transvaal nonintervention was recognition. Such a decision was beyond Warden's authority, but the request was not one to be ignored. If the communication contained a threat, it also offered a hope. Perhaps a settlement with the rebel Boers would be in the interests of the sovereignty. The Reverend Andrew Murray, who had recently visited Pretorius, assured Warden that the Boers of the Transvaal wanted only peace, and that an understanding with them would be a deathblow to the attempts of disaffected Boers in the sovereignty to disturb the government. Though Warden professed to distrust Pre-

---

[50] Smith to Grey, private, Sept. 20, 1851, *ibid.*

[51] Grey to Hogge, private, Oct. 21, 1851, *ibid.*

[52] Russell to Grey, Oct. 20, 1851, *ibid.* Russell wrote: "As the Boers will not defend the Sovereignty, the Sovereignty should be abandoned to Moshesh & the Boers— B. Caffraria shd. be subdued to our rule. Sir H. Smith pleases me less & less. . . ."

[53] Grey to Smith, Oct. 21, 1851, C.O. 48/317, based on a minute by Grey on Smith to Grey, Aug. 20, 1851, Grey Papers. Russell added the statement on "a settled point" (see de Kiewiet, *op. cit.*, p. 60).

torius, he was not disposed to brush aside a prospect for peace. He replied to the delegation that he was submitting their letter to the high commissioner.[54]

Smith and his executive council also recognized the communication as a form of blackmail intended to end the outlawry of Pretorius and gain recognition for the Transvaal republic. They concluded that only extreme necessity would justify submission to such terms. A pardon to the notorious rebel Pretorius would be "a serious shock to British Authority throughout South Africa"; recognition of the republic was a matter for Downing Street's decision.[55] Before he consulted his council, however, Smith had already accepted the possibility that the "extreme necessity" would arise.[56] Though he had no faith in Pretorius, he confided in the assistant commissioners discretionary authority to annul his outlawry. They might deem it expedient to negotiate with Pretorius and they could not treat with an outlaw. If Pretorius was sincere in his avowed object, a peaceful settlement with him might be expedient as a means of ending the "horrors of Barbarian warfare." His overtures in any event could not be dismissed lightly.[57]

Shortly after the assistant commissioners left for the Orange River Sovereignty to ascertain the state of the territory and the full significance of Pretorius' communications, Smith received Grey's dispatch of September, indicating that unless the sovereignty could be made self-sustaining it would be abandoned. Though the later dispatch announcing a definite decision to withdraw had not yet arrived, Smith saw that the fate of his sovereignty was in jeopardy. In forwarding Grey's observations to Hogge and Owen he left them no doubts as to his own views. The abandonment of the sovereignty, he warned, "would be regarded by every man of colour in South Africa as an unprecedented and unlooked-for victory to his race." It would expose those who had been loyal to the vengeance of the disaffected, and would be "a signal for revolt or continued resistance to British authority from Cape Town to the territories and thence to Lake Ngami." [58] As was invariably true when Sir Harry felt strongly (and he usually did), he used hyperbole as others used exclamation marks.

---

[54] This correspondence is enclosed in Smith to Grey, Nov. 5, 1850, C.O. 48/319, P.R.O. For a somewhat different emphasis see de Kiewiet, op. cit., p. 57.

[55] Minutes, Executive Council, Oct. 27, 1851, C.O. 51/76, P.R.O.

[56] Memo by Smith, Oct. 13, 1851, enclosure in Smith to Grey, Oct. 15, 1851, C.O. 48/318, P.R.O.; Smith to Grey, private, Oct. 16, 1851, Grey Papers.

[57] Smith to Hogge and Owen, Nov. 11, 1851, enclosure in Smith to Grey, Nov. 12, 1851, C.O. 48/319, P.R.O.

[58] Ibid.

Hogge and Owen did not share Smith's emotional attachment to the Orange River Sovereignty. Before they left the eastern frontier, Hogge at least had already acquired a most unfavorable impression of the territory and its inhabitants.[59] For the confusion they saw everywhere, they considered two men to be primarily responsible. Sir Harry Smith had imposed British sovereignty on Boers who did not want it. Without the coöperation of the burghers, effective government was impossible. But the Boers were not disposed to coöperate, and their sullenness was transformed into outright hostility by the headstrong, arrogant Major Warden. In the opinion of the commissioners, Warden was incompetent for the position. His council had been unanimously against war with the Basuto, but, influenced by the Wesleyan missionary with Moroko, he had attacked the strongest tribe in South Africa with a totally inadequate force. He had ignored the essential principles of statecraft by alienating the powerful and supporting the weak.[60]

The mission of the commissioners, however, was not to assess blame for the disturbances. They had been sent to propose a course of action that would involve the imperial government in a minimum of liability and expense, and their analysis was essentially Machiavellian. The Basuto, whatever their justification for resisting the resident, must eventually be humbled to restore British prestige. But Moshesh must not be attacked until there was a certainty of success; meanwhile, the policy must be to temporize with him. Pretorius was unscrupulous, and he had undoubtedly incited both Boers and natives to resistance against the Queen's authority; but he should be conciliated if it was in the British interest to do so. Commissioner Hogge had no doubt that the imperial government had been deluded from its true interests in South Africa by pseudo philanthropy. Statesmen had sought to promote Christianity among the natives and to protect them against the whites, but the natives did not welcome political agents or missionaries. There were no friendly tribes in South Africa. Nor could the natives be effectively shielded against the settlers: "The history of the Cape is already written in that of America, and the gradual increase of the white race must eventually though slowly ensure the disappearance of the Black. Providence vindicates this its unalterable law

---

[59] From King Williamstown Hogge wrote to Hawes on Oct. 24, 1851: "Every Dutchman without hardly an exception is a rebel at heart and whatever may have been said, never wished for British sovereignty to be extended over him" (Grey Papers).

[60] Hogge to Grey, March 26, 1852, Grey Papers, copy in C.O. 48/333, P.R.O.

by rendering all the philanthropic efforts that have been made to avert such a destiny subservient to its fulfillment." [61]

Viewed from this perspective an agreement with the Transvaal seemed to offer manifest advantages. A hostile Transvaal would encourage rebellious tendencies in the Orange River Sovereignty. A friendly or neutral Transvaal would discourage disorder. When Hogge and Owen met Pretorius and his fellow commissioners they were convinced that negotiations would be profitable. While their observations of Pretorius confirmed their earlier negative opinions, they were impressed with the good sense of the emigrant council which they believed had restrained him from aggressive action in the past, and with the friendly spirit of the Transvaal deputation. The opportunity to confer as a boon what was already a reality could not be allowed to slip away. The Transvaal Boers were *de facto* independent; Grey's dictum of nonintervention beyond the colony made it evident that they would continue to be so. Thus the commissioners on January 16, 1852, negotiated at Sand River a convention guaranteeing mutual noninterference. The imperial government, in exchange for a promise that there would be no slavery in the Transvaal, disclaimed all alliances "with the coloured nations to the north of the Vaal river." The contracting parties agreed that they would not supply ammunition to the tribes.[62]

In accepting these terms, Hogge and Owen exercised their discretion. But they had little doubt that their action would be approved in London, as it was in accordance with the general policy of nonintervention they had been instructed to promote. Though formally subordinate to Smith the commissioners were answerable to Grey; and they could not have interpreted his wishes more precisely had there been telepathic communication. Shortly before the commissioners had set out for the meeting at Sand River, Grey wrote Owen:

I hope my letters & Dispatches by the Sept. mail may have reached the Colony in time to guide you in your dealings with Pretorius & the boers. I shall rejoice beyond measure if you can make an arrangement by wh. we may be enabled to withdraw & quite agree with you that we must cease to act with such Quixotic philanthropy as to insist on preventing the savages & semi savages (the boers) of Southern Africa from cutting each others throats & thus bringing them all as enemies against ourselves. I have very strongly

[61] Hogge to Grey, private, Dec. 19, 1851, Grey Papers.

[62] For the text of the convention, see G. W. Eybers, *Select Constitutional Documents Illustrating South African History, 1795–1910* (London: Routledge, 1918), pp. 357–359.

expressed this opinion to Sir H. Smith—I see no objection whatever to allowing the boers to form such an independent Govt as they can on our frontier; if they ill treat the natives beyond a certain point the latter will be driven to take refuge in our territory as they do in Natal from Panda. The Boers must trade with us & will supply us with many things we want & contribute to the Colonial Revenue.[63]

The Sand River Convention was the logical consequence of British determination to check the drain of imperial revenue into southern Africa. For many years the official policy had been influenced by humanitarianism on the cheap. But a succession of wars had demonstrated that British entanglement in white-native conflicts was neither cheap nor effectual. It was indeed "Quixotic philanthropy," beneficial to no one, and tremendously expensive. No British government ever contemplated the employment of substantial force beyond the Vaal River, and without such force the effect of humanitarian pronouncements was to infuriate the Boers without protecting the natives. Before Sand River, Boer commandos had scourged the tribes north of the Vaal without hindrance from the imperial government. After the Sand River Convention, they would continue to do so, but with British acquiescence.

Most missionaries denounced the Sand River Convention as a sacrifice of moral principles to expediency. Robert Moffat, working with a tribe of Bechuana who were among the first to be visited by a Boer commando, called it "an act of infatuation which we hope has few parallels in history. . . . it would appear that *extermination* is the motto of the Transvaal farmers and that too under the assumed sanction of the Queen of England." [64] At least one missionary, however, had a different evaluation. Walter Inglis at Matebe, disillusioned by what he considered to be the utter failure of spiritual influence in southern Africa, wrote of the agreement: "I cannot say I rejoice neither am I deeply sorry. Any way you turn . . . in S. Africa—there is blood—If the English rule or misrule you have blood—If the Boers rule or misrule—you have blood—If the natives rule or misrule— you have blood—One & all parties stands in the need of the Spirit of God." [65]

Earl Grey did not consider that the agreement at Sand River and the prospective abandonment of the Orange River Sovereignty meant the sacrifice of moral principles. Rather they were a recognition of the

---

[63] Grey to Hogge, private, Dec. 15, 1851, Grey Papers.
[64] Moffat to Thompson, [Sept., 1852], SAF 27–1, LMS Archives.
[65] Inglis to Directors, LMS, Oct. 10, 1852, *ibid.*

inability of the imperial government to interpose effectively between Boers and natives in the remote interior of southern Africa. Where Britain had the power to restrain the whites, he believed it had a continuing obligation to do so. Grey has been called doctrinaire; the adjective is inappropriate. Aside from his mania on "Sepoy troops," his thought was extremely flexible; if anything, he suffered from a surfeit of imagination. Despite his peremptory instructions against expansion, he was not committed to nonexpansion regardless of circumstances. In December, 1851, as he waited anxiously for word of a settlement with the Transvaal Boers, he was advocating the extension of British sovereignty on the coast. He told Smith that the territory from which the Kaffirs would be expelled should be used for the settlement of "friendly" tribes from the interior who sought refuge from the Boers. Perhaps also the tribes who had proved themselves enemies could be "induced" to move into the interior. These relocation plans made it imperative that Britain control a large portion of the coast between Natal and Cape Colony. Along the coast the imperial power could offer effective protection; in the high veld it could not.[66] Further, without access to the sea, the Boers of the interior were innocuous to British interests.

Sir Harry Smith's view of the Sand River Convention was based upon the possible effects on the Orange River Sovereignty, which was so closely tied to his own prestige. He had no advance knowledge of the treaty, but he insisted that they were in accordance with the principles he had laid down in conversations with the assistant commissioners.[67] In fact, Smith had lost all influence over frontier policy with the arrival of Hogge and Owen.

The contrast between Smith's reports of brilliant victories and the evidence of continued Kaffir resistance had shaken the ministry's faith in his ability and his integrity. Both Grey and Russell were convinced that Smith had prolonged the war by excessive leniency to Hottentot rebels and inadequate vigor against the enemy.[68] Hogge's reports that the governor's dispatches were entirely unreliable and that his conduct of the war was incompetent convinced Grey that Smith must be removed.[69] To Russell the issue was not so simple. Perhaps all that Hogge

---

[66] Grey to Smith, Dec. 15, 1851, Grey Papers.

[67] Smith to Grey, Feb. 16, 1852, C.O. 48/324, P.R.O.

[68] Grey to Russell, Sept. 12, 1851, Russell Papers, PRO 30/22/9, P.R.O.; Russell to Grey, Sept. 13, 1851, Grey Papers.

[69] Grey to Russell, Dec. 12, 1851, Grey Papers. Hogge's low estimate of Smith was widely shared by some of the governor's closest associates. The colonial secretary,

alleged was true, but Smith had an illustrious reputation and he had powerful friends in Parliament. Political considerations dictated that he not be humiliated unless recall was imperative. The war seemed to be approaching an end; it would be preferable to wait and allow the governor to retire gracefully. Russell was willing to recall Smith if Wellington agreed, for the Duke's support of the decision would stifle the attacks of the opposition. Wellington, however, saw no reason to supersede the man whom he considered, with Sir Charles Napier, one of the two most illustrious officers in the British Army, and he brushed aside the accumulation of evidence presented by Grey. Smith had his confidence, and he highly approved of all his operations.[70]

Despite Wellington's opposition,[71] Grey was insistent that Smith must go, and Russell finally consented to bring the issue before the cabinet. In January, 1852, they decided unanimously that Smith should be relieved.[72] After much consideration as to whether the governor of the Cape should be a civilian or a military man,[73] the government decided to appoint Lieutenant General Sir George Cathcart, another intimate of the Duke's.

Within a few weeks Grey himself was out of office. The Russell government, which had survived more by the impotence of its opponents than by its own power, finally fell apart, to be replaced by a Tory administration which maintained an anemic existence for nine months. Grey was succeeded by Sir John Pakington. The new appointee, said

---

John Montagu, wrote to Sir George Napier on Feb. 2, 1852: "A more thorough and lamentable failure in that position [as a statesman] is not to be found. . . . In all he does he is guided by popularity—by favor or by fear—the latter most frequently. No one has the slightest respect for him and no one relies upon anything he says" (Napier Papers, Add. MSS 49167, British Museum).

[70] See his speech of Feb. 5, 1852, *Parliamentary Debates*, 3d series, CXIX, 174.

[71] Wellington to Grey, Jan. 9, 1852, Grey Papers. Sir James Stephen, to whom Grey submitted the correspondence, thought that if the recall of Smith became a subject of debate, "the grave misconduct" of Wellington as commander in chief for resisting the decision should be brought out. Stephen expressed surprise that the Duke had not been admonished that unless he was more careful in the future he would be summarily dismissed. Stephen was no politician. See note by J. S. [Stephen], n.d. [Jan.–Feb., 1852?], Grey Papers.

[72] Memo by Grey, Jan. 8, 1852, *ibid.*

[73] Grey in his journal states that he was first inclined to select Sir Gaspard Le Marchant, who was then about to return to Newfoundland, but decided to appoint a general because a civilian appointment would create "great dissatisfaction" among all the military authorities. Wellington, though continuing to object to Smith's recall, endorsed Cathcart as the best possible successor. See Grey's Journal, March 6, 1852, *ibid.*

the *Times,* had one advantage over his predecessors, "a thorough consciousness of his own ignorance," for he had no discernible qualifications for the office. It was a "strange caprice of fate" which had "entrusted to a gentleman, hitherto principally known at quarter-sessions, the sovereignty over the forty-four colonies of Great Britain." [74]

Pakington had just assumed office when news of the Sand River Convention arrived. The agreement was as gratifying to him as it was to Earl Grey. One of his first official acts had been to send instructions to Cathcart to reverse the outlawry of Pretorius as a preliminary to a convention with the Transvaal,[75] and this decision had been anticipated. Approval of withdrawal south of the Vaal did not necessarily imply acceptance of the previous administration's decision to abandon the Orange River Sovereignty. On this subject Pakington was not prepared to make a final judgment without further information from the assistant commissioners, but he and his subordinates were agreed that whatever the ultimate decision, the Boers must be conciliated. If the burghers were willing to accept the responsibility of self-defense as a price for continued British sovereignty, then perhaps the territory could be retained. If not, Britain should withdraw and leave the inhabitants to their own devices, thus compelling the Boers to accept the responsibility. In either event the imperial government would be relieved of the expense of policing the northern border, as the Boers, "after their own fashion," would "keep the Kaffirs at bay." [76]

A further consideration deterred Hogge and Owen from abandoning the sovereignty immediately. They feared that the result of such withdrawal would be a union of the Boers of the interior and, soon after, a conspiracy for the return of Natal and the establishment of a republic from the high veld to the sea. To prevent the growth of such a menace it seemed expedient to retain the sovereignty, at least for the time. With the Transvaal quiet, disaffected Boers in the Orange River Territory would either subside, or could trek across the river. The new republic would thus be a safety valve for the territory to the south.[77] Herman Merivale, the permanent undersecretary, whose opinions were now heard with greater respect than Grey had accorded

---

[74] *Times,* Feb. 26, 1852.

[75] Pakington to Cathcart, March 10, 1852, C.O. 48/355, P.R.O.

[76] Minutes on Smith to Grey, Jan. 14, 1852, C.O. 48/323. The words are from comments by Lord Desart, parliamentary undersecretary, but the tone was characteristic of the entire staff. Desart was referring in particular to a scheme he had conceived of locating Boers along the frontier as "a cheap and efficient guard" against the natives.

[77] Hogge to Grey, March 26, 1852, Grey Papers; copy in C.O. 48/333, P.R.O.

them, also expressed the fear that a combination of the Boers would create a state of dangerous power on the borders of Cape Colony.[78]

The tendency of the new colonial secretary, like that of the administration, was to avoid decisions rather than to initiate them. Grey had dominated the Colonial Office; the office dominated Pakington. Overwhelmed by the routine and conscious of his own lack of experience, he was inclined to follow the advice of the permanent staff.[79] The future of the Orange River Sovereignty, therefore, remained in doubt.

There were some indications in 1852 that the Sand River Convention might foster a new spirit between the Orange and the Vaal. Many of the settlers expressed alarm that the British government might abandon them and a willingness to bear the burdens required of them. Moshesh manifested eagerness for peace and humbly accepted a fine of cattle imposed on him by Hogge and Owen, though he "dribbled out" the payments in installments. Hogge and Owen set out for Bloemfontein in May, 1852, with the intention of determining whether or not the Boers would accept the burden of self-defense, or, if they would not, of "devising the least disgraceful means of packing out of it." [80] But Hogge died shortly after he reached the sovereignty, and Owen was not able to assume the entire responsibility alone. At the same time Cathcart replaced Warden, who had remained in limbo for months, with Assistant Commissary General Henry Green, who was asked to submit an independent assessment of the state of the territory. Pending this report and the possible appointment of a successor to Hogge, Cathcart devoted his energies to the termination of the Kaffir war and the settlement of the eastern frontier.

When Cathcart arrived at the scene of war at the beginning of April, 1852, he was confronted with the problem of locating the enemy rather than of fighting him. The Slambie tribes, with one exception, had not joined in the war, and those Gaikas who continued to resist had been reduced to marauders or fugitives. They hid from the troops in wooded ravines between the Fish and Keiskama rivers and in the mountainous parts of British Kaffraria. The war had been from the

[78] Minute by Merivale, March 19, [1852], on Smith to Grey, Jan. 14, 1852, C.O. 48/323, P.R.O.

[79] There is a perceptive analysis of the Colonial Office during this period in a minute for Lord Lyndhurst, private, n.d. [1852], unsigned, Gladstone Papers, Add. MSS 44569, British Museum. The writer indicates that Grey was the most formidable foe of the new government, and that he would be a menace to any anti-Whig administration unless the defects of his policies were fully exposed.

[80] Hogge to Grey, May 14, 1852, Grey Papers.

start largely a hunting expedition against an elusive quarry; now it had become a police action. The principal problem was to oust the Kaffirs from the Amatola Mountains and to prevent their returning after their expulsion. These mountains were of no great height but rose abruptly from comparatively open country, forming a circular barrier about forty miles in circumference within which numerous spurs formed deep and heavily wooded ravines.

Cathcart brought the war to a conclusion with relative ease. He led a punitive expedition against Kreli, the Transkeian chief who had supposedly abetted the rebellious Gaikas, and swept up almost 10,000 cattle; his forces then scoured the mountainous areas of Kaffraria, driving all but a handful of fugitives beyond the Kei River. By October, 1852, he could state that the war was at an end. He was now in a position to impose terms of peace.

Like Smith and D'Urban, Cathcart appraised frontier policy from the viewpoint of a military man. He had defeated the enemy, and his object now was to create conditions that would make another war unlikely, or, if it occurred, to minimize the power of the tribes to fight effectively. Unlike his predecessors, he made no pretense of being concerned with the civilization or the Christianization of the natives. Cathcart was neither pronative nor prosettler; the people who inhabited the frontier were important to him to the extent that they related to military security. When he first took command, he had intended to drive all the rebel tribes beyond the Kei River; but, when he discovered that their permanent expulsion would require the maintenance of a large military force, he revised his plans as D'Urban had done in 1835, and assigned them locations in open country between the Keiskama and the Kei, excluding them only from the mountainous areas they had previously occupied. Policy dictated that the chiefs be conciliated; in March, 1853, Cathcart pardoned Sandile, whose deposal had been the immediate cause of the war, and recognized his status as paramount chief.[81]

So far as consistent with the safety of the colony, Cathcart was inclined to leave the tribes of Kaffraria undisturbed. The chiefs must be upheld because they were the leaders of their people; the Kaffirs should be governed by tribal law and custom because interference caused unrest; and intertribal disputes should be settled by the contestants themselves, provided they did not molest the colony.[82] This

---

[81] Cathcart to Secretary of State, Feb. 11, March 15, 1853, both in C.O. 48/337, P.R.O.

[82] Cathcart to Maclean, March 29, 1854, enclosure in Cathcart to Newcastle, April 15, 1854, C.O. 48/353.

laissez-faire policy left untouched the roots of tribal unrest, and Cathcart's land policy intensified it. The removal of the Gaikas from the
Amatola Mountains, and the detachment of some Tembu lands,
intensified pressure on land; and the forfeited territories were granted
to European farmers on the justification that with villages as rallying
points there would be a protection against any future Kaffir aggression. Land taken from the Tembu around the new village of Queens-
town was added to the colony; the rest of Kaffraria remained a separate
jurisdiction. The Kat River settlement was transformed from a Hottentot location to a mixed community by the assignment to Europeans
of lands taken from rebels.[83]

In its broad outlines Cathcart's scheme for the eastern frontier had
an attractive symmetry. Practically all the Kaffirs were now located
beyond the colonial border; only the Fingoes and some Tembu lived
under colonial jurisdiction. Thus there was a clear line of demarcation
between the colony and the tribes. Within British Kaffraria the territory assigned to European occupation was also clearly defined. A
mounted force of 250 men policed the border so effectively that cattle
thievery was almost eliminated.[84] But Cathcart had in fact settled
nothing. The quiet of British Kaffraria was evidence of exhaustion,
not of tranquillity; when Cathcart pardoned Sandile the Gaika chiefs
first expressed their contrition for causing the war and then asked,
"When will you give us back our lands?" [85] Within a year of Cathcart's
departure the Fingoes, on whose inveterate hostility to the Kaffirs
he had relied, were manifesting hostility toward the alien laws of their
British protectors and were contemplating alliance with their ancient
enemies. When Cathcart departed another Kaffir war seemed imminent.

The experience of governors from D'Urban to Cathcart demonstrated
that the problems of the eastern frontier could not be solved by any
governor or by any policy; they would be "solved" only by the reduction of natives to complete subservience. The imperial factor delayed
the process. In time of peace it sought to protect the tribes from their
fate; in war it was compelled to fight with a degree of forbearance
rather than with that decisive ruthlessness by which the Boers imposed
their will. Frontier wars fought by British generals and regular troops
were likely to be protracted and certain to be expensive. At the end of

[83] Memo by Robinson, April 25, 1854, enclosure in Cathcart to Newcastle, April 25,
1854, ibid.

[84] Memo by Cathcart [1854], enclosure in Cathcart to Newcastle, March 14, 1854,
C.O. 48/352, P.R.O.

[85] See speech of Cathcart to the chiefs, March 9, 1853, enclosure in Cathcart to
Secretary of State, March 15, 1853, C.O. 48/337, P.R.O.

the Kaffir war of 1850–1853, Parliament and the imperial government were dedicated to the proposition that this would be the last war to to be fought at British expense; henceforth the Cape, which had just been granted representative government, could fight its own battles.

In Kaffraria there was no question of withdrawing British sovereignty. The issue was assignment of responsibility between the imperial and the colonial government. In the Orange River Sovereignty, to which Cathcart turned his attention with the end of the Kaffir war, the issue was quite different. In Downing Street and at Government House in Cape Town there was unanimity that Smith had blundered in annexing the territory; the imperial government was determined to extricate itself from the responsibility. If, by some miracle, the territory could be made self-sustaining there was yet a chance that it might be retained, but Cathcart's initial impression was that a force of 2,000 infantry supported by cavalry would be required for several years to come to maintain the peace, and this was a price no ministry was prepared to pay.[86] Pakington wrote the governor that "I have heard no arguments in favor of the retention of the sovereignty which would not, as it appears to me, apply with equal force to the Country beyond the Vaal." [87]

There was one important distinction: the Orange River Sovereignty had been annexed, and the Transvaal had not. It was much easier to renounce all pretensions to a territory than to give up a possession. The home government awaited advice from its South African representatives before making a final decision; and Cathcart, engrossed in the Kaffir war, sought guidance from representatives on the spot. After Hogge's death Owen, acting on Cathcart's instructions, convened a meeting in Bloemfontein in June, 1852, attended by seventy-nine delegates including field commandants and field-cornets and three deputies from each field-cornetcy. They agreed to resolutions supporting the establishment of a council with wide powers of self-government, and accepted responsibility for commando duty provided that Britain support them with a sufficient number of troops.[88] Evidently there was widespread desire that the redcoats stay so long as the menace of the Basuto remained.

Since the fiasco at Viervoet, Moshesh and British officials had fenced with each other. The Basuto chief had no wish to provoke a war and sought to escape by minimum compliance with British demands for restitution of cattle allegedly seized from his neighbors. The British

[86] Cathcart to Secretary of State, May 20, 1852, C.O. 48/326, P.R.O.

[87] Pakington to Cathcart, private and confidential, July 26, 1852, *ibid.*

[88] Enclosures in Cathcart to Secretary of State, July 21, 1852, C.O. 48/327, P.R.O.

representative did not press too hard for payment until his hands were free; then he would force the Basuto into submission. Cathcart admitted that Warden's conduct had been inflammatory and that Moshesh, despite strong provocation, had resisted Boer importunities to join them against the British. But the prestige of the British nation, which had sunk as a result of Viervoet, must be restored and Moshesh must be made to pay for his aggressions against his neighbors, though Cathcart admitted there "was scarcely anything tangible" to justify sending troops against him.[89] By November, 1852, the Kaffirs were crushed and Cathcart, with a force of 500 cavalry and 200 infantry, set out for Basuto country to "administer strict justice." He confronted Moshesh with an ultimatum to deliver 10,000 head of cattle within three days or face war, and rejected the chief's plea for an extension of time. When only 3,500 head had been delivered in the specified time, he carried out his threat, with unexpected consequences. At Berea Mountain near Moshesh's stronghold at Thaba Bosiu, the troops barely escaped a major disaster and retired from the field with a healthy respect for the most formidable native foe they had encountered in Africa. Cathcart, who had talked of strict compliance, was content with a total of 6,000 cattle rather than the 10,000 he had demanded, and Moshesh, with great astuteness, gave the governor an opportunity to retreat with honor. In an appeal worthy of his exalted reputation for statesmanship Moshesh humbly sued for peace, and promised to try to keep his people in order in the future. The governor had shown his power and had taken many Basuto cattle; "let it be enough I pray you, and let me be no longer considered an enemy to the Queen." [90] Cathcart acknowledged the words of a great chief, and professed to be satisfied. He retired from the sovereignty, convinced that Britain should abandon it as soon as possible. If there had ever been any doubt as to the retention of the sovereignty, it was resolved at Berea.[91]

Throughout 1852 the Colonial Office had left the issue of the sovereignty in abeyance. As a member of a government holding office on sufferance and averse to any action, Pakington was disposed to inertia, and he could justify deferral of a decision on the basis that he had not received definite recommendations from Governor Cathcart. The governor was not prepared to take any action without instructions from home, but even before Berea he had stated his firm opinion that the burghers beyond the Orange should be granted independence.

[89] Cathcart to Secretary of State, Nov. 14, 1852 (no. 35), C.O. 48/328, P.R.O.
[90] Moshesh to Cathcart, Dec. 20, 1852, Sauer and Theal, *op. cit.*, I, 627.
[91] De Kiewiet, *op. cit.*, p. 69.

If this resulted in their amalgamation with the Transvaal, so much the better. A strong Boer republic could maintain order on the Cape's northern frontier and a sinkhole of endless imperial expense would be converted into a source of profit, for this landlocked republic would be economically dependent on the power that controlled access to the sea.[92]

This was a point of view certain to have strong appeal to the coalition government of Lord Aberdeen, which took office with the collapse of Derby's ministry in December, 1852. Amidst a brilliant array of Whig and Peelite colleagues, the dominant figure was the Chancellor of the Exchequer, William E. Gladstone. The budget he presented in April, 1853, perfectly expressed the ideals of his age by its meticulous attention to economy. Allegedly his five-hour defense of his measures held the members of Parliament "spellbound"; it certainly met with their approval. The dominance of the Chancellor of the Exchequer was significant to the Empire—he became in fact the governor of the imperial engine—and economy dictated retreat south of the Orange River.

The new secretary of state for colonies, the Duke of Newcastle, took office only a few hours after the battle of Berea, but he needed no intelligence of this latest disaster to convince him of the desirability of abandonment. The problem was yet unresolved as to how to accomplish this object with a minimum of unpleasantness. Shortly before he left office, Pakington had asked the law officers of the crown for their opinion as to what steps were necessary to effect withdrawal,[93] and they had advised that an act of Parliament would be required.[94] They arrived at this conclusion on the assumption that letters patent granting a sovereignty had been issued by Sir Harry Smith. In fact the letters patent had been left unissued in Cape Town while Smith was away fighting a war, and Cathcart found them there in January, 1853.[95] This was good news, as it might make a parliamentary debate unnecessary, and the matter was again referred to the law officers. But somehow —the ways of bureaucracy are mysterious—the case was overlooked for six months.[96]

---

[92] Cathcart to Secretary of State, Oct. 12, 1852, C.O. 48/328, P.R.O.

[93] Memo, Pakington to Merivale, Dec. 4, 1852, C.O. 48/326, P.R.O.

[94] Law Officers to Pakington, Dec. 20, 1852, C.O. 48/334, P.R.O.

[95] Cathcart to Secretary of State, Jan. 13, 1853 (no. 47), C.O. 48/337, P.R.O. See also de Kiewiet, op. cit., p. 71.

[96] The matter was submitted to the law officers in March, 1853, and they gave their opinion in September (see Law Officers to Newcastle, Sept. 28, 1853, C.O. 48/350, P.R.O.).

While this delay continued in London the Colonial Office sent another representative to South Africa. Cathcart had no confidence in Owen, whom he considered far inferior to Hogge in knowledge and judgment. To assist Owen in less complicated tasks he appointed a prominent colonist, John B. Ebden,[97] but an able and experienced agent was needed for missions such as the settlement of the Orange River issue or the dangerous problems of native-white settlement in Natal. Pakington left the appointment of a new commissioner to his successor, and after some delay the Duke of Newcastle selected Sir George Russell Clerk, onetime governor of Bombay. Clerk received a dual appointment as special commissioner for the Orange River Territory, where he would be directly responsible to the secretary of state, and as an associate of Owen's in the settlement of the affairs of territories adjacent to the eastern and northeastern frontier. Clerk's functions in the sovereignty were to be the preparation of the native tribes and the burghers for the final abandonment. He would have no legal authority in the arrangements he might make with the inhabitants, but his recommendations were certain to carry great weight.[98]

The basic issue had been settled before Clerk left London: the government had decided to withdraw from the Orange River Sovereignty.[99] It was his responsibility to communicate this unwelcome news to the inhabitants and to settle the problems attendant to abandonment; the wisdom or the unwisdom of the policy did not come within his purview.

Since the Sand River Convention rumors had circulated in Cape Colony of the intended withdrawal from the Orange River area as well, and emphatic opposition had been expressed in newspapers and at public meetings; hostility to the policy was bound to focus on the person of its agent. Clerk undoubtedly accentuated these antagonisms by his frigid manner, but not even the most personable of emissaries could have been well received on such a mission. Colonial disapproval concerned Clerk not at all; he had been sent to carry out a policy "to withdraw if possible in a friendly manner, if not to withdraw anyhow." [100] This policy he himself believed to be in the imperial interest,

[97] Cathcart to Secretary of State, Oct. 12, 1852, C.O. 48/328, P.R.O.

[98] Newcastle to Clerk, private and confidential, April 9, 1853, C.O. 48/338, P.R.O. Cathcart's commission as high commissioner was modified to exclude the Orange River Sovereignty (Newcastle to Cathcart, April 14, 1853, C.O. 48/337, P.R.O.).

[99] Newcastle to Cathcart, March 14, 1853, C.O. 48/337, P.R.O. Eric Walker, *A History of Southern Africa* (London: Longmans, Green, 1957), p. 258, states that Newcastle told Clerk that the issue of abandonment was still an open question. This is contrary to the evidence.

[100] Clerk to Merivale, private, Feb. 14, [1857], C.O. 48/377, P.R.O.

and his experience in the sovereignty reinforced that conviction.[101]

Clerk arrived at Grahamstown to confer with Cathcart on June 22, 1853. He delayed his departure in expectation of receiving word of the law officers' opinion, but after several weeks he left for Bloemfontein, where he arrived on August 8. The scenes that he observed en route must have reinforced his conviction of the sovereignty's worthlessness. Drought had destroyed the grass and parched the earth; the sense of utter hopelessness was accentuated by the hovels in which the pastoral Boers lived.[102]

On the day of his arrival Clerk called a meeting of delegates for September to consider the form of self-government. Before the delegates, seventy-six Boer and nineteen English, convened in the village church, Clerk announced the intention of Her Majesty's government to withdraw and called upon them to agree on a form of government. He was taken aback when they unanimously resolved that they did not wish to be independent and were entitled to continued British protection, and he was unable to give precise answers to their questions as to the extent of his powers and the measures he was prepared to adopt, and whether or not he had the power to absolve them from their allegiance and recognize them as independent.[103]

Clerk's difficulties in responding to the delegates were created by a misunderstanding which continued to plague him for several months. While he was at Plymouth preparing to sail for the Cape, he had received a dispatch informing him that he was to take no final action pending further instructions, which would be sent as soon as the opinion of the law officers was received. He assumed that his responsibility was to effect withdrawal when the ministry, after taking legal counsel, so instructed him, and that in the meantime he could only maintain the *status quo*. When he had acquired all the information he believed requisite on the state of the sovereignty, he requested permission to come home for consultation, leaving Owen as caretaker in his absence.[104] The Colonial Office, on the other hand, had expected him to devote his attention to inquiry and to make recommendations which would be incorporated in the final instructions.[105]

During his first month in the Sovereignty, Clerk acquired the impres-

---

[101] Clerk to Newcastle, Jan. 14, 1854, C.O. 48/364, P.R.O.

[102] Clerk to Newcastle, Aug. 25, 1853, C.O. 48/348, P.R.O.

[103] Clerk to Newcastle, Sept. 10, 1853, and enclosures, *ibid.* Clerk made his announcement on September 5, and the delegates presented him with their resolutions on the following day.

[104] Clerk to Newcastle, private, Sept. 10, 1853, *ibid.*

[105] Minute to Peel on Clerk to Newcastle, Aug. 25, 1853, *ibid.*

sion, confirmed by subsequent observation, that the primary opposition to withdrawal came from the English minority concentrated in and around Bloemfontein, and that the leaders were land speculators and traders who feared that independence would cause them to suffer financial loss. Clerk discovered that 139 proprietors owned 2,500,000 acres; of these only about 40 lived on their properties. Most of this land, he admitted, was of little value for lack of water, but these large holdings nevertheless constituted a significant vested interest. Among a few land barons who owned tremendous acreages, members of the government were prominently represented. Green owned 167,124 acres; the secretary to the registrar of deeds, 29,434; one civil commissioner in the Caledon district, 42,128; and the clerk of the commissioner, 36,000.[106] Not only were officials among the leading speculators but they set a bad example for landholders generally in nonpayment of quitrents; the resident himself was among those who were in arrears. The traders of Bloemfontein, who derived much of their profit from supplying the troops, also opposed withdrawal. Some of these traders were also large-scale land speculators.[107] The fervent loyalty of such people was easily explained. Clerk later recorded that one of the most enthusiastic advocates of British rule, when finally convinced that the decision to withdraw was unalterable, had exclaimed, "Give it up if you like, but leave! oh leave! the troops and the Commissariat." [108]

Among the Boers Clerk found support for British rule to be almost entirely confined to those who had served the British authorities and feared maltreatment under an independent government. He believed that the large majority desired independence.[109] Those Boers at the Bloemfontein meeting who had supported a resolution against independence did so, he insisted, because they had been deceived by the more sophisticated and better-prepared English, who had deluded them into an action that conformed neither to their own views nor to those of the people they professed to represent.[110] During his brief

---

[106] Clerk to Newcastle, Oct. 8, Nov. 10, 1853, both in *ibid*. Clerk's attack on these officials left the impression that they had used their positions for private profit. This was unfair. None of the officials purchased land after they entered government service. But Clerk insisted that the retention of any lands, no matter when bought, was contrary to sound policy. Here is an early application of the "conflict of interest" doctrine. See the resident's defense of his conduct in Green to Secretary of State, Nov. 1, 1854, and minutes thereto, C.O. 48/363, P.R.O.

[107] Clerk to Cathcart, Dec. 27, 1853, C.O. 48/348, P.R.O.

[108] Memo, private, by Clerk, May 22, 1857, C.O. 537/150, P.R.O.

[109] Clerk to Newcastle, Aug. 25, 1853, C.O. 48/348, P.R.O.

[110] Clerk to Newcastle, Nov. 3, 1853, *ibid*.

stay in southern Africa Clerk developed an admiration for the Boers, whom he considered the "pith of the people." It was tragic, he felt, that years of English administration and English arrogance had engendered a hatred of the English nation among the burghers of the sovereignty.[111]

The fate of the sovereignty was not determined by public opinion polls, accurate or inaccurate. The ministry's inaction was caused not by doubts about popular sentiment, but by delay in legal advice as to the means of severing the connection. At the end of September the law officers offered their long-deferred opinion. They found that because the sovereignty had been in fact established before the letters patent had been drawn up, their nonpublication did not affect the question as to how British rule was to be withdrawn. The Crown was legally competent to end its sovereignty in the same manner the sovereignty had been assumed, by proclamation. There might be some moral obligation to those inhabitants who had incurred obligations on the assumption that British rule would continue; if the government decided to indemnify them, an act of Parliament would be required.[112]

In their brief opinion the law officers offered no enlightenment on the nature of the rights that would be compensated, the effect of withdrawal on the status of the inhabitants as British subjects, or its implications for the Cape of Good Hope Punishment Act, which extended over the sovereignty.[113] Requiring further information and awaiting Clerk's report (as Clerk was awaiting his), Newcastle decided to delay the issuance of a proclamation. Finally, in mid-November, Newcastle instructed the commissioner to take formal steps for withdrawal by calling a convention to draft a constitution and negotiate the terms of a treaty like the Sand River Convention. If representatives of the sovereignty showed reluctance to accept separation, they were to be confronted with a *fait accompli* by the unilateral action of the British government. The proposed convention should guarantee to possessors of land the titles to their estates, and should contain a clause prohibiting slavery. As in the Transvaal, the convention would be made with the white community, and the native tribes would resume their former independence. Special arrangements might have to be

---

[111] Memo, private, by Clerk, May 22, 1857, C.O. 537/150, P.R.O.

[112] Law Officers to Newcastle, Sept. 28, 1853, C.O. 48/350, P.R.O. After further discussions with the law officers, Newcastle came to the conclusion that the sovereignty could be abandoned by an order in council and proclamation. An act of Parliament was required to release the inhabitants from their "native allegiance," but this could be deferred until later. See Newcastle to Clerk, confidential, Jan. 14, 1854, C.O. 48/354, P.R.O.

[113] Minutes on Law Officers to Newcastle, Sept. 28, 1853, C.O. 48/350, P.R.O.

made with the Griquas, toward whom the imperial government had incurred special obligations, but these details were left to Clerk's discretion.[114]

Pursuant to these instructions Clerk called another meeting of delegates which, despite the violent protests of the English minority, negotiated a convention at Bloemfontein which established the conditions for the independence of the Orange Free State. The terms were essentially in accordance with Newcastle's instructions. The British government guaranteed the future independence of the new republic and provided that the inhabitants would be free from allegiance to the Crown; Britain stipulated that it had no alliances with any chief north of the Orange River except Kok, and agreed that modifications would be made in its treaty with Kok to allow sales of lands in the "inalienable territory." And, of course, the new state promised that there would be no slavery.[115]

In reporting the treaty, Clerk stated that he had tried to bind the imperial government to as few obligations as possible. This principle he applied with marked success. All obligations to Moshesh arising from Maitland's treaty of 1843 were dismissed as having been eliminated by the battle of Berea. Kok's sham principality he proposed should be allowed to collapse. An excuse for annulling British treaty obligations could be found in the fact that the Griquas had violated the treaties, but the surest way to eliminate the Griqua problem would be to induce Kok and his council to permit their people to sell their property.[116] Clerk had recommended this to Kok in February, but with a rare display of courage, the Griqua council rejected the suggestion that they sign the warrant of execution, despite Kok's initial inclination to yield and the advice of their missionary, Edward Solomon, to sign under protest.[117] Solomon, observing the Griquas struggling against the inevitable, felt deep compassion for "these poor creatures in the grip of forces they could not long resist." [118] When they rejected his terms Clerk left this "medley of idle and impoverished crossbreeds" to whatever fate the Orange Free State might have in store for them,[119] and after a few months all resistance collapsed.

[114] Newcastle to Clerk, Nov. 14, 1853, C.O. 48/348, P.R.O.

[115] The treaty is enclosed in Clerk to Newcastle, Feb. 25, 1854, and is printed in Eybers, *op. cit.*, pp. 281–285.

[116] Clerk to Newcastle, March 28, 1854, C.O. 48/364, P.R.O.

[117] Solomon to Thompson, April 8, 1854, SAF 29–1, LMS Archives.

[118] Solomon to Thompson, April 15, 1854, SAF 28–1, LMS Archives.

[119] Clerk to Secretary to Government, Jan. 20, 1855, enclosure in Grey to Grey, Feb. 2, 1855, C.O. 48/365, P.R.O.

After much argument within the Colonial Office and the Treasury, the imperial government agreed to continue the £300 per year subsidy to Kok and his people.[120] This wrangling over a few pounds was an appropriate conclusion to a sellout of native peoples for the sake of expediency. It had been a complaint of the missionaries in previous years that the moral pretensions of British statesmen lacked substance; in 1854 there was not even a pretense of morality. Clerk was a fitting instrumentality for a British government dedicated to "realism." What had been gained, he asked, by decades of British intervention in race relations? The Boers had been embittered by the moral pretensions of their governors and the natives had been slaughtered by the thousands by their benevolent protectors. The Basuto had paid a heavy penalty for treaties with the Queen; the Kaffirs had lost much of their land. These were powerful arguments by a clear-eyed observer of the South African scene. But perhaps the policy of which Clerk was the agent was too cold-bloodedly realistic in terms of immediate expediency. This was the opinion not only of the misssionary societies, but of some officials, unidentified with "causes," who appraised the decision in terms of statesmanship. Among these were William Porter, attorney general of the Cape, and Sir George Grey, who succeeded Cathcart as governor in 1854.

Porter was one of the ablest public servants in the history of the Cape. A succession of governors sought his advice not only for his legal knowledge but for his judgment, which they invariably found balanced and perceptive. His analysis of the unwisdom of retreat was so trenchant as to elicit the admission from the Duke of Newcastle, who disagreed with some of his conclusions, that he had produced an able state paper. The question, Porter pointed out, was not whether it had been wise or unwise to have intervened in 1848. Intervention had occurred; imperial troops had crossed the Orange River not to bring freedom to the emigrant Boers, but to restrain them from doing what they pleased. Since the Great Trek governments had unwaveringly maintained that the Boers' "allegiance was inalienable and their

---

[120] Even this was not paid in the first year, and when Kok protested the non-payment, the sentiment of the Colonial Office was that the obligation should never have been accepted, and should be transferred to Cape Colony. At the insistence of Governor George Grey, however, the imperial government continued the subsidy (Grey to Labouchere, Sept. 5, 1856, C.O. 48/377, P.R.O.). In 1861 the Griquas, who had previously received Grey's permission, moved to a part of the Cape eastern frontier appropriately named "Nomansland," the modern Griqualand East (see J. S. Marais, *The Cape Coloured People, 1652–1937* [London: Longmans, Green, 1939], pp. 57 ff.).

independence a dream," and that Britain had an obligation to restrain them in accordance with its professed principles, even though that restraint might not be more than moral. Once the Boers of the Transvaal had been given their independence there was no sound reason for continuing to control their brethren between the Orange and the Vaal, but Porter could not escape the conclusion that the decision at Sand River had been a grave mistake.[121]

Sir George Grey came to the same conclusion but for somewhat different reasons. Grey held no brief for the policy pursued before 1852. The government of the Orange River Sovereignty, he admitted, had been neither enlightened nor effective; Warden's policy toward the native tribes had shown a close affinity to the viewpoint of the Boers.[122] But in its haste to disengage itself from costly responsibility the imperial government had overlooked the fact that its actions in one area could not be insulated. Native policy could not be compartmentalized; events beyond the Orange had repercussions along the entire frontier.[123] Sir George Clerk had left the boundaries of the Orange Free State and the Basuto unsettled; they would be determined by war, which was likely to involve the Kaffir tribes with whom Moshesh maintained close association, and thus embroil Cape Colony.

By the conventions the imperial government had in effect bound itself to enter into no treaties with the native tribes and to prevent their acquiring ammunition to defend themselves,[124] but had abdicated all control of the Boers. This, Grey warned, was an invitation to carnage; British honor and British interest dictated that the conventions be revised to provide for restraints on the actions of the republics. In effect, therefore, Grey advocated the reintervention of the imperial factor beyond the Orange River in recognition of the fact that the paramount power in southern Africa could not in its own interests ignore events on the borders of its possessions.[125] Henry Labouchere, secretary of state for colonies, conceded that the independence of the

---

[121] Memo by Porter, Aug. 4, 1852, enclosure in Cathcart to Secretary of State, Nov. 14, 1852, C.O. 48/328, P.R.O.

[122] See Grey to Labouchere, May 3, 1856, C.O. 48/374, P.R.O., in which he describes Warden's assignment of Bushmen and Tembu captives as "apprentices" to Boer farmers.

[123] Grey to Grey, Feb. 2, 1855, C.O. 48/365, P.R.O.

[124] The Bloemfontein Convention made no reference to the denial of ammunition to the natives. Sir George Clerk insisted that the issue was a minor one because the tribes would get ample supplies from smugglers if not from legally authorized sources (Clerk to Merivale, private, Feb. 14, [1857], C.O. 48/377, P.R.O.).

[125] Grey to Labouchere, Nov. 1, 1856, *ibid.*

Orange Free State and the Transvaal tended to complicate the relations between the British colonies and the native tribes.[126] The imperial government, however, had committed itself to a line of policy, and it could "hardly now renounce it, even if it were wise to do so, which I greatly doubt." [127] For twenty years Britain had attempted to maintain order at minimum expense while professing to protect the native tribes against aggression from white settlers. Experience had demonstrated that policy to be exorbitantly expensive without promoting its avowed objects. Now Britain sought to limit responsibility and expense by conferring independence on the two Boer republics. In time the imperial government would recognize that this also was an ill-conceived policy, that weak and poverty-stricken states contributed to disorder, and that the way to decrease British responsibility was to unify the several jurisdictions into a single strong and self-reliant authority. Many years would pass, however, before this conclusion became apparent, and the problems of reunification were far more complicated than the problems of withdrawal.

Sir George Clerk paid out £50,000 to inhabitants of the sovereignty as compensation for claims, moral or legal, against the imperial government.[128] Governor Cathcart commented that withdrawal "would have been cheaply purchased at £200,000." [129] But the price of the resumption of imperial authority was to be thousands of lives, millions of pounds, and a legacy of lasting bitterness.

The tragedy of southern Africa between 1834 and 1854, as subsequently, is not to be explained by the villainy or the blunders of men. Given the characteristics of British society and the nature of the South African problem, no "solution" was possible. The early Victorians were tinged with humanitarianism and dominated by materialism; the combination in South Africa was disastrous.

---

[126] Labouchere to Grey, July 14, 1856, C.O. 48/373, P.R.O.

[127] Minute by Labouchere on Grey to Labouchere, Nov. 1, 1856, C.O. 48/377, P.R.O.

[128] De Kiewiet, *op. cit.*, p. 81.

[129] Clerk to Merivale, private, Feb. 14, 1857, C.O. 48/377, P.R.O.

BIBLIOGRAPHY

MANUSCRIPT SOURCES

BRITISH MUSEUM

   Add. MSS 34581 Bliss Correspondence
   Add. MSS 44586, 44738 Gladstone Papers
   Add. MSS 49167, 49168 Napier Papers
   Add. MSS 40468, 40565, 40589 Peel Papers

CAPE ARCHIVES

   British Kaffraria Correspondence
   Colonial Office Correspondence
   D'Urban Papers
   Government House Correspondence
   Southey Papers

PUBLIC RECORD OFFICE

   Series C.O. 48, 49, 51, 53, 179, 323, 537, 854; W.O. 1, 17
   30/46 Eyre Papers
   30/43 Lowry Cole Papers
   30/22 Russell Papers

ELLICE PAPERS, NATIONAL LIBRARY OF SCOTLAND

   Microfilm copies in Public Archives of Canada and in Library of the
   University of California, Los Angeles

GREY OF HOWICK PAPERS, PRIOR'S KITCHEN, UNIVERSITY OF DURHAM

LONDON MISSIONARY SOCIETY ARCHIVES

   The series of particular value for this study were the South African and
   Philip letters.

METHODIST MISSIONARY SOCIETY ARCHIVES

   The correspondence for this period is more sparse than that of the
   London Missionary Society, but is nevertheless of great value.

PROVINCIAL LIBRARY, CAPE TOWN

D'Urban Typescript

RHODES HOUSE, OXFORD UNIVERSITY

Anti-Slavery Papers
Bourke Papers
Cape Colony Letters

UNIVERSITY OF CAPE TOWN

Philip Transcripts. These are not original letters but summaries and transcripts. The original Philip correspondence, at the University of the Witwatersrand, was destroyed by fire.

UNPUBLISHED THESES

Engels, L. J. "Sir Benjamin D'Urban's Handling of the Frontier Problems, 1834–1836." M.A. thesis, University of Cape Town, 1936.
Renwald, Sister Mary Casilda. "Humanitarianism and British Colonial Policy." Ph.D. dissertation, St. Louis University, 1934.
Roxborough, James. "Colonial Policy on the Northern and Eastern Frontiers of the Cape of Good Hope, 1834–45." Ph.D. dissertation, Oxford, 1953.
Williams, Donovan. "The Missionaries on the Eastern Frontiers of the Cape Colony, 1799–1853." Ph.D. dissertation, University of the Witwatersrand, 1960.

OFFICIAL AND SEMIOFFICIAL PUBLICATIONS

Cape of Good Hope. *Further Correspondence relative to the State of the Tribes, and to the recent outbreak on the Eastern Frontier of the Colony.* Colonial Office, April 29, 1851. Confidential. Printed for the Use of the Cabinet.
————. *Report from the Select Committee on the Defense of the Eastern Frontier.* Cape Town: Solomon, 1854.
————. *Report from the Select Committee on Frontier Defense.* Cape Town: Solomon, 1855.
Documents Relative to the Question of a Separate Government for the Eastern Districts of the Cape. Grahamstown: Godlonton and White, 1847.
Great Britain Confidential Print. Cape. Summary of Correspondence relative to the Policy pursued towards the Native Tribes on the Eastern Frontier of the Cape of Good Hope, including the Wars of 1835 and 1846. Downing Street, April, 1856.

————. Parliament. *Debates, 1834–1854.* London.

————. ————. *Report from the Select Committee on Aborigines (British Settlements); with the Minutes of Evidence.* Ordered by H. of C. to be Printed, 1836, 1837.

————. ————. *Report from the Select Committee on Colonial Military Expenditure.* Ordered by H. of C. to be Printed, Aug. 4, 1835.

————. ————. *Report of the Select Committee on the Kafir Tribes.* Ordered by H. of C. to be printed, 1851.

BOOKS

Addison, William G. *Religious Equality in Modern England.* London: S.P.C.K., 1944.

Agar-Hamilton, John A. I. *The Native Policy of the Voortrekkers.* Cape Town: Maskew Miller, [1928].

————. *The Road to the North, 1852–1886.* London: Longmans, Green, [1937].

The Annual Register . . . of the Year 1848. London: Woodfall, 1849.

Arbousset, Jean T. *Narrative of an Exploratory Tour to the North-East of the Colony of the Cape of Good Hope.* London: Bishop, 1852.

Backhouse, James. *A Narrative of a Visit to Mauritius and South Africa.* London: Hamilton, Adams, 1844.

Barnes, Leonard. *Caliban in Africa.* Philadelphia: Lippincott, 1931.

Bell, Kenneth N., and William P. Morrell. *Select Documents on British Colonial Policy, 1830–1860.* Oxford: Clarendon, 1928.

Benians, Ernest Alfred, James R. M. Butler, Philip Nicholas Seton Mansergh, and Eric A. Walker. *The Cambridge History of the British Empire.* Vol. III. Cambridge: University Press, 1959.

Bird, John. *The Annals of Natal.* Pietermaritzburg: Davis, 1888. 2 vols.

Booth, Charles. *Life and Labour of the People in London.* 3d series. London: Macmillan, 1902. 8 vols.

Bowker, John M. *Speeches, Letters, and Selections from Important Papers.* Grahamstown: Godlonton and Richards, 1864.

Boyce, William B. *Notes on South-African Affairs.* London: Mason, 1839.

Bright, John, and James E. Thorold Rogers. *Speeches on Questions of Public Policy by Richard Cobden, M.P.* London: Macmillan, 1878.

Brookes, Edgar H. *The History of Native Policy in South Africa from 1830 to the Present Day.* Pretoria: Van Schaik, 1927.

Burn, William L. *Emancipation and Apprenticeship in the British West Indies.* London: Cape, 1937.

Buxton, Charles, ed. *Memoirs of Sir Thomas Fowell Buxton.* London: Murray, 1849.

Buxton, Sydney. *Finance and Politics.* London: Murray, 1888. 2 vols.

Calderwood, Henry. *Caffres and Caffre Missions.* London: Nisbit, 1858.

Cana, Frank R. *South Africa from the Great Trek to the Union.* London: Chapman & Hall, 1909.

The Cape of Good Hope Almanac for 1845. Cape Town: Robertson, 1845.

Chase, John C. *The Cape of Good Hope and the Eastern Province of Algoa Bay.* London, Richardson, 1843.

Chisholm, Joseph A. *The Speeches and Public Letters of Joseph Howe.* Halifax: Chronicle Pub. Co., 1909. 2 vols.

Cocks, H. F. Lovell. *The Nonconformist Conscience.* London: Independent Press, 1943.

Cornewall Lewis, George. *Essay on the Government of Dependencies.* Ed. C. P. Lucas. Oxford: Clarendon, 1891.

Cory, George E. *The Rise of South Africa.* London: Longmans, Green, 1921–1930. 5 vols.

———. *The Rise of South Africa.* Vol. VI, chaps. 1–6. In *Archives Year Book for South African History.* Part I. Cape Town: G.P.O., 1939.

Davies, Horton, and Robert Henry Wishart Shepherd, eds. *South African Missions, 1800–1950.* London: Nelson, 1950.

De Kiewiet, Cornelis W. *British Colonial Policy and the South African Republics, 1848–1872.* London: Longmans, Green, 1929.

———. *The Imperial Factor in South Africa.* Cambridge: University Press, 1937.

Dowden, Edward, ed. *Correspondence of Henry Taylor.* London: Longmans, Green, 1888.

Du Plessis, Jacobus S. *Die Onstaan en Ontwikkeling van die Amp van die Staatspresident in Die Zuid-Afrikaansche Republiek.* In *Archives Year Book for South African History.* 18th Year, Vol. I. Cape Town: Govt. Printer, 1955.

Du Plessis, Johannes. *A History of Christian Missions in South Africa.* London: Longmans, Green, 1911.

Edwards, Isobel Eirlys. *The 1820 Settlers in South Africa.* London: Longmans, Green, 1934.

———. *Towards Emancipation: A Study in South African Slavery.* Cardiff: Gomerian Press, 1942.

Eybers, George von Welfling. *Select Constitutional Documents Illustrating South African History, 1795–1910.* London: Routledge, 1918.

Fawcett, John. *Account of an Eighteen Months' Residence at the Cape of Good Hope in 1835–6.* Cape Town: Pike, 1836.

Fawcett, Millicent. *Life of the Right Hon. Sir William Molesworth.* London: Macmillan, 1901.

Godlonton, Robert. *Case of the Colonists of the Eastern Frontier of the Cape of Good Hope, in reference to the Kafir Wars of 1835–36 and 1846.* Grahamstown: Richards, Slater, 1879.

Grampp, William D. *The Manchester School of Economics.* Stanford: Stanford University Press, 1960.

Grey, Henry George, 3d Earl. *The Colonial Policy of Lord John Russell's Administration.* London: Bentley, 1853. 2 vols.

Grobbelaar, Johannes Jacobus Gabriel. *Die Vrystaatse Republiek en die Basoetoe-Vraagstuk.* In *Archives Year Book for South African History.* Part II, 1939. Cape Town: Govt. Printer, 1939.

Halford, Samuel J. *The Griquas of Griqualand.* Cape Town: Juta, n.d.

Hamilton, J. Taylor. *A History of the Church Known as the Moravian Church.* Bethlehem, Pa.: Times Pub. Co., 1900.

Hammond, John L. *Gladstone and the Irish Nation.* London: Longmans, Green, 1938.

Harris, John. *A Century of Emancipation.* London: Dent, 1933.

Hirst, Francis W., Gilbert Murray, and John L. Hammond. *Liberalism and the Empire.* London: Johnson, 1900.

Hoernlé, Reinhold F. Alfred. *South African Native Policy and the Liberal Spirit.* Johannesburg: Witwatersrand University Press, 1945.

Horne, C. Sylvester. *The Story of the L.M.S., 1795–1845.* London: London Missionary Society, 1894.

Howse, Ernest M. *Saints in Politics.* Toronto: University of Toronto Press, 1952.

Hutton, C. W., ed. *The Autobiography of the Late Sir Andries Stockenstrom.* Cape Town: Juta, 1887. 2 vols.

Isaacs, Nathaniel. *Travels and Adventures in Eastern Africa.* Ed. Louis Hermann. Cape Town: Van Riebeeck Society, 1937.

Justus, [Mackenzie Beverley]. *The Wrongs of the Caffre Nation.* London: Duncan, 1837.

Kay, Stephen. *Travels and Researches in Caffraria.* New York: Harper, 1834.

Kinglake, Alexander William. *The Invasion of the Crimea.* Edinburgh: Blackwood, 1863–1887. 8 vols.

Kistner, Wolfram. *The Anti-Slavery Agitation against the Transvaal Republic, 1852–1868.* In *Archives Year Book for South African History.* 15th Year, Vol. II. Cape Town: Govt. Printer, 1952.

Klingberg, Frank J. *The Anti-Slavery Movement in England.* New Haven: Yale University Press, 1926.

Knaplund, Paul. *Gladstone and Britain's Imperial Policy.* New York: Macmillan, 1947.

――――. *James Stephen and the British Colonial System.* Madison: University of Wisconsin Press, 1953.

Knorr, Klaus E. *British Colonial Theories, 1570–1850.* Toronto: University of Toronto Press, 1944.

Lagden, Godfrey. *The Basutos.* London: Hutchinson, 1909. 2 vols.

Lewis, Roy, and Angus Maude. *The English Middle Classes.* New York: Knopf, 1950.

Long, Una. *An Index to Authors of Unofficial, Privately-owned Manuscripts Relating to the History of South Africa, 1812–1912.* Cape Town, 1947. Lithoprinted.

Lovett, Richard. *The History of the London Missionary Society, 1795–1895.* London: Frowde, 1899. 2 vols.

MacCrone, Ian Douglas. *Race Attitudes in South Africa.* London: Oxford University Press, 1937.

Macmillan, William M. *Bantu, Boer, and Briton.* London: Faber and Gwyer, 1929.

———. *The Cape Colour Question.* London: Faber and Gwyer, [1927].

Marais, Johannes Stephanus. *The Cape Coloured People, 1652–1937.* London: Longmans, Green, 1939.

Martin, R. Montgomery. *Statistics of the Colonies of the British Empire.* London: Allen, 1839.

Mellor, George R. *British Imperial Trusteeship, 1783–1850.* London: Faber & Faber, 1951.

Merriman, Nathaniel. *The Kafir, the Hottentot, and the Frontier Farmer.* London: Bell, 1854.

Midgley, John F. *The Orange River Sovereignty (1848–1854).* In *Archives Year Book for South African History.* 12th Year, Part II. Cape Town: Government Printer, 1949.

Moffat, Robert. *Missionary Labours and Scenes in Southern Africa.* London: Snow, 1846.

Moister, William. *Missionary Worthies.* London: Woolmer, 1885.

Morrell, W. P. *British Colonial Policy in the Age of Peel and Russell.* Oxford: Clarendon Press, 1930.

Muller, C. F. J. *Die Britse Owerheid en die Groot Trek.* Cape Town: Juta, [1948].

Napier, Edward Elers. *Excursions in Southern Africa.* London: Shoberl, 1849. 2 vols.

Neumark, S. Daniel. *Economic Influences on the South African Frontier, 1652–1836.* Stanford: Stanford University Press, 1957.

Newman, William A. *Biographical Memoir of John Montagu.* Cape Town: Robertson, 1855.

Northcott, Cecil. *Glorious Company.* London: London Missionary Society, 1945.

Norton, Charles Bowyer Adderley. *Review of "The Colonial Policy of Lord J. Russell's Administration."* London: Stanford, 1869.

Orpen, Joseph M. *Reminiscences of Life in South Africa.* Durban: Davis, 1908.

Overton, John H. *The Evangelical Revival in the Eighteenth Century.* London: Longmans, Green, 1886.

Philip, John. *Researches in South Africa.* London: Duncan, 1828. 2 vols.

Read, James, Jr. *The Kat River Settlement in 1851.* Cape Town: Robertson, 1852.

Reeve, Henry, ed. *The Greville Memoirs. A Journal of the Reigns of King George IV and King William IV.* London: Longmans, Green, 1874. 3 vols.

———. *The Greville Memoirs (Second Part). A Journal of the Reign of*

Queen Victoria from 1837 to 1852. London: Longmans, Green, 1885. 3 vols.

Rogers, J. E. Thorold. *Cobden and Modern Political Opinion.* London: Macmillan, 1873.

Rose, J. Holland, Arthur Percival Newton, and Ernest A. Benians, eds. *The Cambridge History of the British Empire.* Vols. II, VIII. Cambridge: University Press, 1940, 1936.

Rostow, Walt Whitman. *British Economy of the Nineteenth Century.* Oxford: Clarendon Press, 1948.

Russell, Francis Albert Rollo. *Early Correspondence of Lord John Russell, 1805–40.* London: Unwin, 1913. 2 vols.

Russell, George W. E. *A Short History of the Evangelical Movement.* London: Mowbray, 1915.

Sanders, Lloyd C. *Lord Melbourne's Papers.* London: Longmans, Green, 1889.

Sauer, J. W., and George M. Theal, eds. *Basutoland Records.* Cape Town: Richard, 1883. 3 vols.

Schapera, Isaac. *Apprenticeship at Kuruman.* London, 1951.

———, ed. *The Bantu-Speaking Tribes of South Africa.* London, Routledge, 1937.

Schutte, C. E. G. *Dr. Philip's Observations Regarding the Hottentots of South Africa.* In *Archives Year Book for South African History.* Part I. Cape Town: Government Printer, 1940.

Schuyler, Robert L. *The Fall of the Old Colonial System.* London: Oxford University Press, 1945.

Seaver, George. *David Livingstone: His Life and Letters.* London: Lutterworth, 1957.

Shaw, William. *The Story of My Mission in South-Eastern Africa.* London: Hamilton, Adams, 1860.

Sibree, James. *South Africa.* London: Snow, [1882].

Smith, Henry G. W. *The Autobiography of Sir Harry Smith.* Edited with addition of some supplementary chapters by G. C. Moore Smith. London: Murray, 1903.

Soga, John Henderson. *The South-Eastern Bantu.* Johannesburg: Witwatersrand, 1930.

Stock, Eugene. *The History of the Church Missionary Society.* London: Church Missionary Society, 1899. 3 vols.

Stokes, Eric. *The English Utilitarians and India.* Oxford: Clarendon Press, 1959.

Stow, George. *The Native Races of South Africa.* London: Swan Sonnenschein, 1905.

Taylor, Henry. *Autobiography.* London: Longmans, Green, 1885. 2 vols.

Theal, George M. *Documents Relating to the Kaffir War of 1835.* London: Clowes, 1912.

——. *History of South Africa since September, 1795*. London: Swan Sonnenschein, 1907–1910. 5 vols.

——, ed. *Records of the Cape Colony*. Cape Town: G.P.O., 1899–1907.
36 vols.

Van Biljon, Petries. *Grensbakens tussen Blank en Swart in Suid-Afrika*. Cape
Town: Juta, [1947?].

Van der Merwe, Petrus Johannes. *Die Noortwaartse Beweging van die Boere
voor die Groot Trek (1770–1842)*. The Hague: van Stockum, 1937.

——. *Die Trekboer in die Geskiedenis van die Kaapkolonie (1657–1842)*.
Cape Town: Nationale Pers, 1938.

Van der Walt, Andries Jacobus Hendrik, J. A. Wiid, and Alfred L. Geyer.
Geskiedenis van Suid-Afrika. Cape Town: Nasionale Boekhandel, 1955.
2 vols.

Varley, Douglas Harold, and H. M. Matthew. *The Cape Journals of Archdeacon N. J. Merriman, 1848–1855*. Cape Town: Van Riebeeck Society,
1957.

Walker, Eric A. *The Great Trek*. London: Black, 1948.

——. *A History of Southern Africa*. London: Longmans, Green, 1957.

Walpole, Spencer. *A History of England*. London: Longmans, Green, 1879–
1880. 6 vols.

——. *The Life of Lord John Russell*. London: Longmans, Green, 1889.
2 vols.

Wellington, John H. *Southern Africa. A Geographical Study*. Cambridge:
University Press, 1955.

Whiteside, Joseph. *History of the Wesleyan Methodist Church of South
Africa*. London: Stock, 1906.

Willcox, William B. *Star of Empire*. New York: Knopf, 1950.

Williams, Basil. *Record of the Cape Mounted Riflemen*. London: Causton,
1909.

Williams, Eric. *Capitalism and Slavery*. Chapel Hill: University of North
Carolina Press, 1944.

Wilmot, Alexander. *The Life and Times of Sir Richard Southey*. London:
Low, Marston, 1904.

——, and John Centlivres Chase. *History of the Colony of the Cape of
Good Hope*. Cape Town: Juta, 1869.

Woodward, E. L. *The Age of Reform, 1815–1870*. Oxford: Clarendon Press,
1938.

Young, D. Murray. *The Colonial Office in the Early Nineteenth Century*.
London: Longmans, 1961.

ARTICLES

Beaglehole, John C. "The Colonial Office, 1782–1854," *Historical Studies,
Australia and New Zealand*, I (April, 1941), 170–189.

Davey, Cyril J. "Two Hundred Years of Methodism Overseas," *London Quarterly and Holborn Review* (Jan., 1960), pp. 3–8.

Fox-Bourne, Henry R. "South Africa and the Aborigines Protection Society," *Contemporary Review,* (Sept., 1889), pp. 346–360.

Galbraith, John S. "Myths of the 'Little England' Era," *American Historical Review,* LXVII (Oct., 1961), 34–48.

Gallagher, John, and Ronald Robinson. "The Imperialism of Free Trade," *Economic History Review,* 2d series, VI (Aug., 1953), 1–15.

Glaser, John F. "English Nonconformity and the Decline of Liberalism," *American Historical Review,* LXIII (Jan., 1958), 352–363.

Greenberg, Joseph H. "Africa as a Linguistic Area," in William R. Bascom and Melville J. Herskovits, eds., *Continuity and Change in African Cultures.* Chicago: University of Chicago Press, 1959. Pp. 15–27.

Grey, Third Earl. "Past and Future Policy in South Africa," *Nineteenth Century,* V (April, 1879), 583–596.

Grosskopf, Johann F. W. "Vestiging en Trek van die Suid-Afrikaanse Naturelle-Bevolking onder Nuwere Ekonomiese Voorwaardes," *South African Journal of Economics,* I (Sept., 1933), 261–280.

Kitson Clark, G. "The Repeal of the Corn Laws and the Politics of the Forties," *Economic History Series,* 2d series, IV, no. 1 (1951), pp. 1–13.

Knaplund, Paul. "Mr. Oversecretary Stephen," *Journal of Modern History,* I (March, 1929), 39–66.

Lewin, Julius. "Dr. John Philip and Liberalism," *Race Relations Journal* (Johannesburg), XXVII (April–June, 1960), 82–90.

Mackarness, Frederic. "South Africa under Irresponsible Government," *Contemporary Review,* LVI (Aug., 1889), 234–243.

Pappe, H. O. "Wakefield and Marx," *Economic History Review,* 2d series, IV, no. 1 (1951), pp. 88–97.

Robertson, Hector M. "The 1840 Settlers in Natal," *South African Journal of Economics,* XVII (Sept., 1949), 274–288.

Tylden, Major G. "The Cape Coloured Regiments, 1793 to 1870," *Africana Notes and News,* VII (March, 1950), 37–59.

Williams, E. Trevor. "The Colonial Office in the Thirties," *Historical Studies, Australia and New Zealand,* II (May, 1943), 141–160.

————. "James Stephen and British Intervention in New Zealand, 1838–40," *Journal of Modern History,* XIII (March, 1941), 19–35.

PAMPHLETS

Adderley, Charles B. *Some Reflections on the Speech of the Rt. Hon. Lord John Russell on Colonial Policy.* London: Parker, 1850.

Godlonton, Robert, ed. *Sunshine and Cloud.* Cape Town, 1855.

Molesworth, William. *Materials for a Speech in Defence of the Policy of*

Abandoning the Orange River Territory. London: Charles Westerton, 1854.

————. *Observations on the Policy of England as Respects her Possessions at the Cape of Good Hope.* London: Bosworth & Hamilton, 1857.

Stockenstrom, Andries. *Brief Notice of the Causes of the Kaffir War.* London: Saunders, 1851.

————. *Light and Shade.* Cape Town: Solomon, 1854.

NEWSPAPERS AND MAGAZINES

Bankers' Magazine, 1853

Cape Monitor, 1852

Colonial Magazine, 1840, 1841

Economist, 1843–1854

Edinburgh Review, 1834–1854

Evangelical Magazine, 1834–1836

Friend of the Sovereignty, 1851–1854

Grahamstown Journal, 1837–1853

Graaff Reinet Herald, 1853–1854

London Evening Mail, 1851

Missionary Herald (Boston), 1835, 1837–1839

Missionary Magazine, 1836–1854

Missionary Register (London), 1835

Nederduitsch Zuid-Afrikaansch Tijd-schrift (Cape Town), 1834–1835

North British Review, 1851

South African Commercial Adver-tiser, 1834–1854

Times (London), 1834–1854

INDEX